Biological Extinction: New Perspectives

The rapidly increasing human pressure on the biosphere is pushing biodiversity into the sixth mass extinction event in the history of life on Earth. The organisms being exterminated are integral working parts of our planet's life support system, and their loss is permanent. Like climate change, this irreversible loss has potentially devastating consequences for humanity. As we come to recognise the many ways in which we depend on nature, this can pave the way for a new ethic that acknowledges the importance of co-existence between humans and other species. *Biological Extinction* features chapters contributed by leading thinkers in diverse fields of knowledge and practice, including biology, economics, geology, archaeology, demography, and architecture. Drawing on examples from various socio-ecological systems, the book offers new perspectives on the urgent issue of biological extinction, proposing novel solutions to the problems that we face.

PARTHA DASGUPTA is the Frank Ramsey Emeritus Professor of Economics at the University of Cambridge, Chair of the Centre for the Study of Existential Risk, University of Cambridge, and a Fellow of St John's College, Cambridge. He was knighted in 2002 for his services to economics, and is a Fellow of the Royal Society, Foreign Associate of the National Academy of Sciences, and Member of the Pontifical Academy of Social Sciences. He won the Volvo Environment Prize in 2002, the Blue Planet Prize in 2015 and the Tyler Prize in 2016.

PETER H. RAVEN is the President Emeritus of Missouri Botanical Garden and the George Engelmann Professor of Botany Emeritus at Washington University, St Louis. He is a Member of the National Academy of Sciences, Foreign Member of the Royal Society, and Member of the Pontifical Academy of Sciences. He won the Volvo Environment Prize in 1992, the International Cosmos Prize in 2003, and the National Geographic Society's Hubbard Medal in 2018.

ANNA L. MCIVOR completed her Ph.D. in the Department of Zoology, University of Cambridge, and has since worked as a post-doctoral research associate in the Departments of Zoology and Geography at the University of Cambridge.

Biological Extinction: New Perspectives

Edited by
PARTHA DASGUPTA
University of Cambridge
PETER H. RAVEN
Missouri Botanical Garden
ANNA L. MCIVOR
University of Cambridge

CAMBRIDGE
UNIVERSITY PRESS

CAMBRIDGE
UNIVERSITY PRESS

University Printing House, Cambridge CB2 8BS, United Kingdom

One Liberty Plaza, 20th Floor, New York, NY 10006, USA

477 Williamstown Road, Port Melbourne, VIC 3207, Australia

314-321, 3rd Floor, Plot 3, Splendor Forum, Jasola District Centre, New Delhi - 110025, India

79 Anson Road, #06-04/06, Singapore 079906

Cambridge University Press is part of the University of Cambridge.

It furthers the University's mission by disseminating knowledge in the pursuit of education, learning and research at the highest international levels of excellence.

www.cambridge.org
Information on this title: www.cambridge.org/9781108482288
DOI: 10.1017/9781108668675

First published 2019

A catalogue record for this publication is available from the British Library

Library of Congress Cataloging in Publication data
Names: Dasgupta, Partha, editor. | Raven, Peter H., editor. | McIvor, A., editor.
Title: Biological extinction : new perspectives / edited by Partha S. Dasgupta
(University of Cambridge), Peter H. Raven (Missouri Botanical Garden), Anna L.
McIvor (University of Cambridge).
Description: Cambridge ; New York, NY : Cambridge University Press, 2019. |
Includes bibliographical references and index.
Identifiers: LCCN 2019008003 | ISBN 9781108482288 (alk. paper)
Subjects: LCSH: Extinction (Biology) | Evolution (Biology) | Adaptation (Biology)
Classification: LCC QH78 .B56 2019 | DDC 576.8/4–dc23
LC record available at https://lccn.loc.gov/2019008003

ISBN   978-1-108-48228-8   Hardback
ISBN   978-1-108-71181-4   Paperback

To the memory of our friend and colleague Calestous Juma.
His life provides inspiration and gives hope to us all.

Contents

Color plates are to be found between pp. 234 and 235.

Figures

Tables

Contributors

Timothy Beach, Centennial Professor, Geography and the Environment, The College of Liberal Arts, The University of Texas at Austin

John Bongaarts, Vice President and Distinguished Scholar, Population Council, New York

Vanessa Constant, PhD Candidate, Department of Integrative Biology, Oregon State University

Gretchen C. Daily, Co-Director of The Natural Capital Project, Bing Professor in Environmental Science and Senior Fellow, Department of Biology, Stanford Woods Institute for the Environment

Partha S. Dasgupta, Frank Ramsey Professor Emeritus of Economics, Faculty of Economics, University of Cambridge, and Chair of the Management Board, Centre for the Study of Existential Risk, University of Cambridge

Nicholas P. Dunning, Professor, Department of Geography and GIS, University of Cincinnati

Paul R. Ehrlich, Bing Professor of Population Studies Emeritus; President, Center for Conservation Biology; Department of Biology, Stanford University; and Adjunct Professor, University of Technology, Sydney

Brian Heap, Scientific Advisor, Smart Villages Initiative, c/o Trinity College, Cambridge, and Distinguished Fellow, Centre of Development Studies, University of Cambridge

John T. Hoal, Professor of Architecture and Urban Design, and Chair, Urban Design, Graduate School of Architecture and Urban Design, Sam Fox School of Design and Visual Arts, Washington University in St. Louis, and Founding Partner, H3 Studio

John Holmes, Project Co-Leader, Smart Villages Initiative, c/o Trinity College, Cambridge, and Visiting Fellow, Department of Earth Sciences, University of Oxford

Bernie Jones, Project Co-Leader, Smart Villages Initiative, c/o Trinity College, Cambridge

Calestous Juma (deceased), formerly Professor of the Practice of International Development, Belfer Center for Science and International Affairs, Harvard Kennedy School, Harvard University

Ann Kinzig, Professor, School of Life Sciences, Arizona State University

Timothy M. Lenton, Chair in Climate Change and Earth System Science, Earth System Science Group, College of Life and Environmental Sciences, University of Exeter

Jane Lubchenco, Distinguished University Professor, Department of Integrative Biology, Oregon State University

Sheryl Luzzadder-Beach, Professor and Chair of the Department of Geography and the Environment, The College of Liberal Arts, The University of Texas at Austin

Anna L. McIvor, Centre for the Study of Existential Risk, University of Cambridge

Charles Perrings, Professor of Environmental Economics, School of Life Sciences, Arizona State University

Stuart L. Pimm, Doris Duke Professor of Conservation Ecology, Nicholas School of the Environment, Duke University

Prabhu L. Pingali, Professor of Applied Economics, and Director, Tata-Cornell Institute, Cornell University

Stephen Polasky, Regents Professor and Fesler-Lampert Professor of Ecological/Environmental Economics, Department of Applied Economics, University of Minnesota

Peter H. Raven, President Emeritus, Missouri Botanical Garden, St. Louis

Martin Rees, Emeritus Professor of Cosmology and Astrophysics, Institute of Astronomy, University of Cambridge

Neil Shubin, Robert R. Bensley Professor, Department of Organismal Biology and Anatomy, The University of Chicago

Jenna M. Sullivan, PhD Candidate, Department of Integrative Biology, Oregon State University

Mathis Wackernagel, Founder and Chief Executive Officer, Global Footprint Network, Oakland, California

Preface

On our 4.5-billion-year-old planet, life is perhaps as much as 3.7 billion years old, photosynthesis and multi-cellularity (appearing dozens of times independently) around 3.0 billion years old, and plants, animals and fungi emerged onto land perhaps 480 million years ago. Forests appeared around 370 million years ago, and the origin of modern groups such as mammals, birds, reptiles and land plants appeared subsequently about 200 million years ago. The geological record shows that there have been five major extinction events in the past, the first of them about 542 million years ago; the record suggests that 99 per cent of the species that ever lived (perhaps 5 billion of them?) have become extinct. The last major extinction event occurred about 66 million years ago, at the end of the Cretaceous Period, and in general, the number of species on Earth and the complexity of their communities have increased steadily since then until near the present.

Over the past 66 million years, the number of species has grown to an estimated 10–14 million kinds of eukaryotic organisms (those with complex cells) and an unknown but probably much larger number of prokaryotic organisms (archaea and bacteria). The first members of the human evolutionary line split off the African apes about 6–8 million years ago. Our first close relatives, which we call hominids, appear in the fossil record about 2.7 million years ago in Africa. *Homo erectus*, the species most likely to have been the ancestor of our own, migrated out of Africa via the Middle East, starting about 2 million years ago, and apparently gave rise to the Neanderthals and Denisovans in the north. These extinct species were joined about 60,000 years ago by our own species, *Homo sapiens*, which had originated in Africa about 200,000 years ago. *Homo sapiens* spread to Australia soon after their arrival in Eurasia but didn't get to the New World until perhaps 18,000 years ago, and perhaps sooner. By about 30,000 years ago, they had already conquered and killed the other forms of hominids that were present in the Northern Hemisphere, after interbreeding with Neanderthals and Denisovans when they came into contact with them.

For tens of thousands of years after they reached Eurasia, humans lived as hunter-gatherers. During that period, they began to create artistic works and to make weapons, musical instruments and the like, but since they kept moving in search of food, necessarily carrying their babies with them, there was not much chance for them to develop what we consider civilisation today. Dogs were domesticated in Eurasia likely more than 20,000 years ago, and crops were being cultivated by about 12,000 years ago. Along with domestic animals, these crops provided a major source of storable food, one that could see humans through droughts, winters and other unfavourable times. The numbers of people who could live together in a village, town or city were thereby greatly increased, allowing most aspects of what we consider civilisation to develop in these centres. Human dispersal to Australia occurred long before there was any domestication of plants or animals, a practice that never developed there, while dispersal to the New World occurred after the domestication of dogs (Chihuahuas, to eat). No crops were brought to the New World, and in North and South America, crop agriculture was invented independently.

At the time that crops became important elements for human survival some 10,000 years ago, the world population is estimated to have been about 1 million people, with about 100,000 in Europe. Written language was developed about 5000 years ago as distinctive civilisations developed in different parts of the world. Human populations began to grow rapidly and to overwhelm the capacity of many natural systems through cultivating crops and grazing. It is estimated that at the time of Christ, there may have been 300 million people living globally; now, there are nearly 7.6 billion. Some 10 per cent of the world's ice-free land surface has been converted to crop agriculture, with an additional 20 per cent to grazing, most of it unsustainable, on natural grasslands. It is obvious that many of the kinds of organisms that existed 10,000 years ago have already gone extinct and that we are dealing with a reduced set of the organisms that existed when agriculture was first adopted by our ancestors. What percentage would have been lost during this period is unknown, but for some groups on islands (e.g., Pacific birds), it seems to have been a majority, and on continents, a large percentage also, certainly in areas like the Mediterranean Basin.

Current extinction rates of species in relatively well known groups of organisms have been estimated to be 10–1000 times greater than their average rate (about one extinction per million species per year) over the past several million years. That average rate is called the 'background rate' of extinction. Figures for current extinction rates are reached from field studies and from estimates of declines of specific groups of mammals and birds. The latter are arrived at from empirically drawn relationships between the number of species in a geographical area and the size of the area. The relationships are known to vary substantially among communities and habitats, which is why, as the range shows, there are great uncertainties in the estimates. Despite the uncertainties, the figures put the scale of humanity's impact on the Earth system in perspective and explain why most scientists have come to believe that we are witnessing the start of what has been called the Sixth Extinction, following the five earlier ones that occurred before human activities were adding to the destruction.

In recent years, an enormous body of scientific studies, ranging from those of small-scale ecosystems to those of large-scale systems (biomes), has uncovered causal, positive links between biodiversity and the biosphere's productivity, on which we depend. That we do not inflict irreparable damage to the biosphere through destroying species should now be seen to be our central obligation to our descendants. This is why it is remarkable that there is very little available by way of quantitative data relating humanity's demand for the biosphere's goods and services to the biosphere's ability to meet that demand on a sustainable basis. One, inevitably crude estimate is that some five decades ago, we were using about 70 per cent of the Earth's sustainable capacity, but now, we are using about 175 per cent. Nevertheless, 800 million people are chronically malnourished and 100 million are on the verge of starvation at any one time. How have such imbalances, both among contemporaries and between the present and future generations, come about, and how could they possibly be sustained? The problems wouldn't go away if we had another 75 per cent of the size of the Earth to take care of our needs, but we could at least stop eating into the productive capacity of the Earth progressively as the years go by. With a number of nations markedly better off than others, and the wealthy best off everywhere, those who are better off are draining productivity from poor nations in the form of energy, wood and fuel. So there is no possibility of our improving our situation without the widespread adoption of social justice, both as a matter of morality and as a matter of survival. In recent years, the Pontifical Academies have held several colloquia on the subject of social justice, global inequality and deep poverty in the contemporary world. But we haven't addressed the question of whether the Earth system is able to support the demands that humanity has been making on it. The survival of the natural world, and ultimately our survival, depends on our adoption of principles of social justice and sustainability. And sustainability requires care for the biodiversity that supplies the services that enable humanity to live and prosper.

All our food comes directly or indirectly from higher plants, of which there are an estimated 450,000 species. Tens of thousands of these have been cultivated for food at some time by some people, but at present, some 100 of them produce about 90 per cent of our food worldwide, while three kinds of grain, maize, rice and wheat, produce about 60 per cent of the total. We have detailed knowledge of perhaps only one-fifth of the species of plants in the world, and a majority could be gone in nature by the end of the century we entered recently. The same can be said for other groups of organisms, but plants are particularly critical, because we depend on them for many of our medicines, ecosystem services, atmospheric purification, carbon storage and everything that really makes our lives possible.

Even while economists and other social scientists have developed a quantitative grammar for discussing environmental problems, they have in the main neglected to do the same for biodiversity losses. The economics of climate change has advanced to the point where experts are agreed on the ranges in which such ethical parameters as the social rate of discount and the social price of carbon lie. Development economists have arrived at quantitative estimates of income that should be deemed to be the poverty line and have constructed measures of income inequality. But on biodiversity there is nothing comparable. In the absence of the kind of socio-economic reasoning that informs collective decisions affecting other spheres of the social world, direct efforts to preserve biodiversity are the best that is on offer for now. We can continue trying to preserve natural areas, particularly in areas with topographic relief, where the plant and animal inhabitants might have a chance in the face of continued climate change, and we can try to ensure sustainable interactions between the people of given areas and their biodiversity; and we can bring organisms into domestication, cultivation or seed banks to preserve as many of them as possible while they are still there. Cryopreservation may work well for some of them. All of these methods need to be improved and applied based on a continually improving knowledge of organisms, but they will clearly only succeed in the long run when appropriate social conditions have been put in place and we find substitutions for the destabilising competition and aggression toward one another that we and our ancestors have been practising for tens of thousands of years.

The workshop on Biological Extinction at the Vatican Academy in 2017 was designed to collate our current knowledge of the state of biodiversity and the socio-ecological processes that are reducing it. Governments, international organisations and the public at large are anxious to receive policy advice from experts in technical disciplines. But the processes that are shaping current species extinction are so interwoven and complex, and our understanding still so imperfect, that we have been at pains to concentrate on the science of the subject. With but few exceptions (e.g., the reports on smart villages and smart cities), we have avoided discussing policies that could help reduce humanity's aggregate demand for the biosphere's goods and services. With help and advice from our Chancellor and Presidents, we designed a programme that would offer what we felt would be a rounded perspective on the science of species extinction. And we are most grateful to contributors to the volume not only for creating a lively and informative environment at the workshop itself but also for being attentive to the time schedule we proposed to them for submitting their revised papers. The volume would not have been realised, certainly not within the time frame we have managed, without Dr Anna McIvor, who helped with the editorial process. We are most grateful to them all.

Partha S. Dasgupta, University of Cambridge
Peter H. Raven, Missouri Botanical Garden
June 2018

Acknowledgements

The present volume consists of papers presented at a workshop on Biological Extinction, sponsored jointly by the Pontifical Academy of Sciences (PAS) and the Pontifical Academy of Social Sciences (PASS), in Casina Pio IV, Vatican City, 27 February–1 March 2017. We are most grateful to Werner Arber (past President, PAS) and Margaret Archer (President, PASS) for their advice and encouragement in organising the workshop and for participating in it; to the Pontifical Academies, without whose financial support the workshop could not have been held; and to our Chancellor, Bishop Marcelo Sanchez Sorondo, for his advice and help throughout.

We are very grateful to the Centre for the Study of Existential Risk (CSER) at the University of Cambridge for enabling us to invite Dr Anna McIvor to join us in editing the papers for publication.

The usual caveat applies: the opinions expressed in the volume are the authors' own and do not necessarily reflect those of the Pontifical Academies, nor of CSER.

Introduction

PARTHA S. DASGUPTA AND PETER H. RAVEN [*]

Humanity's future will be shaped by the portfolio of capital assets we inherit and choose to pass on to our descendants, and by the balance we strike between the portfolio and the size of our population. So it makes sense to include population on the list of a society's assets and build an overarching study of our relationship with our descendants and with nature by dividing assets into three categories: *produced capital* (buildings, roads, ports, machines, instruments), *human capital* (population, health, education, knowledge and skills) and *natural capital* (biodiversity, ecosystems, subsoil resources). In this Introduction we offer a perspective on the chapters that follow by summarising salient aspects of humanity's troubled relationship with the biosphere.

The Biosphere as a Mosaic of Ecosystems

We may think of the biosphere as a mosaic of ecosystems. Ecosystems combine the abiotic environment with biological communities (plants, animals, fungi and microorganisms) to form functional units. Individual actors in ecosystems include organisms that pollinate, decompose, filter, transport, redistribute, scavenge, fix gases and so on. Most of the organisms that help to produce those services are hidden from view (a gram of soil may contain as many as 10 billion bacterial cells), which is why they are almost always missing from popular discourses on the environment. But their activities enable ecosystems to maintain a genetic library, preserve and regenerate soil, fix nitrogen and carbon, recycle nutrients, control floods, mitigate droughts, filter pollutants, assimilate waste, pollinate crops, operate the hydrological cycle and maintain the gaseous composition of the atmosphere.

---

[*] In preparing this Introduction we have drawn on Dasgupta (2019).

Ecosystems can regenerate, but suffer deterioration (worse, exhaustion) when the rates at which we expropriate the goods and services they produce and the rates at which they are converted directly into produced capital exceed the rates at which they are able to provide a sustainable supply of those goods (e.g., collapse of fisheries). By the same token, restoration and conservation measures (e.g., creating protected areas for marine fisheries) help to increase the biosphere's productivity, as measured by quality or quantity (or both).

There is more to the biosphere of course – technically, it's the part of Earth occupied by living organisms – but regarding it as a gigantic mix of renewable natural resources is a useful way of conceptualising it. Agricultural land, forests, watersheds, fisheries, fresh water sources, estuaries, wetlands, the oceans and the atmosphere are some of the interlocking constituents of the biosphere. We will refer to them generically as 'ecosystems' and, so as to draw attention to populations of species in their habitats, we shall speak of them also, more narrowly, as 'biological communities'.

Ecosystems differ in composition and extent. They can be defined as ranging from the communities and interactions of organisms in your mouth or those in the canopy of a rain forest to all those in Earth's oceans. The processes governing them differ in complexity and speed. There are systems that turn over in minutes, and there are others whose rhythmic time extends to hundreds of years. Some ecosystems are extensive ('biomes', such as the African savanna); some cover regions (river basins); many involve clusters of villages (micro-watersheds); others are confined to the level of a single village (the village pond). In each example there is an element of indivisibility. Divide an ecosystem into parts by creating barriers, and the sum of the productivity of the parts will typically be found to be lower than the productivity of the whole, other things being equal (Loreau et al., 2001; Sodhi et al., 2009; Worm et al., 2006). The mobility of biological populations is a reason. Safe corridors, for example, enable migratory species to survive.

Population extinctions disrupt essential ecosystem services. In tropical forests, for example, dung beetles play an essential role in recycling nutrients. Excessive hunting of mammals in the forests has been found to be a cause of local elimination of dung-dependent beetles (Brook et al., 2008). When subject to excessive stress, once flourishing ecosystems (e.g., biologically rich estuaries) flip into unproductive states (dead zones, resulting from pollution). The stress could be occasioned by an invasion of foreign species or of foreign substances, or it could result from the loss of population diversity in the ecosystem (see below), or it could be triggered by the demise of a dominant species (see below), and so on. Ehrlich and Ehrlich (1981) likened the pathways by which an ecosystem can be tipped out of a stable regime into an unproductive state to a flying aircraft from which rivets are removed, one at a time. The probability that it will crash increases very slowly at first, but then at some unspecifiable number it rises sharply to 1.

Broadly speaking, an ecosystem's productivity and resilience (the flow of goods and services they offer us and their ability to withstand shocks) increases with the diversity of the functional characteristics of its species populations; a mere headcount of species can mislead. Mutual dependence among the species is a reason. For example, many trees produce large, lipid-rich fruits that are adapted for animal dispersal, which means the demise of fruit eating birds can have serious consequences for forest regeneration. Similarly, in a study in Costa Rica, Ricketts et al. (2004) found that coffee yield declined with distance from the forest edge because native forest bees aid pollination. The authors reported that the bees increased coffee yield by 20 per cent in fields within 1 km of the forest edge. Looking elsewhere, about one-third of the human diet in tropical countries is derived from insect-pollinated plants. Consequently, a decline in forest-dwelling insects has an adverse effect on human nutrition. And so on.[1]

In food webs, the relationships are unidirectional. Primary producers in the oceans (phytoplankton, sea weeds) are at the bottom of the food chain, with species at higher trophic levels consuming those that are below. Species whose impact on a community structure is large and disproportionately large relative to their abundance are called 'keystone species' (Power et al., 1996). Keystone species usually occupy the top rungs of a given food chain. When human consumption reduces their populations substantially, the community flips to a different state as prey populations explode. That in turn reduces the diversity of a given community's functional characteristics, and can lead to drastic changes both in its structure and in the species that it can continue to support.

Biological communities can influence their abiotic environment. The Amazon for example generates about half of its own rainfall by recycling moisture 5–6 times as air masses move from the Atlantic across the basin to the west. Mathematicians call this a positive feedback.

Deforestation of the Amazon would be expected to reduce rainfall and to lengthen dry seasons in the region. One estimate has it that 20–25 per cent deforestation of the Amazon can be expected to flip the forests in the east to savanna vegetation (Lovejoy and Nobre, 2018). Palm oil trees are planted increasingly in the Amazon so as to provide substitutes for fossil fuels, only to contribute to a sharp decline in the ability of the Amazon forest to absorb carbon dioxide from the atmosphere. The irony will not escape readers.

In a path-breaking set of publications assessing the state of the world's ecosystems, MEA (2005a, 2005b, 2005c, 2005d) constructed a four-way classification of goods and services we enjoy from them: (1) provisioning services (food, fibre, fuel, fresh water); (2) regulating services (protection against natural hazards such as storms; the climate system); (3) supporting services (nutrient cycling, soil production); and (4) cultural services (recreation, cultural landscapes, aesthetic or spiritual experiences). Cultural services and a variety of regulating services (such as disease regulation) contribute directly to human well-being, whereas others (soil production) contribute indirectly (by providing the means of growing food crops).

The view that the biosphere is a mosaic of renewable natural resources also covers its role as a sink for pollution, contemporary carbon emissions into the atmosphere being an example. Pollutants are the reverse of natural resources. One way to conceptualise pollution is to view it as the depreciation of capital assets. Acid rains damage forests; carbon emissions into the atmosphere trap heat; industrial seepage and discharge reduce water quality in streams and underground reservoirs; sulphur emissions corrode structures and harm human health; and so on. The damage inflicted on each type of asset (buildings, forests, the atmosphere, fisheries, human health) should be interpreted as depreciation. For natural resources depreciation amounts to the difference between the rate at which they are harvested and their regenerative rate; for pollutants the depreciation they inflict on natural resources is the difference between the rate at which pollutants are discharged into the resource base and the rate at which the resource base is able to neutralise the pollutants. The task in either case is to estimate depreciation. 'Resources' are 'goods', while 'pollutants' (the degrader of resources) are 'bads'. Pollution is the reverse of conservation.[2]

Erosion of the Biosphere

Humanity's success in the Modern Era (post 1500 CE) in raising the standard of living has in great measure involved mining and degrading the biosphere. Habitat destruction caused by rising demand for nature's products is the proximate cause of the decline in the biosphere's ability to supply our needs on a sustainable basis. The conversion of land for the production of food, livestock and plantation crops is a prime cause of that decline. Conversion of land into produced capital (e.g., buildings, roads) is another cause.

Erosion of the biosphere usually goes unrecorded in official economic statistics because that most common measure of economic welfare, gross domestic product (GDP), does not record depreciation of capital assets. Destroy an open woodland so as to build a shopping mall, and the national accounts will record the increase in produced capital (the shopping mall is an investment), but not the disinvestment in natural capital. The example is a commonplace. While industrial output increased by a multiple of 40 during the twentieth century, the use of energy increased by a multiple of 16, methane-producing cattle populations grew in pace with human population, fish catch increased by a multiple of 35 and carbon and sulphur dioxide emissions rose by more than 10. It has been estimated that 25–30 per cent of the 130 billion metric tonnes of carbon that are harnessed annually by terrestrial photosynthesis is appropriated for human use (Haberl et al., 2007). Although the rise in the concentration of atmospheric carbon receives much the greater public attention, MEA (2005a, 2005b, 2005c, 2005d) reported that 15 of the 24 ecosystems the authors had reviewed worldwide were either degraded or are being exploited at unsustainable rates.

The statistics we have just summarised for sketching humanity's recent doings differ sharply from the ones that have been on offer in a string of recent books, in which intellectuals have redrawn our attention to the remarkable gains in the standard of living humanity has enjoyed over the past century (Micklethwait and Wooldridge, 2000; Ridley, 2010; Lomborg, 2014; Norberg, 2016; Pinker, 2018). The authors have collated data on growth in scientific knowledge and the accumulation of produced capital and human capital and argued that humanity has never had it so good. But with the exception of rising carbon concentration in the atmosphere, trends in the state of the biosphere accompanying those advances have gone un-noted by the authors. The problem is, global climate change is but one of a myriad of environmental problems we face today. And because it is amenable to technological solutions (e.g., innovating with cheap non-carbon sources of energy and, more speculatively, firing sulphur particulates into the stratosphere to reflect sunlight back to space; Pinker, 2018), it is not representative. Global climate change attracts attention among intellectuals and the reading public not only because it is a grave problem, but also because it is possible to imagine meeting it by using the familiar economics of commodity taxation, regulation and resource pricing without having to forgo growth in living standards in rich countries. The literature on the economics of climate change (e.g., Stern, 2006) has even encouraged the thought that with but little investment in clean energy sources (say 2 per cent of world GDP) we can enjoy indefinite growth in the world's output of final goods and services (global GDP).

And that's a thought to be resisted. At least as grave a danger facing humanity is the unprecedented rate of biological extinctions now taking place. Continued extinctions will damage the biosphere irreparably, and they cannot be prevented by technological fixes. Politics has intervened to prevent even the relatively small global investment that experts suggest is required to stall climate change. So we should expect the problem of biological extinctions to remain off the table, at least until citizens take the matter seriously.

The Biosphere as a Common Property Resource

Reproductive decisions and our use of the natural environment have consequences for others, including our descendants, that are unaccounted for under prevailing institutions and social mores (such as markets, government policy, communitarian engagements and religious injunctions). Economists use the term *externalities* to denote those consequences of our decisions for others that are not accounted for. The qualifier 'not accounted for' means that the consequences in question follow without prior, normative engagement with those who are, or who will be, affected. The required engagements don't have to be face-to-face. Many of our actions can be expected to have consequences for our descendants; but if the actions were taken with due care and concern (we take many actions – for example, saving for the future – with our descendants very much in our mind), they would not give rise to externalities. We begin to engage with future people when we deliberate whether current rates of carbon emissions into the atmosphere will place an unjust burden on our descendants. The presence of externalities explains why and how it can be that a people are settled on a pattern of reproductive behaviour and environmental-resource use they would all prefer to alter but do not because no one has the necessary motivation to change their behaviour unilaterally. Externalities raise deep ethical issues. Not only do they extend to contemporaries and can be expected to extend to future people, it is also that some people will be born in consequence of the decisions we take, while some who would have been born had we acted otherwise will not be born.

Today, growth in atmospheric carbon concentration is the canonical expression of adverse externalities, but humanity faces wider and deeper threats to our future from the species extinctions now taking place, which are also morally even more reprehensible. Proximate causes of extinctions are destruction and fragmentation of natural habitats and overexploitation of biological communities residing there. We are converting land into farms and plantations, destroying forests for timber and minerals, applying pesticides and fertilisers so as to intensify agriculture, introducing foreign species into native habitats and using the biosphere as a sink for our waste. And these activities are taking place at scales that are orders of magnitude greater than they were even 250 years ago.

Adverse externalities associated with our use of the biosphere in great measure arise because nature is mobile: birds and insects fly, water flows, the wind blows and the oceans circulate. That makes it difficult to establish property rights to key components of the biosphere. By property rights we don't only mean private rights, we include communitarian and public rights. This is why much of the biosphere is an 'open-access resource', meaning that it is free to all to do as we like with it. Hardin (1968) famously spoke of the fate of unmanaged common property resources as 'the tragedy of the commons'. But while Hardin's analysis was entirely appropriate for global commons (such as the atmosphere and the oceans), it was less than applicable to geographically confined resources such as woodlands, ponds, grazing fields, coastal fisheries, wetlands and mangroves. Because local commons are geographically confined, their use can be monitored by community members. There were exceptions of course, but in times past those resources were managed by communities, and they were not open-access resources. Reviewing an extensive literature, Feeny et al. (1990) and Ostrom (1990) observed that community management systems enabled societies to avoid experiencing the tragedy of the commons. Social norms of behaviour, including the use of fines and social sanctions for misbehaviour, have guided the use of local common property resources.

In poor countries the commons continue to supply household needs to rural people (such as water, fuelwood, medicinal herbs, fruits and berries, manure and fibres and timber for building material). Some products are also marketed (including fish, fuel wood, dung, wood and fibre products). But as in so many other spheres of social life, communitarian practices have over the years strengthened in some instances (e.g., community forestry in Nepal) and weakened in others. They weakened for example when communal rights were overturned by central fiat. In order to establish political authority after independence (and also to earn rents from timber exports), a number of states in sub-Saharan Africa and Asia imposed rules that destroyed traditional community practices in forestry. Villages ceased to have the authority to enforce sanctions on those who broke norms of behaviour. But knowledge of local ecology is held by those who work on the commons, not by state officials, who in addition can be corrupt. Thomson et al. (1986), Somanathan (1991) and Baland and Platteau (1996), among others, have identified ways in which state authority damaged local institutions and turned local commons into seemingly open-access resources. Then there are subtle ways in which even well-intentioned state policy can cause communitarian practices to weaken (Balasubramanian, 2008; Mukhopadhyay, 2008).[3]

Common Property Resources and Fertility Intentions

Even when commons are managed by the community and outsiders are kept at bay, we should ask whether access to the commons is based on household size or whether each household has a fixed share of its output. It can be argued that when larger households are entitled to a greater share of the commons' goods and services, households have an incentive to convert natural resources excessively into private assets. In sub-Saharan Africa larger households are (or until recently, *were*) awarded a greater quantity of land by the kinship group. That practice encourages fertility.[4] What is true in the case of local commons to which households have access regardless of their size holds true in the case of global commons, to which we all have access regardless of our household size. Even humane systems of property rights can give rise to adverse externalities.

How important are local commons in household income? Despite the importance of the question there is little in the form of quantitative evidence. Casual empiricism suggests they are less significant in advanced industrial countries than in poor rural societies. In the former, local resources are either owned privately or under the jurisdiction of local authorities or, as in the case of places of especial aesthetic value, are national parks. That is not so in rural areas in poor countries. In a pioneering work, Jodha (1986) reported evidence from semi-arid rural districts in Central India that among poor families the proportion of income based directly on local commons was 15–25 per cent. Cavendish (2000) arrived at even higher estimates from a study of villages in Zimbabwe: the proportion of income based directly on local common property resources was found to be 35 per cent, the figure for the poorest quintile being 40 per cent. To not recognise the significance of the local natural-resource base in poor countries is to not understand how the poor live.[5]

Global Ecological Footprint

Studying biogeochemical signatures of the past 11,000 years, Waters et al. (2016) tracked the human-induced evolution of soil nitrogen and phosphorus inventories in sediments and ice. The authors reported that the now-famous figure of the hockey stick that characterises time series of carbon concentration in the atmosphere is also displayed by time series of a broad class of global geochemical signatures. They all show a sharp rise in the middle of the twentieth century. Waters et al. (2016) proposed that the mid-twentieth century should be regarded as the time we entered the Anthropocene.[6]

Their reading is consistent with macroeconomic statistics. World population in 1950 was about 2.5 billion and global output of final goods and services a bit over 8.7 trillion international dollars (at 2011 prices).The average person in the world was poor (annual income was somewhat in excess of 3500 international dollars). Since then the world has prospered beyond recognition. Life expectancy at birth in 1950 was 45, today it is a little over 70. Population has grown to over 7.6 billion and world output of final goods and services is (at 2011 prices) above 110 trillion international dollars, meaning that world income per capita is now more than 15,000 international dollars. A somewhat more than 12-fold increase in global output in a 65-year period helps to explain not only the stresses to the Earth system that we have just reviewed, but it also hints at the possibility that humanity's demand for the biosphere's services has for several decades exceeded sustainable levels.

In a review of the state of the biosphere, WWF (2008) reported that although the global demand for ecological services in the 1960s was less than supply, it exceeded supply in the early years of the present century by 50 per cent. The figure is based on the idea of a 'global ecological footprint', which is the surface area of biologically productive land and sea needed to supply the resources we consume (food, fibres, wood, water) and to assimilate the waste we produce (materials, gases). The Global Footprint Network (GFN) updates its estimates of the global ecological footprint on a regular basis. A footprint in excess of 1 means demand for ecological services exceeds their supply. By GFN's reckoning, maintaining the world's average living standard at the level reached some 10 years ago (roughly 12,000 international dollars) would have required 1.5 Earths, and the number has since grown steadily to over 1.7.[7]

These are inevitably crude estimates. Figures for such socio-economic indicators as GDP, population size, life expectancy and adult literacy are reached by a multitude of national and global institutions, who exchange information and coordinate their work. They are revised regularly and governments and international agencies use them routinely when advocating and devising policy. We all take note of their figures and trust them. For estimates of our global ecological footprint, however, these are early days. What matters is not the exact figure but whether the footprint exceeds 1. On that matter there should be little question. That there is an overshoot in global demand for the biosphere's goods and services is entirely consistent with a wide range of evidence on the state of the biosphere that is summarised in the chapters that follow.

GFN's most recent estimate of the global ecological footprint is 1.76. Sustainable development would require that the footprint must on average be less than 1 over time. Global demand for ecological services can exceed supply for a period, but not indefinitely. Economic development during the past 65 years has raised the average living standard beyond recognition while population has increased by an unprecedented amount; but we have enjoyed that success by leaving a substantially diminished biosphere, and therefore potential for sustainability, for future generations. It would appear we are living at once in the best of times and the worst of times.

Notes

1. Hooper et al. (2005) is an excellent review of the issues. A classic on the subject is Tilman and Downing (1994). See also Tilman (1997), Hector et al. (1999) and Walker et al. (1999).
2. A formal demonstration of the equivalence is in Dasgupta (1982).
3. In recent years democratic movements alongside stakeholders and pressure from international organisations have encouraged a return to community-based systems of management of the local commons. Shyamsundar (2008) presents a synthesis of the findings in nearly 200 articles on the efficacy of a devolution of management responsibilities – from the state to local communities – over the local natural-resource base. Her article focuses on wildlife, forestry and irrigation. The balance of evidence appears to be that devolution leads to better management, other things being equal. Shyamsundar of course offers a discussion of what those other things are.
4. A formal demonstration of the argument is in Dasgupta (2019: Appendix 2).
5. For a study of the population-consumption-environment nexus at both the global and local levels, see Dasgupta (2019).
6. The Anthropocene Working Group has proposed that the immediate post-war years should be regarded as the start of the Anthropocene. See Vosen (2016).
7. In his contribution to the present volume, Mathias Wakernagel explains the methodology adopted by GFN for estimating the global ecological footprint.

References

Baland, J.-M. & Platteau, J.-P. 1996. *Halting Degradation of Natural Resources: Is There a Role for Rural Communities?* Oxford: Clarendon Press.

Balasubramanian, R. 2008. Community tanks vs private wells: Coping strategies and sustainability issues in South India. In R. Ghate,

N. S. Jodha & P. Mukhopadhyay (Eds.), *Promise, Trust and Evolution: Managing the Commons of South Asia*. Oxford: Oxford University Press.

Brook, B. W., Sodhi, N. S. & Bradshaw, C. J. A. 2008. Synergies among extinction drivers under global change. *Trends in Ecology and Evolution*, 23(8): 453–460.

Cavendish, W. 2000. Empirical regularities in the poverty-environment relationships of rural households: Evidence from Zimbabwe. *World Development*, 28(11): 1979–2003.

Dasgupta, P. 1982. *The Control of Resources*. Cambridge, MA: Harvard University Press.

    2019. *Time and the Generations: Population ethics for a diminishing planet*. New York: Columbia University Press.

Ehrlich, P. R. & Ehrlich, A. H. 1981. *Extinction: The Causes and Consequences of the Disappearance of Species*. New York: Random House.

Feeny, D., Berkes, F., McCay, B. J. & Acheson, J. M. 1990. The tragedy of the commons: Twenty-two years later. *Human Ecology*, 18(1): 1–19.

Haberl, H., Erb, K.-H., Krasmann, F., Gaube, V., Bondeau, A., Plutzer, C., Gingrich, S., Lucht, W. & Fisher-Kowalski, M. 2007. Quantifying and mapping the human appropriation of net primary production in Earth's terrestrial ecosystems. *Proceedings of the National Academy of Science*, 104(31): 12942–12947.

Hardin, G. 1968. The tragedy of the commons. *Science*, 162: 1243–1248.

Hector, A., Schmid, B., Beierkuhnlein, C., Caldeira, M. C., Diemer, M., Dimitrakopoulos, P. G., Finn, J. A., Freitas, H., Giller, P. S., Good, J., Harris, R., Högberg, P., Huss-Danell, K., Joshi, J., Jumpponen, A., Körner, C., Leadley, P. W., Loreau, M., Minns, A., Mulder, C. P. H., O'Donovan, G., Otway, S. J., Pereira, J. S., Prinz, A., Read, D. J., Scherer-Lorenzen, M., Schulze, E.-D., Siamantziouras, A.-S. D., Spehn, E. M., Terry, A. C., Troumbis, A. Y., Woodward, F. I., Yachi, S. & Lawton, J. H. 1999. Plant diversity and productivity experiments in European grasslands. *Science*, 286(5442): 1123–1127.

Hooper, D. U., Chapin, F. S., Ewel, J. J., Hector, A., Inchausti, P., Lavorel, S., Lawton, J. H., Lodge, D. M., Loreau, M., Naeem, S., Schmid, B., Setälä, H., Symstad, A. J., Vandermeer, J. & Wardle, D. A. 2005. Effects of biodiversity on ecosystem functioning: A consensus on current knowledge. *Ecological Monographs*, 75(1): 3–35.

Jodha, N. S. 1986. Common property resources and the rural poor. *Economic and Political Weekly*, 21: 1169–1181.

Lomborg, B. (Ed.). 2014. *How Much Have Global Problems Cost the World? A Scoreboard from 1900 to 2050*. Cambridge: Cambridge University Press.

Loreau, M., Naeem, S., Inchausti, P., Bengtsson, J., Grime, J. P., Hector, A., Hooper, D. U., Huston, M. A., Raffaelli, D., Schmid, B., Tilman, D. & Wardle, D. A. 2001. Biodiversity and ecosystem functioning: Current knowledge and future challenges. *Science*, 294(5543): 804–808.

Lovejoy, T. E. & Nobre, C. 2018. Amazon tipping point. *Science Advances*, 4(2): eaat2340.

MEA. 2005a. *Ecosystems and Human Well-Being, I: Current State and Trends*. Ed. R. Hassan, R. Scholes & N. Ash. Washington, DC: Island Press.

　2005b. *Ecosystems and Human Well-Being, II: Scenarios*. Ed. S. R. Carpenter, P. L. Pingali, E. M. Bennet & M. B. Zurek. Washington, DC: Island Press.

　2005c. *Ecosystems and Human Well-Being, III: Policy Responses*. Ed. K. Chopra, R. Leemans, P. Kumar & H. Simmons. Washington, DC: Island Press.

　2005d. *Ecosystems and Human Well-Being, IV: Multiscale Assessments*. Ed. D. Capistrano, C. Samper, M. J. Lee & C. Randsepp-Hearne. Washington, DC: Island Press.

Micklethwait, J. & Wooldridge, A. 2000. *A Future Perfect: The Challenge and Promise of Globalization*. New York: Random House.

Mukhopadhyay, P. 2008. Heterogeneity, commons, and privatization: Agrarian institutional change in Goa. In R. Ghate, N. S. Jodha & P. Mukhopadhyay (Eds.), *Promise, Trust and Evolution: Managing the Commons of South Asia*. Oxford: Oxford University Press.

Norberg, J. 2016. *Progress: Ten Reasons to Look Forward to the Future*. London: One World.

Ostrom, E. 1990. *Governing the Commons: The Evolution of Institutions for Collective Action*. Cambridge: Cambridge University Press.

Pinker, S. 2018. *Enlightenment Now: The Case for Reason, Science, Humanism, and Progress*. New York: Allen Lane.

Power, M. E., Tilman, D., Estes, J. A., Menge, B. A., Bond, W. J., Mills, L. S., Daily, G., Castilla, J. C., Lubchenco, J. & Paine, R. T. 1996. Challenges in the Quest for Keystones. Identifying keystone species is difficult – but essential to understanding how loss of species will affect ecosystems. *BioScience*, 46(8): 609–620.

Ricketts, T. H., Daily, G. C., Ehrlich, P. R. & Michener, C. D. 2004. Economic value of tropical forest to coffee production. *Proceedings of the National Academy of Science*, 101(34): 12579–12582.

Ridley, M. 2010. *The Rational Optimist: How Prosperity Evolves*. London: 4th Estate.

Shyamsundar, P. 2008. Decentralization, devolution, and collective action. In R. Ghate, N. S. Jodha & P. Mukhopadhyay (Eds.), *Promise, Trust and Evolution: Managing the Commons of South Asia.* Oxford: Oxford University Press.

Sodhi, N. S., Brook, B. W. & Bradshaw, C. J. A. 2009. Causes and consequences of species extinctions. In S. A. Levin, S. R. Carpenter, H. C. J. Godfray, A. P. Kinzig, M. Loreau, J. B. Losos, B. Walker & D. S. Wilcove (Eds.), *The Princeton Guide to Ecology.* Princeton, NJ: Princeton University Press

Somanathan, E. 1991. Deforestation, property rights and incentives in Central Himalaya. *Economic and Political Weekly,* 26: PE37–46.

Stern, N. H. 2006. *The Stern Review of the Economics of Climate Change.* Cambridge: Cambridge University Press.

Thomson, J. T., Feeny, D. H. & Oakerson, R. J. 1986. Institutional dynamics: The evolution and dissolution of common property resource management. In National Research Council (Ed.), *Proceedings of Conference on Common Property Resource Management.* Washington, DC: US National Academy of Sciences.

Tilman, D. 1997. Biodiversity and ecosystem functioning. In G. Daily (Ed.), *Nature's Services: Societal Dependence on Natural Ecosystems.* Washington, DC: Island Press.

Tilman, D. & Downing, J. A. 1994. Biodiversity and stability in grasslands. *Nature,* 367: 363–367.

Vosen, P. 2016. Anthropocene pinned down to post war period. *Science,* 353 (6302): 852–853.

Walker, B., Kinzig, A. & Langridge, J. 1999. Plant attribute diversity, resilience, and ecosystem function: The nature and significance of dominant and minor species. *Ecosystems,* 2(2): 95–113.

Waters, C. N., Zalasiewicz, J., Summerhayes, C., Barnosky, A. D., Poirier, C., Gałuszka, A., Cearreta, A., Edgeworth, M., Ellis, E. C., Ellis, M., Jeandel, C., Leinfelder, R., McNeill, J. R., Richter, D. d., Steffen, W., Syvitski, J., Vidas, D., Wagreich, M., Williams, M., Zhisheng, A., Grinevald, J., Odada, E., Oreskes, N. & Wolfe, A. P. 2016. The Anthropocene is functionally and stratigraphically distinct from the Holocene. *Science,* 351(6269): aad2622.

Worm, B., Barbier, E. B., Beaumont, N., Duffy, J. E., Folke, C., Halpern, B. S., Jackson, J. B. C., Lotze, H. K., Micheli, F., Palumbi, S. R., Sala, E., Selkoe, K. A., Stachowicz, J. J. & Watson, R. 2006. Impacts of biodiversity loss on ocean ecosystem services. *Science,* 314(5800): 787–790.

WWF. 2008. *Living Planet Report 2008.* Gland, Switzerland: WWF International.

Prologue

Extinction: What It Means to Us

MARTIN REES [*]

It is a privilege to speak here today. But I do this with diffidence. That is because I am a physicist – trying to understand only the inanimate world. Much of this still baffles us. But it should be an easy task, compared to the complexities of living things and their ecologies. It is the biologists, ecologists and social scientists who face the most daunting intellectual challenges. Those are the disciplines represented at this meeting.

You may think that, as an astronomer, I worry about asteroid impacts. I do, but not very much. It was such an event 65 million years ago that many think did in the dinosaurs. But the probability of such a catastrophe is 1 in 100,000 each century – no bigger now than it was in the remote geological past.

The effects that should worry us more are catastrophes induced by humans – whose probability is now far higher – and is rising fast.

The Earth has existed for 45 million centuries, but this is the first when one species, ours, is so empowered that it can determine the planet's future – the first when technology could enable us all to live in fulfilment. Or – to take a darker view – this is the first century where our follies could foreclose the immense potential for further evolution. We are deep in the Anthropocene.

The choices and decisions we make today will resonate at least into the twenty-second century – and if we get them wrong, we will bequeath future generations a bleak future. We surely need to look ahead, and horizon scan, further than most politicians and planners do.

In particular, if our despoliation of nature causes mass extinctions, by neglect, by error or by malign intention, then, to quote E. O. Wilson, 'it's the action that future generations will least forgive us for'.

---

[*] This was given as an opening address to the Workshop on Biological Extinction in 2017.

Our focus at this workshop will be to address the threats that stem from humanity's ever-heavier collective 'footprint' on the planet, which is depleting resources, impoverishing ecologies and changing the climate. And also we should address the threats stemming from misuse of biotech or other powerful technology.

Even with a cloudy crystal ball there are two things we can predict decades ahead: the world will be more crowded, and it will have a changing climate. A word about these two trends.

Fifty years ago, world population was about 3.5 billion. It is now 7.5 billion. But the growth is slowing. Indeed the number of births per year, worldwide, has levelled off. Nonetheless world population is forecast to rise to 9 to 10 billion by 2050. That is partly because most people in the developing world are young. They are yet to have children, and they will live longer. The age histogram in the developing world is becoming more like it is in Europe.

Experts predict continuing urbanisation: 70 per cent of people in cities by 2050. Even by 2030 Lagos, San Paulo and Delhi will have populations above 30 million. Preventing megacities becoming turbulent dystopias will surely be a major challenge to governance, as it will be to ensure that rural populations are not left behind.

Population growth seems currently under-discussed. That may be partly because it is deemed by some a taboo subject, tainted by association with eugenics in the 1920s and 1930s, with Indian policies under Indira Gandhi, and more recently with China's hard-line one-child policy, and because forecasts of mass starvation have proved premature. Up till now, food production has kept pace: famines stem from wars or maldistribution, not overall shortage.

Can 9 billion people be fed? We will be hearing from experts at this workshop. But my layman's impression is that the answer is yes. Improved agriculture – low-till, water-conserving and perhaps involving GM crops – together with better engineering to reduce waste, improve irrigation and so forth could sustainably feed that number by mid-century. The buzz-phrase is 'sustainable intensification'.

But there will need to be lifestyle changes. The world could not sustain even its present population if everyone lived like Americans do today, each using as much energy and eating as much beef.

But none of us need live as profligately as that. Indeed, all can, by 2050, have a good quality of life, provided that technology is developed appropriately, and deployed wisely. That should be our message – in Gandhi's famous mantra – 'Enough for everyone's need but not for everyone's greed'.

Population trends beyond 2050 are harder to predict. They will depend on what people as yet unborn decide about the number and spacing of their children. John Bongaarts and others will be discussing this.

As we will hear, if families in Africa remain large, then according to the UN, that continent's population could double again by 2100, to 4 billion, thereby raising the global population to 11 billion. Nigeria alone would by then have as big a population as Europe and North America combined, and almost half of all the world's children would be in Africa.

Optimists remind us that each extra mouth brings also two hands and a brain. Nonetheless the higher the population becomes, the greater will be all pressures on resources, especially if the developing world narrows its gap with the developed world in its per capita consumption. And the harder it will be for Africa to escape the 'poverty trap'.

As well as rising population, there is a second firm prediction we can make: the world later this century will be warmer.

Climate change will hit hardest those who have contributed the least to its cause. Heat stress will most hurt those without air conditioning, crop failure will most affect those who already struggle to afford food, extreme weather events will most endanger those whose homes are fragile.

Unlike population trends, climate policies certainly are not under-discussed, even though they are under-acted-upon.

It is still unclear just how fast the climate will change, how much the climatic effects of rising CO_2 are amplified by associated changes in water vapour and clouds.

But despite the uncertainties, most would agree that under 'business-as-usual' scenarios we cannot rule out, later in the century, really catastrophic warming, and tipping pints triggering long-term trends like the melting of Greenland's icecap.

But even those who accept this assertion have diverse views on the policy response. These stem from differences in economics and ethics – in particular, in how much obligation we should feel toward future generations.

Economists who apply 'commercial' discounting (as, for instance, those in Bjorn Lomberg's Copenhagen Consensus do) are in effect writing off what happens beyond 2050, so unsurprisingly they downplay the priority of addressing climate change in comparison with shorter-term efforts to help the world's poor.

But if you care about those who will live into the twenty-second century and beyond, then, as economists like Stern and Weizman argue, you deem it worth paying an insurance premium now, to protect those generations against the worst-case scenarios.

So, even those who agree that there is a significant risk of climate catastrophe a century hence, will differ in how urgently they advocate action today. Their assessment will depend on expectations of future growth, and optimism about technological fixes. But, above all, it depends on an ethical issue: in optimising people's life-chances, should we discriminate on grounds of date of birth?

Consider this analogy. Suppose astronomers had tracked an asteroid, and calculated that it would hit the Earth in 2080, 65 years from now, not with certainty, but with say a 10 per cent probability. Would we relax, saying that it is a problem that can be set on one side for 50 years – people will then be richer, and it may turn out then that it is going to miss the Earth anyway? I do not think we would. There would surely be a consensus that we should start straight away and do our best to find ways to deflect it, or mitigate its effects.

A word now about other threats to the environment that come from new technologies.

Here we cannot make firm forecasts decades ahead – smartphones, for instance, would have seemed magic only 20 years ago. So we cannot conceive what advances might emerge by 2050.

Technology should be our friend. Without applying new science, the world cannot provide food and sustainable clean energy for an expanding and more demanding population. These advances will offer inspirational challenges for young scientists and engineers.

But we need wisely directed technology. Indeed, many of us are anxious that some forms of technology, especially biotech and robotics, are advancing so fast that we may not properly cope with them, and that we will have a bumpy ride through this century.

And there are portents.

The new CRISPR – cas9 gene-editing technique is hugely promising for eliminating harmful genes in humans. And 'gene drive' programmes are being promoted as a method for wiping out species such as mosquitoes that carry diseases, even parasitic imported species like grey squirrels in Britain. But surely caution is in order here. There is a risk of disturbing ecological balances.

These technologies will need regulation, on prudential and ethical grounds.

Back in the early days of recombinant DNA research, a group of biologists met in Asilomar, California, and agreed guidelines on what experiments should and should not be done. This seemingly encouraging precedent has triggered several meetings to discuss the much more powerful recent developments in the same spirit.

But today the research community is far more broadly international, and more influenced by commercial pressures. What I find scary is that biotech involves small-scale dual use equipment. Indeed, biohacking is burgeoning even as a hobby and competitive game. I would worry that whatever regulations are imposed cannot be enforced worldwide, any more than the drug laws can, or the tax laws. Whatever can be done will be done by someone, somewhere. Regulating the huge facilities in the nuclear arena is a doddle in comparison.

Let us recall what is meant by sustainable development. The Bruntland Commission in 1987 introduced this definition: 'development that meets the needs of the present [especially the poor] without compromising the ability of future generations to meet their own needs'.

There seems no *scientific* impediment to achieving a sustainable and secure world, where all enjoy a lifestyle better than those in the 'west' do today. We can be *technological* optimists.

But the intractable politics and sociology – the gap between potentialities and what actually happens – engenders pessimism. Politicians look to their own voters and the next election. We downplay what is happening even now in far-away countries. And we discount too heavily the problems we will leave for new generations.

Our responsibility to our children, to the poorest, and to our stewardship of life's diversity surely demands that we do not leave a depleted and hazardous world.

Here the great religious faiths can be our allies. The Catholic Church, for instance, transcends normal political constraints – there is no gainsaying its global reach, nor its durability and long-term vision, nor its focus on the world's poor. And that is why the Holy Father's

Encyclical on climate and environment was so important. It had huge resonance and smoothed the path toward a consensus at the Paris climate conference in December 2015.

Partha Dasgupta, along with the climate scientist Ram Ramanathan (who sadly could not be at this workshop) achieved great leverage by laying the scientific groundwork through the Study Week on climate and environment.

So, in summary, the pressures of rising populations, climate change and the risks of misusing powerful technologies will aggravate the type of devastation that this workshop is about – the loss of biodiversity.

But let us remind ourselves why this matters. We are clearly harmed if fish stocks dwindle to extinction. There are plants in the rain forest whose genes may be useful to us. But there is a spiritual value too. To quote E. O. Wilson again 'At the heart of the environmentalist world view is the conviction that human physical and spiritual health depends on the planet Earth ... Natural ecosystems – forests, coral reefs, marine blue waters – maintain the world as we would wish it to be maintained. Our body and our mind evolved to live in this particular planetary environment and no other.'

But even this is too anthropocentric a focus. Those who call themselves 'environmentalists' would proclaim that biodiversity, the intricate variety and beauty of the natural world, has intrinsic value over and above its benefit to us humans. And of course the Encyclical affirmed that humans have a duty of care toward the rest of God's creation.

We all surely want to 'sign up' to this goal. But there is a big problem in achieving it, basically because our secular institutions, despite their global range, do not plan long-term enough.

Those who built St Peter's Basilica and Europe's great cathedrals thought the world might only last another thousand years, and they knew of nothing beyond Europe. But despite these constricted horizons, in both time and space, despite the deprivation and harshness of their lives, despite their primitive technology and meagre resources, they built huge and glorious buildings they never lived to see finished, and that uplift our spirits centuries later.

What a contrast to so much of our discourse today! Unlike our forebears, we know a great deal about our world, and indeed about what lies beyond. Technologies that our ancestors could not have conceived enrich our lives and our understanding. Many phenomena still make us fearful, but the advance of science spares us from irrational dread. Unlike our forebears we know that we are stewards of a precious 'pale blue dot' in a vast cosmos, a planet with a future measured in billions of years, whose fate depends on humanity's collective actions this century. So it is shameful that our horizon is shorter than theirs.

Spaceship Earth is hurtling through the void. Its passengers are anxious and fractious. Their life-support system is vulnerable to disruption and breakdowns. There is too little horizon-scanning to minimise long-term risks.

The stakes are high. And the threats are real. It is a wise maxim that 'the unfamiliar isn't the same as the improbable'.

And I give the last word to a secular sage, the biologist Peter Medawar:

'The bells that toll for mankind are . . . like the bells of Alpine cattle. They are attached to our own necks, and it must be our fault if they do not make a tuneful and melodious sound.'

1 | Extinction in Deep Time
Lessons from the Past?

NEIL SHUBIN

The rocks of the world contain a record of more than 3.5 billion years of change to the living world. As new evidence of past life emerges, increasing rigour is brought to the data that tell of species abundance, distribution and relationships through time. In addition, refinements of the stratigraphic record and new insights into past environments illuminate the physical factors that affect the structure and function of ancient ecosystems, particularly how they respond to climate change over time. For these reasons, palaeontological and geological data can be brought to bear on issues central to understanding biodiversity – the rates and patterns of species loss, mechanisms that drive diversity change and features that make some species and times susceptible to extinction. Moreover, the rock and fossil record can inform an understanding of ecosystem recovery after extinctions, revealing how diversity can rebuild after major catastrophes. While ancient fossil records can reveal the physical and biotic factors that underlie extinction, more recent ones are particularly informative. In the right settings, high-resolution recent fossil records can reveal how ecological communities looked and functioned before our own species' arrival.

The planet has encountered and responded to major disturbances for billions of years. The question is, are there lessons that can be drawn from the past?

Our Fragile Earth: A New Idea

The notion of extinction was itself a radical idea that foreshadowed an important revolution in understanding life's diversity. As with most influential ideas, there are many antecedents, but several signposts mark significant changes in thought.

A chain of events was set off when a professor of theology descended into a cave in southern Germany in 1748 (Kurtén, 1995). Accompanied only by a local gamekeeper as a guide, he entered another world, recorded by a poem he originally wrote in Latin that went 'The gruesome, terror-inspiring cavern, the lightless grotto ... as I look down, I see horrendous human bones ... I can see bodies turned to stone and skeletons left lying on the floor' (Kurtén, 1995).

Those strange bones were a mystery, answers to which heralded a new idea in science. Strange bones could reflect ancient monsters that existed prior to Noah, they could reflect creatures still alive on the planet in unexplored regions or they could reflect true monsters. The real meaning of these cave skeletons was to emerge at the hands of the German anatomist Johann Christian Rosenmüller (1771–1820). Rosenmüller had a motto that was to prove vital in his interpretation of the cave bones: 'We should always, when forming opinions about the events in Nature, assume the most natural and common process ... if we believe our senses, we shall have no grounds for self accusation.' This sensibility led Rosenmüller to the conclusion that, with large teeth, jaws and skulls, these remains were from a bear, not a human. But they were different from any bear known to science at that day (Kurtén, 1995). To Rosenmüller, the conclusion was obvious: the bones were from a kind of bear that once lived but then went extinct. Why was this so revolutionary? The whole concept of extinction, something so central of our view of life today, was virtually unknown in his day.

Rosenmüller's notion of extinction was to gain new meaning through the work of the great French anatomist Baron Cuvier (1769–1832) (Rudwick, 1997, 2008). Cuvier was fortunate to be a curator at the Museum of Natural History in Paris during a time of scientific discovery. Creatures, including fossils, were arriving in Paris from a variety of expeditions launched around the world. Many of these were new to science, and some of them drew particular interest. Like the cave bears of Rosenmüller's day, woolly mammoths stood out as being unlike anything alive on the planet. Cuvier saw in these creatures the seeds of a new general theory: one of extinction. These creatures lived in the past and were later eliminated from the planet (Rudwick, 1997). Extinction, to Cuvier, revealed repeated catastrophes in the past.

Charles Darwin built on and modified Cuvier's notions and saw the ubiquity of extinction in the natural world. Indeed, it formed an important basis for his theory of evolution by natural selection

(Darwin, 1859). The acceptance of extinction as a natural process was a fundamental shift. Species were no longer seen as perfect and eternal; they became viewed as impermanent denizens of the natural world. The reality, and indeed the ubiquity, of extinction was essential for Darwin's view of life. Natural selection could only work if species were replaced over time (Darwin, 1859).

Darwin's conception of extinction had several essential features. Extinction was seen to be a gradual process, whereby one species was slowly replaced by another over evolutionary time. Any apparent rapid extinction in the fossil record reflected gaps in the imperfect process of fossilisation. Moreover, to Darwin, extinction was brought about by competition. One species went extinct because it was outcompeted and ultimately replaced by another. Seen in this way, evolution was a slow process of continual struggle for existence among different species.

Even in Darwin's day, the fossil record was revealing sharp breaks in biological diversity (Rudwick, 2008). John Phillips (1800–1874) was a member of a family that mapped rocks and fossils across Britain and Europe, and he saw that the fossil record was not continuous. Not just species but entire faunas appeared in the fossil record only to disappear abruptly. If one took the fossil record literally, a notion supported by the increasing known extent of the strata and fossils in them, extinction was anything but gradual. In this view, discontinuities meant that biotic change could be abrupt, even catastrophic. Through the ideas of Cuvier and Phillips, changes to biodiversity were seen as being sculpted by extinction that was both rapid and global (Rudwick, 2008).

It is hard to overestimate just what fundamental shifts these notions represented for understanding life. The fossil record reveals that species, and by extension the natural world itself, are impermanent and forever changing, often rapidly and episodically. In the years since Darwin, it has been estimated that over 99 per cent of the species that have lived on Earth have gone extinct.

Learning to Read the Rocks

A great expansion of knowledge about the fossil record in the twentieth century brought a new view of extinction. An influential turning point was derived from the construction of a major database of fossil marine animals that lived in the Phanerozoic Aeon, representing the last

541 million years (Newell, 1967; Valentine, 1969; Raup and Sepkoski, 1982; Sepkoski, 1982a, 1982b). Originally assembled at the Linnaean taxonomic level of family, the database, when plotted over geological time, revealed fundamental changes of diversity during marine animal evolution. The marine record was chosen for the quality of its data. Fossils in marine rocks can be extraordinarily abundant and records from the oceans more continuous than those derived from rocks on land. For example, the rock record on land suffers from more erosion than that in the oceans, and with erosion comes gaps in the stratigraphic record that could confound diversity estimates over time.

The analysis reveals fundamental properties of how biological diversity changes over time. These patterns, first observed at higher taxonomic levels, were to withstand the refinement of the data and addition of more fossils, stratigraphic sections and taxonomic rigour (Jablonski, 2001, 2005). The first pattern was the relative ubiquity of extinction over the history of life. Extinction is a continuous property of ecosystems; indeed, the changes in the abundance of species and higher taxonomic categories are seen to reflect the outcome of the rate of origination of new taxa minus the extinction rate of old ones. Changes to the levels of diversity on the planet are an outcome of this dynamic, with background levels of extinction counterbalanced by origination over most of the geologic record.

Against this background of roughly continuous low levels of extinction, several intervals revealed extraordinary patterns of taxon loss (Sepkoski, 1982b; Raup and Sepkoski, 1982). Five episodes emerged as being exceptional and mostly coincided with the boundaries of the major geological periods identified by geologists a century before. Each of these mass extinctions – at the end of the Ordovician, in the terminal phase of the Devonian and at the ends of the Permian, Triassic and Cretaceous – shared several essential properties. First, they revealed significant drops in diversity, ranging from 17 per cent of familial loss at the end of the Cretaceous to 57 per cent at the end of the Permian. In terms of species, the pattern is even more striking. Based on documented losses at the level of genus and family, roughly 90 per cent of marine species are estimated to have been lost. These diversity drops are global and affect multiple environments simultaneously, with entire ecosystems, such as reefs, disappearing (Jablonski, 2005).

The differences between background and mass extinctions are both qualitative and quantitative (Jablonski, 1986, 2005). Because of these dramatic differences in pattern, Earth scientists have long searched for different causes.

Global biological effects have led to the hunt for global causes. Finding the pattern of global drops in diversity led to the quest for causes that (1) have a global effect on diversity and (2) are testable in the rock record. The global extent of extinction drivers led to hypotheses of geological or astronomical events that would change the chemistry of the oceans, atmosphere or both. These include asteroid impacts, major periods of widespread volcanism and tectonic changes.

An asteroid impact, for example, of a bolide 10 km in diameter has been modelled to release energy equivalent to a trillion tonnes of TNT and to inject large amounts of particulate matter into the atmosphere (Alvarez et al., 1980). The result would be a global darkening of the skies and cooling of the climate. Both of these effects would lead to changes across multiple trophic levels, affecting plant biodiversity and abundance, with cascading effects through ecosystems. The asteroid impact hypothesis also made specific predictions in the rock record, namely, that asteroid-specific minerals and elements should be present in an enriched concentration at the extinction horizon. Both of these predictions have proven to hold at the end-Cretaceous event, 66 million years ago. Geological sections from around the world reveal layers enriched in iridium, an element known to be present in certain kinds of meteorites. Likewise, grains of shocked quartz, a type of quartz only produced under the extreme conditions of meteor impacts and nuclear testing sites, are present at the same horizon in a number of localities. Moreover, a known impact site, Chicxulub in Mexico's Yucatán Peninsula, has been dated to the same interval (Renne et al., 2013). The association of the impact site and stratigraphic evidence of a bolide impact at the end of the Cretaceous in association with the extinction horizon, along with a killing mechanism, suggests that the correlation of an asteroid with species loss is a causal one (Renne et al., 2013).

While the hypothesis that an asteroid caused the extinction at the end of the Cretaceous is robust, the same cannot be said for other mass extinctions. Each of the Big Five mass extinctions appears to be the result of different causes or combinations of them. Mass extinctions may involve either a single mechanism or a number of diverse changes acting in concert. For example, the end Permian extinction event is associated with large volcanic events as well as major changes to ocean chemistry (Erwin et al., 2002).

Regardless of the cause, the end result is the same – a sudden pulse of severe extinction that crosses taxonomic, geographic and ecological boundaries (Jablonski, 2005). Beyond the patterns, two fundamental biological questions remain: (1) are there traits that confer resistance to an extinction event or, alternatively, make a taxon more susceptible to going extinct, and (2) how do ecosystems recover over time?

Extinction Survivorship

A deeper understanding of the biology of mass extinction has come from developing model systems to test the biological features that may confer extinction survivorship or resilience. The ideal models have the abundance, diversity and preservation in the fossil record to allow statistical confidence in the interpretation of patterns. In addition, they should have biological traits of interest, ones that are preserved in the fossil record.

For the past three decades, bivalve molluscs have served as a productive model system to explore extinction dynamics (Jablonski, 1986, 2008, 2004, 2005; Edie et al., 2018). These invertebrates are deeply ancient and have been present on Earth throughout the Phanerozoic, and they have witnessed both background extinctions and all of the Big Five mass extinctions. They also have a range of traits preserved in the fossil record that allow robust inferences into major aspects of their ecology, life history and trophic interactions. Given these features, our knowledge of extinction has advanced through the search for robust associations between biological traits and extinction probability (Jablonski, 2005; Payne and Finnegan, 2007).

A number of traits confer advantages to survivorship during background extinctions. Local abundance, i.e., the simple number of individuals in a given area, confers advantages versus species that are more thinly populated in particular regions (Lockwood, 2003; Wing, 2004). In addition, species richness of genera, trophic strategy, body size and generation time all confer robustness during 'normal' extinction (Jablonski, 1986; Smith and Jeffrey, 1998). Species with long generation times are more susceptible to extinction than those with short ones. The same is true for large body size, a trait that may itself often be correlative to long generation time – larger taxa seem to go extinct more readily than smaller ones (Valentine and Jablonski, 1986).

Importantly, none of these features appears to confer any advantage to taxa during the Big Five extinctions (Jablonski, 2005; Payne and Finnegan, 2007). Indeed, the single trait that most clearly confers resistance during a global catastrophe lies in distribution at higher taxonomic levels. Widespread genera, those with species deployed across the globe, preferentially survive extinctions, while those that have geographically restricted species more often are lost during mass extinctions (Payne and Finnegan, 2007; Jablonski, 2005, 2008).

Mass extinctions are evidently times when the normal rules don't apply – taxonomic extinction rates are elevated, global ecosystems collapse and the traits that confer advantages during other times do not necessarily confer advantages to survival or success (Jablonski, 2005). The causes of these shifts may lie in the global scale of the extinction drivers or in the specific nature of the drivers themselves but remain an area of active research.

Recovery from Catastrophe

The Big Five mass extinctions changed the world. One consequence, based on the traits that confer resistance to extinction discussed above, is that long-successful groups that were long dominant, or 'incumbent', are removed, while global ecosystems are deeply perturbed with standing levels of diversity greatly reduced (Jablonski, 2005). A taxon might be extraordinarily well adapted to a particular environment, long dominant on the planet and highly resistant to being displaced by new competitors during normal times. But it is at risk of extinction during a mass extinction for reasons other than the traits that conferred it such advantages during normal times.

Removal of long-lived incumbent taxa can create new opportunities for survivors. Couple that dynamic with the observation that the world's biota is generally depleted in diversity and one would expect a rapid refilling of the world's diversity, albeit with new players, after global catastrophes. Close analysis of some of the most dramatic events reveals a more nuanced and complicated texture to recovery dynamics (Erwin, 2001). In the most dramatic of the mass extinction events, at the end of the Permian – which saw the disappearance of perhaps 90 per cent of species – diversity took at least 10 million years to rebound to pre-event levels (Fraiser and Bottjer, 2007; Payne and Clapham, 2012). The reasons for this delay may relate to characteristics of and interactions between survivors. Likewise, planetary instability resulted in such continued events in the oceans that depleted oxygen levels may have also played a role in the slow recovery. These kinds of factors may explain why rebounds are often uneven and prolonged (Jablonski, 2005).

The pattern of the biotic recovery is also complex. When measured over human timescales, even the most rapid recoveries in the fossil record are extraordinarily slow, happening over millions of years. Moreover, surviving taxa are not assured to be successful; they may not participate in the recovery and suffer a delayed pattern of extinction. If a group survives but its numbers are depleted, it may pass through a catastrophe only to go extinct soon afterward. Importantly, given that incumbent and highly successful taxa have been removed, the recovery can take the biota in new directions.

Entering a Sixth Mass Extinction?

While current species loss, related to the human impacts of climate change, habitat destruction, introduction of invasive alien species and other factors, is extreme, it has been controversial whether the patterns and rates of species loss compare to the Big Five in the past (Barnosky et al., 2011; Ceballos et al., 2015). This is no mere academic taxonomy. Predicting, and even ameliorating, species loss will depend on whether the extinctions are background or mass because the patterns of survivorship and recovery are so very different for the two kinds of events. For background events, we would expect a kind of continual replacement, with successful incumbents remaining in place. For a mass extinction, the expectations are far more serious: not only would incumbents be removed but the longer-term recovery would be exceedingly slow relative to the timescales of human lives and societies.

Recent analysis bears directly on this issue (Ceballos et al., 2015). Using the most stringent criteria to define both background rates of extinction and extinction itself, a troubling comparison emerged. An estimate for continual background extinction rates, using historical records, is two mammal extinctions per 10,000 species per 100 years. Similar figures emerge for birds, amphibians, fish and reptiles. Comparing this background rate with actual species loss today reveals that species loss in recent years is elevated as much as 100 times relative to the background levels. Put another way, the species loss we are seeing today would have taken as much as 10,000 years to happen if humans were not present. These data suggest that, in terms of rates, we are in the process of a sixth mass extinction in the making, something that needs to be averted if we do not want the recovery dynamics to follow those of other mass extinction events. To truly compare these events with mass extinctions means considering factors other than just numbers of species lost (Jablonski, 2005).

The situation may indeed be more serious than the species-level estimates outlined above. Extirpation of populations, or reduction of their levels of abundance and distributions, is not accounted for by species-level taxonomic analyses but is proceeding rapidly (Ceballos et al., 2017). Reduced levels of abundance in populations, or their geographic restriction, can impede the functioning of ecosystems or their delivery for human and planetary well-being. Indeed, anecdotal evidence from amphibians suggests that the population level depletions are extraordinary, despite the fact that higher taxonomic categories are still present.

While it is becoming increasingly difficult to avoid the comparison between the impacts of humans and historical catastrophes on Earth's biota, one issue is becoming clear: if we are entering a mass extinction, then we are also entering a world with all of its properties. Incumbent and long-successful species are at risk. Recovery will be slow and dominated by weedy species before higher trophic levels reassemble. And whatever recovery happens, it would not be one that would transpire on a human timeframe – critical ecosystem services would essentially be gone over a typical human life-span. Perhaps the greatest lesson from mass extinction is one that is most dire for the planet, its species and the humans that depend on them. If the fossil record teaches us anything it is that every ecosystem, no matter how enduring, successful or stable, has a breaking point and can collapse.

Conservation Palaeobiology: Shifting Baselines

The fossil record, particularly the relatively recent one of the past few millennia, can be a valuable resource for assessing current changes in diversity (Dietl and Flessa, 2011, 2018; Kidwell, 2015). By giving us a snapshot of what the world looked like before humans and their environmental impacts, these records can be useful in detecting changes that occurred prior to environmental monitoring and in setting baselines that can serve as targets for restoration or management.

One recent example assessed the impacts of the diversion of the Colorado River on marine communities along the Baja coast downstream. Comparison of the fossil communities and the species in them before and after the diversion reveals dramatic changes in composition, abundance and life history traits. A mollusc that is today endemic and rare was widespread and abundant prior to human impacts. First-year growth rates for a species of clam (as measured by banding of the shell) were faster when there was a more continual supply of freshwater to the estuary. Indeed, the abundances of diverse species in the area are generally reduced. High-resolution fossil records from rivers, ponds, oceans and streams across the world can become an important resource as we measure human impacts, both large and small.

There's a seeming paradox to leveraging the fossil record to understand the present world. Most of the history of life is the history of a world without humans – *Homo sapiens* has only been on the planet for 200,000 years of the 3.5-billion-year history of life. Yet, in that relatively short time, the physical and living worlds have witnessed extraordinary changes. Understanding the world before humans will give us the baselines to understand our effects on the planet but will also reveal the internal dynamics between species, ecosystems and the physical world in which they reside. If the fossil record is any guide, even the most robust and successful species and ecosystems are, over geological time, fragile. That alone is a resonant notion as we evaluate our species' stewardship of the planet.

References

Barnosky, A. D., Matzke, N., Tomiya, S., Wogan, G. O., Swartz, B., Quental, T. B., Marshall, C., McGuire, J. L., Lindsey, E. L., Maguire, K. C., Mersey, B. & Ferrer, E. A. 2011. Has the Earth's sixth mass extinction already arrived? *Nature*, 471: 51–57.

Ceballos, G., Ehrlich, P. R., Barnosky, A. D., García, A., Pringle, R. M. & Palmer, T. M. 2015. Accelerated modern human–induced species losses: Entering the sixth mass extinction. *Science Advances*, 1(5): E1400253.

Darwin, C. (1859) *The Origin of Species*. London: Murray.

Dietl, G. & Flessa, K. 2011. Conservation paleobiology: Putting the dead to work. *Trends in Ecology and Evolution*, 26(1): 30–37.

  2018. *Conservation Paleobiology*. Chicago: University Chicago Press.

Edie, S. M., Jablonski, D. & Valentine, J. W. 2018. Contrasting responses of functional diversity to major losses in taxonomic diversity. *Proceedings of the National Academy of Sciences*, 115(4): 732–737.

Erwin, D. H. 2001. Lessons from the past: Biotic recoveries from mass extinctions. *Proceedings of the National Academy of Sciences*, 98(10): 5399–5403.

Erwin, D. H., Bowring, S. A. & Yugan, J. 2002. End-Permian mass extinctions: A review. *Geological Society of American Special Paper*, 356: 363–383.

Fraiser, M. L. & Bottjer, D. J. 2007. Elevated atmospheric CO_2 and the delayed biotic recovery from the End-Permian extinction. *Palaeogeography, Palaeoclimatology and Palaeoecology*, 252: 164–75.

Jablonski, D. 1986. Background and mass extinctions: The alternation of macroevolutionary regimes. *Science*, 231(4734): 129–133.

2004. The evolutionary role of mass extinctions: Disaster, recovery and something in between. In P. D. Taylor (Ed.), *Extinctions in the History of Life*: 151–177. Cambridge: Cambridge University Press.

2005. Mass extinctions and macroevolution. *Paleobiology*, 31(2): 192–210.

2008. Extinction and the spatial dynamics of biodiversity. *Proceedings of the National Academy of Sciences*, 105(Suppl. 1): 11528–11535.

Kidwell, S. M. 2015. Biology in the Anthropocene: Challenges and insights from young fossil records. *Proceedings of the National Academy of Sciences*, 112(16): 4922–4929.

Kurtén, B. 1995. *The Cave Bear Story*. New York: Columbia University Press.

Lockwood, R. 2003. Abundance not linked to survival across the end-Cretaceous mass extinction: Patterns in North American bivalves. *Proceedings of the National Academy of Sciences*, 100: 2478–2482.

Newell, N. D. 1967. Revolutions in the history of life. In C. C. Albritton Jr (Ed.), *Uniformity and Simplicity: A Symposium on the Principle of the Uniformity of Nature*: 63–91. Boulder CO: Geology Society of America.

Payne, J. L. & Clapham, M. E. 2012. End-Permian mass extinction in the oceans: An ancient analog for the twenty-first century? *Annual Review of Earth and Planetary Sciences*, 40: 89–111.

Payne, J. L. & Finnegan, S. 2007. The effect of geographic range on extinction risk during background and mass extinction. *Proceedings of the National Academy of Sciences*, 104(25), 10506–10511.

Raup, D. & Sepkoski, J. 1982. Mass extinctions in the marine fossil record. *Science*, 215:1501–1503.

Renne, P. R., Deino, A. L., Hilgen, F. J., Kuiper, K. F., Mark, D. F., Mitchell, W. S., III, Morgan, L. E., Mundil, R. & Smit, J. 2013. Time scales of critical events around the Cretaceous–Paleogene boundary. *Science*, 339: 684.

Rudwick, M. 1997. *Georges Cuvier, Fossil Bones and Geological Catastrophes*. Chicago: University of Chicago Press.

    2008. *Worlds before Adam: The Reconstruction of Geohistory in the Age of Reform*. Chicago: University of Chicago Press.

Sepkoski, J. 1982a. A compendium of fossil marine families. *Contributions in Biology and Geology: Milwaukee Public Museum*, 51: 1–125.

    1982b. Mass extinctions in the Phanerozoic oceans: A review. *Geological Society of America Special Paper*, 190: 283–289.

Smith, A. & Jeffery, C. 1998. Selectivity of extinction among sea urchins at the end of the Cretaceous period. *Nature*, 392: 69–71.

Valentine, J. W. 1969. Patterns of taxonomic and ecological structure of the shelf benthos during Phanerozoic time. *Paleontology*, 12: 684–709.

Valentine, J. W. & Jablonski, D. 1986. Mass extinctions: Sensitivity of marine larval types. *Proceedings of the National Academy of Sciences*, 83: 6912–6914.

Wing, S. L. 2004. Mass extinctions in plant evolution. In P. D. Taylor (Ed.), *Extinctions in the History of Life*: 61–97. Cambridge: Cambridge University Press.

2 | Biodiversity and Global Change
From Creator to Victim

TIMOTHY M. LENTON

We owe our very existence to the activities of past and present life forms, which have created a world that we could inhabit (Lenton and Watson, 2011). This is true not just in the evolutionary sense that we are descended from earlier life forms, but in the Earth system sense that the atmosphere would be unbreathable and the climate intolerable were it not for the accumulated actions of other members of the biosphere, past and present (Lenton and Watson, 2011). This fundamental role of biodiversity in maintaining our life-support system is strangely under-recognised by utilitarian arguments for preserving 'nature'. We are part of biodiversity and have been born out of this world, only to be transforming it now in ways that are bad for us and bad for much of the rest of life.

This is not the first time that life has radically transformed the planet with damaging consequences (Lenton and Watson, 2011). However, it is the first time that a single animal species has wielded such world-changing power. Past revolutionary transformations of the biosphere took life to the brink of total extinction in events such as 'snowball Earth'. Our very existence dictates that life survived such past scrapes with disaster (Lenton and Watson, 2011) – but the flipside is that there is no guarantee that the biosphere will necessarily survive what is unfolding now. After past close shaves, it typically took millions of years for the slow workings of Earth system dynamics and the 'blind watchmaker' of natural selection to restore a well-functioning, self-regulating biosphere (Lenton and Watson, 2011). We don't have the luxury of waiting that long. We are meant to be *Homo sapiens* – wise man [*sic*] – instead we are practising an act of cosmic stupidity: in extinguishing biodiversity we are eroding our own life-support system. The irony of this would surely not be lost on any watching deity.

The aim of this paper is to (briefly) tell the history of the Earth system as a means of highlighting how the current biological extinction being caused by human actions could pose an existential risk. The first part of the narrative reviews how life created a world that we could inhabit in the first place, identifying along the way some of the key life forms and functions they perform that are particularly important in creating and maintaining a habitable planet for us. The second part reviews how we *Homo sapiens* came to be planet changers, how the global changes we are causing are impacting biodiversity, and how this could escalate into a threat to the planetary life-support system. This is not intended to shock for the sake of it, but rather to get the reader to appreciate how fundamental our dependence on other life forms is. As the Pope's Encyclical letter on care for our common home makes clear, our lack of collective action on global change thus far suggests a failure in our value system (Pope Francis, 2015). While the narrative here is a scientific rather than a religious one, the conclusion is the same: we need to change our value system to recognise our fundamental dependence on the rest of the biosphere.

Biodiversity as Creator: How Life Created a World We Could Inhabit

The aim of this section is to sketch in broad terms how the past evolution of life has created a world that we could inhabit in the first place (Lenton and Watson, 2011). Along the way we identify some crucial roles of different types of life – from prokaryotes to fellow multicellular eukaryotes – in creating and maintaining a habitable biosphere for advanced multicellular life forms including ourselves. Life and the Earth have co-evolved in the sense that the evolution of life has shaped the planet, changes in the planetary environment have shaped life, and together this can be viewed as one process (Lenton et al., 2004). When we look at this coevolution over Earth history, three revolutionary changes leap out, in which the Earth system was radically transformed (Lenton and Watson, 2011). Each of these revolutionary changes depended on the previous one, and without them we would not be here – and nor would much of the biodiversity that is currently described, and projected to be under threat (i.e., complex eukaryote life forms). To help orientate the reader, Figure 2.1 provides a timeline of major events in Earth history.

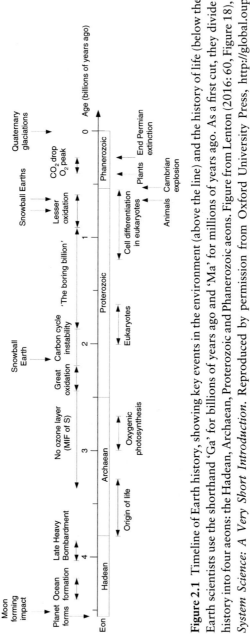

Figure 2.1 Timeline of Earth history, showing key events in the environment (above the line) and the history of life (below the line). Earth scientists use the shorthand 'Ga' for billions of years ago and 'Ma' for millions of years ago. As a first cut, they divide Earth history into four aeons: the Hadean, Archaean, Proterozoic and Phanerozoic aeons. Figure from Lenton (2016: 60, Figure 18), *Earth System Science: A Very Short Introduction*. Reproduced by permission from Oxford University Press, http://global.oup.com. © Oxford University Press.

Origins of the Biosphere

The most fundamental change in the history of the Earth system started with the origin of life, which appeared on Earth remarkably soon after our planet became continuously habitable.

The formation of the solar system is dated from the oldest meteoritic material at 4.567 billion years ago. The Earth and the other planets are younger than this, because they had to form from the gravitational collisions and accumulation of material spinning around the early Sun – in a process called accretion. During the accretion of the Earth there were some truly massive collisions, one (or several) of which formed the Moon 4.470 billion years ago. While the Earth was still forming, the gas giants Jupiter and Saturn had finished accreting. Their gravitational pull disrupted the band of asteroids between Mars and Jupiter, sending some of them off on elliptical orbits that crossed the inner solar system. Crucially, this brought water and other volatile substances, including nitrogen and carbon dioxide, to the early Earth. Remarkably, some tiny bits of the Earth's crust from this time are still present at the surface today, in the form of grains of the mineral zircon that can be precisely dated. The oldest is 4.374 billion years old and was originally part of a granite rock, indicating that the continental crust had started to form in the first 100 million years of the planet's history. Even more remarkably the isotopic composition of oxygen in the zircon suggests that oceans of liquid water were present on the Earth at that early time. However, the onslaught from outer space was not over. The Earth and all the inner solar system suffered a 'Late Heavy Bombardment' by asteroids between about 4.1 and 3.9 billion years ago. Some of these impacts were probably large enough to have evaporated the early oceans and thus temporarily rendered the planet uninhabitable. Thus the Earth only became 'continuously habitable' after the end of this bombardment around 3.85 billion years ago.

The first evidence for life on Earth appears >3.7 billion years ago, remarkably soon after the end of the Late Heavy Bombardment. Indeed as soon as there are sedimentary rocks that could record the presence of life they suggest it is there (Nutman et al., 2016; Dodd et al., 2017). Some of the first evidence takes the form of small particles of graphite – organic carbon – with an isotopic composition ($\delta^{13}C$) consistent with carbon fixation by some form of chemosynthesis or photosynthesis (Rosing, 1999; Ohtomo et al., 2014). Putative microbial structures have also been described from the same rock sequence (Nutman et al., 2016). By 3.5 billion years ago the first putative microscopic fossils of life appear (Schopf, 1993, 2006), although not everyone is convinced the fossil structures were made by biology (Brasier et al., 2002; Brasier et al., 2006). There are also more convincingly biogenic sedimentary structures formed by microbial mats (Noffke et al., 2013). By 3.26 billion years ago there are microfossils of cells caught in the act of division (Knoll and Barghoorn, 1977).

The earliest biosphere was made up exclusively of prokaryotes – bacteria and archaea – two kingdoms of life which divided very early. Metabolically the earliest life forms may have consumed compounds in their environment that could be reacted to release chemical energy, but a shortage of chemical energy on a global scale would have severely restricted the productivity of such a biosphere. One possibility is that early archaea consumed hydrogen and carbon dioxide from the atmosphere to make methane, but such a methanogen-based biosphere would have been restricted to around a thousandth of the productivity of the modern marine biosphere (Kharecha et al., 2005; Canfield et al., 2006).

A more productive global biosphere would have arisen when early life began to harness the most abundant energy source on the planet – sunlight. Photosynthesis fixing carbon dioxide from the atmosphere appears to have evolved very early in the history of life. The >3.7 billion-year-old graphite has a carbon isotopic composition consistent with photosynthesis (Rosing, 1999; Ohtomo et al., 2014), although other explanations are possible. By 3.5 billion years ago the earliest carbonate sediments have an isotopic signature that suggests significant organic carbon burial globally, which must have been supported by photosynthesis.

The first photosynthesis was not the kind we are familiar with, which splits water and produces oxygen as a waste product. Instead, early photosynthesis was 'anoxygenic' – meaning it didn't produce oxygen. It could have used a range of compounds, in place of water, as a source of electrons with which to fix carbon from carbon dioxide and reduce it to sugars, including hydrogen (H_2) or hydrogen sulphide (H_2S) in the atmosphere, or ferrous iron (Fe^{2+}) dissolved in the ancient oceans. The early biosphere fuelled by anoxygenic photosynthesis would have been limited by the supplies of these electron donors, all of which are a lot less abundant than water.

In fact, shortage of materials would have posed a more general problem for life within the early Earth system: the fluxes of materials

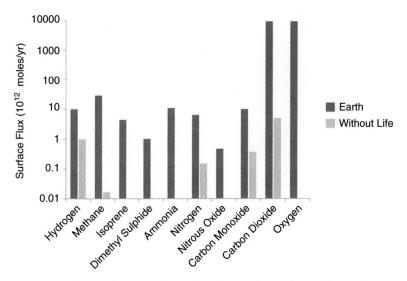

Figure 2.2 Fluxes of gases exchanged at the Earth's surface today and on an abiotic Earth. Illustrates the extraordinary global material recycling due to life – here in the form of gases. Data from Andreae and Crutzen (1997), Mackenzie et al. (1993), Brasseur and Chatfield (1991) and Holland (1978).

coming into the surface Earth system from volcanic and metamorphic processes today are many orders of magnitude less than the fluxes due to life at the surface of the Earth today, indicating that today's biosphere is a phenomenal recycling system (Figure 2.2).

Early life thus had to evolve the means of recycling the materials it needed to metabolise – in other words, to establish global biogeochemical cycles. We have a very scant record of how and when this happened, but a few clues suggest it was very early in the history of life. For example, the phylogenetic tree of prokaryote life suggests that many recycling metabolisms evolved early on, in particular methane production (Vanwonterghem et al., 2016), for which there is geochemical evidence ~3.5 billion years ago (Ueno et al., 2006). The ease or difficulty of evolving recycling has also been explored by seeding computer models with 'artificial life' forms and leaving them to evolve. In these 'virtual worlds' the closing of material recycling loops emerges as a robust result (Williams and Lenton, 2007; Boyle et al., 2012).

If the early biosphere was fuelled by anoxygenic photosynthesis, plausibly based on hydrogen gas, then calculations suggest that once

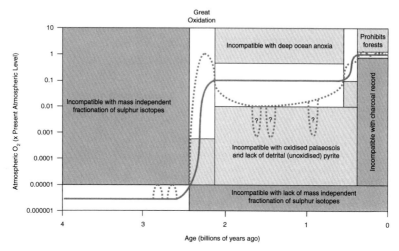

Figure 2.3 Atmospheric oxygen over Earth history. Figure from Lenton (2016: 67, Figure 19), *Earth System Science: A Very Short Introduction*. Reproduced by permission from Oxford University Press, http://global.oup.com. © Oxford University Press.

the biological recycling of this gas had evolved, the early biosphere might have achieved a global productivity up to 1 per cent of the modern marine biosphere (Kharecha et al., 2005; Canfield et al., 2006). If early anoxygenic photosynthesis used the supply of reduced iron upwelling in the ocean then its productivity would have been controlled by ocean circulation and might have reached up to 10 per cent of the modern marine biosphere (Kharecha et al., 2005; Canfield et al., 2006).

All of this early evolution played out in a world essentially devoid of oxygen (Figure 2.3).

The Oxygen Revolution

The innovation that supercharged the early biosphere was the origin of oxygenic photosynthesis, which uses abundant water as an electron donor. This was not an easy process to evolve (Allen and Martin, 2007). To split water requires more energy – i.e., more high-energy photons of sunlight – than any of the earlier anoxygenic forms of photosynthesis. Evolution's solution was to wire together two existing 'photosystems' in one cell and bolt on the front of them a remarkable piece of biochemical machinery that can rip apart water molecules. The result was the first cyanobacterial cell – the ancestor of all organisms performing oxygenic photosynthesis on the planet today.

Current evidence suggests oxygenic photosynthesis took up to a billion years to evolve, with the first compelling evidence appearing around 3–2.7 billion years ago (Lenton and Daines, 2017). The smoking gun is chemical evidence for oxygen leaking into the environment and reacting with metals that are highly sensitive to the presence of oxygen. For example, molybdenum is mobilised from continental rocks by reacting with oxygen and appears for the first time in ocean sediments around 2.7 billion years ago. Once oxygenic photosynthesis had evolved, the productivity of the biosphere would no longer have been restricted by the supply of substrates for photosynthesis, as water and carbon dioxide were abundant. Instead, the availability of nutrients, notably nitrogen and phosphorus, would have become the major limiting factors on the productivity of the biosphere – as they still are today.

Once there was a source of oxygen on the planet it is tempting to assume that the concentration of oxygen in the atmosphere would have steadily risen – a bit like filling a bath with the plug in. But oxygen did not rise in the atmosphere immediately or steadily. Instead it remained a trace gas for hundreds of millions of years. We know this because a very peculiar 'mass independent fractionation' (MIF) of sulphur isotopes is preserved in sediments more than 2.45 billion years old (Farquhar et al., 2000). This MIF signature can still be produced by photochemistry of sulphur gases in the atmosphere today, but it cannot be preserved in today's sediments because all the sulphur first goes through a homogenising reservoir of sulphate in the ocean. Prior to 2.45 billion years ago that sulphate reservoir must have been absent due to a lack of oxygen to produce it. The MIF signature indicates that high-energy ultraviolet radiation streamed through the lower atmosphere and therefore the ozone layer was absent, requiring that oxygen (from which ozone is made) was at a concentration of less than 2 parts per million in the atmosphere (Figure 2.3).

Oxygen could remain at such a low concentration for hundreds of millions of years because there was an excess input flux of reduced materials hungry to react with it, including reduced iron injected into the ocean through mid-ocean ridges, and reduced gases such as hydrogen and hydrogen sulphide entering the atmosphere via volcanoes. The rate of their reaction with oxygen increases with oxygen concentration, thus producing a negative feedback system that stabilised the oxygen concentration at trace levels where the sink of oxygen matched the source (Goldblatt et al., 2006).

This stability broke down after hundreds of millions of years, when atmospheric oxygen jumped up in concentration in an event known as the 'Great Oxidation' around 2.4 billion years ago (Figure 2.3). The mass independent fractionation of sulphur isotopes stops, indicating that oxygen had risen sufficiently to convert all sulphur to sulphate before it was deposited in marine sediments. The fact that the MIF signature has never returned suggests the permanent formation of an ozone layer. Massive deposits of oxidised iron appeared in the form of the first sedimentary 'red beds'. Rusted (oxidised) iron also appeared in ancient soils for the first time. These indicators reveal that oxygen concentration increased by several orders of magnitude from less than a 100,000th to c. 1–10 per cent of its present atmospheric level (Daines et al., 2017). The indicators of oxygen rise all remain with us to the present day, indicating that the Great Oxidation was never reversed.

While the origin of cyanobacteria performing oxygenic photosynthesis was ultimately responsible for the Great Oxidation, there must have been other long-term changes in the Earth system that slowly oxidised the surface Earth system. Fundamental among these was the loss of hydrogen atoms to space. This is a tiny flux on today's Earth, because water is frozen out of the atmosphere at the 'cold trap' between the troposphere and stratosphere. Hence hardly any hydrogen-containing gases make it to the top of the atmosphere. However, much of the organic carbon created by early oxygenic photosynthesis would have been recycled to the atmosphere as methane by archaea. In the resulting methane-rich early atmosphere, much more hydrogen could escape to space and this had the effect of oxidising the surface of the Earth (Catling et al., 2001). This drove the Earth system toward a tipping point (Goldblatt et al., 2006) where the balance of inputs to the atmosphere shifted from an excess of reduced material to an excess of oxygen.

The abruptness of the Great Oxidation suggests that at this point a strong positive feedback process kicked in and propelled the rise of oxygen (Goldblatt et al., 2006; Claire et al., 2006). The formation of the ozone layer was crucial to this transition, because it temporarily suppressed the consumption of oxygen. Ultraviolet radiation catalyses a series of reactions in which oxygen combines with methane to produce carbon dioxide and water (thus reversing the production of oxygen and methane by the biosphere). Without an ozone layer, this process for removing oxygen was rapid and efficient. But once enough oxygen built up for the ozone layer to start to form, this would have shielded the atmosphere below from UV and temporarily slowed down the removal of oxygen. More oxygen would produce more ozone, letting through less UV and further suppressing oxygen consumption in a positive feedback process. Models suggest that this positive feedback was strong enough to temporarily go into 'runaway' producing a rapid oxygen rise (Goldblatt et al., 2006; Claire et al., 2006; Daines and Lenton, 2016). However, the Earth system would soon have stabilised again at a higher oxygen level with the oxygen sinks again matching the sources (Goldblatt et al., 2006).

When oxygen jumped up at the Great Oxidation this caused a decline in atmospheric methane concentration (Daines and Lenton, 2016), slowing the further oxidation of the Earth. This decline in methane could help explain why when oxygen rose there were a series of glaciations. One of these glaciations, 2.2 billion years ago, reached to low latitudes near the equator and was probably the first 'snowball Earth' event. The Great Oxidation was also followed by a large pulse of organic carbon burial recorded in carbon isotopes. This may have been caused by increased oxygen reacting with sulphide in rocks on the continents producing sulfuric acid that dissolved phosphorus out of rocks and fuelled productivity in the oceans (Bekker and Holland, 2012). If so, it reinforced the transition to an oxidising world. By 1.85 billion years ago this instability in the carbon cycle and climate had settled down and the Earth entered a long period of stability known rather unflatteringly as 'the boring billion'.

The Complexity Revolution

The turmoil of the Great Oxidation created a world much more conducive to aerobic (oxygen-utilising) life forms. There was a lot more energy to go around in the post-oxidation world, because respiration of organic matter with oxygen yields an order of magnitude more energy than breaking food down anaerobically. Among the organisms to take advantage of this energy source were the first eukaryotes – complex cells with a nucleus and many other distinct components.

Eukaryotes are profoundly different from the prokaryotes that preceded them, yet they were created from the fusion of once free-living prokaryotes. The mitochondria – the energy factory – in eukaryote cells were once free-living aerobic bacteria, and the plastids in plant and algal cells – where photosynthesis occurs – were once free-living cyanobacteria. These cellular components were acquired in ancient symbiotic mergers. The symbiotic merger that gave rise to mitochondria provided an abundant energy source to the ancestral eukaryote cell. Eukaryotes also rearranged how they copy genetic information – copying many chromosomes in parallel – whereas prokaryotes copy their DNA in one long loop. These innovations enabled eukaryotes to express many more genes than prokaryotes, and this ultimately gave them the capacity to create more complex life forms with multiple cell types.

The origin of eukaryotes is shrouded in mystery and controversy, as biologists do not agree on what marks the start of the lineage or what constitutes fossil evidence for eukaryotes. The earliest claims for biomarker evidence of eukaryotes 2.7 billion years ago are now thought to represent contamination with younger material (Rasmussen et al., 2008). A couple of cryptic 2.5 billion-year-old 'acritarch' fossils might be the resting stages of early eukaryotes, but the name itself means they are of 'confused origin'. Some 1.9 billion-year-old spiral fossils that are visible to the naked eye might be eukaryotic algae (Han and Runnegar, 1992) (called *Grypania*) but could also be colonial cyanobacteria. Molecular clocks suggest the last common ancestor of all eukaryotes lived roughly 1.8–1.7 billion years ago (Parfrey et al., 2011).

Eukaryotes only slowly realised their ability to build more complex life forms with differentiated cell types. Most of the fossils from Earth's middle age – the Proterozoic Aeon – are the rather cryptic 'acritarchs'. Much rarer eukaryote body fossils include 1.5 billion-year-old *Tappania*, which might be a fungus (Butterfield, 2005), and 1.2 billion-year-old *Bangiomorpha pubescens*, which is a multicellular red alga (seaweed) assigned to a modern order (Butterfield, 2000).

Researchers are still puzzling over what held back the evolution of complex life during 'the boring billion', but many see environmental constraints playing a key role. For most of the Proterozoic Aeon the surface ocean remained dominated by prokaryotes and the deep oceans remained anoxic – i.e., devoid of oxygen (Lenton and Daines, 2017). At intermediate depths some of these anoxic waters became 'euxinic', meaning that sulphate in the water was reduced to hydrogen sulphide, which is toxic to many eukaryotes.

Eventually the deadlock was broken in the latter parts of the Neoproterozoic Era (1000–542 million years ago), which witnessed a spell of climatic turbulence, the partial oxygenation of the deep oceans, and the rise of the first animals. The first signs of change began around 740 million years ago, when biomarkers of algae become more prevalent in ocean sediments and the diversity of eukaryote fossils starts to increase (Lenton et al., 2014). This would have made the biological pump of carbon from the surface to the deep ocean more efficient (Lenton et al., 2014). There were also productive microbial ecosystems on the land at the time (Lenton and Daines, 2016) and conceivably eukaryotic fungi, algae and lichens (a symbiotic merger of the two) could have been part of those early land ecosystems – although we have no fossil evidence either way.

Meanwhile, plate tectonics was breaking up the super-continent Rodinia and scattering the resulting land masses in an unusual configuration, with much of the land in the tropics. There was also a massive continental outpouring of volcanic lava (a Large Igneous Province). These geologic factors would have produced very efficient silicate weathering of the continents (Donnadieu et al., 2004), potentially enhanced by biology (Lenton and Watson, 2004). That in turn would have drawn down atmospheric carbon dioxide and cooled the planet. Somehow the climate got so cold that an extreme 'snowball Earth' glaciation – the Sturtian – was triggered around 715 million years ago. Glaciation reached equatorial latitudes and lasted tens of millions of years, consistent with the time it would take to build up enough carbon dioxide to melt the ice.

The climate turmoil did not end there. A second extreme glaciation – the Marinoan – was triggered, ending 635 million years ago. It was followed by a massive deposit of carbonate rock called a 'cap carbonate' – consistent with the snowball Earth hypothesis (Hoffman et al., 1998). In the super-hot and wet aftermath of snowball Earth, weathering would have occurred incredibly rapidly, supplying calcium and magnesium ions to the ocean that would combine with the excess carbon dioxide in the atmosphere and ocean to produce a massive deposit of carbonate sediments.

Perhaps the greatest puzzle about these extreme glaciations is how the ancestors of complex life survived them. Biomarker and molecular clock evidence suggests that simple animals in the form of sponges had already evolved (Love et al., 2009), along with multicellular algae and fungi. Yet complex life did not flourish until after the glaciations. First there are fossils of what are thought to be animal embryos, alongside algae and fungi. Then the first large fossil organisms, the 'Ediacaran biota' appear around 575 million years ago. While their biological affinity is debated, at least some were probably animals. They were followed tens of millions of years later by mobile grazing animals – both on the sediments and as zooplankton in the water column.

What triggered this burst of animal evolution? Relatively large, mobile animals need more oxygen than the sedentary creatures including sponges that came before them (Lenton et al., 2014). Intriguingly, the first evidence for oxygenation of parts of the deep oceans appears 580 million years ago, shortly before the appearance of Ediacaran fossils at depth in the ocean. However, there had been oxygen in the shallow waters of the ocean for more than a billion years before this. It may be that evolution caused oxygenation rather than vice versa (Lenton et al., 2014). By increasing the efficiency of carbon and phosphorus removal into sediments, the rise of sponges and algae may have oxygenated the ocean, improving conditions for ongoing animal evolution. The revolution in biological complexity culminated in the 'Cambrian Explosion' of animal diversity 540 to 515 million years ago, in which modern food webs were established in the ocean. However, as animals began to burrow and bioturbate the ocean sediments this trapped phosphorus in them and ultimately lowered marine productivity and atmospheric oxygen levels (Boyle et al., 2014). As a result anoxia became more widespread in the early Palaeozoic oceans and animals may have limited their own expansion.

The thing that finally created a modern world was the rise of plants on land, beginning around 470 million years ago and culminating in the first global forests by 370 million years ago. Plants accelerated chemical weathering of the land surface, lowering atmospheric carbon dioxide levels and potentially cooling the planet into the Late Ordovician glaciations (Lenton et al., 2012), as well as the later Carboniferous-Permian glaciations (Berner, 1997). The rise of plants doubled global photosynthesis, and with it the long-term source of oxygen from the burial of organic carbon (Lenton et al., 2016a). This increased atmospheric oxygen levels (Lenton et al., 2016a), finally fully oxygenating the deep ocean (Figure 2.3). The record of fossil charcoal starting 420 million years ago tells us that oxygen has remained above 15–17 per cent of the atmosphere since then. This in turn provided one of the necessary conditions for our kind of intelligent life to ultimately evolve: our brains are especially energy-hungry and if the partial pressure of oxygen in the air drops by about a third, brain function really starts to suffer.

Importantly plants and their associated mycorrhizal fungi also appear to have played a key role in regulating both atmospheric oxygen and carbon dioxide levels. Atmospheric oxygen is stabilised by negative feedbacks involving fires suppressing vegetation and thus the long-term source of oxygen (Lenton and Watson, 2000). Atmospheric carbon dioxide is limiting to vegetation productivity which in turn is the key control on the long-term sink of CO_2 from the weathering of silicate rocks, providing a potent negative feedback (Schwartzman and Volk, 1989).

A case can be made that oxygen, carbon dioxide and climate are now more tightly regulated than they have been previously in Earth history, thanks to the involvement of complex life in the feedbacks, and that the resulting stability has provided an important precondition for the further evolution of complex life forms (Lenton and Watson, 2011). Certainly the biodiversity of complex life has been on an impressive up-curve over Phanerozoic time. There have been setbacks of varying sizes – including 'mass' extinctions. However, the background rate at which species are lost has been declining over Phanerozoic time (Harnik et al., 2012), which can be taken as one measure of increasing Earth system stability on the longest timescales.

On the somewhat shorter timescale of mass extinctions, however, Earth system processes can be part of the problem. While scientists tend to look for external causes to mass extinctions – usually in the form of a massive meteorite strike and/or an episode of intense terrestrial volcanism creating a 'large igneous province' of lava flows – such external triggers have clearly been amplified by processes internal to the Earth system, which has at least one Achilles heel: There have been repeated episodes of expanded ocean anoxia that have played a key role in mass extinction events.

The largest mass extinction of all at the end Permian, 252 million years ago, saw widespread ocean anoxia – a reversion back toward the

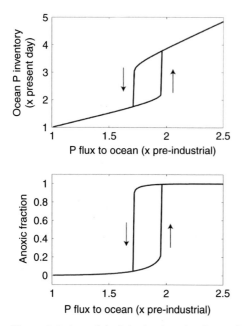

Figure 2.4 A model of tipping into (and out of) an oceanic anoxic event. Figure from Watson et al. (2017). Used under a Creative Commons BY 4.0 licence.

Proterozoic state of the Earth system. Indeed it saw depletion of the ozone layer as well. The spread of ocean anoxia can be propelled by a potent positive feedback process whereby it promotes the recycling of phosphorus from ocean sediments (by biological and chemical means), which when upwelled fuels more productivity, which as it sinks creates more respiratory demand for oxygen consumption (Van Cappellen and Ingall, 1994). This feedback can create a tipping point, whereby a small increase in phosphorus input to the ocean triggers an oceanic anoxic event (Handoh and Lenton, 2003; Watson et al., 2017) (Figure 2.4). The interaction of this relatively fast positive feedback with the slower negative feedbacks that stabilise atmospheric oxygen (Van Cappellen and Ingall, 1996) may have caused the Earth system to oscillate between anoxic and oxygenated oceans for 10 million years after the end Permian, and again later on in the middle of the Cretaceous period when there are a series of oceanic anoxic events (Handoh and Lenton, 2003).

The End Cretaceous extinction, 65 million years ago, finally cleared dinosaurs out of a niche space they had dominated for over 150 million years, allowing mammals to diversify into ecological prominence. In an unusual warm event 55 million years ago – the Palaeocene-Eocene Thermal Maximum – three major mammal orders diversified (Gingerich, 2006), including our own – the Primates – and the odd-toed and even-toed ungulates, many species of which we would ultimately domesticate.

Over the past 40 million years, atmospheric carbon dioxide levels have fallen and the climate has got cooler and drier. The cause of the long-term cooling is still being argued over – with a partial role for the uplift of mountains driving faster weathering rates and associated carbon dioxide uptake (Raymo and Ruddiman, 1992), and also a role for declining long-term inputs of carbon dioxide from volcanic degassing (Mills et al., 2014). The correspondence between CO_2 and climate is not a perfect one on this long timescale as the latest proxies show stable, low CO_2 for the last ~25 million years, while the climate fluctuated and underwent overall cooling (Pagani et al., 2009). One hypothesis argues that the stable low CO_2 was thanks to very strong negative feedback from the role of plants in weathering, because the majority of (C_3) plants were near CO_2 starvation (Pagani et al., 2009).

In this stable low CO_2 world of the Miocene Epoch (23–5.3 million years ago), grasslands expanded abruptly in two phases around 17 and 6 million years ago, such that they now cover about a third of the Earth's productive land surface. These phases of grassland expansion may have been propelled by coevolution with mammal grazers and also by a potent positive feedback involving fires: grasslands encourage fires which encourage grasslands, because frequent fires prevent forests regenerating. In their second phase of expansion, grasslands colonised large parts of Africa including the Great Rift Valley – the place where our evolutionary lineage diverged from chimpanzees, around 6 million years ago (Figure 2.5). Around 4 million years ago in the Pliocene Epoch (5.3–2.6 million years ago) our hominine ancestors began to walk upright – conceivably as an adaptation to moving through the newly created savanna between clumps of woodland.

Just as our ancestors began to develop stone tool use, the Earth's overall cooling trend culminated in a series of Northern Hemisphere ice age cycles of increasing severity and decreasing frequency (Figure 2.6). This change in climate dynamics marks the onset of the Quaternary Period (2.6–0 million years ago). It is important not least because of

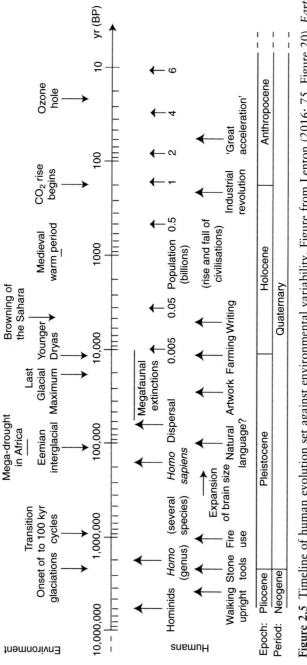

Figure 2.5 Timeline of human evolution set against environmental variability. Figure from Lenton (2016: 75, Figure 20), *Earth System Science: A Very Short Introduction*. Reproduced by permission from Oxford University Press, http://global.oup.com. © Oxford University Press.

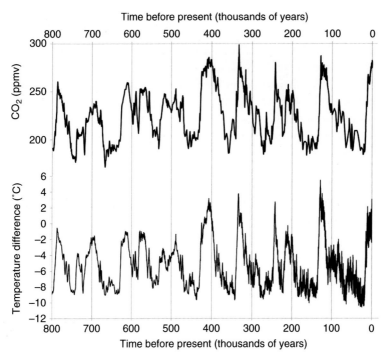

Figure 2.6 Quaternary climate dynamics. The Antarctic ice core record of atmospheric CO_2 and temperature change (the difference in temperature from the average over the last 1000 years), showing the recent 'sawtooth oscillations' of roughly 100 kyr period. Data from Jouzel et al. (2007), Luthi et al. (2008), Monnin et al. (2001), Petit et al. (1999) and Siegenthaler et al. (2005).

what it can tell us about the stability of the 'background' climate system at present. One can read the transition of the Earth system from a single stable climate state in the preceding Pliocene Epoch to the progressively deeper and stronger oscillations of the Quaternary glaciations, as a system that is not only getting cooler but is also destabilising (Lenton and Watson, 2011). The pattern of 'saw tooth' global oscillations (Figure 2.6) whereby the climate cools progressively into an ice age then snaps rapidly out of it, only for the cycle to repeat soon after, is a classic example of a system that, although it is bounded by negative feedback, contains a strong amplifier (positive feedback) – as should be familiar to students of electrical engineering.

Currently our understanding of the key feedbacks involved in the glacial-interglacial cycles is incomplete. Textbooks still emphasise the role of the Milankovitch cycles of changing solar insolation as the cause of the ice ages – but they cannot explain the amplitude or the now dominant 100,000-year period of the glaciations – because the orbital signal is particularly weak at that frequency. Instead, variations in the Earth's orbit are at best an irregular 'pacemaker' of the ice ages, and there may be an inherent, roughly 100,000-year 'relaxation oscillator' in the Earth system's own dynamics (Crucifix, 2012). Current theories for that oscillator invoke either the natural timescale of growth and decay of ice sheets or a long inherent timescale in the carbon cycle. What we can say with more confidence is that at the 'termination' of an ice age, the Earth system goes into near runaway positive feedback, with carbon released from the deep ocean amplifying global climate change.

Biodiversity as Victim: How We Are Causing Global Change Now

There are several key points to take away from the preceding brief history of the biosphere. Firstly, microbes (prokaryotes and unicellular eukaryotes) still play a central role in running all the major biogeo-chemical cycles that sustain life. Secondly, multicellular eukaryotes – plants, fungi and animals – have also played an important role in creating and maintaining an oxygen-rich, CO_2-poor, cool and stable world in which we could ultimately evolve. Thirdly, this is a bad time to be perturbing the Earth system, because it is unusually unstable.

Armed with this information, we now turn from biodiversity as creator to biodiversity as victim – taking an Earth system view of the global change that humans are causing. The underlying premise is that anthropogenic global change is a systemic phenomenon – climate change and other drivers of biodiversity loss, including land use change, invasive species, over exploitation and nutrient loading are all intertwined manifestations of expanding human activities.

A Systemic View of Anthropogenic Global Change Thus Far

The term 'Anthropocene' has been coined to describe a new geological epoch in which human activities are transforming the Earth system at a global scale. While there is much academic debate about whether this really is a new epoch, and if so, when it began, the salient point is that humans are now a planetary force. Here we briefly trace how humans have gone from being just another great ape to planet changers (Figure 2.5), and how today's global changes have their roots in much earlier and more localised innovations.

The Quaternary climate changes (Figure 2.6) provoked widespread speciation in mammals, including our hominine lineage. The resulting environmental instability (Magill et al., 2013) may have played a role in our evolution as unusually intelligent, highly social primates. One idea is that when the environment is changing – but not too frequently or unpredictably – it pays to be smart and to cooperate in social groups to help adapt to the changing conditions.

The intentional use of fire set our ancestors apart from all other species, because it was the first innovation that extended energy use beyond the human body. Controlled use of fire may have started 1.5 million years ago (Wrangham et al., 1999), and was certainly occurring by 800,000 years ago in Africa (Pausas and Keeley, 2009) and by 400,000 years ago in Europe (Roebroeks and Villa, 2011). The use of fire for cooking gave *Homo erectus* more energy in their diet from the cooking of meat and a more diverse diet (by detoxifying foods) (Boyden, 1992). The shift to hunting energy-rich meat in turn triggered the formation of social groups that settled around campsites and divided labour, causing an escalation in human social evolution (Brown et al., 2009).

Between about 400,000 and 250,000 years ago, stone tool technologies became more elaborate and brain size increased rapidly. Anatomically modern humans (*Homo sapiens*) first appeared in East Africa around 200,000 years ago. Sometime after that, our ancestors experienced a bottleneck in population of 10,000 or fewer breeding pairs. Descendants of this founding group emerged out of Africa and began to spread around the world roughly 65,000 years ago. Their migration was facilitated by one of a series of periodic wet phases of the Sahara after a mega-drought in Africa that ended around 90,000 years ago.

As modern humans arrived in new continents, they triggered the extinction of other large mammals or 'megafauna' (Barnosky et al., 2004; Sandom et al., 2014). This began in Australia before 44,000 years ago, in Europe over 30,000 years ago, in North America 11,500 years ago and in South America 10,000 years ago. Extinction was less

severe in Africa, perhaps because existing species were already habitu-
ated to and wary of hunting humans. Fire was the first 'tool' that
enabled early humans to start changing their environment on a large
scale. Human use of fire in hunting shifted ecosystems toward grasslands. This helps explain why herbivores that browse on trees (rather
than eating grasses) suffered most in the megafauna extinctions. Our
ancestors may also have hunted some large herbivores to extinction,
thus leaving carnivores and scavengers to suffer from a lack of food.
Human use of fire in Australia helped maintain desert scrubland over
large areas of the continent. This in turn may have inhibited the return
of the monsoon into the continental interior when the Earth system
entered the present Holocene interglacial epoch (Lynch et al., 2007;
Miller et al., 2005). If so, it may represent the first large-scale impact of
humans on the climate system. Other human fire driven ecosystem
tipping events include rapid landscape transformations in the mesic
environments of New Zealand (McWethy et al., 2010), the wet tropical
forests of the pre-Columbian Amazon (Nevle et al., 2011), and across
the savannas and woodlands of Africa (Archibald et al., 2012).

As the Earth system exited the last ice age there was a major fluctua-
tion in the climate of the Northern Hemisphere. An abrupt warming
around 14,700 years ago was followed by a marked cooling 12,700
years ago and a further abrupt warming 11,500 years ago. During the
cool period known as the 'Younger Dryas', people in the Eastern
Mediterranean region who had been collecting abundant wild cereals
for food began domesticating the first cereal crops, perhaps in response
to the regional drying effects of climate change. As the Earth system
settled into the stable Holocene interglacial state, around 10,500 years
ago, the Sahara re-entered one of its wet and green phases, turning the
region encompassing the Nile, Euphrates and Tigris rivers into the
fabled Fertile Crescent. Farming began there with the domestication
of wheat, barley, peas, sheep, goats, cows and pigs. Farming also arose
independently elsewhere in the world (Diamond and Bellwood, 2003),
around 8500 years ago in South China, 7800 years ago in North China,
4800 years ago in Mexico and 4500 years ago in Peru and Eastern
North America.

The relatively abrupt and independent occurrence of farming all over
the world suggests it may have been held back by environmental conditions before the Holocene. Low ice age levels of carbon dioxide and
the volatile glacial climate would certainly not have helped establish

agriculture. Once established, farming increased the energy input to human societies. This 'Neolithic revolution' caused an increase in human fertility (soon followed by an increase in mortality), which increased the population from 6 million to over 30 million between 6000 and 4000 years ago and perhaps as high as 100 million by 2000 years ago. However, one of the downsides of farming was that sedentary, high-density agricultural civilisations were more sensitive to environmental change than mobile foraging societies. Abrupt shifts in tropical climate during the Holocene have been linked to the collapse of several ancient societies, and intriguingly abrupt fluctuations in Neolithic European populations display the characteristic early warning signals of a system containing destabilizing positive feedbacks (Downey et al., 2016).

The increased population and energy flows due to farming increased the material inputs to, and waste products from, societies. The resulting environmental effects began early in the Holocene, but their scale is much debated (Ellis et al., 2013; Ruddiman, 2013). Irrigation began around 8000 BP in Egypt and Mesopotamia, leading to some localised salination and siltation of the land, reducing crop yields and encouraging a shift in agricultural crop from wheat to more salt-tolerant barley (Jacobsen and Adams, 1958). The use of manure as fertiliser may have begun as early as 9000 BP in SW Asia and 7000 BP in Europe (Ellis et al., 2013; Bogaard et al., 2007). The clearance of forests to create agricultural land and supply biomass energy and wood from 8000 BP onward, reduced the carbon storage capacity of the land, transferring CO_2 to the atmosphere (Kaplan et al., 2011). Cumulative carbon emissions may have approached 300 PgC by 500 BP contributing ~20 ppm to atmospheric CO_2 levels. The biogeophysical effects of forest clearance also affected the climate, regionally and remotely (Devaraju et al., 2015). Anthropogenic sources of methane started around 5000 BP with the irrigation of rice paddies and have contributed to changes in atmospheric CH_4 concentration over the past ~3000 years (Mitchell et al., 2013).

The 'Early Anthropocene' hypothesis (Ruddiman, 2003, 2007) argues that the new epoch began thousands of years ago, with changes in atmospheric CO_2 and CH_4 caused by the Neolithic revolution. However, others argue that natural changes in the climate and carbon cycle can explain most of the changes in atmospheric CO_2 and CH_4 during the Holocene (Stocker et al., 2011; Singarayer et al., 2011). For example, variations in the Earth's orbit meant that 6000 years ago the Northern Hemisphere was warmer than today and therefore supported more vegetation, both in the boreal regions and across much of North Africa – creating a 'green Sahara'. This helps explain somewhat lower atmospheric CO_2 levels in the early Holocene. As the orbital forcing steadily declined there was a relatively abrupt drying and expansion of the Sahara desert, around 5000 years ago. Models predict this was due to a shift between alternative steady states of the vegetation-climate system in North Africa. This 'browning of the Sahara' together with a retreat of boreal forests from the highest northern latitudes added CO_2 to the atmosphere.

Over the past two millennia, our records of past climate change improve, with multiple proxies for climate variability including tree ring and ice core records and temperatures from boreholes. These records reveal slow fluctuations between somewhat warmer and cooler intervals on Northern Hemisphere land surfaces, including the Medieval Warm Period (c. 950–1250 CE) and the Little Ice Age (c. 1550–1850 CE). Intervals of cooler climate correlate with poor agricultural production, war, and population decline (Zhang et al., 2007), and causal links – while still argued over – have been established (Zhang et al., 2011). Ice core records reveal some variations in atmospheric composition including a 10 ppm decline in CO_2 500 years ago, which was also a time when human biomass burning declined, and has been argued to be due to plague-induced human population decline which allowed large areas to reforest and take up carbon. However, the 'Early Anthropocene' hypothesis (Ruddiman, 2003, 2007) continues to be controversial, partly because pre-industrial societies were limited in the energy supplies with which they could transform their environment.

Many researchers link the start of the Anthropocene with the Industrial Revolution, because the accessing of fossil fuel energy greatly increased the impact of humanity on the Earth system. The Industrial Revolution marks the transition from societies fuelled largely by recent solar energy (via biomass, water and wind) to ones fuelled by concentrated 'ancient sunlight'. Although coal had been used in small amounts for millennia, for example for iron making in ancient China, fossil fuel use only took off with the invention and refinement of the steam engine. Thomas Newcomen's demonstration of a working steam engine in 1712, followed by James Watt's improvements to it in 1769, gave a great boost to coal extraction, by draining mines of water. The steam engine was also used to convert fossil fuel energy into mechanical power in manufacturing and transport. This created a potent positive feedback loop that propelled the Industrial Revolution.

The exploitation of concentrated fossil fuel energy triggered a massive expansion of population, food production, material consumption and associated waste products. Human population doubled between 1825 and 1927 from 1 to 2 billion, doubled again by 1975 to 4 billion, and is on course to double again by 2030 to 8 billion. With the Industrial Revolution, food and biomass have ceased to be the main source of energy for human societies. Within 150 years, from 1850 to 2000, global human energy use increased 10-fold (Lenton et al., 2016b) from 56 to 600 EJ yr^{-1}, such that less than a tenth of total energy input to human societies is now contained in annual food production. By year 2000 the annual global energy flux through human societies was one-third of the global terrestrial NPP (Haberl et al., 2007) and greater than the total global energy flux through all non-human heterotrophic biomass (Lenton et al., 2016b).

The step increase in energy capture with industrialisation is associated with fundamental changes in global material cycles. In industrial economies ~80 per cent by weight of the total annual outflow of materials is CO_2, making the atmosphere the largest waste reservoir of the industrial metabolism (Matthews et al., 2000). Between 1850 and 2000 global CO_2 emissions from combustion of fossil fuels and materials processing increased 125-fold from 54 to 6750 TgC yr^{-1} and reached 9140 TgC yr^{-1} in 2010 (Marland et al., 2008). For some elemental cycles our collective activities now exceed the activities of the rest of the biosphere combined. Between 1860 and 2005 anthropogenic creation of reactive nitrogen grew more than tenfold (Galloway et al., 2008), from ~15 to 187 TgN yr^{-1}. The excess reactive nitrogen was transferred to other environmental pools, partly denitrifying to atmospheric N_2 and N_2O, but also contributing to eutrophication and acidification of terrestrial and coastal marine ecosystems, to global warming and to tropospheric ozone pollution. Analogous human-induced acceleration affected the phosphorus cycle. Much of this escalation of human impact on the Earth system has occurred since the end of the Second World War – in a transition dubbed the 'Great Acceleration' – which provides the best stratigraphic basis for defining the start of the Anthropocene epoch (Waters et al., 2016).

Projecting Future Global Change

How the Anthropocene will develop depends critically on human choices now and in the future. Global change will surely continue to be a systemic phenomenon, involving many interacting variables, including the biosphere. That said, much of the current focus is on 'climate change' as the most pervasive global change, consistent with CO_2 being the most massive waste product of the current industrial metabolism. Hence here we briefly summarise the controls on future climate change, before returning to its interactions with the biosphere.

On the short timescale of the next few decades, temperature projections are not very dependent on future greenhouse gas emissions, because the climate system is still responding to the energy imbalance caused by the accumulation of past greenhouse gas emissions. Also, natural variability in heat uptake and storage by the ocean can affect surface temperatures considerably on decadal timescales. However, once we look beyond a couple of decades ahead, the extent of future climate change depends critically on decisions we make now and in the future.

Projections of global temperature change depend fairly linearly on the cumulative emissions of CO_2 up to a given time, i.e., how much fossil fuel we burn without capturing and storing the CO_2 given off (Figure 2.7). Roughly speaking, each 500 billion tonnes of carbon emitted will give 1°C of global warming. Thus, we have burned around 400 billion tonnes of fossil fuel carbon already and have experienced 0.8°C of warming. If we want to stay under 2°C of warming we need to limit our emissions to a trillion (1000 billion) tonnes of carbon, whereas if we burn all 5000 billion tonnes of known fossil fuels we can eventually expect around 10°C of warming. Whether this thought experiment can ever be realised is highly questionable because <10°C warming could be so damaging as to prevent us from burning all the fossil fuel.

On the long timescale of a millennium, temperature change still depends on the total cumulative emissions of carbon (Lenton, 2000). However, by then the Earth system will have apportioned the CO_2 we have added between the atmosphere, ocean and land surface. The fraction remaining in the atmosphere – known as the 'airborne fraction' – will depend on the total amount of carbon we emit. At a minimum it will be about 20 per cent. But simple and intermediate

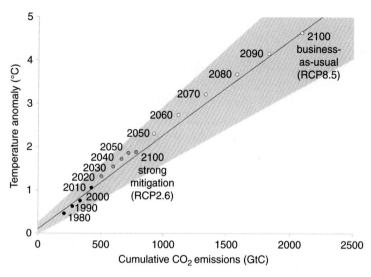

Figure 2.7 Relationship between cumulative carbon emissions and global temperature change (above pre-industrial), showing the range from recent Earth system models (shaded area) and two contrasting future pathways of strong mitigation (RCP2.6; shaded circles) and business-as-usual (RCP8.5; open circles).

complexity models tell us that the fraction increases exponentially with the amount of carbon added. As temperature depends on the natural logarithm of atmospheric carbon these two effects combine to give a linear relationship between carbon emitted and long-term global warming.

The relationship between carbon in the atmosphere and global temperature change is captured in a concept called 'climate sensitivity'. This is defined as the global warming caused by doubling the CO_2 content of the atmosphere, once the heat content of the ocean has adjusted and various 'fast' feedbacks have operated. As early as 1896, Svante Arrhenius calculated that a doubling of atmospheric CO_2 from its pre-industrial concentration would warm the world by around 5°C. This laborious calculation by hand, which took him two years, remains within the range of estimates of 'climate sensitivity' from the latest Earth system models. The current best estimate is that it is near 3°C but it could be in the range 1.5°C–5°C. It is uncertain because models differ over the strength of different feedbacks, and over the long-term heat uptake by the deep ocean, and observations cannot completely constrain these properties. To the 'climate sensitivity' we can add the sensitivity of atmospheric CO_2 concentration to a given CO_2 emission, which depends on feedbacks between the climate and the carbon cycle. As the lifetime of the anthropogenic CO_2 and climate perturbation is expected to stretch into the hundreds of thousands of years (Archer, 2005), there is a long time for 'slow' feedbacks, for example involving the melting of ice sheets, and the thawing of methane hydrates under ocean sediments (Archer et al., 2009), to add to warming. Hence the resulting long-term 'Earth system sensitivity' to CO_2 could be considerably larger than the climate sensitivity (Lunt et al., 2010).

While much of the behaviour of the Earth system can be described as 'linear' and predictable with current models, there is a class of 'non-linear' change that is much harder to predict and potentially much more dangerous. It involves 'tipping points' – where a small perturbation triggers a large response from a part of the Earth system – leading to abrupt and often irreversible changes (Lenton et al., 2008). Tipping points can occur when there is strong positive feedback within a system, which creates alternative stable states for a range of boundary conditions. When changes in the boundary conditions cause the current state of a system to lose its stability, a tipping point occurs, triggering a transition into the alternative stable state. Several sub-systems of the Earth system are thought to exhibit alternative stable states and tipping points – and I have dubbed those parts of the Earth system that can exhibit tipping points 'tipping elements' (Lenton et al., 2008). Among them are several candidates that could be tipped by human-induced global change (Figure 2.8). They can be divided into those involving abrupt shifts in modes of circulation of the ocean or atmosphere (or the two of them coupled together), those involving abrupt loss of parts of the cryosphere, and those involving abrupt shifts in the biosphere – which we return to below.

Thankfully it is very difficult to pass a tipping point at the planetary scale. Rare examples from Earth history are the switches into (and out of) 'snowball Earth' events, or into (and out of) oceanic anoxic events (Handoh and Lenton, 2003). Nevertheless, the possibility of a future planetary tipping point triggered by human activities should not be discounted. Already, the long lifetime of the anthropogenic CO_2 and climate perturbation may have prevented the next ice age (Archer and

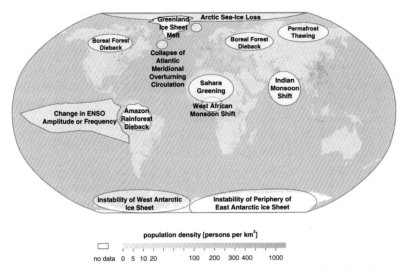

Figure 2.8 Map of some potential tipping elements in the Earth's climate system. Adapted from Lenton et al. (2008).

Ganopolski, 2005), and if CO_2 emissions continue unabated for centuries then the corresponding climate forcing could exceed anything the Earth has experienced in the last 420 million years since the rise of plants (Foster et al., 2017). If so, then we can expect the consequences to be as dramatic as those associated with the rise of plants, and we should take seriously the possibility of switching the Earth into an alternative 'hothouse' mode (Kidder and Worsley, 2012) like those associated with past oceanic anoxic events and mass extinctions.

Consequences of Global Change for Biodiversity

Given this shocking but seemingly distant possibility let us turn to review current projections of the consequences of global change for biodiversity. The corresponding body of work is overwhelmingly focused on much nearer-term timescales and on taking a bottom-up approach that aggregates projected losses of species under smooth scenarios of change, with a particular focus on terrestrial plant and animal species. Such a bottom-up approach is defensible if we believe the world is a simple system that responds linearly to forcing without significant feedbacks between its living and non-living parts. However, if we accept that the world is a complex, non-linear system, in which the living and non-living components are tightly coupled, then it could miss potentially important tipping points. Furthermore, while the focus on terrestrial plants and animals is understandable given that these are the best described species, it misses whole kingdoms of life – archaea and bacteria (prokaryotes), protists (unicellular eukaryotes), and fungi – that are fundamental to the functioning of the Earth system and may respond quite differently to global change.

Thus far, habitat loss due to land use change has been the most important cause of species loss, although climate change is already affecting species distributions and phenology (Parmesan and Yohe, 2003). Looking ahead, climate and land use change are expected to interact together, and with other dimensions of global change, in a systemic way to threaten biodiversity (Oliver and Morecroft, 2014).

Climate change is generally agreed to pose a major future threat to biodiversity of complex life forms, especially terrestrial ones, despite ongoing arguments over methodology (Bellard et al., 2012). Early projections focused on the loss of terrestrial plant and animal (mostly mammal) species, based on the projected movement – and often contraction – of their 'bioclimatic envelope' (i.e., the area defined by the correlation between climate variables and observed distribution) under a given climate change scenario (Thomas et al., 2004). This was combined with the well-known species-area relationship, to project 'committed extinction' (Thomas et al., 2004). Limits of maximum dispersal rates and no dispersal were considered, giving alarming lower-upper estimates of 15–37 per cent committed extinction under a mid-range 2050 climate warming scenario (Thomas et al., 2004). This would put climate change on a par with habitat loss from land use change (Sala et al., 2000), as the greatest threat to terrestrial biodiversity. No timescale was assigned to how long it would take the 'committed' extinctions to unfold, thus opening the possibility that if global temperature could be brought down in the future – either by natural or artificial (geoengineering) means – this could save species (Thomas et al., 2004), by bringing their bioclimatic envelope back to where they are.

Those versed in recent Earth history have noted that the abrupt climate changes of the Quaternary period provoked nothing like the level of species extinction being projected under smaller levels of future climate change. Instead the megafauna extinctions that did occur are mostly (if not universally) attributed directly to human activities, occurring as they do synchronously with the spread of *Homo sapiens* across the planet (Sandom et al., 2014). This begs the question of how species kept up with the movement of their bioclimatic envelope in the past. One line of reasoning is that past climate changes were less rapid giving more time for migration/dispersal or genetic adaptation of populations. However, while this is true for the overall pace of deglaciation, some past abrupt warming events (e.g., at the end of the Younger Dryas), while not fully global in scale, were more rapid than anything considered in the future projections. Despite this, several relatively sedentary (e.g., tree) species in the most affected regions were able to move at an impressive rate. This suggests a critical role for rare long-range dispersal events (Nathan, 2006) (and/or for nascent islands of cryptic diversity outside recognised climate envelopes).

Many subsequent studies – reviewed elsewhere (Bellard et al., 2012) – have attempted to project extinction risk from climate change. The great majority still use bioclimatic envelope models to project changes in range, although IUCN status methods and dose-response relationship models have also been used to assess loss of species. A few studies have used more aggregated dynamic global vegetation models to project shifts in biomes and then downscaled from that to assess extinction risk. Early on it was noted that the lack of consideration of distinct ecotypes within a species, each having a more restricted bioclimatic envelope than the species as a whole, could lead to underestimation of species loss (Harte et al., 2004). Conversely the lack of consideration of acclimation (phenotypic plasticity) and genetic adaptation could lead to an overestimation of committed extinction.

The fundamental question of 'can life adapt?' to global change has become the focus of a rapidly expanding recent body of work (Parmesan, 2006; Hoffmann and Sgro, 2011). Here 'adapt' is taken in the broad sense to cover both physiological acclimation and genetic adaptation. The question is particularly pertinent for the marine ecosystem as it is based fundamentally on microbial primary producers with considerable phenotypic plasticity, and (thanks to short generation times) considerable potential for rapid evolutionary adaptation. Thus, global change will affect the phytoplankton, but changes in function may be more pertinent than levels of extinction. For example, modelling of the physiological acclimation of phytoplankton cells to ocean warming, based on molecular genetic insights into the temperature sensitivity of core biochemistry, predicts that the ribosomal content of cells will decline in a warmer ocean and with that their N:P ratio will go up (Daines et al., 2014; Toseland et al., 2013). Such a fundamental change in the composition of organisms at the base of the marine food chain is likely to have a range of biogeochemical and ecological consequences, including triggering greater nitrogen depletion of ocean waters and a resulting selective pressure for increased nitrogen fixation.

As this brief review reveals, the bottom-up approach to projecting global change effects on biodiversity can clearly suggest global consequences. However, major questions remain unanswered, such as, would relatively high levels of projected species loss compromise the functioning of ecosystems and the biosphere, and to what degree? Given the preceding review of the crucial role that plants, fungi and animals have played in creating a high-O_2, low-CO_2 world it would seem logical to infer that a major loss of their biodiversity will impact the regulation of the Earth system. Equally the bottom-up approach may miss the possibility that the greatest global change threats to biodiversity could come at larger levels of biological organisation than the individual or the species – including the possibility of wholesale loss of ecosystems and biomes due to the passing of tipping points.

Starting on the land surface, some biomes (particularly in the tropics) are strongly coupled to the atmosphere through positive feedbacks. For example, the 'green Sahara' state that was present 6000 years ago supported an atmospheric circulation that brought moisture into what is now a desert. Today the Amazon rainforest recycles water to the atmosphere thus helping maintain the rainfall that supports the forest. It also suppresses fires. However, if the climate dries regionally – as was seen in recent Amazon drought years (2005, 2010) – this can lead to dieback of trees and a shift to a more devastating fire regime. If grasses begin to encroach into the forest these encourage fires which destroy tree saplings and support an alternative grassland or savanna state (a positive feedback). Grasslands are already thought to be an alternative stable vegetation state for large parts of the Amazon basin under present rainfall (Hirota et al., 2011; Staver et al., 2011). In the future, if the region dries out, widespread dieback of the Amazon rainforest has been projected in some models (Cox et al., 2000; Jones et al., 2009).

Biomes may also pass climate thresholds to their viability, due to the dominant organisms reaching physiological limits or due to abrupt increases in disturbance factors linked to climate change. Currently several regions of temperate and boreal forests are experiencing widespread tree dieback due to drought and heat stress (Allen et al., 2010) and to attack by bark beetles that are thriving in a warmer climate (Kurz et al., 2008a; Kurz et al., 2008b). In some future projections, large areas at the southern boundary of the boreal forests are abruptly lost and replaced with steppe grasslands (Joos et al., 2001; Lucht et al., 2006), as the summers become too hot for the dominant trees and disturbance by fires and bark beetle attacks increases. Abrupt dieback of large areas of forests would clearly negatively impact the biodiversity they contain and could happen faster than the movement of species' bioclimatic envelopes. Loss of large areas of tropical or boreal forests would also feedback CO_2 to the atmosphere, making a significant contribution to cumulative CO_2 emissions and temperature rise.

Turning to the ocean, coral reefs are under threat of large-scale loss due to a combination of drivers, including ocean warming and acidification (Hoegh-Guldberg et al., 2007; Veron et al., 2009). Coral bleaching events have become much more widespread and detrimental in recent decades, and marine biologists are already talking about tropical coral reefs being at a 'point of no return' (Veron et al., 2009). Cold-water corals that grow down to 3000 m depth will be the first to be affected by ocean acidification as the saturation horizon of aragonite (the crystalline form of calcium carbonate out of which they are constructed) shallows. Once bathed in corrosive waters, under saturated in aragonite, the skeletons and shells may dissolve and the reefs collapse. With unabated CO_2 emissions an estimated 70 per cent of the presently known deep-sea coral reef locations will be in corrosive waters by the end of this century (Guinotte et al., 2006).

An even larger-scale tipping point threat to ocean ecosystems comes from the increased input of phosphorus (and nitrogen) to the land for food production, which is already fuelling anoxic conditions in freshwaters and some shelf seas. Ocean anoxia is further encouraged by warming of the ocean, which reduces the solubility of oxygen in the water and tends to stratify the ocean, isolating deeper deoxygenating waters from the atmosphere. If humans continue to refine all the known phosphate rock reserves and turn them into fertiliser over the coming centuries, then this will significantly increase the phosphorus content of the ocean (Watson et al., 2017). Augmented by climate change–driven acceleration of phosphorus weathering rates, this risks triggering

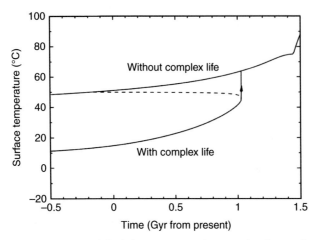

Figure 2.9 A model of alternative steady states for the Earth's temperature and the life span of the biosphere under a steadily brightening Sun (Lenton & von Bloh, 2001). Figure from Lenton (2016: 126, Figure 29), *Earth System Science: A Very Short Introduction*. Reproduced by permission from Oxford University Press, http://global.oup.com. © Oxford University Press.

a global oceanic anoxic event (Figure 2.4) on a millennial timescale (Watson et al., 2017), thanks to the potent positive feedback whereby anoxia enhances phosphorus recycling from shelf-sea sediments fuelling more productivity and anoxia (Handoh and Lenton, 2003; Watson et al., 2017). As the fossil record attests, widespread ocean anoxia causes marine mass extinction, and at the end Permian it fed back through the Earth system to contribute to extinctions on land.

In the worst-case scenario, a large enough anthropogenic perturbation to the land surface, climate and biogeochemical cycling could conceivably tip the Earth system into an alternative stable hot state that cannot support complex eukaryote life forms (Lenton and von Bloh, 2001) (Figure 2.9). In the standard model for the life span of the biosphere, the steady brightening of the Sun eventually causes complex life to overheat, in about 1 billion years, and the Earth system tips into a much hotter steady-state. However, that steady-state is already predicted to be stable now, if we were to remove the biological enhancement of rock weathering which profoundly lowers CO_2 and global temperature. This implies that if we seriously impair the effect of plants and fungi on rock weathering, combined with a very large global warming perturbation, then we could irreversibly tip the Earth into a hot state, unable to support complex eukaryote life forms (Lenton and von Bloh, 2001). Such existential risks may seem distant by human timescales, but from the perspective of geologic time they could be imminent.

Conclusion: Where Next?

While human transformation of the planet was initially unwitting, now we are collectively aware of it. We have conscious foresight that (as far as we know) has never been part of the Earth system before. This changes the Earth system fundamentally, because it means that one species can – in principle at least – consciously, collectively shape the future trajectory of our planet. We know our current way of living is both unsustainable and is eroding biodiversity (in many senses of the word). I have made the case that we depend completely on the biosphere for our very existence and furthermore that the global changes and extinctions that we have begun to cause now could threaten our very life-support system. This should be more than enough existential threat to be triggering a rear guard action, yet little real change is happening. As the Pope's Encyclical letter on care for our common home makes clear, this must be due to a failure in our value system (Pope Francis, 2015).

Specifically, we fail to recognise and embody in our social and economic systems the fundamental existential value of the biosphere. That said it doesn't take much, even within the current narrow paradigm of economic valuation, to get a very different result. For example, if we simply recognise that the biosphere provides essential services to us that cannot be substituted by something in the market place (Sterner and Persson, 2008), and furthermore that a part of those services is under threat of irreversible loss (Lenton et al., 2008), then even if we barely value those services in market terms, they should still be exerting a huge influence on our 'social planning' – including triggering policy decisions to work much harder and faster to mitigate climate change (Cai et al., 2015). This is because the irreplaceable and unsubstitutable biosphere does not grow like the economy – hence even in mainstream economics it effectively becomes scarcer and therefore more precious the longer we continue in a growth paradigm (Hoel and Sterner, 2007).

Whether the current growth paradigm thus contains the intellectual seeds of its own demise is a moot point given the current political economy of knowledge. Nevertheless, it seems worth reflecting if we could change our value system to properly embrace our reliance on the biosphere, and see ourselves as an integral part of it, could we chart a very different way forward? In particular, rather than heading (now with our eyes open) toward an impending apocalypse, or frantically trying to retreat into lower energy and material consumption, could we help create a positive revolutionary change of the Earth system (Lenton and Watson, 2011)? And could such a 'good Anthropocene' be truly good for all and not just some rich elite (Pope Francis, 2015)? As a scientist I think that a future world powered by sustainable energy with near-closed recycling of materials could conceivably support billions of people and allow the rest of the biosphere to flourish (Lenton and Watson, 2011). As a human being I want to believe that it could also be a more equitable future world (Pope Francis, 2015). What I am sure of is that these are the questions we have to collectively address as we shape the future of this remarkable biosphere.

References

Allen, C. D., Macalady, A. K., Chenchouni, H., Bachelet, D., Mcdowell, N., Vennetier, M., Kitzberger, T., Rigling, A., Breshears, D. D., Hogg, E. H., Gonzalez, P., Fensham, R., Zhang, Z., Castro, J., Demidova, N., Lim, J.-H., Allard, G., Running, S. W., Semerci, A. & Cobb, N. 2010. A global overview of drought and heat-induced tree mortality reveals emerging climate change risks for forests. *Forest Ecology and Management*, 259: 660–684.

Allen, J. F. & Martin, W. 2007. Evolutionary biology: Out of thin air. *Nature*, 445: 610–612.

Andreae, M. O. & Crutzen, P. J. 1997. Atmospheric aerosols: Biogeochemical sources and role in atmospheric chemistry. *Science*: 276, 1052–1058.

Archer, D. 2005. Fate of fossil fuel CO_2 in geologic time. *Journal of Geophysical Research: Oceans*, 110(C9): C09S05.

Archer, D., Buffett, B. & Brovkin, V. 2009. Ocean methane hydrates as a slow tipping point in the global carbon cycle. *Proceedings of the National Academy of Sciences USA*, 106: 20596–20601.

Archer, D. & Ganopolski, A. 2005. A movable trigger: Fossil fuel CO_2 and the onset of the next glaciation. *Geochemistry Geophysics Geosystems*, 6: doi:10.1029/2004GC000891.

Archibald, S., Staver, A. C. & Levin, S. A. 2012. Evolution of human-driven fire regimes in Africa. *Proceedings of the National Academy of Sciences*, 109: 847–852.

Barnosky, A. D., Koch, P. L., Feranec, R. S., Wing, S. L. & Shabel, A. B. 2004. Assessing the causes of Late Pleistocene extinctions on the continents. *Science*, 306: 70–75.

Bekker, A. & Holland, H. D. 2012. Oxygen overshoot and recovery during the early Paleoproterozoic. *Earth and Planetary Science Letters*, 317–318:295–304.

Bellard, C., Bertelsmeier, C., Leadley, P., Thuiller, W. & Courchamp, F. 2012. Impacts of climate change on the future of biodiversity. *Ecology Letters*, 15: 365–377.

Berner, R. A. 1997. The rise of plants and their effect on weathering and atmospheric CO_2. *Science*, 276: 544–546.

Bogaard, A., Heaton, T. H. E., Poulton, P. & Merbach, I. 2007. The impact of manuring on nitrogen isotope ratios in cereals: Archaeological implications for reconstruction of diet and crop management practices. *Journal of Archaeological Science*, 34: 335–343.

Boyden, S. V. 1992. *Biohistory: The Interplay Between Human Society and the Biosphere, Past and Present*. Carnforth, UK: Parthenon Publishing Group.

Boyle, R. A., Dahl, T. W., Dale, A. W., Shields-Zhou, G. A., Zhu, M., Brasier, M. D., Canfield, D. E. & Lenton, T. M. 2014. Stabilization of the coupled oxygen and phosphorus cycles by the evolution of bioturbation. *Nature Geoscience*, 7: 671–676.

Boyle, R. A., Williams, H. T. P. & Lenton, T. M. 2012. Natural selection for costly nutrient recycling in simulated microbial metacommunities. *Journal of Theoretical Biology*, 312: 1–12.

Brasier, M. D., Green, O. R., Jephcoat, A. P., Kleppe, A. K., van Kranendonk, M. J., Lindsay, J. F., Steele, A. & Grassineau, N. V. 2002. Questioning the evidence for Earth's oldest fossils. *Nature*, 416: 76–81.

Brasier, M. D., Mcloughlin, N., Green, O. & Wacey, D. 2006. A fresh look at the fossil evidence for early Archaean cellular life. *Philosophical Transactions of the Royal Society of London Series B – Biological Sciences*, 361.

Brasseur, G. P. & Chatfield, R. B. 1991. The fate of biogenic trace gases in the atmosphere. In T. D. Sharkey, E. A. Holland & H. A. Mooney (Eds), *Trace Gas Emission from Plants*: 1–27. San Diego, CA: Academic.

Brown, K. S., Marean, C. W., Herries, A. I. R., Jacobs, Z., Tribolo, C., Braun, D., Roberts, D. L., Meyer, M. C. & Bernatchez, J. 2009. Fire

As an Engineering Tool of Early Modern Humans. *Science*, 325: 859–862.

Butterfield, N. J. 2000. *Bangiomorpha pubescens* n. gen., n. sp.: Implications for the evolution of sex, multicellularity, and the Mesoproterozoic/ Neoproterozoic radiation of eukaryotes. *Paleobiology*, 26: 386–404.

  2005. Probable Proterozoic fungi. *Paleobiology*, 31: 165–182.

Cai, Y., Judd, K. L., Lenton, T. M., Lontzek, T. S. & Narita, D. 2015. Environmental tipping points significantly affect the cost–benefit assessment of climate policies. *Proceedings of the National Academy of Sciences*, 112: 4606–4611.

Canfield, D. E., Rosing, M. T. & Bjerrum, C. 2006. Early anaerobic metabolisms. *Philosophical Transactions of the Royal Society B: Biological Sciences*, 361: 1819–1836.

Catling, D. C., McKay, C. P. & Zahnle, K. J. 2001. Biogenic methane, hydrogen escape, and the irreversible oxidation of early Earth. *Science*, 293: 839–843.

Claire, M. W., Catling, D. C. & Zahnle, K. J. 2006. Biogeochemical modelling of the rise in atmospheric oxygen. *Geobiology*, 4: 239–269.

Cox, P. M., Betts, R. A., Jones, C. D., Spall, S. A. & Totterdell, I. J. 2000. Acceleration of global warming due to carbon-cycle feedbacks in a coupled climate model. *Nature*, 408: 184–187.

Crucifix, M. 2012. Oscillators and relaxation phenomena in Pleistocene climate theory. *Philosophical Transactions of the Royal Society A: Mathematical, Physical and Engineering Sciences*, 370: 1140–1165.

Daines, S. J., Clark, J. R. & Lenton, T. M. 2014. Multiple environmental controls on phytoplankton growth strategies determine adaptive responses of the N:P ratio. *Ecology Letters*, 17: 414–425.

Daines, S. J. & Lenton, T. M. 2016. The effect of widespread early aerobic marine ecosystems on methane cycling and the Great Oxidation. *Earth and Planetary Science Letters*, 434: 42–51.

Daines, S. J., Mills, B. & Lenton, T. M. 2017. Atmospheric oxygen regulation at low Proterozoic levels by incomplete oxidative weathering of sedimentary organic carbon. *Nature Communications*, 8: 14379.

Devaraju, N., Bala, G. & Modak, A. 2015. Effects of large-scale deforestation on precipitation in the monsoon regions: Remote versus local effects. *Proceedings of the National Academy of Sciences*, 112: 3257–3262.

Diamond, J. & Bellwood, P. 2003. Farmers and their languages: The first expansions. *Science*, 300: 597–603.

Dodd, M. S., Papineau, D., Grenne, T., Slack, J. F., Rittner, M., Pirajno, F., O'Neil, J. & Little, C. T. S. 2017. Evidence for early life in Earth's oldest hydrothermal vent precipitates. *Nature*, 543: 60–64.

Donnadieu, Y., Godderis, Y., Ramstein, G., Nedelec, A. & Meert, J. 2004. A 'snowball Earth' climate triggered by continental break-up through changes in runoff. *Nature*, 428: 303–306.

Downey, S. S., Haas, W. R. & Shennan, S. J. 2016. European Neolithic societies showed early warning signals of population collapse. *Proceedings of the National Academy of Sciences*, 113: 9751–9756.

Ellis, E. C., Kaplan, J. O., Fuller, D. Q., Vavrus, S., Klein Goldewijk, K. & Verburg, P. H. 2013. Used planet: A global history. *Proceedings of the National Academy of Sciences*, 110: 7978–7985.

Farquhar, J., Bao, H. & Thiemens, M. 2000. Atmospheric Influence of Earth's Earliest Sulfur Cycle. *Science*, 289: 756–758.

Foster, G. L., Royer, D. L. & Lunt, D. J. 2017. Future climate forcing potentially without precedent in the last 420 million years. *Nature Communications*, 8: 14845.

Galloway, J. N., Townsend, A. R., Erisman, J. W., Bekunda, M., Cai, Z., Freney, J. R., Martinelli, L. A., Seitzinger, S. P. & Sutton, M. A. 2008. Transformation of the nitrogen cycle: Recent trends, questions, and potential solutions. *Science*, 320: 889–892.

Gingerich, P. D. 2006. Environment and evolution through the Paleocene-Eocene thermal maximum. *Trends in Ecology & Evolution*, 21: 246–253.

Goldblatt, C., Lenton, T. M. & Watson, A. J. 2006. Bistability of atmospheric oxygen and the great oxidation. *Nature*, 443: 683–686.

Guinotte, J. M., Orr, J., Cairns, S., Freiwald, A., Morgan, L. & George, R. 2006. Will human-induced changes in seawater chemistry alter the distribution of deep-sea scleractinian corals? *Frontiers in Ecology and the Environment*, 4: 141–146.

Haberl, H., Erb, K. H., Krausmann, F., Gaube, V., Bondeau, A., Plutzar, C., Gingrich, S., Lucht, W. & Fischer-Kowalski, M. 2007. Quantifying and mapping the human appropriation of net primary production in Earth's terrestrial ecosystems. *Proceedings of the National Academy of Sciences*, 104: 12942–12947.

Han, T. M. & Runnegar, B. 1992. Megascopic eukaryotic algae from the 2.1-billion-year-old negaunee iron-formation, Michigan. *Science*, 257.

Handoh, I. C. & Lenton, T. M. 2003. Periodic mid-Cretaceous Oceanic Anoxic Events linked by oscillations of the phosphorus and oxygen biogeochemical cycles. *Global Biogeochemical Cycles*, 17: 1092.

Harnik, P. G., Lotze, H. K., Anderson, S. C., Finkel, Z. V., Finnegan, S., Lindberg, D. R., Liow, L. H., Lockwood, R., McClain, C. R., McGuire, J. L., O'Dea, A., Pandolfi, J. M., Simpson, C. & Tittensor, D. P. 2012. Extinctions in ancient and modern seas. *Trends in Ecology & Evolution*, 27: 608–617.

Harte, J., Ostling, A., Green, J. L. & Kinzig, A. 2004. Biodiversity conservation: Climate change and extinction risk. *Nature*, 430.

Hirota, M., Holmgren, M., van Nes, E. H. & Scheffer, M. 2011. Global resilience of tropical forest and savanna to critical transitions. *Science*, 334: 232–235.

Hoegh-Guldberg, O., Mumby, P. J., Hooten, A. J., Steneck, R. S., Greenfield, P., GOMEZ, E., Harvell, C. D., Sale, P. F., Edwards, A. J., Caldeira, K., Knowlton, N., Eakin, C. M., Iglesias-Prieto, R., Muthiga, N., Bradbury, R. H., Dubi, A. & Hatziolos, M. E. 2007. Coral reefs under rapid climate change and ocean acidification. *Science*, 318: 1737–1742.

Hoel, M. & Sterner, T. 2007. Discounting and relative prices. *Climatic Change*, 84: 265–280.

Hoffman, P. F., Kaufman, A. J., Halverson, G. P. & Schrag, D. P. 1998. A Neoproterozoic snowball Earth. *Science*, 281: 1342–1346.

Hoffmann, A. A. & Sgro, C. M. 2011. Climate change and evolutionary adaptation. *Nature*, 470: 479–485.

Holland, H. D. 1978. *The Chemistry of the Atmosphere and Oceans.* New York: Wiley.

Jacobsen, T. & Adams, R. M. 1958. Salt and silt in ancient Mesopotamian agriculture: Progressive changes in soil salinity and sedimentation contributed to the breakup of past civilizations. *Science*, 128: 1251–1258.

Jones, C., Lowe, J., Liddicoat, S. & Betts, R. 2009. Committed ecosystem change due to climate change. *Nature Geoscience*, 2: 484–487.

Joos, F., Prentice, I. C., Sitch, S., Meyer, R., Hooss, G., Plattner, G.-K., Gerber, S. & Hasselmann, K. 2001. Global warming feedbacks on terrestrial carbon uptake under the Intergovernmental Panel on Climate Change (IPCC) emissions scenarios. *Global Biogeochemical Cycles*, 15: 891–907.

Jouzel, J., Masson-Delmotte, V., Cattani, O., Dreyfus, G., Falourd, S., Hoffmann, G., Minster, B., Nouet, J., Barnola, J. M., Chappellaz, J., Fischer, H., Gallet, J. C., Johnsen, S., Leuenberger, M., Loulergue, L., Luethi, D., Oerter, H., Parrenin, F., Raisbeck, G., Raynaud, D., Schilt, A., Schwander, J., Selmo, E., Souchez, R., Spahni, R., Stauffer, B., Steffensen, J. P., Stenni, B., Stocker, T. F., Tison, J. L., Werner, M. & Wolff, E. W. 2007. Orbital and millennial Antarctic climate variability over the past 800,000 years. *Science*, 317(5839): 793–796.

Kaplan, J. O., Krumhardt, K. M., Ellis, E. C., Ruddiman, W. F., Lemmen, C. & Klein Goldewijk, K. 2011. Holocene carbon emissions as a result of anthropogenic land cover change. *The Holocene*, 21: 775–791.

Kharecha, P., Kasting, J. & Siefert, J. 2005. A coupled atmosphere–ecosystem model of the early Archean Earth. *Geobiology*, 3: 53–76.

Kidder, D. L. & Worsley, T. R. 2012. A human-induced hothouse climate? *GSA Today*, 22: 4–11.

Knoll, A. H. & Barghoorn, E. S. 1977. Archean microfossils showing cell division from the Swaziland system of South Africa. *Science*, 198: 396–398.

Kurz, W. A., Dymond, C. C., Stinson, G., Rampley, G. J., Neilson, E. T., Carroll, A. L., Ebata, T. Safranyik, L. 2008a. Mountain pine beetle and forest carbon feedback to climate change. *Nature*, 452: 987–990.

Kurz, W. A., Stinson, G., Rampley, G. J., Dymond, C. C. & Neilson, E. T. 2008b. Risk of natural disturbances makes future contribution of Canada's forests to the global carbon cycle highly uncertain. *Proceedings of the National Academy of Sciences*, 105: 1551–1555.

Lenton, T. M. 2000. Land and ocean carbon cycle feedback effects on global warming in a simple Earth system model. *Tellus*, 52B: 1159–1188.

2016. *Earth System Science: A Very Short Introduction*. Oxford: Oxford University Press.

Lenton, T. M., Boyle, R. A., Poulton, S. W., Shields, G. A. & Butterfield, N. J. 2014. Co-evolution of eukaryotes and ocean oxygenation in the Neoproterozoic era. *Nature Geoscience*, 7: 257–265.

Lenton, T. M., Crouch, M., Johnson, M., Pires, N. & Dolan, L. 2012. First plants cooled the Ordovician. *Nature Geoscience*, 5: 86–89.

Lenton, T. M., Dahl, T. W., Daines, S. J., Mills, B. J. W., Ozaki, K., Saltzman, M. R. & Porada, P. 2016a. Earliest land plants created modern levels of atmospheric oxygen. *Proceedings of the National Academy of Sciences*, 113: 9704–9709.

Lenton, T. M. & Daines, S. J. 2016. Matworld: The biogeochemical effects of early life on land. *New Phytologist*, doi:10.1111/nph.14338.

2017. Biogeochemical transformations in the history of the ocean. *Annual Review of Marine Science*, 9: 31–58.

Lenton, T. M., Held, H., Kriegler, E., Hall, J., Lucht, W., Rahmstorf, S. & Schellnhuber, H. J. 2008. Tipping Elements in the Earth's Climate System. *PNAS*, 105: 1786–1793.

Lenton, T. M., Pichler, P. P. & Weisz, H. 2016b. Revolutions in energy input and material cycling in Earth history and human history. *Earth System Dynamics*, 7: 353–370.

Lenton, T. M., Schellnhuber, H. J. & Szathmáry, E. 2004. Climbing the co-evolution ladder. *Nature*, 431: 913.

Lenton, T. M. & Von Bloh, W. 2001. Biotic feedback extends the life span of the biosphere. *Geophysical Research Letters*, 28: 1715–1718.

Lenton, T. M. & Watson, A. J. 2000. Redfield revisited: 2. What regulates the oxygen content of the atmosphere? *Global Biogeochemical Cycles*, 14: 249–268.

2004. Biotic enhancement of weathering, atmospheric oxygen and carbon dioxide in the Neoproterozoic. *Geophysical Research Letters*, 31: L05202.

2011. *Revolutions That Made the Earth*. Oxford, Oxford University Press.

Love, G. D., Grosjean, E., Stalvies, C., Fike, D. A., Grotzinger, J. P., Bradley, A. S. Kelly, A. E., Bhatia, M., Meredith, W., Snape, C. E., Bowring, S. A., Condon, D. J. & Summons, R. E. 2009. Fossil steroids record the appearance of Demospongiae during the Cryogenian period. *Nature*, 457: 718–721.

Lucht, W., Schaphoff, S., Erbrecht, T., Heyder, U. & Cramer, W. 2006. Terrestrial vegetation redistribution and carbon balance under climate change. *Carbon Balance and Management*, 1: 6.

Lunt, D. J., Haywood, A. M., Schmidt, G. A., Salzmann, U., Valdes, P. J. & Dowsett, H. J. 2010. Earth system sensitivity inferred from Pliocene modelling and data. *Nature Geoscience*, 3: 60–64.

Luthi, D., Le Floch, M.,Bereiter, B., Blunier, T., Barnola, J.-M., Siegenthaler, U., Raynaud, D., Jouzel, J., Fischer, H., Kawamura, K. & Stocker, T. F. 2008. High-resolution carbon dioxide concentration record 650,000–800,000 years before present. *Nature*, 453, 379–382.

Lucht, W., Schaphoff, S., Erbrecht, T., Heyder, U. & Cramer, W. 2006. Terrestrial vegetation redistribution and carbon balance under climate change. *Carbon Balance and Management*, 1: 6.

Lunt, D. J., Haywood, A. M., Schmidt, G. A., Salzmann, U., Valdes, P. J. & Dowsett, H. J. 2010. Earth system sensitivity inferred from Pliocene modelling and data. *Nature Geoscience*, 3: 60–64.

Lynch, A. H., Abramson, D., Görgen, K., Beringer, J. & Uotila, P. 2007. Influence of savanna fire on Australian monsoon season precipitation and circulation as simulated using a distributed computing environment. *Geophysical Research Letters*, 34: L20801.

Mackenzie, F. T., Ver, L. M., Sabine, C., Lane, M. & Lerman, A. 1993. C, N, P, S global biogeochemical cycles and modelling of global change. In

R. Wollast, F. T. Mackenzie & L. Chou (Eds.), *Interactions of C, N, P and S Biogeochemical Cycles and Global Change*: 1–61. Berlin: Springer.

Magill, C. R., Ashley, G. M. & Freeman, K. H. 2013. Ecosystem variability and early human habitats in Eastern Africa. *Proceedings of the National Academy of Sciences*, 110: 1167–1174.

Marland, G., Andres, R. J. & Boden, T. A. 2008. Global CO_2 emissions from fossil-fuel burning, cement manufacture, and gas flaring: 1751–2005. In *Trends: A Compendium of Data on Global Change*. Oak Ridge National Laboratory, Oak Ridge, TN: Carbon Dioxide Information Analysis Center.

Matthews, E., Amann, C., Bringezu, S., Fischer-Kowalski, M., Huttler, W., Kleijn, R., Moriguchi, Y., Ottke, C., Rondenburg, E., Rogich, D., Schandl, H., Schutz, H., van der Voet, E. & Weisz, H. 2000. *The Weight of Nations. Material Outflows from Industrial Economies*. Washington, DC: World Resources Institute.

McWethy, D. B., Whitlock, C., Wilmshurst, J. M., McGlone, M. S., Fromont, M., Li, X., Dieffenbacher-Krall, A., Hobbs, W. O., Fritz, S. C. & Cook, E. R. 2010. Rapid landscape transformation in South Island, New Zealand, following initial Polynesian settlement. *Proceedings of the National Academy of Sciences*, 107: 21343–21348.

Miller, G., Mangan, J., Pollard, D., Thompson, S., Felzer, B. & Magee, J. 2005. Sensitivity of the Australian Monsoon to insolation and vegetation: Implications for human impact on continental moisture balance. *Geology*, 33: 65–68.

Mills, B., Daines, S. J. & Lenton, T. M. 2014. Changing tectonic controls on the long-term carbon cycle from Mesozoic to present. *Geochemistry, Geophysics, Geosystems*, 15: 4866–4884.

Mitchell, L., Brook, E., Lee, J. E., Buizert, C. & Sowers, T. 2013. Constraints on the Late Holocene anthropogenic contribution to the atmospheric methane budget. *Science*, 342: 964–966.

Monnin, E., Indermühle, A., Dällenbach, A., Flückiger, J., Stauffer, B., Stocker, T. F., Raynaud, D. & Barnola, J.-M. 2001. Atmospheric CO_2 concentrations over the Last Glacial Termination. *Science*, 291(5501): 112–114.

Nathan, R. 2006. Long-distance dispersal of plants. *Science*, 313: 786–788.

Nevle, R. J., Bird, D. K., Ruddiman, W. F. & Dull, R. A. 2011. Neotropical human-landscape interactions, fire, and atmospheric CO_2 during European conquest. *The Holocene*, 21: 853–864.

Noffke, N., Christian, D., Wacey, D. & Hazen, R. M. 2013. Microbially induced sedimentary structures recording an ancient ecosystem in the ca. 3.48 billion-year-old dresser formation, Pilbara, Western Australia. *Astrobiology*, 13: 1103–1124.

Nutman, A. P., Bennett, V. C., Friend, C. R. L., van Kranendonk, M. J. & Chivas, A. R. 2016. Rapid emergence of life shown by discovery of 3,700-million-year-old microbial structures. *Nature*, 537: 535–538.

Ohtomo, Y., Kakegawa, T., Ishida, A., Nagase, T. & Rosing, M. T. 2014. Evidence for biogenic graphite in early Archaean Isua metasedimentary rocks. *Nature Geoscience*, 7: 25–28.

Oliver, T. H. & Morecroft, M. D. 2014. Interactions between climate change and land use change on biodiversity: Attribution problems, risks, and opportunities. *Wiley Interdisciplinary Reviews: Climate Change*, 5: 317–335.

Pagani, M., Caldeira, K., Berner, R. & Beerling, D. J. 2009. The role of terrestrial plants in limiting atmospheric CO_2 decline over the past 24 million years. *Nature*, 460: 85–88.

Parfrey, L. W., Lahr, D. J. G., Knoll, A. H. & Katz, L. A. 2011. Estimating the timing of early eukaryotic diversification with multigene molecular clocks. *Proceedings of the National Academy of Sciences*, 108: 13624–13629.

Parmesan, C. 2006. Ecological and evolutionary responses to recent climate change. *Annual Review of Ecology, Evolution, and Systematics*, 37: 637–669.

Parmesan, C. & Yohe, G. 2003. A globally coherent fingerprint of climate change impacts across natural systems. *Nature*, 421: 37–42.

Pausas, J. G. & Keeley, J. E. 2009. A burning story: The role of fire in the history of life. *BioScience*, 59: 593–601.

Petit, J. R., Jouzel, J., Raynaud, D., Barkov, N. I., Barnola, J. M., Basile, I., Bender, M., Chappellaz, J., Davis, M., Delaygue, G., Delmotte, M., Kotlyakov, V. M., Legrand, M., Lipenkov, V. Y., Lorius, C., Pépin, L., Ritz, C., Saltzman, E., & Stievenard, M. 1999. Climate and atmospheric history of the past 420,000 years from the Vostok ice core, Antarctica. *Nature*, 399: 429.

Pope Francis, 2015. *Laudato Si': On Care for Our Common Home* [Encyclical]. Vatican City, Italy: Vatican Press. http://w2.vatican.va/con tent/francesco/en/encyclicals/documents/papa-francesco_20150524_en ciclica-laudato-si.html

Rasmussen, B., Fletcher, I. R., Brocks, J. J. & Kilburn, M. R. 2008. Reassessing the first appearance of eukaryotes and cyanobacteria. *Nature*, 455: 1101–1104.

Raymo, M. E. & Ruddiman, W. F. 1992. Tectonic forcing of late Cenozoic climate. *Nature*, 359: 117–122.

Roebroeks, W. & Villa, P. 2011. On the earliest evidence for habitual use of fire in Europe. *Proceedings of the National Academy of Sciences*, 108: 5209–5214.

Rosing, M. T. 1999. 13C-depleted carbon microparticles in >3700-Ma sea-floor sedimentary rocks from West Greenland. *Science*, 283: 674–676.

Ruddiman, W. F. 2003. The anthropogenic greenhouse era began thousands of years ago. *Climatic Change*, 61: 261–293.

2007. The early anthropogenic hypothesis: Challenges and responses. *Reviews of Geophysics*, 45: RG4001.

2013. The Anthropocene. *Annual Review of Earth and Planetary Sciences*, 41: 45–68.

Sala, O. E., Chapin, F. S. I., Armesto, J. J., Berlow, E., Bloomfield, J., Dirzo, R., Huber-Sanwald, E., Huenneke, L. F., Jackson, R. B., Kinzig, A., Leemans, R., Lodge, D. M., Mooney, H. A., Oesterheld, M. Ì. N., Poff, N. L., Sykes, M. T., Walker, B. H., Walker, M. & Wall, D. H. 2000. Global biodiversity scenarios for the year 2100. *Science*, 287: 1770–1774.

Sandom, C., Faurby, S., Sandel, B. & Svenning, J.-C. 2014. Global late Quaternary megafauna extinctions linked to humans, not climate change. *Proceedings of the Royal Society B: Biological Sciences*, 281.

Schopf, J. W. 1993. Microfossils of the Early Archean apex chert: New evidence of the antiquity of life. *Science*, 260: 640–646.

2006. Fossil evidence of Archaean life. *Philosophical Transactions of the Royal Society B*, 361: 869–885.

Schwartzman, D. W. & Volk, T. 1989. Biotic enhancement of weathering and the habitability of Earth. *Nature*, 340: 457–460.

Siegenthaler, U., Stocker, T. F., Monnin, E., Luthi, D., Schwander, J., Stauffer, B., Raynaud, D., Barnola, J.-M., Fischer, H., Masson-Delmotte, V. & Jouzel, J. 2005. Stable carbon cycle–climate relationship during the Late Pleistocene. *Science*, 310(5752): 1313–1317.

Singarayer, J. S., Valdes, P. J., Friedlingstein, P., Nelson, S. & Beerling, D. J. 2011. Late Holocene methane rise caused by orbitally controlled increase in tropical sources. *Nature*, 470: 82–85.

Staver, A. C., Archibald, S. & Levin, S. A. 2011. The global extent and determinants of savanna and forest as alternative biome states. *Science*, 334: 230–232.

Sterner, T. & Persson, U. M. 2008. An even sterner review: Introducing relative prices into the discounting debate. *Review of Environmental Economics and Policy*, 2: 61–76.

Stocker, B. D., Strassmann, K. & Joos, F. 2011. Sensitivity of Holocene atmospheric CO_2 and the modern carbon budget to early human land use: analyses with a process-based model. *Biogeosciences*, 8: 69–88.

Thomas, C. D., Cameron, A., Green, R. E., Bakkenes, M., Beaumont, L. J., Collingham, Y. C., Erasmus, B. F. N., De Siqueira, M. F., Grainger, A., Hannah, L., Hughes, L., Huntley, B., van Jaarsveld, A. S., Midgley, G. F., Miles, L., Ortega-Huerta, M. A., Townsend Peterson, A., Phillips, O. L. & Williams, S. E. 2004. Extinction risk from climate change. *Nature*, 427: 145–148.

Toseland, A., Daines, S., Clark, J. R., Kirkham, A., Strauss, J., Uhlig, C., Lenton, T. M., Valentin, K., Pearson, G., Moulton, V. & Mock, T. 2013. The impact of temperature on marine phytoplankton resource allocation and metabolism. *Nature Climate Change*, 3: 979–984.

Ueno, Y., Yamada, K., Yoshida, N., Maruyama, S. & Isozaki, Y. 2006. Evidence from fluid inclusions for microbial methanogenesis in the early Archaean era. *Nature*, 440: 516–519.

van Cappellen, P. & Ingall, E. D. 1994. Benthic phosphorus regeneration, net primary production, and ocean anoxia: A model of the coupled marine biogeochemical cycles of carbon and phosphorus. *Paleoceanography*, 9: 677–692.

   1996. Redox stabilisation of the atmosphere and oceans by phosphorus-limited marine productivity. *Science*, 271: 493–496.

Vanwonterghem, I., Evans, P. N., Parks, D. H., Jensen, P. D., Woodcroft, B. J., Hugenholtz, P. & Tyson, G. W. 2016. Methylotrophic methanogenesis discovered in the archaeal phylum Verstraetearchaeota. *Nature Microbiology*, 1: 16170.

Veron, J. E. N., Hoegh-Guldberg, O., Lenton, T. M., Lough, J. M., Obura, D. O., Pearce-Kelly, P., Sheppard, C. R. C., Spalding, M., Stafford-Smith, M. G. & Rogers, A. D. 2009. The coral reef crisis: The critical importance of <350ppm CO_2. *Marine Pollution Bulletin*, 58: 1428–1437.

Waters, C. N., Zalasiewicz, J., Summerhayes, C., Barnosky, A. D., Poirier, C., Gałuszka, A., Cearreta, A., Edgeworth, M., Ellis, E. C., Ellis, M., Jeandel, C., Leinfelder, R., Mcneill, J. R., Richter, D. D., Steffen, W., Syvitski, J., Vidas, D., Wagreich, M., Williams, M., Zhisheng, A., Grinevald, J., Odada, E., Oreskes, N. & Wolfe, A. P. 2016. The Anthropocene is functionally and stratigraphically distinct from the Holocene. *Science*, 351.

Watson, A. J., Lenton, T. M. & Mills, B. J. W. 2017. Ocean de-oxygenation, the global phosphorus cycle, and the possibility of human-caused large-scale ocean anoxia. *Philosophical Transactions of the Royal Society A*, 375: 20160318.

Williams, H. T. P. & Lenton, T. M. 2007. The Flask model: Emergence of nutrient-recycling microbial ecosystems and their disruption by environment-altering 'rebel' organisms. *Oikos*, 116: 1087–1105.

Wrangham, R. W., Jones, J. H., Laden, G., Pilbeam, D. & Conklin-Brittain, N. L. 1999. The raw and the stolen: Cooking and the ecology of human origins. *Current Anthropology*, 40: 567–590.

Zhang, D. D., Brecke, P., Lee, H. F., He, Y.-Q. & Zhang, J. 2007. Global climate change, war, and population decline in recent human history. *Proceedings of the National Academy of Sciences USA*, 104: 19214–19219.

Zhang, D. D., Lee, H. F., Wang, C., Li, B., Pei, Q., Zhang, J. & An, Y. 2011. The causality analysis of climate change and large-scale human crisis. *Proceedings of the National Academy of Sciences*, 108: 17296–17301.

3 | The State of the World's Biodiversity

STUART L. PIMM AND PETER H. RAVEN

In this chapter, we ask several simple questions. How many species are there, both named and unnamed? How fast are species now going extinct? How fast do species go extinct normally? And how fast do they diversify and thus might be able to recover from the current massive losses? Finally, where are extinctions concentrated, and how can we use this information to prevent extinctions?

How Many Species Are There?

This deceptively simple question has a rich – and even theological – pedigree. Westwood (1833) speculated 'On the probable number of species of insects in the Creation'. In the last few decades, studies have drawn widely varying conclusions (Gaston, 1991; May and Beverton, 1990; Mora et al., 2011; Stork, 1993). A recent, thorough compilation of previous estimates by Chapman (2009), plus new studies that propose novel methods of estimation, motivated a review of progress (Scheffers et al., 2012). Table 3.1 simplifies the latter's compilation of previous estimates of species. To it, we add additional data to illustrate key debates.

We deal here only with eukaryotic organisms. We are far from being able to make similar estimates for Eubacteria and Archaea, where the definition of species is problematic. The numbers of forms might even reach one trillion (Locey and Lennon, 2016).

In Table 3.1, the column 'Currently Catalogued' counts the numbers of species that have been named within various taxonomic groupings. Deriving such estimates, even for well-studied groups like birds, is not straightforward. There are two kinds of problems. First, far more species exist than taxonomists have named. Second, taxonomists have also complicated matters inadvertently by giving multiple names

Table 3.1 *Estimates of species numbers*

Kingdom	Phylum/division	Within phylum	Major division	Currently catalogued	Described species range	Estimated
Plants	Pteridophytes, lycophytes			400,000		460,000
	Bryophytes (mosses, hepatics, hornworts)			12,000		14,000
				19,900		20,000
Fungi	Lichen-forming Fungi			98,998	45,173–300,000	1.5M[a]
				19,400		28,000
Animals	Porifera			~6000	5500–10,000	~18,000
	Cnidaria			9795	9000–11,000	NA
	Mollusca			~85,000	50,000–120,000	~200,000
	Annelida			16,763	12,000–16,763	~30,000
	Arthropoda					
		Arachnida		102,248	60,000–102,248	~600,000[a]
		Myriapoda		16,072	8160–17,923	~90,000

Table 3.1 (*cont.*)

Kingdom	Phylum/division	Within phylum	Major division	Currently catalogued	Described species range	Estimated
Animals (cont.)		Insecta		~1M	720,000–>1 M	5 M[a]
			Coleoptera	360,000–400,000		1.1M
			Diptera	152,956		240,000[a]
			Hemiptera	80,000–88,000		
			Hymenoptera	115,000		>300,000[a]
			Lepidoptera	174,250		300,000–500,000
		Crustacea		47,000	25,000–68,171	150,000
	Platyhelminthes			20,000	20,000–25,000	(~80,000)
	Nematoda			<25,000	12,000–80,000	~500,000[a]
	Echinodermata			7003	6100–7003	~14,000
	Chordata			64,788		~80,500
			Mammals	5487	4300–5487	~5500
			Birds	9990	9000–9990	>10,000
			Birds	10,052		
			Reptiles	8734	6300–8734	~10,000
			Amphibians	6515	4950–6515	~15,000
			Fishes	31,269	25,000–31,269	~40,000

[a] These estimates are very uncertain.
Source. Updated from Chapman (2009), Scheffers et al. (2012) and estimates discussed in the text.

to many species. For large groups of poorly studied species, the determination of the number of such synonyms is difficult.

The completeness of global inventories varies greatly (see 'Estimated' in Table 3.1). Inventories are ~97 per cent complete for mammals, 85 per cent for flowering plants, 79 per cent for fish, 67 per cent for amphibians and no more than ~30 per cent for arthropods (Hamilton et al., 2010; Joppa et al., 2010; Mora et al., 2008) (Table 3.1). Taxonomic effort is near evenly distributed among vertebrates, plants and invertebrates, yet plants have roughly 10 times, and invertebrates at least 100 times more species than vertebrates.

The Hyper-Estimates of Species Numbers

The greatest uncertainties in species numbers involve 'hyper-estimates' – by which we mean individual totals of 5 million species or more. For one example, Grassle and Maciolek (1992) used the relationship between the numbers of invertebrates found in samples of areas of increasing extent to extrapolate the total number of species in the deep sea. They suggested the world's deep seafloor could have up to 10 million species – a total that is several orders of magnitude larger than that found in their geographically restricted sample.

Numbers this large invite scientific controversy. In the case of marine invertebrates, such extrapolations from local to global seafloor diversity were unwarranted because of the obvious difficulties about scaling up from a small to a much larger geographical scale. That an area of size A, has S species, does not mean that an area of 10 times A has 10 times S species. Moreover, the known, non-linear relationships between numbers of species within areas of a given size vary by circumstance (Rosenzweig, 1995). Several authors have raised general concerns about the limitations of scaling up from estimates collected at a single spatial scale (ØDegaard, 2000; Gering et al., 2007; Lambshead and Boucher, 2003).

Certainly, marine diversity is a challenge because it is so taxonomically diverse. Appeltans et al. (2012) assembled 120 experts covering all the phyla and major groups. They estimated 0.7–1.0 million marine species with 226,000 described and another 70,000 in collections awaiting description

For a second example, Erwin (1982) estimated there might be 30 million species of arthropods. His calculation starts with his assertion that 13.5 per cent of the beetle species he found might be restricted to a single species of tree in Panama, then extrapolates to more trees species and other arthropod groups. His estimate generated much criticism, primarily from those concerned about the assumptions underlying such a 'small to large' extrapolation. The method, however, spawned considerable interest and research.

Fundamental to the controversy was the degree of host specificity of herbivorous insects on their food plants, i.e., 13.5 per cent for the beetles he studied. Novotny et al. (2007), ØDegaard (2000) and others found considerably lower host specificity than this, perhaps by a factor of four or five. Subsequent global estimates of insect species numbers have consequently been considerably lower. The subject requires much further study before a reasonable degree of precision can be attained.

Hamilton et al. (2010) highlighted the sensitivity of Erwin's model to its input parameters. As with earlier studies, their estimate requires values for the average effective specialisation of herbivorous beetle species across all tree species, a correction factor for beetle species that are not herbivorous, the proportion of canopy arthropod species that are beetles, the proportion of all arthropod species found in the canopy and the number of tropical tree species. Their approach uniformly and randomly sampled plausible ranges for each of these numbers. Some 90 per cent of these parameter combinations fell between 3.6 and 11.4 million species (Novotny et al., 2007).

Fungi are another poorly known group. Hawksworth (1991) started with the 6:1 ratio of fungi to flowering plant species found in Britain, where both groups are well known, and extrapolated this ratio to the global total for flowering plants, yielding an estimate of 1.62 million species of fungi globally. May (1991) was sharply critical of this estimate. A key concern, he argued, is that the species-rich tropics are unlikely to have the same ratio of fungi to plants as does Britain. (Elsewhere, the ratio is even higher; Taylor et al., 2014.) Even if the ratio were only 6:1, then collections of fungi from the tropics should find that >95 per cent of the species encountered would be new, given that only ~70,000 fungi had been catalogued globally to that date. May noticed that actual percentages of new species from tropical samples were much smaller. An alternative approach by Mora et al. (2011) estimates ~611,000 fungal species globally and seemingly supports May's more conservative estimate of ~500,000 fungal species.

Such low estimates of fungi species have spawned strident counters. First, small, quickly obtained samples of species will not be random ones but dominated by well-known, widespread species. Only when sampling is intensive will it uncover species unique to that area. Second, Hawksworth (1991) emphasised not just fungal and plant associations, but the strong associations of fungi with insects. Each beetle species might have a unique fungus, for example. Third, Bass and Richards (2011) point out that over the past decade, new methods in molecular biology and environmental probing have substantially increased the rate of species' descriptions. Such techniques can also estimate what fractions of genomes from samples match species with descriptions. The answers are often only a minority (Hibbett, 2016), which also suggests many unknown species.

Cannon (1997) estimates that there are 9.9 million species of fungi. O'Brien et al. (2005) estimate 3.5 to 5.1 million species (Blackwell, 2011). The very high genetic diversity of fungi in soil samples – 491 distinct fungal genomes in pine-forest soil samples, and 616 in soils from mixed-hardwood forests, respectively – initiate these hyper-estimates. They emerge, as before, from extrapolating ratios from local to global scales, so the concerns about scaling also apply here. At present, there are no comparable genomic surveys in tropical moist forests showing exceptionally high fungal richness there, as would be expected. Moreover, no one has yet shown how communities of fungal genomes change over large geographical areas.

Robert Lucking (personal communication) estimates that there are about 19,400 valid species of lichen-forming fungi known. He estimates that the total number will climb to about 28,000 eventually.

Finally, we note that comparable concerns apply to nematodes and mites. They are both poorly known, while informed experts expect large numbers of species to be uncovered eventually.

Quantitative Methods

There have been several attempts to estimate species numbers using various large-scale relationships.

Mora et al. (2011) used the rates of description to fit asymptotic regression models to taxon-accumulation curves over time for phyla, classes, orders, families and genera. Using the asymptotic estimates for animals, the ratios of classes per phyla, orders per class, families per order and genera per family were strikingly similar. On this basis, they posited that the ratio of species per genus would be the same globally and so predicted 8,750,000 terrestrial and 2,210,000 marine species. There is no theoretical reason to make this final supposition about the species to genus ratio, but to the extent that they could compare the best estimates of numbers of species within phyla, there was broad agreement with their predictions.

Estimating the total number of species in a taxon would seem to be a straightforward task from the rates of their discovery. These rates should slow as the number of as yet undescribed species falls and so the cumulative number of species should asymptote (Costello and Wilson, 2011; Ricotta et al., 2002; Solow and Smith, 2005). For birds globally, and for some taxa regionally, the rates of description are slowing over time, whence asymptotic approaches provide reasonable estimates. Mora et al. (2011) employ this approach to estimate the numbers of higher taxa as well – as described above.

Quite unexpectedly, for many taxa, not only are the rates of species description increasing, they are doing so exponentially. This precludes estimates of asymptotes. While there are widespread concerns that the numbers of taxonomists are decreasing, the numbers of individuals who describe species are, in fact, also increasing and doing so exponentially. (The pattern holds for mammals, amphibians, spiders, marine snails of the genus *Conus* [Joppa et al., 2011b], parasitic wasps [Bacher, 2012] and several other invertebrate taxa for which taxonomists have given Pimm access to their data.) The discrepancy is surely that there are fewer dedicated taxonomists now than in the past for some groups, but that many more individuals likely describe species as part of their other research.

To account for this increase in the numbers of individuals describing species, a mechanistic model accounts for taxonomic effort and for changing taxonomic efficiency. Initially proposed by Joppa et al. (2010, 2011a), this model defines *taxonomic effort* as the number of people involved in describing species and *taxonomic efficiency* as an increase in the number of species described per person, adjusted for the continually diminishing pool of as yet unknown species. Rates of species description divided by taxonomic effort generally decline. This allows statistical estimation of the likely number of species in the taxon.

How well does this model perform? For plants, validating it by expert opinion revealed broad agreement with its predictions of how many species remained to be described (Joppa et al., 2010). In some plant taxa and for parasitic wasps, the numbers of species described per taxonomist remains roughly constant even as the pool of missing species inevitably declines. Taxonomists can describe only so many species in a year – regardless of how many missing species there are – and work through the backlog of undescribed species methodically, genus by genus.

Finally, the first description of a species is merely the first step. The number of recognised bird species has continued to rise, even though birds are the best-known taxon. Some of this increase represents genuinely new discoveries, but much is the recognition that what was once one species should now be best viewed as several. And, some of those changes stem from changing ideas of whether distinct allopatric populations should be considered the same or different species. Even for mammals, many species could not be considered to be well known and for other taxa only a small fraction has been studied in detail.

Plants

Because plants are the base of the living food chain they demand special attention. The expected large numbers of herbivorous insects likely depend on how many plant species there are, for example. For plant species, collaboration between Kew and the Missouri Botanic Garden created the Global Plant List www.plantlist.org. It lists 351,000 species of plants, made up of 304,000 flowering plants, 1100 species of gymnosperms, 10,600 species of ferns and lycopods, and 35,000 species of mosses and liverworts.

Plant taxonomists are working through the lists of plant species family-by-family to resolve synonyms. For the families assessed to date, there are about twice as many synonyms as valid names. For the species in the families not yet assessed, adding half the names to the already assessed total, we estimate approximately 400,000 vascular plant species (Pimm et al., 2014; Pimm and Raven, 2017).

How many plant species remain to be named? Expert opinion (Libing Zhang, personal communication) suggests there might be 14,000 species of ferns and lycopods. Marshall Crosby and Matt von Konrat (personal communications) suggest 19,900 valid bryophyte species have been described, with a total of about 20,000. The total number of valid moss species is falling, while that of hepatics is rising at about the same rate.

The rate of description of new species of plants shows the taxonomic catalogue is far from complete. Both expert opinion and the Joppa et al. models suggest there will be another 15 per cent more species – and so a total of 460,000 species of plants (Pimm and Raven, 2017). If there are another 60,000 or so species to be named, perhaps half of them are already present as specimens in herbaria (Brummitt et al., 2015).

Where Are the Missing Species?

As we show below, knowing where species live is vital for understanding future rates of species extinction – and setting international priorities for conservation. Incomplete information might leave us unable effectively to prioritise where to allocate conservation efforts. For example, the 'biodiversity hotspots' (Myers et al., 2000) combine a measure of exceptional habitat destruction (<30 per cent relatively intact habitat remaining) with the numbers of *known* endemic flowering plant species (>1500) (Pimm et al., 2014). Recent studies by Joppa et al. (2011a) suggest the plant species still undescribed will be concentrated in the biodiversity hotspots – places such as Central America, the northern Andes and South Africa.

Prospects

There are several encouraging trends.

1 Herbaria clearly harbour many of the remaining undescribed species of plants. For example, Bebber et al. (2007) found that existing herbarium material typically took decades to describe and estimated that perhaps half of all missing plant species were already represented in herbaria.

2 Recent advances in DNA barcoding facilitate the detection of similar species (Hebert et al., 2004) by revealing breaks in the patterns of variation. This in turn has led to improved understanding of the patterns of variation in many different groups.

3 Communities of taxonomists working with some groups of organisms are now placing their lists and taxonomic decisions into the public domain, especially on websites. These include sites for flowering plants (www.kew.org/wcsp/), spiders (research .amnh.org/oonopidae/catalog/) amphibians (research.amnh.org/h erpetology/amphibia/index.php), birds (www.birdlife.org/data zone/info/taxonomy) and mammals (www.bucknell.edu/msw3/). A few groups other than plants and vertebrates are likewise being sorted so that we can better understand what is known about them, but for the large, poorly known groups, sorting what is known can be seen only as a meagre and very preliminary step: neither the specimens nor the people to study them are available.

4 Global efforts to catalogue all species, such as All-Species (www .allspecies.org), GBIF (www.gbif.org), Species 2000 (www .sp2000.org) and Tree of Life (www.tolweb.org/tree/phylogeny .html), are now being made available online, but can do relatively little for most groups of organisms.

5 Efforts to map where species occur are progressing. Smart phones and software-website applications such as iNaturalist (www.inaturalist.org) link data directly into IUCN Red Lists, the Global Biodiversity Information Facility, and other pre-existing databases. Crowd-sourcing of species mapping could greatly expand these databases, which are major contributions to our knowledge of where species live. Such databases are already promoting the discovery of new species, revealing those that do not fit known descriptions, but they work well only for groups of organisms that are relatively well known. The enormous task of bringing the knowledge of other groups into adequate register cannot be completed, as we demonstrate later in this paper, until most of the species that exist now have disappeared forever.

6 Unlike most other groups of organisms, plants can be preserved effectively by growing them in gardens, in seed banks or in tissue culture. Perhaps a quarter of the total number of species have already been preserved in one of these ways, and there is great hope that nearly all might be rescued from extinction in the coming decades if we accelerate our efforts to accomplish this important goal.

How Fast Are Species Going Extinct?

... a mass extinction crisis, with a rate of extinction now 1000 times higher
than the normal background rate.
Al Gore (2006: 152) in the Academy Award–winning
documentary *An Inconvenient Truth*

As Gore's remark testifies, it has become standard to quantify present
extinctions as rates and then to compare them to some background that
typifies geological history. Mass extinction events are understood to be
exceptions. Gore's and similar statements emerged via secondary
sources originally derived from Pimm et al. (1995) who estimated
'recent extinction rates are 100 to 1000 times their pre-human levels'.

Before 1995, the literature quoted statistics on current extinctions in
'species per day'. Estimates ranged from a 'minimum' of three (Myers,
1989) to 'a hundred species per day' (Stork, 2010). More than uncertainties about the extinctions themselves, the numbers reflected the wide
range of estimates for how many eukaryote species exist (see above).

The uncertainty in the 'species per day' estimates also posed problems when dealing with critics of environmental concerns who
demanded the scientific names of those recently extinct (Stork, 2010).
Of course, taxonomists have described only a small fraction of species,
while the IUCN's Red List (www.iucnredlist.org) has assessed an even
smaller fraction of those – ~53,000 species. To avoid the necessarily
complex caveats for extinctions per day estimates, Pimm et al. (1995)
deliberately chose to replace this metric with a proportional rate that
they could calculate for a given taxon.

Estimating the current rates of extinctions is a straightforward process: one follows a cohort of species for some specified interval and
records what fraction succumbed (Pimm et al., 1995, 2006, 2014). For
numerical convenience, we calculate extinctions per million species-
years (E/MSY). This method does not count species, such as the dodo,
that went extinct before the 1750s, when the current system of Latin
names was first applied to organisms. For example, taxonomists have
described 1230 species of birds since 1900, of which 13 have become
extinct (Table 3.2). This cohort accumulated 98,334 species-years –
meaning that an average species has been known for 80 years – and so
the extinction rate is $13 \times 10^6/98,334 = 132$ E/MSY.

Extinction rates from cohort analyses average about 100 E/MSY
(Table 3.2). Local rates from regions at great risk can be much higher,

for example, rates for fish and gastropods in North American rivers and lakes and rates for cichlid fishes in Africa's Lake Victoria (Pimm et al., 2014). Given that most species are still undescribed and many species with small ranges are recent discoveries, these numbers are bound to be underestimates for the living world as a whole. Many, if not most, species will have gone or be going extinct before they are given Latin names. (This happens even for well-known birds; Lees and Pimm, 2015.) The extinction rates of species described after 1900 are considerably higher than the rates for those described earlier, reflecting the fact that particularly in well-known groups, those species described more recently will on average be rare and restricted in range (Table 3.2).

Rates of extinction increase with improved knowledge – since taxonomists describe widespread common species before local and rare ones, and the latter are more vulnerable to human actions. Thus, recent extinction rates based on poorly known taxa (such as insects) are bound to be substantial underestimates since so many species remain undescribed. (Widespread species likely dominate the fossil record, which further clouds estimates of extinction rates derived from it – see below.)

Finally, in addition to species deemed extinct, there are substantial fractions of species that are critically endangered (Table 3.2). Some of these may indeed be already extinct, while others survive only through energetic conservation efforts.

How Fast Should Species Be Going Extinct?

De Vos et al. (2015) explored three lines of evidence toward achieving the more difficult task of estimating this 'background rate' of extinction. By this, we mean the geologically recent rates of extinction before human actions inflated them.

Extinction Rates from the Fossil Record

The fossil record provides essential information, but it is very limited in temporal resolution and taxonomic breadth (Purvis, 2008). Moreover, most palaeontological studies assess genera, not species (Flessa and Jablonski, 1985). The one conclusion one can draw from Barnosky et al. (2011) are the large uncertainties in the extinction rates that fossils provide.

Alroy (1996) found the mean rate for Cenozoic mammals to be 0.165 extinctions of genera per million genera years (see his Figure 6).

Table 3.2 *Extinction rates calculated by cohort analysis and fractions of species that are critically endangered (CR)*

When Described	Species	Extinctions	Species-years	Extinction Rate	CR	% CR
Birds						
Before 1900	8922	93	1,812,897	51	123	1.4
1900 to present	1230	13	98,334	132	60	4.9
Amphibians						
Before 1900	1437	18	212,348	85	22	1.5
1900 to present	4967	121	206,149	587	379	7.6
Mammals						
Before 1900	3048	37	499,101	74	55	1.8
1900 to present	2486	32	174,512	183	100	4.0

Note. All species thought to be 'possibly extinct', 'extinct in the wild' and 'possible extinction in the wild' are counted as extinctions.
Source. Pimm et al. (2014).

Harnik et al. (2012) examined a variety of marine taxa. What they call 'extinction rate' is, in fact, a dimensionless extinction fraction, the natural logarithm of the fractional survival of genera measured over an average stage length of 7 million years. Converting these fractions to their corresponding rates yields values for the last few million years of 0.06 genera extinctions per million genera-years for cetaceans, 0.04 for marine carnivores, and for a variety of marine invertebrates between the values of 0.001 (brachiopods) and 0.01 (echinoids). Put another way, 1 per cent of echinoid genera are lost per million years, were we to make the interpolation.

There are many caveats.

First, fossil estimates suffer the obvious bias that genera may be present somewhere before they are first recorded and after they are last recorded. Thus, unless corrected, longevities are potentially underestimated and the extinction rates are overestimated (Foote and Raup, 1996). Fossil data likely most accurately reflect rates during events, such as the five mass extinctions, when extinction rates were episodically high.

Second, whether it is reasonable to interpolate fractional survivorship based on stages averaging several million years to shorter intervals of a million years is problematical. For this reason, Barnosky et al. (2011) show estimates as a function of the interval over which they calculated them. Any interpolation imputes homogenous rates of extinction across geological stages, while evidence suggests extinction rates are pulsed toward their end (Alroy, 2008; Foote, 2005). Indeed, changes in floras and faunas often define when one stage ends and the other starts. If so, for millions of years the rates would be even lower than reported values, followed by episodes when they are higher.

In any case, comparing rates of generic extinctions to species extinction is complex (Russell et al., 1998). For mammals, with 4.4 species per genus, were all genera to have four species in them, binomial probabilities show that a species rate of 0.63 E/MSY would give the observed rate of 0.165 extinctions of genera per million genera years (Alroy, 1996), and for five species, 0.69. There are two problems with this. Most generic extinctions are likely those in monotypic genera. Second, these calculations assume statistical independence. As Russell et al. show, species extinctions within a genus are highly contingent. Some genera and some places are much more vulnerable than others. Combined, these considerations would lead to the species extinction rate being close to the generic rate, i.e., 0.165 E/MSY.

In short, in comparing the extinction rates of fossils with present biota, we are contrasting genera with species, and, of course, typically very different taxa and often marine with terrestrial ecosystems.

Species Extinction Rates from Molecular Phylogenies

Molecular phylogenies provide an appealing alternative to the fossil record's shortcomings, covering a large range of taxa, time periods and environments. The simplest case expects a single lineage to grow to a clade size of N species, during time t, according to

$$N = \exp(r \times t) \tag{3.1}$$

The net diversification rate, r, is the speciation, λ, minus the extinction rate, μ, $(\lambda - \mu)$:

$$(\lambda - \mu) = r = \frac{\ln(N)}{t} \tag{3.2}$$

Can one *separately* estimate the speciation and extinction rates, not just their difference? Equation (3.1) expects the plot of the logarithm of the number of lineages through time (LTT) to be linear, with slope $\lambda - \mu$ but with an important qualification. In the limit of the present day, there are no extinctions of the most recent taxa – they have not yet happened. Thus, near the present, the LTT slope should increase and approach λ, the speciation rate (Nee, 2006). This allows the separate calculation of the speciation and extinction rates.

Practice is considerably more complicated than this simple theory (Etienne et al., 2012; Morlon et al., 2011): λ and μ may be time-dependent, be functionally related, both may depend on the number of species already present, and they will likely vary from place-to-place and among different taxa. McPeek (2008) found that 80 per cent of the studies compiled have LTT graphs that curve *downward* on the log-linear scale.

Such studies yield a maximum likelihood estimate of zero extinction, but we can reasonably ask how certain are these estimates. Not all the LTT graphs involve smooth increases in the numbers of species over time. Many show irregularities that increase the uncertainty of the estimates, widening the probable ranges of parameters. That complication means we must employ methods that explore the probability distributions of the parameters we estimate, rather than inferring a most likely point estimate. There are also concerns about how many species might be missing from the clades analysed.

To address these concerns, De Vos et al. (2015) undertook an extensive set of simulations of known diversifications, with varying fractions of species removed from these modelled clades, and in some cases, different rates of diversification. At best, their simulations demonstrate that the underestimation of extinction due to complex diversification processes may be only slight: they always recovered the correct order of magnitude of absolute extinction across replicate phylogenies, even though individual estimates were associated with large uncertainties. They concluded that phylogenies of extant taxa should contain at least some information on extinction rates (Pyron and Burbrink, 2013).

Finally, taxonomists may fall short of recognising all lineages that will give rise to new species in the future (Phillimore and Price, 2008). The entirely arbitrary taxonomic decision of whether to group geographically isolated populations as one species or split them into several recently derived species will affect estimates of extinction rates.

Despite those difficulties, an important conclusion emerges. Of the 140 phylogenies that De Vos et al. (2015) analysed, all but four had median estimated extinction rates of <0.4 E/MSY and only two (one arthropod and one mollusc) had rates >1 and those were <1.5. These estimates match those of Weir and Schluter (2007) who estimated bird and mammal extinctions that range from 0.08 E/MSY at the equator – where there are the most species – to ~0.4–0.6 E/MSY at 50° latitude – where they are far fewer. Thus, despite the methodological hurdles and the potentially confounding whims of taxonomists, there is consistent evidence that background extinction rates are below one extinction per million species-years and most likely much less than this.

How Fast Can Species Diversify?

In contrast to the methodological complexities of separating speciation and extinction rates, it is relatively easy to calculate their difference – the rates of diversification. Consequently, there are many estimates of diversification. Table 3.3 shows median diversification rates from

Table 3.3 *Various studies, their sample sizes and the median rates of species diversification*

Study	Sample size	Net diversification rate
Summary of previous studies		
Plants (Ferrer and Good, 2012)	204	0.060
Birds (Phillimore and Price, 2008)	45	0.147
Mammals	121	0.047
Results of De Vos et al. (2015)		
Chordata	45	0.204
Plants	37	0.088
Arthropods	34	0.173
Mammals	16	0.066
Mollusca	8	0.135

Source. After De Vos et al. (2015). See this for details.

~0.05 to ~0.2 new species per species per million years for disparate groups of animals and plants. Rates >1.0 are exceptional.

Valente et al. (2010) explicitly addressed the issue of how fast taxa can diversify. They analysed the genus *Dianthus* (carnations, Caryophyllaceae) and found net diversification rates of up to 16 new species per species per million years. This puts them well above 11 other plant groups, to which they compared them, the highest rate of which was Andean *Lupinus* (lupines, Fabaceae) at ~2 (Koenen et al., 2013). For birds, the record holder is the group of Southeast Asian *Zosterops* (white-eyes, Zosteropidae), at 2.6 new species per species per million years. Others classify some of these 'species' as subspecies, which would reduce that rate; the distinction is quite arbitrary.

Valente et al. (2010) also discuss the cichlids of east African lakes that have speciated rapidly, with estimates of stem diversification up to six new species per species per million years for Lake Malawi. They notice that rates roughly 10 times these for Lake Victoria are possible if the ~500 species now present are all descended from just one ancestor after the lake dried out 14,700 years ago. To achieve such rates, however, one must completely exclude the possibility of several species surviving that desiccation in small, permanent pools. An additional example is the rapid divergence of *Enallagma* damselflies, which have added 23 new species from seven lineages in the last 250,000 years (Turgeon et al., 2005). In contrast are lineages such as *Ginkgo*, which appears to have changed little since the Jurassic (Zhou and Zheng, 2003).

Synthesis

We have reviewed three lines of evidence to help us obtain an order-of-magnitude estimate of the background rate of extinction. We certainly recognise that this rate will vary over time, space and taxon. Fossil data are the most direct, but their analysis presents many limitations. Separating extinction and speciation rates from phylogenies is methodologically difficult and generates ongoing, vigorous debate. Rates of diversification provide less direct information, but there are many compilations across different taxa and ecosystems. Diversification rates are ~0.05 to ~0.2 new species per species per million years, with exceptional rates of >1. The question is what these tell us about extinction rates.

We notice that the fossil record shows that overall species richness is increasing over time (Rosenzweig, 1995). Certainly, some clades are shrinking – Quental and Marshall (2011) list examples – but these are fewer than those that are increasing. The direct estimates of extinction rates from phylogenies listed above are also low. The insights from our simulation models show that when averaged across a set of phylogenies, the models placed these rates within the right order of magnitude. In short, what we see in observed phylogenies also precludes high extinction rates.

Simply, there is no widespread evidence for high recent extinction rates from either the fossil record or from molecular phylogenies. Thus, overall, extinction rates cannot exceed diversification rates. Combining the evidence from the fossil record, from the separation of speciation and extinction rates from molecular phylogenies, and overall diversification rates, we conclude that background extinctions rates are approximately 0.1 extinctions per million species per year, a rate that indicates that current extinction rates are 1000 times higher than the historical background.

How Fast Will Species Become Extinct in the Future?

The best guide to future extinctions is the IUCN Red List (IUCN, 2016). It assigns species to classes of Least Concern, through Near-

Threatened to three progressively escalating categories of Threatened species (Vulnerable, Endangered, Critically Endangered) and Extinct. Other than the last category, these constitute an expert system of the relative likelihood of how soon species will become extinct in the future, given present conditions. The most important criteria in determining risk are the size of a species' geographic range and the degree to which the effects of human actions (including climate change) are shrinking its habitat. Other factors include whether humans hunt, collect or kill the species for other reasons. There are two major problems with the Red List: the incompleteness of the data and the inconsistency of the assessments.

Incompleteness

By January 2017, IUCN had considered 85,604 of >1.7 million named species. Groups of vertebrate animals get the most attention (~45,000), invertebrates constitute another 19,000, while plants ~22,000. Of the 63,303 total animals assessed, 11,923 were judged to be data deficient – meaning there is not enough information to know their status. This often means that they are rare, so that a large fraction of them may be threatened with extinction. Of the remaining 51,380, 1285 were extinct or probably so, while 12,630 were threatened, with 2696 of them deemed critically endangered. Birds, mammals and amphibians constitute ~23,000 of the species assessed and are mostly terrestrial or partially terrestrial species. They are the only groups for which there are comprehensive species distribution maps (www.biodiversitymapping.org).

Efforts are expanding the limited data from oceans for which only 2 per cent of species are assessed compared to 3.6 per cent of all known species. Peters et al. (2013) assessed snails of the genus *Conus* and Carpenter et al. (2008) assessed corals. Dulvy et al. (2014) assessed 1041 known shark and ray species: 17.4 per cent are threatened, most by overexploitation, and most of them large-bodied, shallow water, coastal species. Only 37.4 per cent of species were deemed of Least Concern, the lowest fraction in any vertebrate group assessed.

For plants, Kew (2016) tabulates the various estimates of how many species are threatened with extinction, and these fall mostly in the 20–33 per cent range. This highlights the complexities. First, the

IUCN Red List has assessed a sample of only ~22,000 species, of which 7 per cent had insufficient data, and 52 per cent were deemed threatened. Kew (2016) argues that this is too high an estimate for all plants because those compiling the Red List had understandably emphasised taxa at particular risk of extinction.

An estimate of 20 per cent of species being threatened is broadly comparable with the percentage determined for well-known vertebrate taxa, for which one can separately calculate extinction rates directly by following species fates from their year of scientific description (see above). For these vertebrates, human actions are now driving species extinct at rates which are a thousand times faster than their normal background rates of extinction. If plants have similar rates of extinction, these would also be one thousand times faster than the rates of plant speciation derived from molecular phylogenies (De Vos et al., 2015).

Kew's (2016) tabulations show higher percentages of species at risk when one sensibly adds in the predicted numbers of species as yet unknown to the total of threatened species. They are likely to be rare, which is why we have not yet found them. Moreover, they are likely to be where recent discoveries are being made – see above – places where habitat loss is proceeding rapidly.

The alarming question is whether these as yet unknown species will survive long enough for us to collect them. To illustrate, Tom Croat and Doug Stevens, two active plant taxonomists at the Missouri Botanical Garden, who have been working and collecting plants, mostly in Latin America, for nearly a half-century each, agree that only a small percentage of the localities where they collected still hold natural forest today. Given that so many plant species have small geographical ranges, it is likely that in areas with massive habitat loss, none of their original habitat remains.

For plants, as we noted above, and unlike most other groups of organisms, ex situ preservation is relatively simple. Seed samples gathered from maternal parents, say, 20 from a population, will reasonably represent the genetic diversity of the population. With cryopreservation and the other special techniques available, practically any plant can be preserved in a seed bank for decades or more. Another option is tissue culture. Plants can of course also be maintained in cultivation, even though it is difficult to maintain sufficient genetic diversity to support a species or even a population that way.

Inconsistency

While the IUCN Red List classifies a species risk of extinction, using an open, democratic and rule-based approach, it suffers from a lack of consistency. In particular, Ocampo-Peñuela et al. (2016) show that important geospatial data do not enter this process explicitly or efficiently. Rapid growth in availability of remotely sensed observations provides fine-scale data on elevation and increasingly sophisticated characterisations of land cover and its changes. These data readily show that species are likely not present within many areas within the overall envelopes of their distributions. Additionally, global databases on protected areas inform how extensively ranges are protected. Ocampo-Peñuela et al. (2016) selected 586 endemic and threatened forest bird species from six of the world's most biodiverse and threatened places (Atlantic Forest of Brazil, Central America, Western Andes of Colombia, Madagascar, Sumatra and Southeast Asia). The Red List deems 18 per cent of these species to be threatened (15 critically endangered, 29 endangered and 64 vulnerable). Inevitably, after refining ranges by elevation and forest cover, ranges shrink. Do they do so consistently? For example, refined ranges of critically endangered species might reduce by (say) 50 per cent, but so might the ranges of endangered, vulnerable and non-threatened species. Critically, this is not the case. Ocampo-Peñuela et al. (2016) found that 43 per cent of species fall below the range threshold where *comparable* species are deemed threatened. Some 210 species of bird belong to a higher threat category than current Red List placement, including 189 species that are currently deemed non-threatened. Incorporating readily available spatial data substantially increases the numbers of species that should be considered at risk. Likely the Red List has also seriously underestimated the fractions of other taxa that are at risk of extinction.

Where Are the Species That Are at Risk of Extinction?

These concerns motivate the next question of asking where species are at risk of extinction. There are several 'laws' to describe the geographical patterns of where species occur. By 'law', we mean a general, widespread pattern, that is, one found across many groups of species and many regions of the world. Wallace (1855) famously provides the first one, in describing the general patterns of evolution in his famous 'Sarawak Law' paper:

LAW 1. 'the following law may be deduced from these [preceding] facts: – Every species has come into existence coincident both in space and time with a pre-existing closely allied species'. He would uncover natural selection, as the mechanism behind this law, a few years later, independently of Darwin. There are other laws too.

LAW 2. Most species' ranges are very small; few are very large. Pimm et al. (2014) show that range sizes of flowering plants, amphibians, mammals, birds and the marine gastropod genus *Conus* are highly skewed. There are species with very large ranges – some >10 million km^2, for example. However, for example, over half of all amphibian species have ranges smaller than 4300 km^2. The comparable medians for the other taxa range from ~115,602 km^2 (mammals) to ~729,770 km^2 (plants). For plants, the number is certainly a substantial overestimate, since the range data come from coarse regions (e.g., single countries) and a plant species will not likely occur everywhere within a given region.

LAW 3. Species with small ranges are locally scarce. There is a well-established relationship across many geographical scales and groups of species that link a species' range to its local abundance. The largest-scale study is that of Manne and Pimm (2001) who used data on bird species across South America. A species is 'common' if one is nearly guaranteed to see it in a day's fieldwork, then 'fairly common', 'uncommon' down to 'rare' – meaning it likely takes several days of fieldwork to find one even in the appropriate habitat. Almost all bird species with ranges greater than 10 million km^2 are 'common', while nearly a third of species with ranges of less than 10,000 km^2 are 'rare' and very few are 'common'.

LAW 4. Species with small ranges are geographically concentrated, and LAW 5. Those concentrations are generally not where the greatest numbers of species are fond. The simplest expectation is that where there are more species, there will be more large-ranged, more small-ranged species – and more threatened species. Reality is strikingly different.

Figure 3.1 shows the patterns for all species, small-ranged species and threatened species of mammals on land and in the oceans. (By small-ranged, we mean less than the median range size for the taxon in question.) Small-ranged species are geographically concentrated, and do not merely mirror the patterns for all species (of which, they

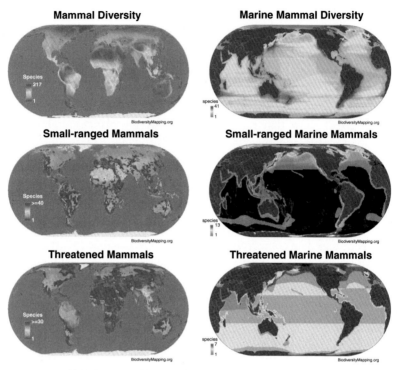

Figure 3.1 Global maps of terrestrial and marine mammal diversity, small-ranged mammal diversity, and numbers of threatened mammals (Jenkins et al., 2013; Jenkins and Van Houtan, 2016; Pimm et al., 2014). Maps from BiodiversityMapping.org, used with permission from Clinton Jenkins. Source of data used in terrestrial maps is IUCN, July 2013 update. Source of data used in marine maps is IUCN, August 2014 update. (A black and white version of this figure will appear in some formats. For the colour version, please refer to the plate section.)

constitute exactly half). Moreover, the concentrations of small-ranged species are, generally, not where the greatest numbers of species are. Finally, the patterns of threatened species very closely resemble those of small-ranged species. Similar terrestrial patterns are found in birds and mammals, and at much coarser spatial resolution, they mirror the patterns for plants (Jenkins et al., 2013).

Several interesting consequences emerge. Most of the species at greatest risk of extinction concentrate geographically and, broadly, such species in different taxa concentrate into the same places – the hotspots. This is of huge practical significance for it means that conservation efforts can be concentrated in these special places. Moreover, priorities set for one taxonomic group may be sensible for others, at least at this geographical scale. These ideas were first developed by Norman Myers (Myers, 1988).

Other things being equal, extinctions will concentrate where there are many species with small ranges. Other things are not equal of course and the other important driver is human impact. Myers added the second – and vital criterion – that these regions have less than 30 per cent of their natural vegetation remaining. Myers's idea is a very powerful one. It creates the 'number of small-ranged species times habitat loss equals extinction' idea with another key and surprising insight. What surprises is that there are few examples of concentrations of small-ranged species that do not also meet the criterion of having lost 70 per cent of more of their natural habitat. The island of New Guinea is an exception, though habitat losses there are quickly depriving it of that distinction. Hotspots have disproportionate human impact measured in other ways besides their habitat loss. Cincotta et al. (2000) show that hotspots generally have higher than human population densities and that almost all of them have annual population growth rates that are higher (average = 1.6 per cent per annum) than the global average (1.3 per cent per annum).

We considered each of the 25 hotspots using the statistics on endemic bird species, original area and the current area of remaining natural vegetation (Pimm and Raven, 2000). This provides a best-case scenario of what habitat might remain. We predicted that ~1700 species of birds should be lost eventually just from the loss of habitat to date – a number similar to current estimates of the number of threatened species.

Species can obviously linger in small habitat fragments for decades before they expire (Brooks et al., 1999; Ferraz et al., 2003; Pimm and Brooks, 2013). Based on these rates of species loss, perhaps three-quarters of these species – 1250 – will likely go extinct this century. If so, Pimm and Raven (2000) estimated future extinction rates of ~1000 E/MSY from human actions to date – about 10 times larger than the ones we currently observe. Put another way, extinction rates should accelerate.

Two extrapolations are possible. The worst-case scenario for the hotspots assumes that the only habitats that will remain intact will be the areas currently protected. This assumption increases the prediction of the number of extinctions to 2200 (Pimm and Raven, 2000).

The second adds in species from areas not already extensively deforested. These changes would even further accelerate the rates of
extinction.

Other Causes of Extinction

There are various other causes of extinction that will add to the totals
suggested from habitat destruction. The accidental introduction of the
brown tree snake (*Boiga irregularis*) to Guam eliminated the island's
birds in a couple of decades (Savidge, 1987). In the oceans, increases in
long-line fisheries are a relatively new and very serious threat to three-
quarters of the 21 albatross species and other seabirds. Chestnut blight
fungus (*Cryphonectria parasitica*) has essentially eliminated the
American chestnut (*Castanea dentata*) from its often sub-dominant
role in the forests of eastern North America. Our hunting and gathering
of organisms from nature for any purpose may likewise exterminate
them locally or even generally.

Global Change and Extinction

One of the most significant factors in the extinction of species will
undoubtedly be climate change, a factor not included in any of the
estimates presented above. Current estimates of how many species will
go extinct vary widely, in part, because the underlying mechanisms are
complex (Pereira et al., 2010). More detailed, regional modelling exer-
cises in Australia (Williams et al., 2007) and South Africa (Erasmus
et al., 2002) have led to predictions of the extinction of many species
with narrowly restricted ranges during this or longer intervals.

In addition to species moving upward in elevation and toward the
poles as the climate warms, climate disruption also involves changing fire
regimes, the loss of pollinators, increases in herbivores, the changing
phenologies of a plant's pollinators and herbivores, and many other
factors, all relevant to the chances of becoming extinct (Pimm, 2009).

The critical question is whether these extinctions, which are
predominantly of small-ranged species, are the same as those predicted from habitat destruction or whether they are additional. In
many cases, they are certainly the latter (Pimm, 2008). All species
restricted in range to the southern edges of the southern continents
are in danger of extinction from climate change as their habitats

simply disappear. The southern borders of Africa and Australia are very rich in endemic plant species for which moving south as the climate warms is not an option. Whether those species that occur at the higher altitudes on mountains are likely to become extinct depends on their possibility of migrating to other suitable habitats through distance dispersal or other means. For specific communities, such as coral reefs, attuned to narrow temperature regimes, the danger may be extreme, as the devastating losses recently demonstrated in the corals that make up Australia's Great Barrier Reef so vividly illustrate. Similarly, any species in onshore communities maintained in part by fog drip, such as the coastal redwoods of California (*Sequoia sempervirens*), will be endangered by changes in offshore water temperatures.

Human Growth and Consumption

Finally, of overarching concern is the growth in human pressure on the biosphere, and especially human consumption levels, which are leading directly to the rapid deterioration of the world's physical condition. The Global Footprint Network (www.footprintnetwork.org) estimates that we are using approximately 170 per cent of the world's sustainable productivity now, up from an estimated 70 per cent in 1970. Consequently, much higher estimates of future extinction – say, within this century – appear warranted than those based on current conditions. The highest estimates of threat (up to 60 per cent) come from assuming that all species endemic to a country may be at risk because of their presumed small ranges and ongoing habitat loss (Pitman and Jørgensen, 2002) as the conditions just enumerated accelerate. If global warming approaches 4°C–6°C, which is possible unless nations agree to cooperate strongly to ameliorate this problem, rates of extinction could climb much higher. All in all, it seems reasonable to assume that half of all species, most of them unknown at the time of their loss, may disappear within the remainder of this century.

References

Alroy, J. 1996. Constant extinction, constrained diversification, and uncoordinated stasis in North American mammals. *Palaeogeography, Palaeoclimatology, Palaeoecology*, 127(1): 285–311.

2008. Dynamics of origination and extinction in the marine fossil record. *Proceedings of the National Academy of Sciences*, 105(Supplement 1): 11536–11542.

Appeltans, W., Ahyong, S. T., Anderson, G., Angel, M. V., Artois, T., Bailly, N., Bamber, R., Barber, A., Bartsch, I. & Berta, A. 2012. The magnitude of global marine species diversity. *Current Biology*, 22(23): 2189–2202.

Bacher, S. 2012. Still not enough taxonomists: Reply to Joppa et al. *Trends in Ecology and Evolution*, 27(2): 65–66.

Barnosky, A. D., Matzke, N., Tomiya, S., Wogan, G. O. U., Swartz, B., Quental, T. B., Marshall, C., McGuire, J. L., Lindsey, E. L. & Maguire, K. C. 2011. Has the Earth's sixth mass extinction already arrived? *Nature*, 471(7336): 51–57.

Bass, D. & Richards, T. A. 2011. Three reasons to re-evaluate fungal diversity 'on Earth and in the ocean'. *Fungal Biology Reviews*, 25(4): 159–164.

Bebber, D. P., Marriott, F. H. C., Gaston, K. J., Harris, S. A. & Scotland, R. W. 2007. Predicting unknown species numbers using discovery curves. *Proceedings of the Royal Society B: Biological Sciences*, 274(1618): 1651–1658.

Blackwell, M. 2011. The Fungi: 1, 2, 3 … 5.1 million species? *American Journal of Botany*, 98(3): 426–438.

Brooks, T. M., Pimm, S. L. & Oyugi, J. O. 1999. Time lag between deforestation and bird extinction in tropical forest fragments. *Conservation Biology*, 13 (5): 1140–1150.

Brummitt, N. A., Bachman, S. P., Griffiths-Lee, J., Lutz, M., Moat, J. F., Farjon, A., Donaldson, J. S., Hilton-Taylor, C., Meagher, T. R. & Albuquerque, S. 2015. Green plants in the red: A baseline global assessment for the IUCN sampled Red List Index for plants. *PLoS One*, 10(8): e0135152.

Cannon, P. F. 1997. Diversity of the Phyllachoraceae with special reference to the tropics. In K. D. Hyde (Ed.), *Biodiversity of Tropical Microfungi*: 255–278. Hong Kong: Hong Kong University Press.

Carpenter, K. E. & et al. 2008. One-third of reef-building corals face elevated extinction risk from climate change and local impacts. *Science*, 321 (5888): 560–563.

Chapman, A. D. 2009. *Numbers of Living Species in Australia and the World*, 2nd ed. Canberra, Australia: Report for the Australian Biological Resources Study.

Cincotta, R. P., Wisnewski, J. & Engelman, R. 2000. Human population in the biodiversity hotspots. *Nature*, 404(6781): 990–992.

Costello, M. J. & Wilson, S. P. 2011. Predicting the number of known and unknown species in European seas using rates of description. *Global Ecology and Biogeography*, 20(2): 319–330.

De Vos, J. M., Joppa, L. N., Gittleman, J. L., Stephens, P. R. & Pimm, S. L. 2015. Estimating the normal background rate of species extinction. *Conservation Biology*, 29(2): 452–462.

Dulvy, N. K. & et al. 2014. Extinction risk and conservation of the world's sharks and rays. *eLife*, 3.

Erasmus, B. F., Van Jaarsveld, A. S., Chown, S. L., Kshatriya, M. & Wessels, K. J. 2002. Vulnerability of South African animal taxa to climate change. *Global Change Biology*, 8(7): 679–693.

Erwin, T. L. 1982. Tropical forests: Their richness in Coleoptera and other arthropod species. *The Coleopterists Bulletin*, 36(1): 74–75.

Etienne, R. S., Haegeman, B., Stadler, T., Aze, T., Pearson, P. N., Purvis, A. & Phillimore, A. B. 2012. Diversity-dependence brings molecular phylogenies closer to agreement with the fossil record. *Proceedings of the Royal Society B: Biological Sciences*, 279(1732): 1300–1309.

Ferraz, G., Russell, G. J., Stouffer, P. C., Bierregaard, R. O., Pimm, S. L. & Lovejoy, T. E. 2003. Rates of species loss from Amazonian forest fragments. *Proceedings of the National Academy of Sciences*, 100(24): 14069–14073.

Ferrer, M. M. & Good, S. V. 2012. Self-sterility in flowering plants: Preventing self-fertilization increases family diversification rates. *Annals of Botany*, 110(3): 535–553.

Flessa, K. W. & Jablonski, D. 1985. Declining Phanerozoic background extinction rates: Effect of taxonomic structure? *Nature*, 313(5999): 216–218.

Foote, M. 2005. Pulsed origination and extinction in the marine realm. *Paleobiology*, 31(1): 6–20

Foote, M. & Raup, D. M. 1996. Fossil preservation and the stratigraphic ranges of taxa. *Paleobiology*, 22(2): 121–140.

Gaston, K. J. 1991. The magnitude of global insect species richness. *Conservation Biology*, 5(3): 283–296.

Gering, J. C., DeRennaux, K. A. & Crist, T. O. 2007. Scale dependence of effective specialization: Its analysis and implications for estimates of global insect species richness. *Diversity and Distributions*, 13(1): 115–125.

Gore, A. 2006. *An Inconvenient Truth: The Planetary Emergency of Global Warming and What We Can Do about It.* New York: Rodale Books.

Grassle, J. F. & Maciolek, N. J. 1992. Deep-sea species richness: Regional and local diversity estimates from quantitative bottom samples. *The American Naturalist*, 139(2): 313–341.

Hamilton, Andrew J., Basset, Y., Benke, Kurt K., Grimbacher, Peter S., Miller, Scott E., Novotny, V., Samuelson, G. A., Stork, Nigel E.,

Weiblen, George D. & Yen, Jian D. L. 2010. Quantifying uncertainty in estimation of tropical arthropod species richness. *The American Naturalist*, 176(1): 90–95.

Harnik, P. G., Lotze, H. K., Anderson, S. C., Finkel, Z. V., Finnegan, S., Lindberg, D. R., Liow, L. H., Lockwood, R., McClain, C. R., McGuire, J. L., O'Dea, A., Pandolfi, J. M., Simpson, C. & Tittensor, D. P. 2012. Extinctions in ancient and modern seas. *Trends in Ecology & Evolution*, 27(11): 608–617.

Hawksworth, D. L. 1991. The fungal dimension of biodiversity: Magnitude, significance, and conservation. *Mycological Research*, 95(6): 641–655.

Hebert, P. D. N., Penton, E. H., Burns, J. M., Janzen, D. H. & Hallwachs, W. 2004. Ten species in one: DNA barcoding reveals cryptic species in the neotropical skipper butterfly Astraptes fulgerator. *Proceedings of the National Academy of Sciences of the United States of America*, 101(41): 14812–14817.

Hibbett, D. 2016. The invisible dimension of fungal diversity. *Science*, 351 (6278): 1150–1151.

IUCN. 2016. *The IUCN Red List of Threatened Species*. www.iucnredlist.org.

Jenkins, C. N., Pimm, S. L. & Joppa, L. N. 2013. Global patterns of terrestrial vertebrate diversity and conservation. *Proceedings of the National Academy of Sciences*, 110(28): E2602-E2610.

Jenkins, C. N. & Van Houtan, K. 2016. Global and regional priorities for marine biodiversity protection. *Biological Conservation*, doi:10.1016/j. biocon.2016.10.005.

Joppa, L. N., Roberts, D. L., Myers, N. & Pimm, S. L. 2011a. Biodiversity hotspots house most undiscovered plant species. *Proceedings of the National Academy of Sciences*, 108(32): 13171–13176.

Joppa, L. N., Roberts, D. L. & Pimm, S. L. 2010. How many species of flowering plants are there? *Proceedings of the Royal Society B: Biological Sciences*, 278(1705): 554.

2011b. The population ecology and social behaviour of taxonomists. *Trends in Ecology & Evolution*, 26(11): 551–553.

Kew, R. 2016. *The State of the World's Plants Report – 2016*. Kew, UK: The Board of Trustees of the Royal Botanic Gardens.

Koenen, E. J. M., de Vos, J. M., Atchison, G. W., Simon, M. F., Schrire, B. D., de Souza, E. R., de Queiroz, L. P. & Hughes, C. E. 2013. Exploring the tempo of species diversification in legumes. *South African Journal of Botany*, 89: 19–30.

Lambshead, P. J. D. & Boucher, G. 2003. Marine nematode deep-sea biodiversity: Hyperdiverse or hype? *Journal of Biogeography*, 30(4): 475–485.

Lees, A. C. & Pimm, S. L. 2015. Species, extinct before we know them? *Current Biology*, 25(5): R177–R180.

Locey, K. J. & Lennon, J. T. 2016. Scaling laws predict global microbial diversity. *Proceedings of the National Academy of Sciences*, 113(21): 5970-5975.

Manne, L. L. & Pimm, S. L. 2001. Beyond eight forms of rarity: Which species are threatened and which will be next? *Animal Conservation*, 4 (3): 221–229.

May, R. M. 1991. A fondness for fungi. *Nature*, 352(6335): 475–476.

May, R. M. & Beverton, R. J. H. 1990. How many species? [and Discussion]. *Philosophical Transactions of the Royal Society of London. Series B: Biological Sciences*, 330(1257): 293–304.

McPeek, M. A. 2008. The ecological dynamics of clade diversification and community assembly. *The American Naturalist*, 172(6): E270-E284.

Mora, C., Tittensor, D. P., Adl, S., Simpson, A. G. B. & Worm, B. 2011. How many species are there on Earth and in the ocean? *PLoS Biology*, 9(8): e1001127.

Mora, C., Tittensor, D. P. & Myers, R. A. 2008. The completeness of taxonomic inventories for describing the global diversity and distribution of marine fishes. *Proceedings of the Royal Society B: Biological Sciences*, 275(1631): 149–155.

Morlon, H., Parsons, T. L. & Plotkin, J. B. 2011. Reconciling molecular phylogenies with the fossil record. *Proceedings of the National Academy of Sciences*, 108(39): 16327–16332.

Myers, N. 1988. Threatened biotas: 'Hot spots' in tropical forests. *Environmentalist*, 8(3): 187–208.

1989. Extinction rates past and present. *BioScience*, 39(1): 39–41.

Myers, N., Mittermeier, R., Mittermeier, C., da Fonseca, G. & Kent, J. 2000. Biodiversity hotspots for conservation priorities. *Nature*, 403: 853–858.

Nee, S. 2006. Birth-death models in macroevolution. *Annual Review of Ecology, Evolution, and Systematics*, 37(1): 1–17.

Novotny, V., Miller, S. E., Hulcr, J., Drew, R. A. I., Basset, Y., Janda, M., Setliff, G. P., Darrow, K., Stewart, A. J. A., Auga, J., Isua, B., Molem, K., Manumbor, M., Tamtiai, E., Mogia, M. & Weiblen, G. D. 2007. Low beta diversity of herbivorous insects in tropical forests. *Nature*, 448 (7154): 692–695.

O'Brien, H. E., Parrent, J. L., Jackson, J. A., Moncalvo, J.-M. & Vilgalys, R. 2005. Fungal community analysis by large-scale sequencing of environmental samples. *Applied and Environmental Microbiology*, 71 (9): 5544–5550.

Ocampo-Peñuela, N., Jenkins, C. N., Vijay, V., Li, B. V. & Pimm, S. L. 2016. Incorporating explicit geospatial data shows more species at risk of extinction than the current Red List. *Science Advances*, 2(11): e1601367.

ØDegaard, F. 2000. How many species of arthropods? Erwin's estimate revised. *Biological Journal of the Linnean Society*, 71(4): 583–597.

Pereira, H. M., Leadley, P. W., Proença, V., Alkemade, R., Scharlemann, J. P., Fernandez-Manjarrés, J. F., Araújo, M. B., Balvanera, P., Biggs, R. & Cheung, W. W. 2010. Scenarios for global biodiversity in the 21st century. *Science*, 330(6010): 1496–1501.

Peters, H., O'Leary, B. C., Hawkins, J. P., Carpenter, K. E. & Roberts, C. M. 2013. *Conus*: First comprehensive conservation red list assessment of a marine gastropod mollusc genus. *PLoS One*, 8(12): e83353.

Phillimore, A. B. & Price, T. D. 2008. Density-dependent cladogenesis in birds. *PLoS Biology*, 6(3): e71.

Pimm, S. L. 2008. Biodiversity: Climate change or habitat loss – which will kill more species. *Current Biology*, 18(3): R117-R119.

2009. Climate disruption and biodiversity. *Current Biology*, 19(14): R595–R601.

Pimm, S. L. & Brooks, T. 2013. Conservation: Forest fragments, facts, and fallacies. *Current Biology*, 23(24): R1098–R1101.

Pimm, S. L., Jenkins, C. N., Abell, R., Brooks, T. M., Gittleman, J. L., Joppa, L. N., Raven, P. H., Roberts, C. M. & Sexton, J. O. 2014. The biodiversity of species and their rates of extinction, distribution, and protection. *Science*, 344(6187): 1246752.

Pimm, S. L. & Raven, P. 2000. Biodiversity: Extinction by numbers. *Nature*, 403(6772): 843–845.

2017. The fate of the world's plants. *Trends in Ecology & Evolution*, 32 (5): 317–320.

Pimm, S., Raven, P., Peterson, A., Şekercioğlu, Ç. H. & Ehrlich, P. R. 2006. Human impacts on the rates of recent, present, and future bird extinctions. *Proceedings of the National Academy of Sciences*, 103 (29): 10941–10946.

Pimm, S., Russell, G. J., Gittleman, J. & Brooks, T. M. 1995. The future of biodiversity. *Science*, 269: 347–350.

Pitman, N. C. & Jørgensen, P. M. 2002. Estimating the size of the world's threatened flora. *Science*, 298(5595): 989–989.

Purvis, A. 2008. Phylogenetic approaches to the study of extinction. *Annual Review of Ecology, Evolution, and Systematics*, 39: 301–319.

Pyron, R. A. & Burbrink, F. T. 2013. Phylogenetic estimates of speciation and extinction rates for testing ecological and evolutionary hypotheses. *Trends in Ecology & Evolution*, 28(12): 729–736.

Quental, T. B. & Marshall, C. R. 2011. The molecular phylogenetic signature of clades in decline. *PLoS One*, 6(10): e25780.

Ricotta, C., Ferrari, M. & Avena, G. 2002. Using the scaling behaviour of higher taxa for the assessment of species richness. *Biological Conservation*, 107(1): 131–133.

Rosenzweig, M. L. 1995. *Species Diversity in Space and Time*. Cambridge: Cambridge University Press.

Russell, G. J., Brooks, T. M., McKinney, M. M. & Anderson, C. G. 1998. Present and future taxonomic selectivity in bird and mammal extinctions. *Conservation Biology*, 12(6): 1365–1376.

Savidge, J. A. 1987. Extinction of an island forest avifauna by an introduced snake. *Ecology*, 68(3): 660–668.

Scheffers, B. R., Joppa, L. N., Pimm, S. L. & Laurance, W. F. 2012. What we know and don't know about Earth's missing biodiversity. *Trends in Ecology & Evolution*, 27(9): 501–510.

Solow, A. R. & Smith, W. K. 2005. On estimating the number of species from the discovery record. *Proceedings: Biological Sciences*, 272(1560): 285–287.

Stork, N. E. 1993. How many species are there? *Biodiversity and Conservation*, 2(3): 215–232.

2010. Re-assessing current extinction rates. *Biodiversity and Conservation*, 19(2): 357–371.

Taylor, D. L., Hollingsworth, T. N., McFarland, J. W., Lennon, N. J., Nusbaum, C. & Ruess, R. W. 2014. A first comprehensive census of fungi in soil reveals both hyperdiversity and fine-scale niche partitioning. *Ecological Monographs*, 84(1): 3–20.

Turgeon, J., Stoks, R., Thum, R. A., Brown, J. M. & McPeek, M. A. 2005. Simultaneous Quaternary radiations of three damselfly clades across the Holarctic. *The American Naturalist*, 165(4): E78–E107.

Valente, L. M., Savolainen, V. & Vargas, P. 2010. Unparalleled rates of species diversification in Europe. *Proceedings of the Royal Society B: Biological Sciences*, 277(1687): 1489–1496.

Wallace, A. R. 1855. XVIII. – On the law which has regulated the introduction of new species. *Journal of Natural History*, 16(93): 184–196.

Weir, J. T. & Schluter, D. 2007. The latitudinal gradient in recent speciation and extinction rates of birds and mammals. *Science*, 315(5818): 1574–1576.

Westwood, J. 1833. On the probable number of species of insects in the creation; together with descriptions of several minute Hymenoptera. *The Magazine of Natural History and Journal of Zoology, Botany, Mineralogy, Geology and Meterology*, 6: 116–123.

Williams, J. W., Jackson, S. T. & Kutzbach, J. E. 2007. Projected distributions of novel and disappearing climates by 2100 AD. *Proceedings of the National Academy of Sciences*, 104(14): 5738–5742.

Zhou, Z. & Zheng, S. 2003. Palaeobiology: The missing link in Ginkgo evolution. *Nature*, 423(6942): 821–822.

4 Extinction Threats to Life in the Ocean and Opportunities for Their Amelioration

JENNA M. SULLIVAN, VANESSA CONSTANT
AND JANE LUBCHENCO

The Ocean Harbours Riches We Are Still Discovering

'The oceans not only contain most of the planet, but also most of the wide variety of living things' (Pope Francis, 2015). With this statement, Pope Francis summarised a central point about life on Earth: we cannot understand and protect Earth's biodiversity without considering the ocean. Covering over 70 per cent of the Earth's surface, the ocean represents an estimated 99 per cent of its habitable living space (Costanza, 1999). The ocean harbours a remarkably rich diversity of species, with almost twice as many major groups, or phyla, of animals living in the ocean as on land. (Of the 34 known phyla of animals, 33 are found in the ocean and only 12 are found on land.) A single type of marine habitat, the coral reef, holds over 50 per cent more phyla than all terrestrial and freshwater habitats combined, despite having a surface area more than 460 times smaller (Birkeland, 2015). Life in the ocean is also more evenly distributed across groups than is life on land. A single phylum, Arthropoda (e.g., insects, arachnids), accounts for 90 per cent of all terrestrial animal species. In striking contrast, it takes eight phyla – Mollusca, Arthropoda, Chordata, Annelida, Nematoda, Cnidaria, Bryozoa and Porifera – to account for 90 per cent of all known marine species (Jaume and Duarte, 2006).

Given the immensity of the ocean's available living space and the fact that humans are terrestrial, it is not surprising that we know far less about marine biodiversity than we do about terrestrial biodiversity. In fact, we have explored only 5 per cent of the ocean (Miller and Spoolman, 2009). New discoveries abound and await the curious. Forty years ago, in 1977, scientists stunned the world with the discovery that completely unknown macroscopic life forms were thriving in the deep, dark ocean and at scalding water temperatures. Far removed from sunlight, life in these hydrothermal vent ecosystems utilises chemosynthesis instead of photosynthesis to convert energy into organic compounds. Specifically, bacteria use some of the chemicals dissolved in the super-hot water that emerges along tectonic plate boundaries; in turn, giant tubeworms, clams, limpets and shrimp feed on the bacteria. Hundreds of new species have been described from dozens of hot-vent ecosystems found at plate boundaries or volcanic hot vents in waters ranging from 60°C to 464°C. Five years after hot-vent ecosystems were discovered, scientists announced another stunning discovery: 'cold seeps', places where hydrogen sulphide and methane percolate up from fissures in the seafloor. These chemicals support yet more chemosynthetic bacteria that in turn feed other organisms such as mussels, clams and tubeworms. Cold-seep ecosystems have been found throughout the oceans of the world, with water temperatures ranging from ambient to just a few degrees above ambient. Just within the past two years, scientists have reported a third type of vent system, this one characterised by warm water (~60°C), with a range of associated species, including octopuses (Orcutt, 2016).

Technology has enabled exploration of new places in the ocean and provided novel ways of understanding what lives there. Molecular methods such as DNA barcoding are opening up exciting avenues for discovering and monitoring biodiversity (e.g., Leray and Knowlton, 2015; Sun et al., 2016). Molecular analysis recently led to the discoveries of a new species of beaked whale (Morin et al., 2017) and oceanic sunfish, the largest bony fish in the world (Nyegaard et al., 2017). Analysis of acoustic data facilitated the discovery of new-to-science populations of the largest species on Earth, the blue whale, living just off the coast of Australia (Balcazar et al., 2015). Innovative technologies enable deeper explorations and discoveries of the ocean's biodiversity; surveys of abyssal zone sediments routinely find new species, e.g., 90 per cent of copepods, isopods and nematodes sampled there are new to science (Higgs and Attrill, 2015; McIntyre, 2010).

Life in the Ocean Is Threatened as Never Before – with Immense Consequences

Humans have historically viewed the ocean as so immense that it is an inexhaustible source of resources and dumping grounds, impervious to our actions. People have depended on marine resources throughout human history. In just the last half-century, however, developments in technology, wasteful practices and the explosive growth in human consumption as reflected in humanity's demand on the biosphere have combined to deplete and disrupt life in the ocean to the extent that marine life and our own future are now at stake. The individual and cumulative impacts of activities on and in the ocean – fishing, aquaculture, coastal development, oil, gas and mineral extraction, some kinds of recreation and shipping – interact with and exacerbate the impacts of land-based activities ranging from agriculture to energy production. Collectively, they are taking a significant toll on life in the ocean. As humans have become better at exploiting ocean and planetary resources, threats to ocean life and habitats have accelerated.

If we continue on this trajectory, we risk losing not only entire species and habitats, but also the life-support services humans require from healthy ocean ecosystems. The ocean provides a wealth of services, including food production, fibre, medicines, coastal protection, water purification, carbon sequestration, climate regulation, recreation, tourism and cultural value. These services are the product of interactions among the plants, animals and microbes in the ocean and between those species and their environments. When species are removed; when biogeochemical cycles are altered; when the ocean becomes warmer, more acidic or less oxygenated; and when excess nutrients, plastic waste, toxins and noise increase, the functioning of marine ecosystems is altered and the provision of the benefits humans want and need is affected.

Threats Are Numerous, and They Interact

Historically, the greatest threat to ocean biodiversity has been overfishing, and it continues to have huge impacts on ocean life. Decades of increasingly intensive and often wasteful fishing have resulted in a legacy of depleted stocks, destroyed habitats and disrupted ecosystems. Fishing has both direct and indirect impacts on biodiversity. For example, bluefin tuna and most shark species are threatened directly by overfishing, whereas many sea turtles, birds and marine mammals are threatened indirectly because they are caught accidentally in nets and on hooks (and some of these are already reduced in numbers from past fishing). In addition, by preferentially eliminating large-bodied predators, fishing effects cascade throughout food webs as the loss of predators affects their prey and other species with which they interact.

Through fishing activities, humans function as a unique marine 'super-predator' (Darimont et al., 2015) or 'hyper-keystone species' (Worm and Paine, 2016). Human fisheries exploit prey at a median rate that is 14.1 times higher than that of other marine predators (Darimont et al., 2015). Because of the scale of this impact and the implications of overharvesting entire food webs and ecosystems, fishing in the ocean is currently a greater threat to biodiversity than is hunting on land.

Habitat disruption and habitat loss pose another major threat to ocean life. This includes physical removal or alteration of the seafloor, water column or living structures as well as chemical perturbations. For example, destructive fishing practices (e.g., trawling or dynamite fishing) alter the seabed and the water column, as do mining, construction of artificial islands and reefs, and conversion to aquaculture ponds. Noise from energy exploration or vessel traffic (Nelms et al., 2016; Williams et al., 2015), entanglement in active or discarded fishing gear and energy generation (wind, tidal or wave) pose different threats to a wide range of species. Excess nutrient runoff from land and aquaculture can trigger zones of hypoxia (low dissolved oxygen) or anoxia (essentially no dissolved oxygen) in coastal waters as well as causing harmful algal blooms. Plastic and toxic pollution, mostly from terrestrial sources, pose additional threats. The magnitude and rates of many of the activities that disrupt habitat vary by location, but in general have accelerated in recent decades. The area of ocean floor lost or degraded by bottom trawling is estimated to be 150 times greater than the area of forest impacted by clearcutting on land (Dulvy et al., 2003). Each year approximately 1–9 per cent of coral reefs (Bellwood et al., 2004; Gardner et al., 2003) and 1.8 per cent of mangroves (Polidoro et al., 2010; Valiela et al., 2001) are lost. An estimated 29 per cent of the total cover of seagrass beds in North America, Europe and Australia has disappeared since initial data recording began in 1879 (Waycott et al., 2009). These habitats harbour significant biodiversity and often serve as nursery grounds for many ecologically and economically important seafood species. The adverse effects of habitat loss and modification can be compounded by other human-caused threats facing the ocean such as invasive species and, on a broader scale, climate change and ocean acidification.

Habitat degradation through human-induced modifications can homogenise landscapes, change energy and nutrient dynamics, and simplify food webs. This is especially true where invasive species are common. Invasive species tend to grow and reproduce rapidly, out-compete native species for resources and face few natural enemies (Parker et al., 2013). They are extremely successful at colonising per-turbed systems. Following introduction, invasive species can displace native species, reduce native habitat and productivity, and disrupt essential ecosystem processes (Katsanevakis et al., 2014), negatively impacting the ecosystem in multiple ways and leaving it more vulner-able to additional stressors.

Globally, climate change and ocean acidification are direct conse-quences of anthropogenic greenhouse gas emissions that can amplify and exacerbate other threats to marine biodiversity. Since the Industrial Revolution, the ocean has absorbed almost 30 per cent of anthropogenic carbon dioxide emissions, altering ocean chemistry and increasing ocean acidity by nearly 30 per cent (Logan, 2010). In addi-tion, because water holds more heat than air, over 90 per cent of excess heat stored on Earth since the 1970s is in the ocean (Gleckler et al., 2016; Levitus et al., 2005). As a result, surface waters have warmed at a median rate of 0.07°C/decade (Burrows et al., 2011) and deeper waters are warming at an accelerating pace (Gleckler et al., 2016). Warmer waters are altering historic, seasonal patterns of water move-ment throughout the ocean. Warm spring temperatures are arriving sooner (Parmesan and Yohe, 2003). Likewise, cold fall temperatures are arriving later, with larger effects in the ocean than on land (Burrows et al., 2011). The direct effects of climate warming are likely to be as great in the oceans as on land at comparable latitudes, and greater in the ocean around the equator (Burrows et al., 2011). For instance, reef-building corals are experiencing increasingly frequent bleaching events, higher susceptibility to disease and impaired reproduction and calcifi-cation (see review by Spalding and Brown, 2015). Species are shifting ranges 1.5–5 times faster in the ocean than on land (Cheung et al., 2009). Moreover, these range shifts are not expected to follow simple projections based on expected changes in physical conditions due to other key factors such as altered species' interactions and interactions between species and their environment (Burrows et al., 2011).

An increasingly acidified ocean creates additional challenging condi-tions, particularly for species such as corals and oysters that build skeletons and shells out of calcium carbonate. Carbonate ions decrease in availability as seawater becomes more acidic. Ocean acidification can also disrupt the ability of prey to sense and behaviourally avoid predators (e.g., Watson et al., 2013; Munday et al., 2014; Jellison et al., 2016), or of predators to detect and capture prey (e.g., Watson et al., 2017), potentially altering species interactions, food web dynamics and community structure and functioning.

These local and global stressors are not uniform throughout the ocean. For example, Ramírez and colleagues showed that marine biodiversity hotspots often correspond directly with those areas that are fished most intensively and are also most heavily affected by climate change (Ramírez et al., 2017). Those areas also tend to be places experiencing the greatest velocities of warming and seasonal temperature shifts (Burrows et al., 2011). Locations with high human impact, such as frequently disturbed coastal habitats (Molinos et al., 2016), are particularly vulnerable. Nearly 40 per cent of the global human population lives within 100 km of the coast and population densities in these regions are steadily increasing (Crossland, 2006), making coastal areas increasingly vulnerable as well as important to people. Many coastal habitats provide key ecosystem services such as mangroves, salt marshes, oyster and coral reefs and kelp forests providing protection from storm surge and sequestration of carbon. For this reason, coastal areas are also places where smart action to protect and restore habitats could bring benefits to people as well as other species.

The sum of these stressors on ocean ecosystems and their interactive effects can lead to complex changes in the distribution, behaviour, physiology, ecological role and survival of many marine organisms and processes. The compounding burden of these stressors on marine organisms increases the potential for species declines and extinctions. Together, these threats to life in the ocean are unprecedented in their collective intensity and spatial scale. They are also arguably more diverse than those threats confronting life on land. Whereas terrestrial flora and fauna are now challenged with land use change as the primary driver of extinction, followed closely by climate change and chemical pollution (Knapp et al., 2017), life in the ocean is being hammered simultaneously by all of these interacting threats as well as significant pressures from overharvesting and acidification, which are not major global threats on land. Marine species are at an increasing risk of population decline, loss of genetic diversity and extinction. The mantra 'Expect the unexpected' captures the collective impact of these stressors on marine species and their distributions.

Marine Species May Be More Vulnerable to Extinction than Previously Assumed

Based on interpretations of the fossil record and recent evidence of extinctions, scientists have assumed that extinction in the ocean is far less likely than on land. However, a more thorough examination of both the deep and the recent past suggest this assumption may not be valid in today's world.

The fossil record suggests that 'normal' species extinction (i.e., excluding the five mass extinction events) is inversely related to geographic range size (Harnik et al., 2012; Orzechowski et al., 2015). Thus, because marine species today tend to have greater potential for dispersal than do terrestrial species (Kinlan and Gaines, 2003) and many have very broad geographic ranges, they have been assumed to be more resilient to environmental changes. On the surface of it, recent evidence of extinctions would appear to support that assumption. The International Union for Conservation of Nature (IUCN) has recognised over 30 times more animal species extinctions on land than in the ocean (514 vs. 15, respectively, as of 2014) in the past approximately 500 years (McCauley et al., 2015).

However, new analyses have triggered a re-examination of the assumptions and conclusions. We examine five recent lines of evidence. (1) Low documented rates of recent marine extinctions may simply reflect our lack of knowledge of the ocean rather than lower vulnerability of marine species, as previously assumed. For example, Webb and Mindel (2015) concluded that the risk of extinction for the best assessed marine species is around 20–25 per cent, which is comparable to that for land species. Of the estimated 0.7–1.0 million species in the ocean, only about 243,000 valid extant species have been scientifically described (of approximately 400,000 total named species, including synonyms) (Appeltans et al., 2012; Costello and Chaudhary, 2017). Of those 243,000, scientists know the extinction risk status of only ~3 per cent. This is partly because species conservation assessments tend to focus primarily on well-known and described groups. Most of these assessments have not historically included marine species (Webb and Mindel, 2015).

(2) Many marine species with broad geographic ranges may still be quite vulnerable to extinction if their different life history stages are specialised to specific habitats that are threatened. A number of species

require multiple, distinct habitats throughout various life stages. For example, the Bocaccio rockfish depends on five separate habitats: nearshore eelgrass beds, boulder fields, deep-water caves, drifting kelp and open water habitats (Love et al., 2002; Lubchenco et al., 2007). Loss of any one of these habitats might compromise the ability of the species to survive and reproduce. Thus, despite a broad biogeographic range, a species dependent upon specific habitats at different stages might actually be quite susceptible to local disappearance and eventual extinction.

(3) Throughout history the response of marine species to climate change, as supported by the fossil record, has involved geographic range shifts (Jablonski et al., 2017). However, human activities in recent years have blocked or depleted escape routes, inhibiting the option of species range shifts in response to climate change. (4) Whereas species extinction has been inversely related to geographic range size (Harnik et al., 2012; Orzechowski et al., 2015), these factors are decoupled in the face of the mass-scale climate perturbations such as ocean acidification and thermal stress (Jablonski et al., 2013), and perhaps low dissolved oxygen. (5) Furthermore, whereas past extinction events in the ocean were either non-selective or preferentially removed smaller-bodied species, one major current extinction threat in the ocean (overfishing) is uniquely selective against larger-bodied vertebrate species, with important implications for ecosystem functioning (Payne et al., 2016).

Finally, even though many species have not yet been driven entirely to global extinction, many marine ecosystems still experience biodiversity loss. Destructive human practices have caused local extinctions (where species are lost entirely from specific regions), ecological extinctions (where population sizes are reduced greatly – e.g., marine fish have declined by an estimated 38 per cent and baleen whales by 80–90 per cent) and commercial extinctions (where abundances are too low for economically feasible commercial harvest) (McCauley et al., 2015).

A number of experts have thus suggested that mass extinctions in the ocean are likely if current threats continue and their rates of change continue to accelerate (Barnosky et al., 2011). Extinction may be especially likely if population declines and extirpations are under way at multiple locations (Ceballos et al., 2017). Additionally, range contractions may give the appearance of locally stable population densities, and thus short-circuit the normal feedbacks that prevent overharvesting to extinction (Burgess et al., 2017a; but see Burgess et al., 2017b; Le Pape et al., 2017). Moreover, as Ceballos and colleagues point out, the consequences of this 'biological annihilation' (population declines and extirpations) may entail significant negative cascading impacts on local ecosystem functioning and delivery of ecosystem services (Ceballos et al., 2017).

New science, awareness and action are beginning to address causes of potential extinctions.

We now understand that many of our historical paradigms – that ocean resources are inexhaustible, that the ocean is too massive to be affected by human actions, and that marine species are invulnerable to extinction – are wildly inaccurate. The ocean's rich biodiversity and many of the ecosystem services provided by marine environments are increasingly at risk due to escalating demands for marine resources. The essential questions now are, 'Can we use the ocean equitably without using it up? Can we avoid mass extinctions in the ocean? Is there cause for hope?'

Securing productive and resilient ocean ecosystems for future generations will require protecting biodiversity and working toward sustainable, equitable and healthy ocean-use practices.

While achieving these goals is not impossible, it will require research, management, engagement, leadership and innovation. In proposing solutions and not just identifying problems, scientists have risen to the challenge. Natural and social scientists are increasingly collaborating with each other and with colleagues in the humanities, arts, civil society, government and industry to pursue solutions that acknowledge the complexity of the problems we face. For example, recognising that ecological systems in the ocean are modified by, and in turn modify, economic and social systems in a complex adaptive systems framework allows scientists, managers and policymakers to promote connections and feedbacks that can help increase systemwide resilience (see Lubchenco et al., 2016a). Furthermore, aligning social incentives with ecological goals can convert a vicious cycle of unsustainable practices to a virtuous cycle of sustainable practices. These incentives can be economic, for example, where behaviour that has conservation benefits also makes good fiscal sense, or they can take the form of changes in societal or personal norms, in which individual actors behave in a sustainable manner to enhance their reputation or align their ethics and self-image (Lubchenco et al., 2016a; Nyborg et al., 2016).

Below, we outline brief examples of strategies that are successfully helping protect and restore ocean species, ecosystems, and the services they provide, and therefore benefitting people. We touch on only a few of the many strategies under way to address immediate threats. None of these solutions is at the scale needed to stem the biological annihilation under way, but each provides a model that can be replicated and scaled up, and – of equal importance – each provides hope that it might be possible to transition to a world of smart stewardship of biodiversity.

Fisheries Reforms

Because overfishing is the most immediate threat to ocean biodiversity in many places, achieving sustainable fisheries is of paramount importance. Fortunately, making fisheries sustainable has strong potential to benefit not only conservation but also the people-centric outcomes of poverty alleviation, improved nutrition, job opportunities, economic benefits and food security. In fact, it is this triple alignment of environmental, economic and societal interests that presents a globally important and timely opportunity. With more than three billion people worldwide reliant on seafood for a significant fraction of their daily protein (FAO, 2016) – most of them in the developing world – restoring ocean ecosystems to a healthier condition would bring significant human as well as biodiversity benefit.

Globally, all general categories of fisheries – industrial-scale, small-scale and artisanal – are significantly depleted. In light of the urgency of addressing food security globally, but especially for poor people, this problem deserves greater attention than it has received. It is dire, but far from unsolvable. Recent success and analyses suggest that despite the depredations, it is possible to reverse the historic trends and recover most depleted fisheries. The analyses suggest that doing so could be achieved rapidly once appropriate fishery policies and practices are in place. Moreover, recovered fisheries could reap benefits 10 times greater than the costs of restoring them, produce >20 per cent more food and >300 per cent more profits, compared to business-as-usual practices (Costello et al., 2016). The likelihood of achieving these successful outcomes depends in part on reforming fisheries soon, while recovery is still possible. The fact that there is a positive economic outcome could incentivise industry and governments if policies are properly structured.

However, there are major social, political, economic and knowledge impediments to the adoption of effective fishery reforms globally. The enabling conditions for success are diverse and challenging: awareness of the possibility of recovering depleted fisheries, financing to transition to more sustainable practices, attention to and respect for the realities of life for small-scale and artisanal fishers, political stability, leadership (political, civil society, industry and community), scientific knowledge and advice that can monitor and adapt to changing conditions, and a policy framework (with appropriate legal authorities and financing) to incentivise and guide reforms and subsequent implementation and enforcement.

Given the difficulties in meeting these enabling conditions, one might ask how any reforms have succeeded. Analyses of the successful ventures suggest that one key element is an appropriate policy that can be embraced by multiple stakeholders and political leaders and that removes some of the perverse incentives that drive overfishing.

Several successful fishery reform policy models have evolved, many of which involve the use of rights-based approaches to management (see reviews by Barner et al., 2015; Lubchenco et al., 2016a). In this approach, a dedicated share of the scientifically determined total allowable fish catch is allocated to individuals, groups or communities. This contrasts with a 'common-pool' management strategy, whereby fishers compete with one another for fish until the quota for the year is reached. In a common-pool strategy, fishers are in a 'race to fish' that incentivises fast, hard fishing without regard for ecological impact or consequences to future fishing. In contrast, rights-based management provides fishers with an economic incentive for good stewardship because they have a clear stake in the future of fish stocks. Successful implementation of rights-based approaches requires careful design, with attention to equitable allocation, smooth transition, adequate financing and strong accountability and monitoring. In addition, and very importantly, science-based catch limits that are adequately enforced and modified in response to ecosystem considerations and changing ocean conditions are key. In some cases, spatially explicit rights-based management is combined with fully protected areas to achieve both fishery improvement and conservation goals (Barner et al., 2015).

Recent experiences in the US provide examples of the successes that can arise through rights-based management strategies that align economic, social and ecological incentives and are backed by science (see Lubchenco et al., 2016a). Building on the 1996 and 2006 Congressional mandate to end overfishing in US federal waters by setting and enforcing annual catch limits based only on science, the US National Oceanic and Atmospheric Administration in 2010 facilitated wider adoption of rights-based fisheries management in many US fisheries (Grimm et al., 2012; Conathan and Siciliano, 2016). The reforms have resulted in slashing overfishing by 60 per cent and recovering many depleted fisheries much faster than predicted (Barner et al., 2015; Lubchenco et al., 2016b; NOAA Fisheries, 2016a).

For example, the West Coast groundfish fishery, which was declared a federal fishery disaster in 2000 due to a long history of overexploitation, implemented a rights-based management programme in 2011. This led to dramatic environmental, social and economic benefits. Fishery profits increased (Matson, 2014) and populations of many species involved in the fishery – including the majority of the groundfish species that were previously overfished – recovered (NOAA, 2017; NOAA Fisheries, 2016b). Similarly, the commercial red snapper fishery in the Gulf of Mexico switched to rights-based management in 2007. It has since enjoyed 70 per cent higher profits, catch limits that are more than doubled with more than 50 per cent less discards, almost threefold higher spawning potential, and an improved designation for sustainability through the Monterey Bay Aquarium's Seafood Watch certification programme (Fisher, 2013; NMFS, 2015).

Similar efforts are under way in disparate parts of the world. Inspired in part by the US successes, the European Union recently reformed its fishery management policies and is now in the process of implementing the reforms. Belize's experiments with fishery reforms in a few fishing communities were so successful that they have been adopted country-wide (Lubchenco et al., 2016a; see also below). The Philippines is seeing great outcomes in a few test regions, and based on those successes, is exploring scaling up these approaches. Globally, as of 2013, there are almost 200 rights-based fisheries that involve over 500 species in 40 countries (EDF Fisheries Solutions Center, 2017). Many of these efforts have produced impressive results, but they are not yet at the scale needed to address the magnitude of the global problems of depleted fisheries and threatened biodiversity. Fortunately, awareness of the existence of solutions, and identification of key elements for success (see Costello et al., 2016; Lubchenco et al., 2016a), are increasingly contributing to more positive outcomes.

In these and other cases, ending overfishing has led to multiple benefits, including enhancements of the status of endangered and threatened species that were previously vulnerable to accidental by-catch in the fishery. Incentivised by the catch-share programme to avoid those species, fishers have become more innovative in sharing information and avoiding fishing grounds where the threatened/endangered species are more likely to be accidentally caught in nets. Changing the incentives for fishers has resulted in better conservation outcomes as well as smarter fishing.

None of these reforms were easy, but the fact that they were successful and are now providing impressive triple bottom-line outcomes should spur additional efforts. Moreover, the fact that reforms have worked in both developed and developing nations, and with industrial as well as small-scale and artisanal fisheries, provides hope that a global turn-around might be possible.

Aquaculture

In addition to recovering depleted fisheries, sustainable aquaculture will be an essential component of global and local food security. The demand for fish protein is projected to increase over the next several decades as appetite and population size swell (OECD/FAO, 2014). From 1974 to 2004, aquaculture production increased by 32 per cent (FAO, 2016); just in the decade between 1987 and 1997, global production of farmed fish (including shellfish) more than doubled in weight and value (Naylor et al., 2000). In 2014, the world's population consumption of farmed fish surpassed that of wild caught fish for the first time (FAO, 2016). More than 220 species of finfish and shellfish have successfully been farmed (Naylor et al., 2000), ranging from filter feeders to herbivores and omnivores to carnivores. Significant improvements in aquaculture have been made in recent years to increase production efficiency while also minimising adverse environmental impacts, but much remains to be done to provide the incentives needed for aquaculture to achieve its potential. A number of promising initiatives are under way to promote more sustainable practices and policies in seafood production, e.g., the new Seafood Business for Ocean

Stewardship (SeaBOS) initiative which is a partnership between scientists through the Stockholm Resilience Center and industry leaders, specifically the Chief Executive Officers (CEOs) of the world's largest seafood companies (http://keystonedialogues.earth/).

Restoration

Efforts to reform fisheries and sustainably farm seafood can be further supported through the restoration of degraded habitats. This is particularly true for coastal wetlands and mangroves that, in addition to providing critical habitat for many economically important fisheries species, also provide buffers to sea level rise and storm surge, sequester carbon and provide habitat for birds and other species. As mangrove forests disappear at an increasingly alarming rate – a result of clearing, harvesting, pollution, climate change and other human-caused threats – efforts to repair them must accelerate. Sri Lanka provides a recent success story: following the 2004 Indian Ocean tsunami, particular attention was given to the re-establishment of green infrastructure along coastlines to improve coastal resilience against natural disasters. As with many of the fishery reforms, the success of this initiative was largely attributable to the participation of coastal communities and local conservation groups, sustained care of the habitat post-rehabilitation, and attention to suitable implementation conditions (Kodikara et al., 2017).

Protected Areas

Parallel efforts are under way to directly protect biodiversity and the habitats upon which it depends through Marine Protected Areas (MPAs), especially a specific type of MPA called a Marine Reserve (MR) that is fully protected from any extractive activity. MRs have been shown, time and again, to bring far greater benefit to biodiversity than lightly protected MPAs (Lubchenco et al., 2016b; Lubchenco and Grorud-Colvert, 2015; Sala and Giakoumi, 2017).

Scientific analyses of MRs suggest they lead to impressive outcomes, within and outside the protected area. In general, MRs increase the size, biomass, number of individuals and diversity of species inside a MR, relative to the outside (Lester et al., 2009; Sciberras et al., 2015). In many cases, the bounty inside a MR spills out to adjacent fished areas, bringing additional fishery enhancement or recovery of depleted fisheries. In addition, MRs can enhance ecological resistance and resilience to climate and other environmental changes (Roberts et al., 2017). For example, when the Gulf of California abalone fishery was confronted with a climate-driven low-oxygen event, the large, fecund individuals in a MR were able to provide a source of juveniles to replenish populations and thereby recovered faster than abalone in unprotected areas (Micheli et al., 2012). Abalone in the reserve also maintained higher genetic diversity and avoided a bottleneck that afflicted populations outside the reserve (Munguía-Vega et al., 2015).

Marine Reserves were initially small areas situated close to shore. Through time and experience, three general patterns have emerged. First, small MRs in coastal waters are being established by fishing communities, states or nations. Second, much larger MRs are being created by nations in more remote portions of their Exclusive Economic Zones (EEZs). Finally, one very large MR has been established on the high seas, in this case by the action of 25 governments through a regional fishery management organisation's jurisdiction in the Ross Sea, Antarctica. There are increased calls for more, very large MRs on the high seas, beyond any country's jurisdiction, or even converting the entire high seas area to one super-large MR (White and Costello, 2014).

The creation of protected areas can be enabled and incentivised in many ways. Recently, there has been a flurry of designations by a number of Heads of State across the world of extremely large MPAs within their nations' EEZs (see Lubchenco and Grorud-Colvert, 2015), perhaps in part motivated by personal incentives on the part of these leaders to protect spectacular places and also leave a legacy (Lubchenco et al., 2016a). This has resulted in dramatic increases in the percentage of ocean protected: in the year 2000, only an estimated 0.9 per cent of the ocean was protected, with 0.1 per cent strongly protected in a MR; in contrast, by 2015, almost 4 per cent of the ocean was under some form of protection and 1.9 per cent of that was in a MR, representing more than an order-of-magnitude increase in MR area (Lubchenco and Grorud-Colvert, 2015). Nonetheless, the fraction protected is far less than the 10 per cent target adopted by governments of the world most recently in the UN Sustainable Development Goal 14 and much less than the 20–50 per cent target that many scientists say is needed (Lubchenco and Grorud-Colvert, 2015).

Because so little of the ocean is currently protected, most species and populations remain vulnerable, and increasingly so. For example, we know that large marine reserves help protect shark populations (White et al., 2017), but 70 nations would need to expand MPAs by 3 per cent to protect half of the geographic ranges of 99 threatened species of sharks, rays and chimeras (Davidson et al., 2017). A recent study showed that 97.4 per cent of species studied have less than 10 per cent of their geographic range inside a protected area (Klein et al., 2015). Efforts to create fully protected areas in the ocean need to be accelerated, and getting incentives right can help. Reforming fisheries so they are sustainable will certainly lessen the threats to many species – especially those caught as by-catch – but will not restore and protect habitats nor restore the integrity of food webs. Hence, both fishery reform and creation of very large fully protected MRs are necessary. Neither is sufficient alone.

A recent innovation combines a MR in the centre of a region surrounded by a fished area that is managed through a type of rights-based fishery management. Called TURF-Reserves (for Territorial User Rights for Fisheries-Marine Reserves), these areas are created by local communities who, in exchange for exclusive access to the fishing areas, agree to fully protect an area inside the fishing grounds. This strategy allows fishers to take advantage of the spillover of fish from the Marine Reserve, aligning economic, social and ecological incentives (Barner et al., 2015). A success story of this type of management comes from the shallow-water reef fisheries in Belize, where local fishing communities collaborated with government and non-governmental organisations (NGOs) in 2011 to implement a pilot TURF-reserve programme. It has been a resounding success, due in large part to the integral role of fishers in the policy design. Because of their involvement in the design process and their desire to maintain their livelihood and cultural values, fishers have personal and social incentives for ocean stewardship. The programme resulted in a 60 per cent decrease in illegal fishing (Weigel et al., 2014), and in 2016 Belize adopted the programme at a national scale.

A number of nations are exploring a variation on the TURF-reserve: the area immediately offshore is reserved for exclusive use by local fishers and the balance of the EEZ outside the fishing grounds is a fully protected MR. In 2015, the island nation of Palau announced the crea-tion of an immense MR called the Palau Marine Sanctuary adjacent to fishing grounds reserved exclusively for Palauans. Chile and the Rapa Nui people of Chile are considering a variation on this idea.

One message is clear from the above fishery reform and MR endea-vours: existing tools have the power to be much more effective in protecting biodiversity if they are more widely adopted. Analyses have demonstrated that changing social and economic incentives have been key to triggering many of the successes to date. Nonetheless, a quantum leap in the use of these tools may well require an additional perspective: moral leadership.

Biodiversity Protection Needs Moral Leadership and Inspiration

The threat of extinction in the ocean is real and accelerating. The concomitant loss is already having very real consequences to the most vulnerable people on Earth. The biggest immediate threat is overfish-ing, but habitat destruction, climate change and ocean acidification, pollution and invasive species all contribute significantly. As the above examples illustrate, tools exist to address most of the drivers of this depletion, disruption and degradation, but they are not deployed at a scale commensurate with the problem.

'Each year sees the disappearance of thousands of plant and animal species which we will never know, which our children will never see, because they have been lost forever. The great majority become extinct for reasons related to human activity. Because of us, thousands of species will no longer give glory to God by their very existence, nor convey their message to us. We have no such right' (Pope Francis, 2015). This quote, from Pope Francis's second Encyclical, illustrates his overall message that humankind has a moral obligation to address climate change and biodiversity loss. This type of moral authority matters. Recent research showed that US survey respondents were more likely to agree that climate change is a moral issue when they were presented with a picture of Pope Francis before the survey (Schuldt et al., 2017).

The match that could ignite a firestorm of awareness and action to protect biodiversity is yet to be lighted. We posit that the moral responsibility we all share for all people and for nature holds the power to strike this match. The scientific case is clear. The long-term economic case is clear. The policy, economic, social and scientific tools are available. But the powerful ethical case for saving marine biodiversity – for people and for all of creation – has not been heard. Much hangs in the balance. Moral leadership and inspiration are urgently needed.

Acknowledgements

We thank Drs Peter Raven and Partha Dasgupta, the organisers of the Vatican Workshop on Biological Extinction; Professors Werner Arber and Margaret Archer, Presidents of the Pontifical Academy of Sciences (PAS) and the Pontifical Academy of Social Sciences (PASS), respectively; Monsignor Marcelo Sánchez Sorondo, Chancellor of PAS and PASS; members of PAS and PASS; and the workshop participants for the opportunity to contribute and for lively and engaging presentations and discussions. We are grateful to His Holiness Pope Francis for his respect for science and his global efforts to connect people and nature in a time of environmental and social change. We are grateful to workshop organisers and participants and especially to reviewers Drs David Jablonski, Nancy Knowlton and Timothy Sullivan for helpful feedback on our paper. All three authors have been supported by Provostial funds from Oregon State University to JL.

References

Appeltans, W., Ahyong, S. T., Anderson, G., Angel, M. V., Artois, T., et al. 2012. The magnitude of global marine species diversity. *Current Biology*, 22(23): 2189–2202.

Balcazar, N. E., Tripovich, J. S., Klinck, H., Nieukirk, S. L., Mellinger, D. K., et al. 2015. Calls reveal population structure of blue whales across the southeast Indian Ocean and the southwest Pacific Ocean. *Journal of Mammalogy*, 96(6): 1184–1193.

Barner, A., Lubchenco, J., Costello, C., Gaines, S., Leland, A., et al. 2015. Solutions for recovering and sustaining the bounty of the ocean: Combining fishery reforms, rights-based fisheries management, and marine reserves. *Oceanography*, 25(2): 252–263.

Barnosky, A. D., Matzke, N., Tomiya, S., Wogon, G. O. U., Swartz, B., et al. 2011. Has the Earth's sixth mass extinction already arrived? *Nature*, 471: 51–57.

Bellwood, D. R., Hughes, T. P., Folke, C. & Nyströ, M. 2004. Confronting the coral reef crisis. *Nature*, 6994: 827–33.

Birkeland, C. 2015. *Coral Reefs in the Anthropocene*. Dordrecht, Netherlands: Springer.

Burgess, M. G., Costello, C., Fredston-Hermann, A., Pinsky, M. L., Gaines, S. D., et al. 2017a. Range contraction enables harvesting to extinction. *Proceedings of the National Academy of Sciences*, 114(15): 3945–3950.

Burgess, M. G., Fredston-Hermann, A., Pinsky, M. L., Gaines, S. D. & Tilman, D. 2017b. Reply to Le Pape et al.: Management is key to preventing marine extinctions. *Proceedings of the National Academy of Sciences*, 114(31): E6275–E6276.

Burrows, M. T., Schoeman, D. S., Buckley, L. B., Moore, P., Poloczanska, E. S., et al. 2011. The pace of shifting climate in marine and terrestrial ecosystems. *Science*, 334(6056): 652–655.

Ceballos, G., Ehrlich, P. R. & Dirzo, R. 2017. Biological annihilation via the ongoing sixth mass extinction signaled by vertebrate population losses and declines. *Proceedings of the National Academy of Sciences*, 114 (30): E6089–E6096.

Cheung, W. W. L., Lam, V. W. Y., Sarmiento, J. L., Kearney, K., Watson, R., et al. 2009. Projecting global marine biodiversity impacts under climate change scenarios. *Fish and Fisheries*, 10(3): 235–251.

Conathan M & Siciliano A. 2016. *America's Blueprint for Sustainable Fisheries*. Washington, DC: Center for American Progress. www .americanprogress.org/issues/green/reports/2016/09/14/144126/ameri cas-blueprint-for-sustainable-fisheries/.

Costanza, R. 1999. The ecological, economic, and social importance of the oceans. *Ecological Economics*, 31: 199–213.

Costello, C., Ovando, D., Clavelle, T., Strauss, C. K., Hilborn, R., et al. 2016. Global fishery prospects under contrasting management regimes. *Proceedings of the National Academy of Sciences*, 113(18): 5125–5129.

Costello, M. J. & Chaudhary, C. 2017. Marine biodiversity, biogeography, deep-sea gradients, and conservation. *Current Biology*, 27(11): R511–R527.

Crossland, C. J. 2006. *Coastal Fluxes in the Anthropocene*. Berlin: Springer.

Darimont, C. T., Fox, C. H., Bryan, H. M. & Reimchen, T. E. 2015. The unique ecology of human predators. *Science*, 349(6250): 858–860.

Davidson, L. N. K., Dulvy, N. K., Dulvy, N. K., Barker, B. & Brodie, P. 2017. Global marine protected areas to prevent extinctions. *Nature Ecology & Evolution*, 1(2): 6.

Dulvy, N. K., Sadovy, Y. & Reynolds, J. D. 2003. Extinction vulnerability in marine populations. *Fish and Fisheries*, 4(1): 25–64.

EDF Fisheries Solutions Center. 2017. *Database | Fishery Solutions Center.* http://fisherysolutionscenter.edf.org/database.

FAO. 2016. *The State of World Fisheries and Aquaculture 2016. Contributing to Food Security and Nutrition for All.* Rome. www .fao.org/3/a-i5555e.pdf.

Fisher, R. 2013. *Gulf of Mexico/South Atlantic Final Seafood Recommendation.* www.seafoodwatch.org/-/m/sfw/pdf/reports/s/mba _seafoodwatch_gulfofmexicosnapperreport.pdf.

Gardner, T. A., Côté, I. M., Gill, J. A., Grant, A. & Watkinson, A. R. 2003. Long-term region-wide declines in Caribbean corals. *Science*, 301 (5635): 958–960.

Gleckler, P. J., Durack, P. J., Stouuer, R. J., Johnson, G. C. & Forest, C. E. 2016. Industrial-era global ocean heat uptake doubles in recent decades. *Nature Climate Change*, 6: 394–398.

Grimm, D., Barkhorn, I., Festa, D., Bonzon, K., Boomhower, J., et al. 2012. Assessing catch shares' effects evidence from Federal United States and associated British Columbian fisheries. *Marine Policy*, 36 (3): 644–657.

Harnik, P. G., Lotze, H. K., Anderson, S. C., Finkel, Z. V., Finnegan, S., et al. 2012. Extinctions in ancient and modern seas. *Trends in Ecology & Evolution*, 27(11): 608–617.

Higgs, N. D. & Attrill, M. J. 2015. Biases in biodiversity: wide-ranging species are discovered first in the deep sea. *Frontiers in Marine Science*, 2: 61.

Jablonski, D., Belanger, C. L., Berke, S. K., Huang, S., Krug, A. Z., et al. 2013. Out of the tropics, but how? Fossils, bridge species, and thermal ranges in the dynamics of the marine latitudinal diversity gradient. *Proceedings of the National Academy of Sciences*, 110(26): 10487–10494.

Jablonski, D., Huang, S., Roy, K. & Valentine, J. W. 2017. Shaping the latitudinal diversity gradient: New perspectives from a synthesis of paleobiology and biogeography. *The American Naturalist*, 189(1): 1–12.

Jaume, D. & Duarte, C. M. 2006. General aspects concerning marine and terrestrial biodiversity. In C. M. Duarte (Ed.), *The Exploration of Marine Biodiversity Scientific and Technological Challenges*: 17–30. Bilbao: Fundacion BBVA.

Jellison, B. M., Ninokawa, A. T., Hill, T. M., Sanford, E. & Gaylord, B. 2016. Ocean acidification alters the response of intertidal snails to a key sea star predator. *Proceedings of the Royal Society of London B: Biological Sciences*, 283(1833): 20160890.

Katsanevakis, S., Wallentinus, I., Zenetos, A., Leppakoski, E., Cinar, M. E., et al. 2014. Impacts of invasive alien marine species on ecosystem services and biodiversity: a pan-European review. *Aquatic Invasions*, 9 (4): 391–423.

Kinlan, B. P. & Gaines, S. D. 2003. Propagule dispersal in marine and terrestrial environments: a community perspective. *Ecology*, 84(8): 2007–2020.

Klein, C. J., Brown, C. J., Halpern, B. S., Segan, D. B., McGowan, J., et al. 2015. Shortfalls in the global protected area network at representing marine biodiversity. *Scientific Reports*, 5(1): 17539.

Knapp, S., Schweiger, O., Kraberg, A., Asmus, H., Asmus, R., et al. 2017. Do drivers of biodiversity change differ in importance across marine and terrestrial systems – Or is it just different research communities' perspectives? *Science of the Total Environment*, 574: 191–203.

Kodikara, K. A. S., Mukherjee, N., Jayatissa, L. P., Dahdouh-Guebas, F. & Koedam, N. 2017. Have mangrove restoration projects worked? An in-depth study in Sri Lanka. *Restoration Ecology*, 25(5): 705–716.

Le Pape, O., Bonhommeau, S., Nieblas, A.-E. & Fromentin, J.-M. 2017. Overfishing causes frequent fish population collapses but rare extinctions. *Proceedings of the National Academy of Sciences*, 114 (31): E6274.

Leray, M. & Knowlton, N. 2015. DNA barcoding and metabarcoding of standardized samples reveal patterns of marine benthic diversity. *Proceedings of the National Academy of Sciences*, 112(7): 2076–2081.

Lester, S., Halpern, B., Grorud-Colvert, K., Lubchenco, J., Ruttenberg, B., et al. 2009. Biological effects within no-take marine reserves: A global synthesis. *Marine Ecology Progress Series*, 384: 33–46.

Levitus, S., Antonov, J. & Boyer, T. 2005. Warming of the world ocean, 1955–2003. *Geophysical Research Letters*, 32(2): L02604.

Logan, C. A. 2010. A review of ocean acidification and America's response. *BioScience*, 60(10): 819–828.

Love, M. S., Yoklavich, M. M. & Thorsteinson, L. K. 2002. *The Rockfishes of the Northeast Pacific*. Berkeley: University of California Press.

Lubchenco, J., Cerny-Chipman, E. B., Reimer, J. N. & Levin, S. A. 2016a. The right incentives enable ocean sustainability successes and provide hope for the future. *Proceedings of the National Academy of Sciences*, 113(51): 14507–14514.

Lubchenco, J., Gaines, S. D., Grorud-Colvert, K., Airamé, S., Palumbi, S. R., et al. 2007. *Science of Marine Reserves Second Edition: United States Version*. www.piscoweb.org/sites/default /files/SMR_US_LowRes.pdf.

Lubchenco, J. & Grorud-Colvert, K. 2015. Making waves: The science and politics of ocean protection. *Science*, 350(6259): 382–383.

Lubchenco, J., Guidetti, P., Grorud-Colvert, K., Giakoumi, S., Gaines, S. D., et al. 2016b. *Science of Marine Reserves – Mediterranean Version.* www .piscoweb.org.

Matson, S. E. 2014. *West Coast Groundfish, Shorebased IFQ Program September 2014 Catch Report.* www.westcoast.fisheries.noaa.gov/pub lications/fishery_management/trawl_program/analytical_docs/ifqcat chreport-sept2014.pdf.

McCauley, D. J., Pinsky, M. L., Palumbi, S. R., Estes, J. A., Joyce, F. H., et al. 2015. Marine defaunation: Animal loss in the global ocean. *Science*, 347 (6219): 1255641.

McIntyre, A. D. 2010. *Life in the World's Oceans: Diversity, Distribution, and Abundance.* Chichester, UK: Wiley-Blackwell.

Micheli, F., Sáenz-Arroyo, A., Greenley, A., Vazquez, L., Espinoza-Montes, J. A., et al. 2012. Evidence that marine reserves enhance resilience to climatic impacts (A. P. Klimley, Ed.). *PLoS One*, 7(7): e40832.

Miller, G. T. & Spoolman, S. 2009. *Living in the Environment: Concepts, Connections, and Solutions*, 16th ed. Belmont, CA: Brooks/Cole.

Molinos, J. G., Halpern, B. S., Schoeman, D. S., Brown, C. J., Kiessling, W., et al. 2016. Climate velocity and the future global redistribution of marine biodiversity. *Nature Climate Change*, 6: 83–90.

Morin, P. A., Scott Baker, C., Brewer, R. S., Burdin, A. M., Dalebout, M. L., et al. 2017. Genetic structure of the beaked whale genus *Berardius* in the North Pacific, with genetic evidence for a new species. *Marine Mammal Science*, 33(1): 96–111.

Munday, P. L., Cheal, A. J., Dixson, D. L., Rummer, J. L. & Fabricius, K. E. 2014. Behavioural impairment in reef fishes caused by ocean acidification at CO_2 seeps. *Nature Climate Change*, 4: 487–492.

Munguía-Vega, A., Sáenz-Arroyo, A., Greenley, A. P., Espinoza-Montes, J. A., Palumbi, S. R., et al. 2015. Marine reserves help preserve genetic diversity after impacts derived from climate variability: Lessons from the pink abalone in Baja California. *Global Ecology and Conservation*, 4: 264–276.

Naylor, R. L., Goldburg, R. J., Primavera, J. H., Kautsky, N., Beveridge, M. C. M., et al. 2000. Effect of aquaculture on world fish supplies. *Nature*, 405(6790): 1017–1024.

Nelms, S., Piniak, W., Weir, C. & Godley, B. 2016. *Biological Conservation.* https://ore.exeter.ac.uk/repository/handle/10871/23049.

NMFS. 2015. *2014 Gulf of Mexico Red Snapper Individual Fishing Quota Annual Report Executive Summary.* http://sero.nmfs.noaa.gov/sustaina ble_fisheries/ifq/documents/pdfs/annual_reports/2014_rs_annualreport .pdf.

NOAA. 2017. *Rebuilding Success Continues for West Coast Groundfish.* www.westcoast.fisheries.noaa.gov/stories/2017/19_06192017_.html.

NOAA Fisheries. 2016a. *Status of Stocks 2016.* www.nmfs.noaa.gov/sfa/fisher ies_eco/status_of_fisheries/archive/2016/status-of-stocks-2016-web.pdf.

2016b. *Rebuilding Plans Pay Off for West Coast Groundfish Fishery.* www.westcoast.fisheries.noaa.gov/stories/2016/22_04222016_rebuil ding_rockfish.html.

Nyborg, K., Anderies, J. M., Dannenberg, A., Lindahl, T., Schill, C., et al. 2016. Social norms as solutions. *Science*, 354(6308): 42–43.

Nyegaard, M., Sawai, E., Gemmell, N., Gillum, J., Loneragan, N. R., et al. 2017. Hiding in broad daylight: molecular and morphological data reveal a new ocean sunfish species (Tetraodontiformes: Molidae) that has eluded recognition. *Zoological Journal of the Linnean Society*, 56: 232–244.

OECD. 2014. OECD-FAO Agricultural Outlook 2014. https://doi.org/10 .1787/agr_outlook-2014-en.

Orcutt, B. 2016. *Dr Beth Orcutt on the Discovery of a New Habitat on the Ocean Seafloor.* www.youtube.com/watch?v=bM_BSInK2C8.

Orzechowski, E. A., Lockwood, R., Byrnes, J. E. K., Anderson, S. C., Finnegan, S., et al. 2015. Marine extinction risk shaped by trait-environment interactions over 500 million years. *Global Change Biology*, 21(10): 3595–3607.

Parker, J. D., Torchin, M. E., Hufbauer, R. A., Lemoine, N. P., Alba, C., et al. 2013. Do invasive species perform better in their new ranges? *Ecology*, 94(5): 985–994.

Parmesan, C. & Yohe, G. 2003. A globally coherent fingerprint of climate change impacts across natural systems. *Nature*, 421(6918): 37–42.

Payne, J. L., Bush, A. M., Heim, N. A., Knope, M. L. & McCauley, D. J. 2016. Ecological selectivity of the emerging mass extinction in the oceans. *Science*, 353(6305): 1284–1286.

Polidoro, B. A., Carpenter, K. E., Collins, L., Duke, N. C., Ellison, A. M., et al. 2010. The loss of species: Mangrove extinction risk and geographic areas of global concern. (D. M. Hansen, Ed.). *PLoS One*, 5(4): e10095.

Pope Francis. 2015. *Laudato Si': On Care for Our Common Home* [Encyclical]. Vatican City, Italy: Vatican Press. http://w2.vatican.va/con tent/francesco/en/encyclicals/documents/papa-francesco_20150524_en ciclica-laudato-si.html.

Ramírez, F., Afán, I., Davis, L. S. & Chiaradia, A. 2017. Climate impacts on global hot spots of marine biodiversity. *Science Advances*, 3(2): e1601198.

Roberts, C. M., O'Leary, B. C., McCauley, D. J., Cury, P. M., Duarte, C. M., et al. 2017. Marine reserves can mitigate and promote adaptation to climate change. *Proceedings of the National Academy of Sciences*, 114 (24): 6167–6175.

Sala, E. & Giakoumi, S. 2017. No-take marine reserves are the most effective protected areas in the ocean. *ICES Journal of Marine Science*. https://doi.org/10.1093/icesjms/fsx059.

Schuldt, J. P., Pearson, A. R., Romero-Canyas, R. & Larson-Konar, D. 2017. Brief exposure to Pope Francis heightens moral beliefs about climate change. *Climatic Change*, 141(2): 167–177.

Sciberras, M., Jenkins, S. R., Mant, R., Kaiser, M. J., Hawkins, S. J., et al. 2015. Evaluating the relative conservation value of fully and partially protected marine areas. *Fish and Fisheries*, 16(1): 58–77.

Spalding, M. D. & Brown, B. E. 2015. Warm-water coral reefs and climate change. *Science*, 350(6262): 769–771.

Sun, S., Li, Q., Kong, L., Yu, H., Zheng, X., et al. 2016. DNA barcoding revel patterns of species diversity among northwestern Pacific molluscs. *Scientific Reports*, 6: 33367.

Valiela, I., Bowen, J. L., York, J. K., et al. 2001. Mangrove forests: One of the world's threatened major tropical environments. *BioScience*, 51 (10):807.

Watson, S.-A., Fields, J. B. & Munday, P. L. 2017. Ocean acidification alters predator behaviour and reduces predation rate. *Biology Letters*, 13(2): 20160797.

Watson, S.-A., Lefevre, S., McCormick, M. I., Domenici, P., Nilsson, G. E., et al. 2013. Marine mollusc predator-escape behaviour altered by near-future carbon dioxide levels. *Proceedings of the Royal Society of London B: Biological Sciences*, 281(1774): 20132377.

Waycott, M., Duarte, C. M., Carruthers, T. J. B., Orth, R. J., Dennison, W. C., et al. 2009. Accelerating loss of seagrasses across the globe threatens coastal ecosystems. *Proceedings of the National Academy of Sciences*, 106(30): 12377–12381.

Webb, T. J. & Mindel, B. L. 2015. Global patterns of extinction risk in marine and non-marine systems. *Current Biology*, 25(4): 506–511.

Weigel, J.-Y., Mannle, K. O., Bennett, N. J., Carter, E., Westlund, L., et al. 2014. Marine protected areas and fisheries: Bridging the divide. *Aquatic Conservation: Marine and Freshwater Ecosystems*, 24(S2): 199–215.

White, C. & Costello, C. 2014. Close the high seas to fishing? *PLoS Biology*, 12(3): e1001826.

White, T. D., Carlisle, A. B., Kroodsma, D. A., Block, B. A., Casagrandi, R., et al. 2017. Assessing the effectiveness of a large marine protected area for reef shark conservation. *Biological Conservation*, 207: 64–71.

Williams, R., Wright, A. J., Ashe, E., Blight, L. K., Bruintjes, R., et al. 2015. Impacts of anthropogenic noise on marine life: Publication patterns, new discoveries, and future directions in research and management. *Ocean & Coastal Management*, 115: 17–24.

Worm, B. & Paine, R. T. 2016. Humans as a hyperkeystone species. *Trends in Ecology & Evolution*, 31(8): 600–607.

5 | Out of the Soil

Soil (Dark Matter Biodiversity) and Societal 'Collapses' from Mesoamerica to Mesopotamia and Beyond

TIMOTHY BEACH, SHERYL LUZZADDER-BEACH
AND NICHOLAS P. DUNNING

Plowed ground smells of earthworms and empires.

Justin Isherwood

We know more about the movement of celestial bodies than about the soil underfoot.

Leonardo da Vinci

The Latin name for man, homo, [is] derived from humus, the stuff of life in the soil.

Dr Daniel Hillel

Much of what we can say about the ebbs and flows of ancient societies comes embedded in and directly from the soil. The soil provides evidence about its past and about the qualities it provided for ecological health and human resources. This is important to the topic of this book because the soil, or the pedosphere, is the ultimate domain of ecosystem services and holds the Earth's highest biodiversity. In this chapter, we begin with a review of biodiversity and erosion in the underappreciated soil ecosystem and then consider societal collapses, extinctions in a sense, mainly through the lenses of geoarchaeology or archaeology using many tools of the geosciences.

Our synthesis presents two equal and complementary theses. First, humanity has squandered soil resources and ecosystems in many cases insidiously and sometimes more palpably in the forms of badlands and deep gullies. All forms of soil degradation lead to the depletion of the pedosphere as well as aboveground and aquatic ecosystems. Soil degradation refers to land use changes that deplete soils by many means, diminishing soil habitats, and of course soil truncation or erosion and removal of whole ecosystems. A well-known axiom is that the offsite costs of soil erosion are at least equal to the on-site costs. This means the damage that eroded soil does as it cascades from its point of origin through watersheds to lakes or seas is on a par with the myriad losses from where it eroded. Moreover, eroded soil is the largest water pollutant from local water bodies to coastal dead zones (Pimental et al., 1995).

The second thesis of this chapter is that many indigenous societies and cultures have exuded resilience and sustainability, building enduring 'landesque capital' and adaptation capital providing examples of successful human adaptation to large-scale changes. Landesque capital is the idea of capital invested in the land that persists long after the initial investment (Sen, 1959; Blaikie and Brookfield, 1987). One example is ancient Maya agricultural terracing that has persisted in landscapes for millennia and built-up soil beds that in some areas have taller forests with fewer gaps and greater vertical diversity than do unterraced slopes today (Hightower et al., 2014). Adaptation capital is landesque capital that was also a successful adaptation to overcome a natural hazard or environmental change. An apt example of this is that ancient Maya farmers built wetland fields with canals and soil beds in the face of rising water tables that flooded their formerly dryland farms (Beach, 2016). There is no place here for Pollyannaish optimism because there are also many landscapes of failure where humanity suffered during past episodes of environmental change. We do argue that societies around the world have conserved and even modified environments through the novel creation of agroecosystems that evolved greater biodiversity over time. Such past cultures may provide us with roadmaps of successful and less successful adaptations to both the wide swings of natural and human-accelerated environmental hazards, such as sea level rise and droughts. We caution as well that the archaeological record may be too fuzzy and provide no clear answers about human responses to environmental change. The patterns we excavate in the soil may imply only equifinalities or multiple possible pathways to the ends we dig out of the ground.

Soils: The Dark Matter of Biodiversity

Soils are living ecosystems that are generally half air and water, 45 per cent minerals and 5 per cent organic matter. Of that 5 per cent organic matter, only 10 per cent is life, but this makes up some of the greatest biodiversity by several measures on our planet, though humans recognise this form of biodiversity the least. This hidden component of the living world is also a key player in ecosystem services for carbon and nitrogen storage, nutrient cycles, supplying most of the water for plant growth, cleaning water and aboveground plant health and biodiversity. Soil water, moreover, makes up 65 per cent of the world's freshwater and is the source for 90 per cent of the Earth's farm production (Amundson et al., 2015).

Soil ecosystems parallel terrestrial and marine ecosystems in the forms and functions of their food webs and trophic levels. Also similar to the oceans, most of soil life exists near its surface but microbes persist at far deeper levels. Soil ecosystems start like most ecosystems from primary producers that shed leaf litter on the soil surface and root matter through the rhizosphere, where the roots interact with the soil and its primary consumers and food web. The enormous networks of mycorrhizae, or mutualistic fungi that connect rootlets to a wider array of soil nutrients and water, form one of the nature's greatest ecosystem services. Nitrogen fixation, another of the greatest ecosystems services, fertilises this environment by making inert gas from the air into a form of nitrogen, the most important macronutrient, usable in the food chain. These nitrogen fixing organisms are especially important in the tropical forests, which otherwise often have low-fertility soils (Hedin et al., 2009).

Many sources recount the extraordinary biodiversity of soil ecosystems, and soil communities may account for much of the biodiversity on the planet (Wall et al., 2010). Nonetheless, we simply know little about the 'dark matter' of the Earth's biodiversity (Bardgett and van der Putten, 2014). Most of the living soil biomass comes from algae, bacteria and fungi, and Decaëns et al. (2006) estimated that more than 25 per cent of the Earth's species live only in the soil or soil litter and that soil species may be multiple orders of magnitude more diverse than the rainforest above them.

We also know that soil diversity, the soil classification types based on a soil's factors of formation, are remarkably varied (Amundson et al., 2015). Soil diversity includes 20,000 soil types or 'Series' in the US and more than 300,000 globally. One example of a soil type that has gained global interest are anthropogenic soils with high fertility and biodiversity associations across the world, especially the Amazonian Dark

Earth (*Terra Preta*) soils that create islands of fertility in a sea of low-fertility soils (Glaser, 2007).

Another aspect of soil biodiversity are the useful drugs that soils have provided. Selman Waksman won the Nobel Prize in 1951 for discovering a soil actinobacteria that made actinomycin, which led to hundreds more antibiotics, especially from the genus *Streptomyces*. Indeed, soil is a major reservoir for medicines with about 78 per cent of antibacterial agents and 60 per cent of new cancer drugs approved between 1983 and 1994 having had their origins in the soil, as did about 60 per cent of all newly approved drugs between 1989 and 1995 (Pepper et al., 2009). Although new drugs from soil microbes had declined since the 1960s, Ling et al. (2015) in *Nature* reported a scientific breakthrough that will likely renew antibiotic discovery.

In spite of the great biodiversity of the pedosphere, soil biodiversity losses have been alarming. We can estimate soil biodiversity loss through combined estimates of the different types of soil organism degraders. These include many of the well-known broader factors of biological extinction like habitat fragmentation, invasive species and climate change but for soil biodiversity; we add soil erosion, soil pollution, urban sprawl over soils (sealing) and organic matter decline (Orgiazzi et al., 2016). These more soil specific factors of extinction are smaller factors for aboveground ecosystems. The soil-focused factors of biodiversity loss, however, are key ones for soils and aquatic ecosystems because the key type of soil erosion, sheet and rill erosion, preferentially removes the surface where the most biodiversity, carbon sequestration and the wider web of ecosystem services exists. Moreover, soil degradation accelerates runoff and erosion moves this organic, macronutrient-rich sediment to water bodies, which has led to eutrophication and hypoxia (or oxygen collapse) in aquatic ecosystems worldwide (Rabalais et al., 2014). We know little about the impact of soil sealing (paving and urbanisation) on biodiversity but it covers, removes and generally degrades many of the soil's ecosystem services.

Soil degradation also leads to the attrition of soil health, health that arises from the vitality and diversity of the life within soil (Nannipieri et al., 2003). In essence, soil health refers to the continued capacity of soil to function as a vital living ecosystem that sustains plants, animals and humans. While soil erosion is an often highly visible manifestation of degradation, changes that negatively affect soil ecosystems degrade the health of soil – and in turn its primary productive potential (Hauser and Norgrove, 2016). Many forms of modern industrialised agriculture with their continual reliance on pesticides, herbicides and synthetic fertilisers negatively influence soil, thereby effectively reducing the sustainability of soil health and productivity.

The role of soil and soil erosion in global warming is also clearly important because of the great stocks and flows of carbon and nitrogen into and from soils. For example, Lal (2003) estimated that soils contain up to 80 per cent of terrestrial carbon, and Chappell et al. (2015) estimated that up to 25 per cent of our uncertainty in the flux of global carbon is from soil erosion. Soils and biomass burning were the first anthropogenic sources of greenhouse gas, and fossil fuels as greenhouse gas sources only surpassed them in the twentieth century (Amundson et al., 2015). Soils often lose 50 per cent of their carbon with conversion to agriculture (Stockmen et al., 2013). The soil's potential to remain high or increase as a greenhouse gas source will likely continue because of the increasing demand for more food without commensurately increasing crop yields. Indeed, agriculture in its impacts on soil was also the first step in human impacts on planetary climate change, some would call the Early Anthropocene, by 5000 years ago (Ruddiman et al., 2016).

Erosion of Soils and Biodiversity and Human History

Nearly all of humanity over history depended on soil resources and, aside from written archives, most scholarship on the trajectories of ancient cultures came from excavations and cores into soils and sediments. We argue that soil is the frequently ignored but ultimate natural resource because of its hidden but unparalleled ecosystem services. Writers have speculated on past societal collapses since at least the West's ancient Classical period, and now centuries of archaeological excavations and a century of paired geoscientific investigations have documented environmental changes associated with different societies around the world (Butzer and Endfield, 2012).

One of the earliest and best-known narratives of collapse comes from Plato's *Critias*, which calls upon soil erosion as an example of the lost glories of a once great Attica: 'all the richer and softer parts of the soil having fallen away, and the mere skeleton of the land being left' (Critias by Plato). Most scholars see this as a commentary on the greatness of the past squandered by a less enlightened, later generation (Grove and

Rackham, 2001: 288). In any case, Plato chose soil, the most basic resource for food and life, for a key part of his *Dialogue*. There are many such commentaries on soil from transformative minds through history from Leonardo da Vinci's statement on the ignorance of soils in the quote at the beginning of this chapter to a focus on soil's importance to past and present society in many recent works such as Dotterweich (2013), Montgomery (2007a, 2007b, 2017) and McNeill and Winiwarter (2006). These works synthesise and provide cases from around the world showing the vast losses of soils and their attendant and largely unknown ecosystems. The underlying theme that comes out of these studies is the regretful ignorance of soil in light of its importance in terms of biodiversity, ecosystem services and basic food since it provides humanity with 99.7 per cent of its food calories (Pimentel and Burgess, 2013).

Although many still debate whether the Anthropocene is a new geological epoch, anthropogenic soils and erosion are important metrics for defining the impacts of humans (Certini and Scalenghe, 2011). Bolstering this claim of soil erosion induced biodiversity loss is research that has demonstrated that soil erosion is the largest geomorphic agent on the planet today (Hooke, 2000) and research that estimated that erosion occurs now at the highest rate in the last 500 million years (Wilkinson and McElroy, 2007). Natural erosion occurs at different rates depending on factors like plant cover, slope gradient, soil texture and rainfall intensity. Soil erosion is usually slow in stable ecosystems, but accelerates with vegetation removal from land use changes such as deforestation. The World Wildlife Fund estimated that some half of all topsoils have eroded in the past 150 years, which makes the case for the Anthropocene Epoch stronger (WWF, 2017). Although there are few studies of lost biodiversity from soil erosion, the high global rates and many cases of large-scale erosion imply high biodiversity losses.

Although worldwide studies probably underestimate soil erosion, a typical estimate is that 75 billion tonnes of soil erode annually at a rate 13–40 times background rates of erosion before human-accelerated erosion (Zuaso et al., 2009). Some studies estimate most (80 per cent) of the globe's farmland has moderate to severe erosion, first from water and secondarily from wind (Chappell et al., 2015). Wetlands hold specific types of soils and global losses of wetlands have been high, up to 87 per cent globally since 1700 CE (Davidson, 2014).

Figure 5.1 Denuded landscape of Iceland with two remnant soil pedestals (rofabards) that are about 2 m high, showing a landscape largely eroded of its soil. Photograph by Timothy Beach. (A black and white version of this figure will appear in some formats. For the colour version, please refer to the plate section.)

Highly productive wetlands and soils will suffer more losses due to many aspects of climate change like sea level rise. Nevertheless, global case studies of soil and wetland losses are better at quantifying the mass of soil losses than they are at identifying specific soil species. This shows the need to integrate more soil biodiversity studies with soil erosion studies.

Studies that show the on-site impacts of soil erosion on biodiversity include areas with features like badlands, hoodoos like rofabards (Figure 5.1) and other landscapes made skeletal by erosion of all kinds. Likewise, studies that show offsite impacts of soil erosion are legion, including worldwide coastal hypoxic zones, sediment covered zones of aquatic environments (Tomašových and Kidwell, 2017), and the damage to coral reefs (Maina et al., 2013) and wetlands (Davidson, 2014), two other biodiversity hotspots like soils being lost at high rates globally. Specific examples of offsite impacts of soil erosion, together with other human elevated nitrogen and phosphorous, are that global oceans lost about 2 per cent of their oxygen between 1960 and 2010

(Schmidtko et al., 2017), and hypoxia has spread exponentially since the 1960s (Díaz and Rosenberg, 2008).

Cases of Erosion and Human History

Cases of on-site soil erosion that imply biodiversity losses are widespread and here we consider cases ranging from the tropics to the Mediterranean and to Iceland. Iceland provides an interesting example of intense soil erosion and then collapse of biodiversity both of the unknown soil species and the affected aboveground ecosystems. Almost half of Iceland's soils are Andisols, volcanic and less cohesive, which makes them prone to human-induced erosion (Arnalds, 2005). Another 17 per cent of Iceland has Vitrisols (Arnalds, 2008) or low-organic and low-fertility, sandy volcanic soils that past human-induced erosion created and continue to be a main source for erosion (Arnalds et al., 2001).

We argue that pioneers have often caused soil degradation, as well as species collapses, around the world because of unfamiliarity with the ecosystems they entered. For example, when the Norse first entered Iceland in about 874 CE, the island was about 65 per cent vegetated. Vegetation cover dropped to 25 per cent and forest cover dropped to 1 per cent of its original extent (Blöndal, 1987; Arnalds, 2005) due to deforestation and overgrazing, mainly by sheep (Arnalds, 2005). Thus the combination of deforestation, trampling and overgrazing started early and lasted to the present (Thórhallsdóttir et al., 2013). A classic assessment found that more than half of the Island's soil had experienced 'considerable' to 'extremely severe erosion' (Arnalds et al., 2001: 43).

Today, many parts of Iceland's soil surface lies truncated, eroded to its parent materials. Since by far the most soil biodiversity occurs near a soil's surface, this means a high proportion of the soil life no longer exists in these degraded landscapes. Many landscapes have remnant pedestals called 'rofabards' (Figure 5.1) of past soil cover that stands out above the largely barren landscapes. Estimating the lost extent of pristine forest is complicated but Iceland lost about 95 per cent of its Birch (*Betula pubescens* and *nana*) woodlands (Gísladóttir et al., 2010; Greipsson, 2012). Some studies have also argued that there were winners and losers in Icelandic erosion history with inland and upland sites eroded, losing forests and habitation sites, while lowland and coastal sites gained eroded sediment and inhabitants (Catlin, 2016). Despite these vast losses, Catlin (2016) argued that Iceland was sustainable for a thousand years for humans, though human suffering was high and ecosystems became depauperate. Human winners and losers aside, much of the landscape lost its forest and its soil cover, meaning soils and biodiversity in and on these soils were the biggest losers.

The Mediterranean world provides many examples of soil erosion and a long history of so-called ruined landscapes, which Butzer and Harris (2007) and Grove and Rackham (2001: 288) consider critically. One example in Turkey's Hatay Province showed ancient Roman agricultural terraces and roads eroded down by 1 m or more creating deep gullies and leaving 1-m-high hoodoos in the uplands and 2-m-deep sedimentation on the coastal plain that buried ancient Roman roads. Erosion and sedimentation here started much earlier because Bronze Age sites lay buried by 5 m of sediment in some places (Beach and Luzzadder-Beach, 2008; Beach et al., 2017). Despite this degradation history, agriculture today is intense and productive along the coastal plain that had been buried by sediment but patchy in the eroded foothills, in parallel with the Icelandic example of uphill losers and downhill winners.

Similar studies of skeletal landscapes of gullies and hoodoos associated with human-induced erosion history include the highlands of Colombia (Mora Pacheco, 2012), Central Mexico (Rincon, 1999), and the US Piedmont and Coastal Plain (Sutter, 2015). Spanish colonial records implicate livestock expansion in the seventeenth century in the eroded, desertlike landscape of the Valle de Leyva, Colombia (Figure 5.2) (Mora Pacheco, 2012), though we have no soil studies that give firm dates to erosion and sedimentation in this highland terrain. Similarly, some studies implicated livestock in the erosion of the Mezquital in highland central Mexico (Melville, 1994) but research has shown that erosion rates were also high in pre-Columbian times (Butzer, 1992). Cordova and Parsons (1997) and Rincon Maunter (1999: 664) described fields with a few soil pedestals, remnants of pre-eroded surfaces, sticking out above the mostly eroded surface (Figure 5.3). Similarly, Providence Canyon in the coastal plain of the US state of Georgia started gullying soon after deforestation occurred in the nineteenth century, and Charles Lyell, a founding father of geology, was on hand nearby in 1846 to record similar gullies forming, which became an iconic section in his seminal book the *Principles of Geology*. Lyell

Figure 5.2 Denuded landscape of Colombia's Northern Andes with a remnant soil pedestal that is about 1.5 m high, showing a landscape largely eroded of its soil. Photograph by Timothy Beach. (A black and white version of this figure will appear in some formats. For the colour version, please refer to the plate section.)

reported a gully formed in 20 years that was about 17 m deep and up to 55 m wide. Providence Canyon by the early twentieth century was even larger, up to 53 m deep (Sutter, 2015: 33).

Many of these soil erosion cases are severe, yet commonplace, examples of anthropogenic erosion multiplied by natural factors, especially steep slopes and intensive rainfall in the Colombian highlands and US South, steep slopes in Central Mexico and Turkey, and easy to erode volcanic soils in Iceland. But these cases and multiple others worldwide stand testimony to deep former soils and their lost productivity and biodiversity and the fact that human land use change triggered these episodes of runaway degradation and 'dark matter biodiversity' loss.

There are diverse perceptions about soil erosion because it can be unseen (or insidious) in landscapes, large areas of flat terrain have low erosion, and many people are ignorant of or hold negative perceptions about soil (Brevik and Hartemink, 2010). Nonetheless, many cultures through history have developed soil conservation in myriad forms that can be obvious

Figure 5.3 Denuded badlands landscape of the Central Mexican Highlands with a remnant soil pedestal rising above the badlands. Photograph by Timothy Beach. (A black and white version of this figure will appear in some formats. For the colour version, please refer to the plate section.)

or hidden in landscapes. Later, we explore many aspects of soil conservation in ancient Mesoamerica, and such early efforts arose around the world, though written documentation of professional soil conservation only goes back to the 1700s in Germany (Dotterweich, 2013).

One of the heydays of efforts to stem soil erosion was the US New Deal of the 1930s, when government leveraged science, economics and the humanities to put people to work and conserve soil (McLeman et al., 2014). A key figure in this effort was Hugh Hammond Bennett, who possessed an unparalleled combination of scientific knowledge and leadership and showed why soils and conserving them were necessary. His genius was to recognise a grassroots approach using the intelligence of local farmers with government support and a system of incentives to help spread conservation. He mastered communication to publicise the problem and implementation in the use of demonstration projects and suggestion, instead of command and control. The 1930s had the twin misfortunes of the Great Depression and the Dust Bowl, or the worst economic decline and the worst environmental disaster in American History, when parts of the Great Plains lost three-fourths of their topsoils (Hornbeck, 2012). In a famous display of political acuity, Bennett delayed his testimony before Congress to the day when he knew Midwestern soils would blow with the winds through Washington, DC during a congressional session. He showed Congress the dust from those eroding farms flying by the windows as they were debating funds for soil conservation. The measure passed and money for soil conservation solved two problems, preserving soils and putting people back to work (Helms, 2010).

Another innovative approach was to publicise the importance of – or shock at – soil erosion by paying artists to render images of the calamity of soil erosion. This helped spawn a movement of similar imagery, including Alexandre Hogue's famous painting of a naked *Mother Earth Laid Bare* as sculpted by gullies (White, 2006). Since then, we argue that soil erosion has not risen to the forefront of concern about environmental destruction as much as other causes of biological extinction, despite many attempts to warn against soil degradation over the decades (e.g., Bennett, 1939; Pimentel, 1995, 2013; Montgomery, 2007a, 2007b, 2017). We can only speculate that indifference has been due to soil's lack of charisma and association with rural professions practised by fewer and fewer in a rapidly urbanising world.

Connecting soil erosion studies to the decline of civilisations has a long history, exemplified in work by D. Montgomery (2007a and 2007b), H. H. Bennett (1939) and W. C. Lowdermilk (1953) in the twentieth century and George Perkins Marsh (1864) in the nineteenth century. Bennett wrote his magnum opus *Soil Conservation* in 1939, a large tome that described mainly US erosion and conservation but two chapters discussed world erosion.

Despite all of this global evidence for soil erosion, many have commented that agriculture prevailed and food production has only increased in recent human history (McNeill, 2000). Butzer and Harris (2007) wrote this about the Mediterranean and Lindert (2000) wrote this about China and Indonesia. Many areas of extreme erosion may be of limited importance because of their small size or because soil amendments could partly compensate for soil depletion. We are left with a tension between what we know has been a history of extreme soil erosion in many places around the world and the history of soil conservation and evolving sustainability as cultures developed myriad soil conserving and enhancing features and sustainable agroecosystems. The social science side of human-soil history has many positives: increasing landesque capital and humanised, intensified farming systems and anthropogenic soils that can sequester carbon and hold more water. But this does not disprove or compensate the large-scale degradation of soil landscapes and the loss of 'dark matter' biodiversity, which increases unabated in many places on Earth. This means that humanity has fewer land use choices on the eroded landscapes and we are ignorant of what we have lost and what we are losing.

Cases of Collapse in Historical Science

James Hutton in the eighteenth century and later Charles Lyell developed the concept of uniformitarianism, epitomised as 'the present is the key to the past', which implies we can read the Earth's history based on the processes we can observe today. A Permian sand dune from 275 million years ago operated much as one in Patagonia does today. Moreover, we could study the patterns in those fossilised dunes to understand modern dune patterns. Likewise, using the historical sciences to study past cultural-environmental interactions increases our sample size to understand these relationships in the present. The past, however, will include many fuzzy examples with unclear results. Even cases that some have called clear examples of environmentally caused historical collapses find counter-arguments with complicated explanations. Natural science should be fair in interpreting archaeology and ancient history and realise much of the evidence may tell us little about the processes of societal collapse. The evidence we find may be the product of multiple pathways and thus show only equifinality rather than morals to stories.

These multiple paths weave through spiritual, economic, political and environmental relationships to crises, and lead to multiple potential outcomes of collapse, resilience and/or sustainability. For example, Butzer (2012) notes that a literature arose from a major societal transformation in ancient Egypt's First Intermediate Period (2181–2055 BCE). These texts, while not necessarily accurate, still had the impact to create a lasting 'cultural memory of a painful transition' (Butzer 2012: 3633) relating Nile River failure with civil upheaval and health crises, among other human tragedies. In another case study from much more recent history, Endfield (2012) found in her archival study of colonial Mexico, that with climate variation, both seasonal and extreme, societies may gain from periods of crisis by enhancing their ability to respond to hardship, to recognise their vulnerabilities and to plan contingencies for future challenges. These findings offer optimism (Endfield, 2012). Understanding these historical human responses can help us to avoid despair. We must, however, guard against forgetting the suffering and losses in our hope for a silver lining.

It is reasonable to suppose that Pleistocene humans suffered the greatest impacts from natural hazards. The Pleistocene experienced much greater amplitudes of environmental change, and these changes were especially abrupt in the Late Pleistocene, when temperature changes were near the high-end predictions of today's global warming crisis. For example, during the Younger Dryas in the last vestiges of the Ice Age, c. 12,900 to c. 11,700 calendar years ago (BP), even the equatorial Cariaco Basin cooled by 3°C (Lea et al., 2003). At this time many parts of the Northern Hemisphere became abruptly colder and dryer for a millennium before abruptly warmer and wetter conditions at the start of the Holocene (Rosen and Rivero-Collazo, 2012).

Connecting these changes to culture and climate, Weiss and Bradley (2001) referred to the Younger Dryas as 'the earliest well-documented example of societal collapse'. But Rosen and Rivero-Collazo (2012) applied the model of adaptive change (resilience theory) to the Younger Dryas in the Levant. Based on four phases they interpreted: release/collapse (Ω); reorganisation (α), when the system restructures itself after a catastrophic stimulus through innovation and social memory – a period of greater resilience and less vulnerability; exploitation (r); and conservation (K), representing an increasingly rigid system that loses flexibility to change. Following this same region into the early Holocene during two abrupt but less intense cooling and drying events at 9.2 ka (1 ka is 1000 years ago) and 8.2 ka, Flohr et al. (2016) found farming communities were again resilient.

Over the Late Pleistocene some of the greatest human impacts on ecosystems until recent times occurred with the Pleistocene Megafaunal extinctions. These extinctions also have complex explanations because of overlapping climate and ecosystem changes but the correlation of humans or better killing technologies entering continents at the time of these extinctions is suspicious. Two aspects about these extinctions stand out. First, all the New World megaherbivores over 1000 kg, and 64 to 81 per cent of large megaherbivores, 45–999 kg, went extinct as *Homo sapiens sapiens* with their hunting and butchering technology entered the New World. In contrast, only 43 per cent of Old World African megaherbivores and 22 per cent of African large herbivores went extinct (Gill et al., 2009; Malhi et al., 2016). We should note that the large seesaw of climate changes from the Last Glacial to Interglacial occurred many times before in the Americas without humans present and without similar extinctions. The Late Pleistocene was the first time humans, an unimpressive looking predator, had entered the picture, unlike the Old World where megafauna and *H. sapiens* had co-evolved. Thus, it seems likely that human overhunting played some role in the megafauna extinctions, which impaired biodiversity and ecosystem functions (Malhi et al., 2016), but humans again adapted with new technologies, ways of life and animal and plant exploitation. The largest and clearest human impacts on species extinctions often occurred on vulnerable islands rather than large tropical forests (Roberts et al., 2017).

The Green Sahara, also called the Neolithic Subpluvial and the Holocene Wet Phase, refers to a period from 9 to 3000 years ago when the Sahara and Arabia in the the Northern Hemisphere subtropics became wetter and hosted higher biodiversity and human numbers; they then dried to present conditions (Kruper and Kröpelin, 2006; Kröpelin et al., 2008). This is perhaps the best example of a past climate change that correlated with large-scale human settlement and population changes. One of the great engines of natural climate periodicity, Precession, generated more solar radiation in the Northern Hemisphere summer. This caused the monsoon to intensify and draw in moist Atlantic air masses that intensified rainfall in the summer period. These patterns created significantly wetter conditions for half the Holocene, expanding the great African savanna populations, including humans, into the now desolate Sahara and Rub Al-Khali (DeMonical et al., 2000).

Although opinion varies on how abruptly this period ended (e.g., deMenocal et al., 2000, argue for abrupt, and Kröpelin et al., 2008, argue for gradual), the Holocene Wet Phase and the Middle–Late Holocene Boundary ended from c. 6000 to 3000 years ago (Kröpelin et al., 2008; Tierney et al., 2017). By this time, the region had dried out to its present conditions and vegetation decreased from covering around 70 per cent to less than 10 per cent of the surface (Claussen et al., 1999). Possibly ushering in the desiccation of the late Holocene was the 5.9 ka event, which appears as an abrupt transition similar to the earlier 9.2 and 8.2 ka events. Studies correlate this aridification with human migration from diffuse Saharan settlements to more concentrated settlement along the Nile, where the earliest complex, organised, state-level cultures appeared during the sixth millennium BP (Brooks, 2006). Over the same time, Arabian inland sites disappeared during the 'Dark Millennium' while coastal sites along the Arabian Gulf also persisted (Parker et al., 2006).

Perhaps the last gasp of the Green Sahara was the 4.2 ka event in Mesopotamia and surrounding areas with possibly similar aridity or cold conditions around the world (Weiss, 2016). Some of the societal transitions that correlated with the 4.2 ka event are the decline of Akkadian Mesopotamia and the Old Kingdom of Egypt, with the latter associated with very low Nile floods (Stanley et al., 2003). We note contention exists between scholars about environmental triggers associated with these societal transitions (Butzer, 2012). Indeed, because we have a wealth of written information about Egypt that shows a tremendously complex picture of collapse and resilience, it warns us about correlations between environmental change and collapse where we have limited information and where there may be a wide range of dating errors (Butzer and Endfield, 2012). Human agency, including 'poor leadership, administrative dysfunction, and ideological ambivalence' (Butzer, 2012: 3638), frequently couples with and amplifies other collapse triggers in non-linear ways.

Although evidence for disappearing human settlements is clear from the collapse of the Green Sahara, some sources find resilience and new forms of social complexity across this broad time span and geographic span. Weiss (2016), for example, finds evidence for collapse and abandonment for the 4.2 ka event, but societies adapted by moving to wetter refuges of the Euphrates and Orontes river valleys. Zerboni et al. (2016) show from the drying African Sahara and South Asian Thar deserts at the end of the Green Sahara period that cultures adapted with new forms of social complexity and sustenance that allowed them to shift to evolving resources. Archaeological evidence shows that settlement patterns changed but habitation abided without collapses. Thus evidence often points to continuity of occupation, but with changes in settlement patterns, rather than full-fledged abandonment (Zerboni et al., 2016).

Settlements also shifted toward water sources and evidence exists for innovation of water technology correlating with periods of aridity

(Magee, 2004). One example of resilience and innovation in the face of the 4.2 ka aridity event was the development of a groundwater collection system in the floodplains and wetlands of La Mancha, Spain (Mejías Moreno et al., 2014). Here, a series of Bronze Age habitation hills 'motillas' on floodplains with wells that tapped into a deep, perennial aquifer developed coincident with the 4.2 ka aridity and became abandoned coincident with the wetter Late Bronze age.

Another example from the Middle East that underscores the complexity of environmental impacts on societal transformations is the differential salinisation of ancient Mesopotamia and Egypt. Both of these arid civilisations developed on the back of irrigation from exotic rivers. Some have argued that salinisation caused the eventual decline of Mesopotamian city-states (Jacobsen, 1982; Artzy and Hillel, 1988), which did not occur in the equally arid and irrigation-dependent Egypt. They based this on evidence from salinised soils and cuneiforms that tell of a shift to salt-tolerant barley in place of wheat and the eventual decline even of the barley. Others, however, argued the technologies existed to leach salinity from soils (Powell, 1985). The different geographies of the Egyptian Nile did not produce as high a level of salinisation as in Mesopotamia, which allowed Egyptian societies to persist. In Egypt, the fields lay above the Nile and flood irrigation recedes back to the river taking salts with it, except where floodwater evaporated without draining salts as in the Fayum Depression (Hillel, 1994). Egypt persisted for millennia of course, but written records here give us more insight into the suffering of these successes, including the many famines when the floods failed (Butzer, 1976).

Connecting the two sections of this chapter, soil erosion and biodiversity collapses and societal transitions or collapses, are cases from Iceland and Greenland. Here, the distinction between short-term disaster and collapse comes from time and persistence. Dugmore et al. (2012) favour the concept of decline over collapse in their study of Norse Greenland, delineating it as a long-term process on the scale of decades to centuries (Dugmore et al., 2012: 3658). They also emphasise that decline affects different members of a human society at different rates, and that human societies rarely 'collapse to the point of extinction'. Therefore, the focus shifts away from a biological extinction model to one of human societal transformation (Dugmore et al., 2012). Traditional ecological knowledge, deliberate choices and societal memory are key elements of the decline and collapse of Norse

Greenland, which is an outcome from multiple intersecting human causes (changes in the global economy, 'regional political change, cultural contact', and environmental triggers; Dugmore et al., 2012). In contrast, an overlapping team of scientists found a measure of resilience in pre-modern Icelandic society, despite epidemics, the vast soil erosion discussed earlier, disruptive volcanic activity and demographic fluctuations (Streeter et al., 2012).

Finally, bringing these cases to the present, Hsiang et al. (2013) in a meta-study over long periods and wide geographic scope found that climate change of one sort or another was always a factor in societal declines. Nevertheless, even the most recent events may have very fuzzy and hard to prove connections. For example, recent studies have connected the ongoing Syrian conflict to a series of droughts and rising greenhouse gases that preceded it (Gleick, 2014; Kelley et al., 2015). There are, however, both journalistic and academic critiques of this view (Selby et al., 2017). This should not dissuade research from studying such cases but help us recognise the convolution of factors associated with collapse.

Morals of the Mayacene: Droughts, Degradation, Landesque Capital

Among the best-known examples of 'collapse' is that of ancient Classical Maya Civilisation about a millennium ago (Dunning et al., 2012; Luzzadder-Beach et al., 2012; Turner and Sabloff, 2012). Ancient Maya civilisation emerged around 3000 years ago in a tropical forested lowland and many Maya people and Mayan languages are still alive today. This ancient culture was complex, developed the concept of the zero, hieroglyphic writing, diverse art and a remarkable infrastructure of cities, canals and field systems across the Yucatán Peninsula and adjacent areas (Houston and Inomata, 2009). The Maya and surrounding peoples lived in a hazardous area. Remarkably, the Chicxulub asteroid impact, the cause of the last great biodiversity die-off, still shapes this region 65 million years later (Perry et al., 2009). The shooting gallery of common natural hazards includes earthquakes, hurricanes, droughts and volcanic eruptions (Dunning et al., 2012). Like other ancient cultures, how the Maya persisted and developed in their tropical forest landscape against these hazards is more interesting to many than are their 'collapses'. For example,

Central Americans persisted through multiple devastating volcanic eruptions and evinced resilience in many cases (Sheets, 2008) and some of the region's high soil fertility is the by-product of these past eruptions (Tankersley et al., 2016). Still, the idea of 'collapse' can provoke attention to what were the tipping points for different kinds of extinction. For the Maya, what became extinct were prominent aspects of culture: the act of carving dynastic stone monuments or stelae with writing (the last dated to 909–910 CE; Fuente et al., 1999: 186), many of their cities across a large region, and many intensive agricultural systems.

The factors associated with 'collapse' in Maya civilisation, over the last hundred years of research, have been legion. A short list of the causes of 'collapse' includes warfare, disease, climate change, over-population and environmental degradation, and all of these and many of the others not listed could be interrelated or compounding (Dunning et al., 2012; Luzzadder-Beach et al., 2012; Turner and Sabloff, 2012). The two main periods associated with 'collapse' were the end of the Terminal Preclassic about 250 CE and Terminal Classic about 900 CE. There still is no consensus on what were the causes of, or to what degree they were even, collapses. There were indeed 'drastic population declines in the elevated interior region (EIR), cessation of support for divine kings, and an accompanying priority shift to commerce' (Luzzadder-Beach et al., 2016). This description certainly fits the EIR in the Terminal to Post Classic (800–1000 CE), but less so the Terminal Preclassic (100–250 CE). Both periods of disruption coincided with significant droughts, which are equivalent in some climate records. The EIR is important here because many relict cities here lie prone, far above the water table with no perennial water sources where the dry season may last five months or more (Beach et al., 2015). Such places would be susceptible to drought and collapse, but many other Maya cities lay just above the freshwater table on the coastal plain.

In our own age of global warming and ever-present conflict, the most common interpretations in the literature for the Maya 'collapse' are drought and warfare, which, of course, are interrelated like the other causes of societal transition. One strength of these hypotheses is that they have spawned many studies to look for evidence of climate change and warfare, but the weakness of the hypotheses is their tendency too often to become linear, deterministic explanations (Kennett and Beach, 2014; Luzzadder-Beach et al., 2016).

Most focus has been on drought in the Terminal Classic from 800 to 900 CE when drought evidence overlaps large-scale abandonment. But, some records indicate the Post Classic drought is the most severe from 1000 to 1100 CE, which may be the final blow for the EIR and even the Northern Yucatán cities such as Chichen Itza. Some scholars even connect the rise of another Yucatán city, Mayapan, to the return of moist conditions after 1100 CE and collapse there again to drought in the fifteenth century (Hoggarth et al., 2016). We can also connect the Maya collapses to warfare, especially in the Late and Terminal Classic (Douglas et al., 2016). Warfare was an obvious cause of the collapse of Mesoamerican indigenous societies with European Conquest. One lucid example of warfare causing a kind of collapse was Bishop de Landa burning most of the Maya books still in use at that time at an Inquisition in Mani, Yucatán in 1562. Although four books or codices survive, scholars only translated this written Mayan language again in the 1950s, ironically, with the aid of de Landa's book, which he wrote after burning most of the Maya books (Houston and Inomata, 2009).

Environmental degradation models of collapse were more common in the 1970s and 1980s and they remain relevant. These models evolved to consider resilience and adaptation as scholarship changed and studies found more nuanced understanding of how Maya landscapes developed over time (Beach et al., 2015). Collapse hypotheses based on environmental degradation and overpopulation have deep histories in Maya research. For example, in the early part of the twentieth century scientists pointed out the region's skeletal soils may have been the product of ancient soil erosion, which may indeed be correct for some parts of the Maya Lowlands. But evidence of higher erosion in the Maya Preclassic and lower erosion in the Maya Classic period, when populations were highest and soil conservation features were proliferating, indicates innovation and sustainability and possibly source reduction from earlier soil erosion. Since many places in the Maya Lowlands have low gradient slopes, below the thresholds of much erosion, the soil erosion-degradation hypothesis could only apply to some areas (Beach et al., 2009). This smaller subset of the Maya world, however, included its heartland in the Petén of Guatemala and adjacent Belize, Mexico and Honduras, where many key cities sit along steep ridges next to or in depressions. Thus, Tikal, El Zotz, Calakmul, Caracol, Copán, El Mirador and many more cities sat prone to erosion, though some large, lowland cities like Chichen Itza,

Figure 5.4 The ancient Maya wetland field known as the Birds of Paradise, a form of landesque capital built as polycultural, intensive agroecosystems in the Maya Late Classic c. 700 CE (Beach et al., 2009). Photograph by Dr Jon Lohse, 2004. Used with permission. (A black and white version of this figure will appear in some formats. For the colour version, please refer to the plate section.)

Dzibilchaltun and Chunchucmil were on flat plains with much less potential for erosion (Beach et al., 2017). Whether prone to erosion or not, all of these ancient cities became abandoned.

During the Maya Classic period, one clear change was the widespread growth of infrastructure including reservoirs and intensively managed agricultural fields – that is landesque capital. This produced intensive, polycultural farming systems, many water management systems, wetland fields (Figure 5.4), and extensive forest garden systems. Decades of geoarchaeological and palaeoecological study have given us insights into the knowledge it took to build and maintain these systems (Beach et al., 2015). Moreover, ethnographic studies of modern and historical Maya farmers (Nigh and Diement, 2013) show the profound knowledge involved with today's indigenous agriculture and insight into past knowledge.

The extent of Maya landesque capital is becoming clearer with recent studies using LiDAR, a form of laser mapping that can penetrate through forest canopies and map the surface. LiDAR mapping has revealed even larger areas of agricultural terracing, road networks, and reservoirs (Chase et al., 2014). We knew about these in many areas before LiDAR, but we now can begin to map the full extent and connectivity of such systems. What are now turning out to be widespread conservation and intensive agricultural features from the Classic period were technologies that long preceded the Classic period. Just as Maya writing, habitation sites and population expanded in the Classic period, much of the diffusion of intensive agriculture also occurred then. The period of LiDAR research applied to the Maya world, after about 2010, is a renaissance for understanding Maya land use and a major new lens on ancient Maya environmental and cultural interaction.

The large quantity of Maya terraces, reservoirs and wetland fields implies considerable investment in labour for multiple reasons. Some terrace systems must have been adaptations to eroded or depleted landscapes, as demonstrated by examples perched on slopes above depressions containing deep sediments derived from earlier upslope erosion, and by examples of terrace walls built on bare bedrock, with soils formed behind the walls only since the Maya built them. One environmental niche that became a focus for intensive cultivation in the Classic period were areas downslope from the escarpments on the margins of depressions where years of upslope erosion beginning in the Preclassic inadvertently created deep, 'cumulic' soils (Dunning et al., 2015). The Maya adapted to this redistribution of soil cover by transforming this altered landscape further, investing in terraces, field walls and drainage ditches – a landesque capital that would persist beyond abandonment centuries later.

Studies of wetland fields give us some indication about what motivated their construction (Beach et al., 2015). Here evidence suggests many areas had been dry, and even dry land agricultural fields preceded these wetland field systems, which became wet with water table rise induced by sea level rise (Beach et al., 2009). Thus, at least some of these fields were adaptations to changing environments, which many coastal and lowland areas around the world have experienced because of sea level rise from melting of Pleistocene glaciers during the Holocene. That many wetland field systems arose in the Classic period after slope erosion may also indicate innovation and adaptation by developing new forms of farming after depletion of slopes by erosion (Beach, 2016). Wetland canals at Angkor Wat, another tropical civilisation, leave evidence of damage from floods that may have devastated these hydraulic systems (Buckley et al., 2010).

Many of the Maya agroecosystems diminished in the Terminal Classic, once again as did writing, urbanism and population. Thus, the large-scale abandonment of complicated farming systems in the Terminal Classic was a kind of extinction in terms of lost knowledge that was required to manage these systems and the evidence they held for adaptation to changing environments. The fact that much land-esque capital is still functioning a thousand years later implies some level of sustainability, if not for the Maya, then for ecosystems. Water still runs through canals next to fields in wetlands, terraces still anchor slopes and both have fertile soil beds. Thus, evidence suggests more that landesque capital diffused rapidly after the main thrust of soil erosion rather than soil erosion led to any collapse. Muddying this issue, however, is the evidence that reservoirs have metres of Classic period sediment, indicating continued erosion and lack of mainte-nance that would have diminished water holding capacity and quality long before abandonment (Luzzadder-Beach et al., 2016). Moreover, many slopes and depressions indicate continued soil erosion in the Classic period (Beach et al., 2018). Thus, there is evidence for and against soil erosion correlating with the societal decline in the Late and Terminal Classic, though we argue the evidence supports that widespread diffusion of soil conservation correlates with overall soil erosion declines.

Before, during and after the Terminal Classic of the ninth century CE, climate was changing across much of the Maya world, and evi-dence for drought has grown steadily for these periods. The evidence for drought and warfare based on inscriptions and archaeology corre-late with this period of rearrangement (Kennett and Beach, 2014). But while warfare and regional collapses existed before evidence for the onset of drought, this does not preclude drought as a factor of political instability and collapse in the Late Classic Petén in the EIR (Douglas et al., 2016). Later drought in the Post Classic from 1000 to 1100 CE also correlated with decline in Northern Yucatán cities. Drought may also have remained a push factor against resettlement of the Petén and EIR as trade networks had shifted to the coasts (Beach et al., 2016). Even wetland fields on the coastal plain that retained their advantage of wetness during drought in the Terminal Classic, largely collapsed with minimal re-entry by later Maya groups (Luzzadder-Beach et al., 2012).

Ironically, for this volume on extinction, renewed soils and forests and, in places, increased biodiversity grew up on this collapsed cultural landscape of cities and intensive agroecosystems (Beach et al., 2015). Indeed, many contemporary Maya farmers grow crops preferentially on ancient ruins because these ruins often provide greater fertility from leftover macronutrients, charcoal, organic matter and better drainage in many places (Beach et al., 2017). This ancient enrichment of soil among ruins is likely the result of long-term nutrient transfer and sequestration from hinterlands to population centres within the ancient agricultural economy.

Conclusions: Extinctions in Soils and Societies

Two related concepts compelled this chapter: soil biodiversity and destruction, and societal transitions or collapses. First, soil biodiversity is the 'dark matter' of the Earth's biodiversity, because it is so vast and a little known sphere of life on Earth. The aspects of soil biodiversity include ecosystem structure and function, number of species, key eco-system services, types of soils and the great resource for drugs that can help against disease. For example, soils store up to 80 per cent of terrestrial carbon, are the only habitat for more than one-quarter of the planet's species, and soil organisms were and may become again the chief sources of many antibiotics and other drugs.

Icelandic rofabards (Figure 5.1) and their many comparable features around the world are emblematic of soil degradation. These small remnant soil pedestals show whole landscapes that have lost most of their soil, biodiversity, forests and ecosystem services. These landscapes and those of badlands and gullies are obvious examples of soil devasta-tion, but areas of sheet and rill erosion, often subtle or unnoticed, destroy a much wider landscape. Altogether, world soil degradation is alarming: about 66 per cent of global soils have degraded to a measurable degree (Gibbs and Salmon, 2015) and soil depletion will accelerate in the decades ahead if current trends continue (FAO and ITPS, 2015). Arguably, humankind faces a 'soil degradation para-dox' by destroying global soil resources at precisely the time humanity needs soils and their vast ecosystem services more than ever – as population levels and food demand soar (Delong et al., 2015).

Soil deterioration is very likely one of the greatest pathways for biological extinction, because there are so many types of soil degradation, it is so widespread and it started early especially with agricultural pioneers in many places around the world. We have few studies, however, that give us a baseline for species in the soil now or in earlier times since most of the diversity is microbial and it is less noticeable and inspires less concern than other species with more charisma, an important impetus for conservation. Since soils are foundational for other terrestrial ecosystems, are the chief source of pollution for aquatic ecosystems, and the soil ecosystems themselves are so diverse, we need to reinvigorate soil conservation by leveraging it with broader biodiversity efforts. Testifying to the currency of this problem, the front page of the New York Times on 30 July 2017, carried a report about soil degradation in Africa (Gettleman, 2017).

Soils also connect to civilisations because most civilisations and societies lived off soils and their often ignored ecosystem services. We still do, but dwindling human populations work tethered to the professions of the land. This reality further removes humans from the essential facts of their existence and an appreciation of soils. Studying past examples of societal innovation, resilience, adaptation and collapse connects us to these essential facts through this essential resource base. Moreover, some studies link declines of past civilisations to soil losses (Montgomery, 2007b), which if correct mean that extinctions happened to both some unknown parts of soil biodiversity and to some part of that civilisation's cultural knowledge. Others agree that soil erosion has been severe but question how important that is given that food production has grown and become sufficient. They also note that soil erosion led to winners (areas that gained soils) and losers (denuded areas) and did not change the long-term sustainability of places like Iceland and the Mediterranean. Such views ignore the offsite impacts of soil erosion in water pollution, the degraded soil biodiversity and the losses of ecosystem services, like water cleansing, infiltration and storage in denuded areas.

While past societies would not have been conscious of the scientific basis of soil health, especially the biological basis of soil ecosystems, ancient farmers like farmers today surely observed the adverse effects of erosion and declining crop yields as soilscapes deteriorated. In many cases these farmers responded intuitively, stabilising slopes, improving drainage and adding organic amendments – responses that paid both short and long-term dividends. Our first motivation for this chapter is to make the case that it would be unforgivable if we, with our vastly increased knowledge base, fail to respond to the present-day soil crisis at least as effectively.

The second reason for this chapter is that we can learn crucial lessons from the methods and findings of the societal extinctions or 'collapse' literature, even in the cases that societies did not really collapse.

First, the ancient societal trajectories we study through excavation are extremely complex and many have unclear, non-linear connections to environmental stresses. Many findings have equifinalities or results that multiple pathways could produce. We may never divine the role specific environmental changes played in cultural changes, but we can get closer correlation with more precise dating. Even when events correlate in time, they may not be related; we can only make logical inferences about connections. Where we do have archival sources, they may or may not implicate a myriad of non-environmental factors for times of collapse correlated with environmental changes. In either case, these do not negate or prove environmental triggers.

Second, even when the past is unclear, we can show humanity was able to endure and eventually flourish despite some major downturns that were as large as the high-end scenarios of today's global warming. In Mesopotamia and Africa, humans outlasted the cold and dry of the Younger Dryas and the collapse of the Green Sahara by migration and habitat tracking. In Prehispanic Central America, humans rapidly retreated and rebuilt elsewhere when confronted with volcanic eruptions (Sheets, 2008). Within these positive examples, we must also recognise the severe human suffering that accompanied them.

Third, human cultures over time have developed immense landesque capital, such as farming terraces and reservoirs, ultimately to provide more food and water, but the proximate measures were to improve soil and water conditions. Landesque capital therefore links civilisation dynamics to the sustainable management of soil and water. Landesque capital systems may allow us to date changes within these systems and compare them with other lines of evidence. For example, did ancient farmers build canals or reservoirs after major droughts? Did canal alterations correlate with droughts or floods (Buckley et al., 2010)? We may also infer cultural or religious meaning in such features like field systems growing smaller or dams growing taller over time, or religious icons buried in a field (Berry and McAnany, 2007). We argue that ancient landesque capital is too often an under-recognised type of human knowledge that can provide insight into past human experience with environmental change and hazards.

Fourth, we hypothesise adaptation capital or a landscape memory of successful adaptation to a large environmental change. For example, in La Mancha, Spain, water management innovation grew out of the 4.2 ka aridity. In addition, terrace systems around the world are successful adaptations to a world of eroded slopes.

Finally, ancient Maya civilisation provides examples of all of these lessons from its long interaction with its tropical forest in the shooting gallery of natural hazards of Central America. Maya studies provide many examples of equifinality and complex human-environmental interactions. For example, the Late Preclassic drought from c. 200 CE correlated with Maya societal transformation, but we cannot conclude whether this was successful because of an externality like the drought's severity or an internality like Mayan resilience in developing widespread reservoir systems. We are also unsure as to what degree decreased soil erosion in the Classic period is due to soil conservation or source reduction. The Maya certainly endured and flourished through extreme environmental changes such as the Late Preclassic drought, hurricanes, earthquakes, volcanic eruptions and other calamities we have yet to excavate or otherwise discover. We also know the Maya developed immense landesque capital, and developed the rarer adaptation capital. They built agricultural terracing, reservoirs, forest gardens, transportation networks and intensive and extensive farming systems. Of the adaptation capital, we know of webs of terraces and wetland field and canal systems, which Maya farmers built when soils eroded and water tables flooded their erstwhile dryland fields. We can also say that our knowledge of these systems has grown exponentially with recent acquisition of LiDAR imagery, which we are only beginning to explore.

This immense landesque capital developed by cultures over history is the second reason for this chapter. What we have discovered through scientific archaeology thus far are human successes against changes as large as the high-end predictions of climate change. But, as with soil biota lost with erosion and languages lost with cultural die offs, we are losing much landesque capital through deforestation and many other land use changes. What we are losing thus is evidence of successful and unsuccessful human interaction with the nature and the resilience capital that accrues from cases of success in this hazardous world.

References

Amundson, R., Berhe, A. A., Hopmans, J. W., Olson, C., Sztein, A. E. & Sparks, D. L. 2015. Soil and human security in the 21st century. *Science*, 348: 1261071-1-6.

Arnalds, A. 2005. Approaches to landcare : A century of soil conservation in Iceland. *Land Degradation and Development*, 16: 113–125.

2008. Soils of Iceland. *Jökull*, 58: 409–421.

Arnalds, Ó., Gísladóttir, F. O. & Sigurjonsson, H. 2001. Sandy deserts of Iceland: An overview. *Journal of Arid Environments*, 47: 259–371.

Artzy, M. & Hillel, D. 1988. A defense of the theory of progressive soil salinization in ancient Mesopotamia. *Geoarchaeology*, 3(3): 235–238.

Bardgett, R. D. & van der Putten, W. H. 2014. Below ground biodiversity and ecosystem functioning. *Nature*, 515: 505–511.

Beach, T. 2016. Morals to the story of the 'Mayacene' from geoarchaeology and paleoecology. In *Exploring Frameworks for Tropical Forest Conservation: Managing Production and Consumption for Sustainability*. Paris: UNESCO.

Beach, T. & Luzzadder-Beach, S. 2008. Aggradation around Kinet Höyük, an archaeological mound in the Eastern Mediterranean, Turkey. *Geomorphology*, 101(3): 416–428.

Beach, T., Luzzadder-Beach, S., Cook, D., Dunning, N., Kennett, D., Krause, S., Terry, R., Trein, D. & Valdez, F. 2015. Ancient Maya impacts on the Earth's surface: an early anthropocene analog? *Quaternary Science Reviews*, 124: 1–30.

Beach, T., Luzzadder-Beach, S., Cook, D., Krause, S., Doyle, C., Eshleman, S., Wells, G., Dunning, N., Brennan, M., Brokaw, N., Cortes-Rincon, M., Hammond, G., Terry, R., Trein, D. & Ward, S. 2018. Stability and instability on Maya Lowlands tropical hillslope soils. *Geomorphology*, 205: 185–208.

Beach, T., Luzzadder-Beach, S., Dunning, N., Jones, J., Lohse, J., Guderjan, T., Bozarth, S., Millspaugh S. & Bhattacharya T. 2009. A review of human and natural changes in Maya Lowlands wetlands over the Holocene. *Quaternary Science Reviews*, 28: 1710–1724.

Beach, T., Luzzadder-Beach, S. & Flood, J. 2017. Synthesis of geoarchaeological research around Kinet Höyük, Hatay, Turkey. In E. Kozal, M. Akar, Y. Heffron, Ç. Çilingiroğlu, T. E. Şerifoğlu,

C. Çakırlar, S. Ünlüsoy & É. Jean (Eds.), Festschrift for Marie-Henriette and Charles Gates, *Veröffentlichungen zur Kultur und Geschichte des Alten Orients und des Alten Testaments*: 771–802. Münster, Germany: Ugarit Verlag.

Beach, T., Luzzadder-Beach, S., Sweetwood, R. V., Farrell, P., Mazeau, D. & Terry, R. E. 2017. Soils and agricultural carrying capacity. In S. Hutson (Ed.), *Ancient Maya Commerce: Multidisciplinary Research at Chunchucmil*: 197–219. Boulder: University Press of Colorado.

Bennett, H. H. 1939. *Soil Conservation*. New York: McGraw-Hill.

Berry, K. A. & McAnany, P. 2007. Reckoning with the wetlands and ancient Maya society. In V. L. Scarborough & J. E. Clark, *The Political Economy of Ancient Mesoamerica: Transformations in the Formative and Classic Periods*. Albuquerque: University of New Mexico Press.

Blaikie, P. & Brookfield, H. C. 1987. *Land Degradation and Society*. London: Methuen.

Blöndal, S. 1987. Afforestation and reforestation in Iceland. *Arctic and Alpine Research*, 19(4): 526–529.

Brevik, E. C., Hartemink, A. E. 2010. Early soil knowledge and the birth and development of soil science. *Catena*, 83(1): 23–33.

Brooks, Nick. 2006. Cultural responses to aridity in the Middle Holocene and increased social complexity. *Quaternary International*, 151(1): 29–49.

Buckley, B., Anchukaitis, K., Penny, D., Fletcher, R., Cook, E., Sano, M., Nam, L., Wichienkeeo, A., Minh, T. & Hong, T. 2010. Climate as a contributing factor in the demise of Angkor, Cambodia. *Proceedings of the National Academy of Science*, 107(15): 6748–6752.

Butzer, K. W. 1976. *Early Hydraulic Civilization in Egypt: A Study in Cultural Ecology*. Chicago: University of Chicago Press.

1992. The Americas before and after 1492: An introduction to current geographical research. *Annals, Association of American Geographers*, 82: 345–368.

2012. Collapse, environment and society. *Proceedings of the National Academy of Sciences*, 109: 3632–3639.

Butzer, K. & Endfield, G. 2012. Critical perspectives on historical collapse, *Proceedings of the National Academy of Sciences*, 109: 3628–3633.

Butzer, K. W. & Harris, S. 2007. Geoarchaeological approaches to the environmental history of Cyprus: Explication and critical evaluation. *Journal of Archaeological Science*, 34: 1932–1952.

Catlin, K. A. 2016. Archaeology for the Anthropocene: Scale, soil, and the settlement of Iceland. *Anthropocene*, 15: 13–21, http://dx.doi.org/10.1016/j.ancene.2015.12.005.

Certini, G. & Scalenghe, R. 2011. Anthropogenic soils are the golden spikes for the Anthropocene. *Holocene*, 2(8): 1269–1274.

Chappell, A., Baldock, J. & Sanderman, J. 2015. The global significance of omitting soil erosion from soil organic carbon cycling schemes. *Nature Climate Change*, 6: 187–191, doi:10.1038/ncimate2829.

Chase, A. F., Chase, D. Z., Awe, J. J., Weishampel, J. F., Iannone, G., Moyes, H., Yaeger, J. & Brown, M. K. 2014. The use of LiDAR in understanding the ancient Maya landscape: Caracol and Western Belize. *Advances in Archaeological Practice* 2(3): 147–160.

Claussen, M., Kubatzki, C., Brovkin, V., Ganopolski, A., Hoelzmann, P. & Pachur, H. J. 1999. Simulation of an abrupt change in Saharan vegetation in the mid-Holocene. *Geophysical Research Letters*, 26(14): 2037–2040.

Cordova, C. E. & Parsons, J. 1997. Geoarchaeology of an Aztec dispersed village. *Geoarchaeology*, 12(3): 177–210.

Davidson, N. C. 2014. How much wetland has the world lost? Long-term and recent trends in global wetland area. *Marine and Freshwater Research*, 65: 934–941.

Decaëns, T., Jimenez, J. J., Gioia, C., Measey, G. J. & Lavelle, P. 2006. The values of soil animals for conservation biology. *European Journal of Soil Biology*, 42: S23–S38.

DeLong, C., Cruse, J. & Weiner, J. 2015. The soil degradation paradox: Compromising our resources when we need them the most. *Sustainability*, 7: 866–879.

deMenocal, P. B., Ortiz, J., Guilderson, T., Adkins, J., Sarnthein, M., Baker, L. & Yarusinsky, M. 2000. Abrupt onset and termination of the African Humid Period: Rapid climate responses to gradual insolation forcing. *Quaternary Science Reviews*, 19: 347–361.

Díaz, R. J. & Rosenberg R. 2008. Spreading dead zones and consequences for marine ecosystems. *Science*, 321: 926–929.

Dotterweich, M. 2013. The history of human induced soil erosion: Geomorphic legacies, early descriptions and researches, and the development of soil conservation – a global synopsis. *Geomorphology*, 201: 1–34.

Douglas, P. M., Demarest, A. A., Brenner, M. & Canuto, M. A. 2016. Impacts of climate change on the collapse of lowland Maya civilization. *Annual Review of Earth and Planetary Sciences*, 44: 613–645.

Dugmore, A. J., McGovern, T. H., Vestereinsson, O., Arneborg, J., Streeter, R. & Keller C. 2012. Cultural adaptation, compounding vulnerabiltiies and conjunctures in Norse Greenland. *Proceedings of the National Academy of Sciences*, 109(10): 3658–3663.

Dunning, N., Beach, T. & Luzzadder-Beach, S. 2012. Kax and kol: Collapse and resilience in lowland Maya civilization. *Proceedings of the National Academy of Science*, 109: 3652–3657.

Dunning, N., Griffin, R., Jones, J., Terry, R., Larsen, Z. & Carr, C. 2015. Life on the edge: Tikal in a Bajo landscape. In D. Lentz, N. Dunning &

V. Scarborough (Eds.), *Tikal: Paleoecology of an Ancient Maya City*: 95–123. Cambridge: Cambridge University Press.

Endfield, G. H. 2012. The resilience and adaptive capacity of social-environmental systems in Colonial Mexico. *Proceedings of the National Academy of Sciences.* 109(10): 3676–3681.

FAO and ITPS. 2015. *Status of the World's Soil Resources (SWSR) – Main Report.* Rome, Italy: Food and Agriculture Organization of the United Nations and Intergovernmental Technical Panel on Soils.

Flohr, P., Fleitmann, D., Matthews, R., Matthews, W. & Black, S. 2016. Evidence of resilience to past climate change in Southwest Asia: Early farming communities and the 9.2 and 8.2 ka events, *Quaternary Science Review*, 136: 23–39.

Fuente, B. de la, Staines, C. L. & Hernández, A. A. 1999. Art: Sentries of eternity. In A. Arellano Hernández., B. de la Fuente & C. L. Staines (Eds.), *The Mayas of the Classical Period*: 141–226. Mexico City: Consejo Nacional para la Cultura y las Artes (CONACULTA).

Gettleman, J. 2017. Loss of fertile land fuels 'looming crisis' across Africa. *New York Times*, 29 July 2017, 1. www.nytimes.com/2017/07/29/wo rld/africa/africa-climate-change-kenya-land-disputes.html.

Gibbs, H. K. & Salmon, J. M. 2015. Mapping the world's degraded land. *Applied Geography*, 57: 12–21.

Gill, J. L., Williams, J. W., Jackson, S. T., Lininger, K. B. & Robinson, G. S. 2009. Pleistocene megafaunal collapse, novel plant communities, and enhanced fire regimes in North America. *Science*, 326(5956): 1100–1103.

Gisladottir, G., Erlendsson, E., Lal, R. & Bigham, J. 2010. Erosional effects on terrestrial resources over the last millennium in Reykjanes, southwest Iceland. *Quaternary Research*, 73: 20–32.

Glaser, B. 2007. Prehistorically modified soils of Central Amazonia: A model for sustainable agriculture in the 21st century? *Philosophical Transactions of the Royal Society, Series B*, 362: 187–196.

Gleick, P. H. 2014. Water, drought, climate change, and conflict in Syria. *Weather, Climate, and Society*, 6: 331–340.

Greipsson, S. 2012. Catastrophic soil erosion in Iceland: Impact of long-term climate change, compounded natural disturbances and human driven land-use changes. *Catena*, 98: 41–54.

Grove, A. T. & Rackham, O. 2001. *The Nature of Mediterranean Europe: An Ecological History*. New Haven, CT: Yale University Press.

Hauser, S. & Norgrove, L. 2016. The sustainability of the world's soils. In B. Pritchard, R. Ortiz & M. Shekar (Eds.), *Routledge Handbook of Food and Nutrition Security*: 201–213. London: Earthscan/ Routledge.

Hedin, L. O., Brookshire, E. N. J., Menge, D. N. L. & Barron, A. R. 2009. The nitrogen paradox in tropical forest ecosystems. *Annual Review of Ecology, Evolution, and Systematics*, 40: 613–635.

Helms, D. 2010. Hugh Hammond Bennett and the creation of the Soil Conservation Service. *Journal of Soil and Water Conservation*, 65(2): 37A–47A.

Hightower, J. N., Butterfield, A. C. & Weishampel, J. F. 2014. Quantifying ancient Maya land use legacy effects on contemporary rainforest canopy structure. *Remote Sensing*, 6: 10716–10732.

Hillel, D. 1994. *Rivers of Eden: The Struggle for Water and the Quest for Peace in the Middle East*. New York: Oxford University Press.

Hoggarth, J. A., Breitenbach, S. F. M., Culleton, B. J., Ebert, C. E., Masson, M. A. & Kennett, D. J. 2016. The political collapse of Chichén Itzá in climatic and cultural context. *Global and Planetary Change*, 138: 25–42.

Hooke, R. LeB. 2000. On the history of humans as geomorphic agents. *Geology*, 28: 843–846.

Hornbeck, R. 2012. The enduring impact of the American dust bowl: Short- and long-run adjustments to environmental catastrophe. *American Economic Review*, 102(4): 1477–1507.

Houston, S. & Inomata, T. 2009. *The Classic Maya*. Cambridge World Archaeology Series. Cambridge: Cambridge University Press.

Hsiang, S. M., Burke, M. & Miguel, E. 2013. Quantifying the influence of climate on human conflict. *Science*, 341: 1235367.

Jacobsen, T. 1982. *Salinity and Irrigation Agriculture in Antiquity: Diyala Basin Archaeological Report on the Essential Results, 1957–1958*. Bibliotheca Mesopotamia 14. Malibu: Udenda.

Kelley, C. P., Mohtadi, S., Cane, M. A., Seager, R. & Kushnir, Y. 2015. Climate change in the fertile crescent and implications of the recent Syrian drought. *Proceedings of the National Academy of Sciences*, 112: 3241–3246.

Kennett, D. & Beach, T. 2014. Archaeological and environmental lessons for the Anthropocene from the Classic Maya collapse. *Anthropocene*, 4: 88–100.

Kröpelin, S., Verschuren, D., Lézine, A. M., Eggermont, H., Cocquyt, C., Francus, P., Cazet, J. P., Fagot, M., Rumes, B., Russell, J. M., Darius, F., Conley, D. J., Schuster, M., von Suchodoletz, H. & Engstrom, D. R. 2008. Climate-driven ecosystem succession in the Sahara: The past 6000 years. *Science*, 320(5877): 765–768.

Kuper, R. & Kröpelin, S. 2006. Climate-controlled Holocene occupation in the Sahara: Motor of Africa's evolution. *Science*, 313(5788): 803–807.

Lal, R. 2003. Soil erosion and the global carbon budget. *Environment International*, 29: 437450.

Lea, D. W., Pak, D. K., Peterson, L. C. & Hughen K. A. 2003. Synchroneity of tropical and high-latitude atlantic temperatures over the Last Glacial Termination. *Science*, 301: 1361–1364.

Lindert, P. H. 2000. *Shifting Ground: The Changing Agricultural Soils of China and Indonesia.* Cambridge, MA: MIT Press.

Ling, L. L., Schneider, T., Peoples A. J., Spoering, A. L., Engels, I., Conlon, B. P., Mueller, A., Schäberle, T. F., Hughes, D. E., Epstein, S., Jones, M., Lazarides, L., Steadman, V. A., Cohen, D. R., Felix, C. R., Fetterman, K. A., Millett, W. P., Nitti, A. G., Zullo, A. M., Chen, C. & Kim Lewis, K. 2015. A new antibiotic kills pathogens without detectable resistance. *Nature*, 517: 455–459.

Lowdermilk, W. C. 1953. *Conquest of the Land through Seven Thousand Years.* Washington, DC: United States of America Department of Agriculture. http://landcare.sc.egov.usda.gov/pdf.asp?productI D=109&ConquestThru7000.pdf.

Luzzadder-Beach, S., Beach, T. & Dunning, N. 2012. Maya models and distant mirrors: Wetland fields, drought, and the Maya abandonment. *Proceedings of the National Academy of Sciences*, 109: 3646–3651.

Luzzadder-Beach, S., Beach, T., Hutson, S. & Krause, S. 2016. Sky-Earth, lake-sea: Climate and water in Maya history and landscape. *Antiquity*, 90: 426–442. doi:10.15184/aqy.2016.38.

Magee, P. 2004. The impact of southeast Arabian intra-regional trade on settlement location and organization during the Iron Age II period. *Arabian Archaeology and Epigraphy*, 15: 24–42.

Maina, J., de Moel, H., Zinke, J., Madin, J., McClanahan, T. & Vermaat, J. 2013. Human deforestation outweighs future climate change impacts of sedimentation on coral reefs. *Nature Communications*, 4: 1986 doi:10.1038/ncomms2986.

Malhi Y., Doughty C. E., Galetti M., Smith F. A., Svenning J.-C. & Terborgh J. W. 2016. Megafauna and ecosystem function from the Pleistocene to the Anthropocene. *Proceedings of the National Academy of Sciences*, 113(4): 838–846.

Marsh, G. P. 1864. *Man and Nature: or, Physical Geography as Modified by Human Action.* New York: Charles Scribner.

McLeman, R. A., Dupre, J., Berrang Ford, L., Ford, J., Gajewski, K. & Marchildon, G. 2014. What we learned from the Dust Bowl: Lessons in science, policy, and adaptation. *Population and Environment*, 35(4): 417–440.

McNeill, J. R. 2000. *Something New under the Sun: An Environmental History of the 20th-Century World.* New York: Norton.

McNeill, J. R. & Winiwarter, V. (Eds.). 2006. *Soils and Societies: Perspectives from Environmental History*. United Kingdom: White Horse Press.

Mejías Moreno, M., Benítez de Lugo, E. L., del Pozo Tejado, J. & Moraleda Sierra, J. 2014. Los primeros aprovechamientos de aguas subterráneas en la Península Ibérica. Las motillas de Daimiel en la Edad del Bronce de La Mancha. *Boletín Geológico y Minero*, 125(4): 455–474.

Melville, E. G. 1994. *A Plague of Sheep: Environmental Consequences of the Conquest of Mexico*. Cambridge: Cambridge University Press.

Montgomery, D. R. 2007a. Soil erosion and agricultural sustainability. *Proceedings of the National Academy of Sciences*, 104: 13268–13272.

2007b. *Dirt: Erosion of Civilizations*. Berkeley: University of California Press.

2017. *Growing a Revolution: Bringing Our Soil Back to Life*. New York: Norton.

Mora Pacheco, K. G. 2012. Livestock farming in the Saquencipá Valley, new kingdom of Granada, Colombia in the 16th and 17th centuries. *Pastos*, 42(2): 251–272.

Nannipieri, I., Ascher, J., Ceccherini, M. T., Landi, L., Pietramellara, G. & Renella, G. 2003. Microbial diversity and soil functions. *European Journal of Soil Science*, 54: 655–670.

Nigh, R. & Diemont, S. A. W. 2013. The Maya milpa: Fire and the legacy of living soil. *Frontiers in Ecology and the Environment*, 11 (s1): e45–e54.

Orgiazzi, A., Panagos, P., Yigini, Y., Dunbar, M. B., Gardi, C., Montanarella, L. & Ballabio, C. 2016. A knowledge-based approach to estimating the magnitude and spatial patterns of potential threats to soil biodiversity. *Science of the Total Environment*, 545–546: 11–20.

Pepper I. L., Gerba C. P., Newby D. T. & Rice C. W. 2009. Soil: A public health threat or saviour? *Critical Reviews in Environmental Science and Technology*, 39: 416–432.

Perry, E., Payton, A., Pederson, B. & Velazquez-Oliman, G. 2009. Groundwater geochemistry of the Yucatan Peninsula, Mexico, constraints on stratigraphy and hydrogeology. *Journal of Hydrology*, 367: 27–40.

Pimentel, D. & Burgess, M. 2013. Soil erosion threatens food production. *Agriculture*, 3: 443–463.

Pimentel, D., Harvey, C., Resosudarmo, P., Sinclair, K., Kurz, D., McNair, M., Crist, S., Shpritz, L., Fitton, L., Saffouri, R. & Blair, R. 1995. Environmental and economic costs of soil erosion and conservation benefits. *Science*, 267: 1117–1123.

Powell, M. A. 1985. Salt, seed and yields in Sumerian agriculture: A critique of the theory of progressive salinization. *Zeitschrift der Assyrologie*, 75: 7–38.

Rabalais, N. N., Cai, W.-J., Carstensen, J., Conley, D. J., Fry, B., Quiñones-Rivera, X., Rosenberg, R., Slomp, C. P., Turner, R. E., Voss, M., Wissel, B. & Zhang, J. 2014. Eutrophication-driven deoxygenation in the coastal ocean. *Oceanography*, 70: 123–133.

Rincon Maunter, C. 1999. Man and the environment in the Coixtlahuaca Basin of northwestern Oaxaca, Mexico: Two thousand years of historical ecology. Unpublished PhD dissertation, University of Texas at Austin.

Roberts, P., Hunt, C., Arroyo-Kalin, M., Evans, D. & Boivin, N. 2017. The deep human prehistory of global tropical forests and its relevance for modern conservation. *Nature Plants*, 3: 17093.

Rosen, A. M. & Rivera-Collazo, I. 2012. Climate change, adaptive cycles and the persistence of foraging economies during the Late Pleistocene/Holocene transition in the Levant. *Proceedings of the National Academy of Sciences*, 109(10): 3640–3645.

Ruddiman, W. F., Fuller, D. Q., Kutzbach, J. E., Tzedakis P. C., Kaplan J. O., Ellis E. C., Vavrus, S. J., Roberts, C. N., Fyfe, R., He, F., Lemmen C. & Woodbridge J. 2016. Late Holocene climate: Natural or anthropogenic? *Reviews of Geophysics*, 53: 93–118.

Schmidtko, A., Stramma, L. & Visbeck, M. 2017. Decline in global oceanic oxygen content during the past five decades. *Nature*, 542: 335–339.

Selby, J., Dahi, O. S., Frohlich, C. & Hulme, M. 2017. Climate change and the Syrian civil war revisited. Political Geography 60: 232–244.

Sen, A. K. 1959. The choice of agricultural techniques in underdeveloped countries. *Economic Development and Cultural Change*, 7(3): 279–285.

Sheets, P. 2008. Armageddon to the Garden of Eden: Explosive volcanic eruptions and societal resilience in ancient Middle America. In D. H. Sandweiss & J. Quilter (Eds.), *El Niño, Catastrophism, and Culture Change in Ancient America*: 167–186. Cambridge, MA: Harvard University Press.

Stanley, D. J., Krom, M. D., Cliff, R. A. & Woodward J. C. 2003. Nile flow failure at the end of the Old Kingdom Egypt: Strontium isotopic and petrologic evidence. *Geoarchaeology: An International Journal*, 18–3:395–402.

Stockmann, U., Adams, M. A., Crawford, J. W., Field, D. J., Henakaarchchi, N., Jenkins, M., Minasny, B., McBratney, A. B., de Courcelles, V. de R., Singh, K., Wheeler, I., Abbott, L., Angers, D. A., Baldock, J., Bird, M., Brookes, P. C., Chenu, C., Jastrow, J. D., Lal, R.,

Lehmann, J., O'Donnell, A. G., Parton, W. J., Whitehead, D. & Zimmerman, M. J. 2013. The knowns, known unknowns and unknowns of sequestration of soil organic carbon. *Agriculture, Ecosystems and Environment*, 164: 80–99.

Streeter, R., Dugmore, A. & Vesteinsson, O. 2012. Plague and landscape resilience in premodern Iceland. *Proceedings of the National Academy of Sciences*, 109(10): 3664–3669.

Sutter, Paul. 2015. *Let Us Now Praise Famous Gullies: Providence Canyon and the Soils of the South*. Athens: University of Georgia Press.

Tankersley, K. B., Dunning, N. P., Scarborough, V., Huff, W. D., Lentz, D. & Carr, C. 2016. Catastrophic volcanism and its implication for agriculture in the Maya Lowlands. *Journal of Archaeological Science Report*, 5: 465–470.

Thórhallsdóttir, A. G., Júlíusson, A. D. & Ögmundardóttir, H. 2013. The sheep, the market, and the soil: Environmental destruction in the Icelandic highlands, 1880–1910. In D. Jørgensen & S. Sörlin (Eds.), *Northscapes: History, Technology, and the Making of Northern Environments*: 155–173. Vancouver: UBC Press.

Tierney, J. E., Pausata, F. S. R. & deMenocal, P. B. 2017. Rainfall regimes of the Green Sahara. *Science Advances*, 3: e1601503.

Tomašových, A. & Kidwell, S. M. 2017. Nineteenth-century collapse of a benthic marine ecosystem on the open continental shelf. *Proceedings of the Royal Society B*, 284: 20170328.

Turner, B. L. & Sabloff, J. A. 2012. Classic Period collapse of the Central Maya Lowlands: Insights about human-environment relationships for sustainability. *Proceedings of the National Academy of Science*, 109: 13908–13914.

Wall, D. H., Bardgett, R. D. & Kelly E. 2010. Biodiversity in the dark. *Naure Geoscience*, 3: 297–298.

Weiss, H. 2016. Global megadrought, societal collapse and resilience at 4.2–3.9 ka BP across the Mediterranean and West Asia. *PAGES (Past Global Changes)*, 24(02): 62–63.

Weiss, H. & Bradley, R. S. 2001. What drives societal collapse? *Science*, 291: 609–610.

White, M. A. 2006. Alexandre Hogue's passion: Ecology and agribusiness in the Crucified Land. *Great Plains Quarterly*, 26(2): 67–83.

Wilkinson, B. H. & McElroy, B. J. 2007. The impact of humans on continental erosion and sedimentation. *Geological Society of America Bulletin*, 119(1): 140–156.

World Wildlife Fund. 2017. Soil erosion and degradation. www.worldwildlife.org/threats/soil-erosion-and-degradation.

Zerboni, A., Biagetti, S., Lancelotti C. & Madella M. 2016. The end of the Holocene Humid Period in the central Sahara and Thar deserts. *PAGES (Past Global Changes)*, 24(02): 60–61.

Zuazo, V. H. D. & Pleguezuelo, C. R. R. 2009. Soil-erosion and runoff prevention by plant covers: a review. In E. Lichtfouse, M. Navarette, P. Debaeke, S. Veronique & C. Alberola (Eds.), *Sustainable Agriculture*: 785. Paris: Springer.

6 | The Green Revolution and Crop Biodiversity

PRABHU L. PINGALI [*]

The pattern of crop diversity in the fields of the developing world has changed fundamentally over the past 200 years with the intensification and commercialisation of agriculture. This process accelerated with the advent of the Green Revolution (GR) in the 1960s when public sector researchers and donors explicitly promoted the international transfer of improved seed varieties to farmers in developing countries. Since the GR, the germplasm that dominates the area planted to the major cereals has shifted from 'landraces' or the locally adapted populations that farmers have historically selected from seed they save, to 'modern varieties' or the more widely adapted seed types produced by scientific plant breeding programmes and purchased by farmers.

The yield-enhancing seed types enabled the intensification of agriculture in areas of the world with high population densities. Initially they diffused through the environments best suited for their production, spreading later – and unevenly – into less favoured areas (Pingali and Smale, 2001). Landraces continue to be grown in the latter and in regions with lower population densities and limited market linkages.

The developing world is at the cusp of a Green Revolution 2.0 (GR 2.0), one that extends the benefits of improved crop technologies into areas that have been bypassed by the first Green Revolution and expands the set of improved crops beyond the major three staples – rice, wheat and maize (Pingali, 2012). Sub-Saharan Africa stands out as the region that has benefited the least from GR technologies, despite facing chronic food deficits for decades. The demand for intensification and hence the need for land productivity enhancing seed varieties was low at the start of the GR in the 1960s (Pingali, 2012). Also, in the decades of the 1960s and 1970s, the GR research was not focused on

---

[*] Reprinted with permission from Hunter, D., Guarino, L, Spillane, C.& McKeown, P. C. (Eds.). 2017. *The Handbook of Agricultural Biodiversity*. London: Earthscan/Routledge.

crops important to African smallholders, such as sorghum, millets, cassava and tropical maize (Evenson and Gollin, 2003). In the last decade there has been a significant rise in the introduction and adoption of improved varieties of these crops (Walker and Alwang, 2015). At the same time in Asia, lower potential rice lands are witnessing the rapid spread of improved drought and flood tolerant varieties (Pandey, 2015).

The advent of GR 2.0 has significant implications for crop biodiversity and genetic diversity. One of the primary outcomes of the original GR was that by intensifying crop production on favourable agricultural lands it allowed significant areas of unfavourable land to be moved out of agriculture. Stenvenson et al. (2013) estimate that the GR saved an estimated 18–27 million hectares from being brought into agricultural production. Will the land sparing benefits hold as the GR 2.0 spreads into more marginal production environments? Also, farming systems in less favourable environments tend to be very diverse and are home to a significant number of landraces of traditional food crops, such as millets. Will improved stress tolerant varieties change that system and promote monocultures as has happened in the favourable environments?

This paper outlines some of the implications of agricultural intensification and the adoption of GR technologies on crop biodiversity and genetic diversity. The first part of the paper describes the drivers of agricultural intensification and its consequences for land use change and crop choice. The second part of the paper describes the spatial and temporal patterns of modern variety diffusion and examines its impact on genetic diversity across modern varieties and within varieties. The final part of the paper presents the prospects for a Green Revolution 2.0 with a focus on areas bypassed by the original GR, and discusses its potential consequences for crop biodiversity.

Agricultural Intensification, Land Use Change and Crop Diversity

Intensification of agriculture refers to the increase in output per unit of land used in production, or land productivity. Population densities, expressed as the ratio of labour to land, explain much about where and under which conditions this process has occurred (Boserup, 1981). The transition from low-yield, land-extensive cultivation systems to land-intensive, double- and triple-crop systems is only profitable in societies where the supply of uncultivated land has been exhausted. It is no accident that the modern seed-fertiliser revolution has been most successful in densely populated areas of the world, where traditional mechanisms for enhancing yields per unit area have been exhausted (Hayami and Ruttan, 1985).

Intensive cultivation will also be observed in areas with lower population densities provided that soil conditions are suitable and markets are accessible. Intensification occurs in the less densely populated areas for two reasons: (1) higher prices and elastic demand for output imply that the marginal utility of effort increases, hence farmers in the region will begin cultivating larger areas; and (2) higher returns to labour encourage migration into well-connected areas from neighbouring regions with higher transport costs. Examples of regions with low population density but intensive, market-oriented production are the Central Plains of Thailand and parts of South America's Southern Cone. If the conditions described are not present, labour and other costs associated with intensive agriculture are substantially higher than its incremental economic returns. Intensification of land use and the adoption of yield-enhancing technologies have occurred in traditional as well as modern agricultural systems (Pingali and Smale, 2001).

Agricultural intensification influences the extent of crop diversity in two ways: first through changes in land use patterns; and second, through crop choice changes. Lands that have high agricultural productivity potential, such as the irrigated and high rainfall lowlands, and lands with high soil fertility tend to become the focus of intensification efforts as population densities rise. One also witnesses the concentration of crops that are responsive to intensification pressures, i.e., crops whose productivity can be enhanced through increases in input use. Hence the choice of staple grain crops, such as rice and wheat, over millets and root crops. This change in cropping pattern preceded the Green Revolution, but the advent of high-yielding varieties certainly accelerated the process. Hence the Green Revolution induced ubiquitous monoculture systems in the favourable production environments. The crowding out of traditional millets and pulses from the Indo-Gangetic plains of South Asia, in favour of intensive rice and wheat production is a classic example of such cropping pattern changes (Pingali, 2012).

The lower productive rain-fed environments, on the other hand, continue to maintain diversity of crops grown, and for individual staple grain crops, diversity in traditional varieties and land races. Crops grown in the less favourable environments are generally lower yielding and do not respond to higher input use as compared to those grown in the more favourable environments and under higher levels of intensity. These crops, such as traditional millets and sorghum, tend to be better adapted to harsher environmental stresses, such as drought, high temperatures or flooding, and hence are better suited to the unfavourable environments. Unlike the monoculture systems that are prevalent in the irrigated lands, the stress prone environments tend to have multiple crops on the same field at the same time. The *Milpa* system of Mexico is a great example of inter-cropping of maize, beans and squash in order to ensure farm household food security and diet quality. Furthermore, *milpas* generate public economic value by conserving agrobiodiversity, especially that of maize landraces, which have the potential to contribute unique traits needed by plant breeders for future crop improvement (Birol et al., 2007).

Spatial and Temporal Patterns of Diffusion of Modern Varieties

The change in the crop genetic landscape from predominantly traditional to largely modern patterns of genetic variation occurred over the past 200 years and at an accelerated rate since the 1960s with the advent of the Green Revolution (Pingali and Smale, 2001).[1] Evenson and Gollin (2003) show that adoption of modern varieties (for 11 major food crops averaged across all crops) increased rapidly during the two decades of the GR, and even more rapidly in the following decades, from 9 per cent in 1970 to 29 per cent in 1980, 46 per cent in 1990 and 63 per cent by 1998. Moreover, in many areas and in many crops, first-generation modern varieties have been replaced by second- and third-generation modern varieties (Evenson and Gollin, 2003).

Spatial and temporal patterns in the adoption of modern varieties are largely determined by the economic factors affecting their profitability and by the performance of agricultural research institutions and seed industries (Pingali and Smale, 2001). The adoption of these varieties has been most widespread in land-scarce environments with high population densities and/or in areas well-connected to domestic and international markets, where the intensification of agriculture first began. Even in these areas, the profitability of modern variety adoption has been conditioned by the potential productivity of the land under cultivation. For instance, while modern rice and wheat varieties spread rapidly through the irrigated environments, their adoption has been less spectacular in the less favourable environments – the drought-prone and high-temperature environments for wheat, and the drought- and flood-prone environments for rice. For all three cereals, traditional landraces continue to be cultivated in the less favourable production environments across the developing world (Pingali and Heisey, 2001).

Improved varieties for crops such as sorghum, millets, pulses and cassava were not available until the 1980s (Evenson and Gollin, 2003). Hence the limited expansion of the Green Revolution beyond the favourable irrigated lands. The limited penetration of the Green Revolution into sub-Saharan Africa up until the 1990s was partly also due to the lack of suitable improved varieties for the traditional staples, especially tropical maize, millets and cassava. The situation has changed dramatically since then. Recent evidence indicates that sub-Saharan Africa is well on its way toward adopting modern varietal technology (Walker and Alwang, 2015).

For instance, the area planted to improved cassava varieties in sub-Saharan Africa doubled from 18 per cent in 1998 to 36 per cent in 2009, and the area under improved maize varieties was at 57 per cent by 2009 in West and Central Africa (Alene et al., 2015). Fuglie and Marder (2015) report that the area under improved varieties doubled from 20 to 40 million hectares between 2000 and 2010. 'This was achieved by deepening the pool of improved varieties available to farmers, both in terms of their adaptability to more environments but especially to a wider set of crops beyond the major cereal grains, including oilseeds, legumes, roots, tubers and bananas' (Fuglie and Marder, 2015: 356). But sub-Saharan Africa still has improved variety diffusion rates that are significantly below those of rain-fed areas in other parts of the World. The converse to this statement is of course, that sub-Saharan Africa is still home to significant diversity in traditional varieties and land races of food crops.

In the case of rain-fed environments in South Asia, Pandey et al. (2015) indicate that the adoption of modern rice varieties, specifically targeted for those environments, has increased substantially since 1998. By 2010 modern varieties occupied over 80 per cent of the rain-fed lowland rice growing area in the region, an average annual increase in adoption level in the range of 1–3 per cent between 1998 and 2010. The rapid spread of improved varieties in the stress prone environments raises concerns about the crowding out of crop diversity in favour of staple grain monoculture systems. A potential repeat of the Green Revolution experience could be witnessed in the irrigated lowlands of Asia.

Narrowing of Crop Genetic Diversity?

Crop genetic diversity broadly defined refers to the genetic variation embodied in seed and expressed when challenged by natural and human selection pressure. In applied genetics, diversity refers to the variance among alternative forms of a gene (alleles) at individual gene positions on a chromosome (loci), among several loci, among individual plants in a population or among populations (Brown et al., 1990). Diversity can be measured by accessions of seed held in gene banks, lines or populations utilised in crop-breeding programmes, or varieties cultivated by farmers (cultivars). But crop genetic diversity cannot be literally or entirely observed at any point in time; it can only be indicated with reference to a specific crop population and analytical perspective (Smale, 1997).

Whether the changes in crop varietal adoption induced by the Green Revolution have resulted in a narrowing of genetic diversity is an issue that remains largely unresolved due to conceptual and practical difficulties. Scientists disagree about what constitutes genetic narrowing or when such narrowing may have occurred. Several dimensions of diversity must be considered in this regard, including both the spatial and temporal variation between landraces and modern elite cultivars and the variation within modern cultivars (Fu, 2015).

According to Smale (1997), the adoption of modern varieties has been characterised first by a concentration on a few varieties followed by an expansion in their numbers as more varieties became available. Porceddu et al. (1988) described two major stages of genetic narrowing in wheat during modern times. The first occurred in the nineteenth century when scientific plant breeding responded to the demand for new plant types. Farming systems emerged that were based on the intensive use of land and labour, livestock production and the use of organic manure. Changes in cultivation methods favoured genotypes that diverted large amounts of photosynthates into the ear and grain.

Bell (1987) reports that the engineering innovations of the late nineteenth century led to the establishment of extensive wheat-growing areas in North America, Australia and parts of South America. Mechanisation of agriculture dictated uniformity in plant type.

According to Porceddu et al. (1988), a second stage of narrowing occurred in the twentieth century, when genes were introduced to produce major changes in plant type. Use of the dwarfing genes Rht1 and Rht2, for example, conferred a positive genotype-by-environment interaction in which yield increases proved greater given a certain combination of soil moisture, soil fertility and weed control. Varieties carrying these dwarfing genes were developed by Norman Borlaug with the national breeding programme in Mexico and later by the CIMMYT (International Maize and Wheat Improvement Center, Mexico). They became known as the Green Revolution wheat or modern wheat varieties.

As the process of modernisation proceeded and the offerings of scientific breeding programmes expanded, the pattern of concentration declined in many European and North American countries (Lupton, 1992; Dalrymple, 1988, cited in Smale, 1997). Similarly in the early years of the GR, the dominant cultivar occupied over 80 per cent of the wheat area in the Indian Punjab, but this share fell below 50 per cent by 1985. By 1990, the top five bread wheat cultivars covered approximately 36 per cent of the global wheat area planted to modern varieties (Smale, 1997).

Comparing counts of landraces and modern varieties over time may not provide a meaningful index of genetic narrowing. They also imply that even if reliable samples of the landraces originally cultivated in an area could be obtained, analyses comparing their genetic diversity might provide only part of the answer regarding genetic narrowing. While the landrace in the farmers' field is a heterogeneous population of plants, it is derived from generations of selection by local farmers and is therefore likely to be local in adaptation (Pingali and Smale, 2001).

Evenson and Gollin's (1997) summary of the history of rice breeding suggests a process of continual expansion and narrowing of the genetic pool. Organised breeding efforts probably date earlier than 1000 CE in China. Modern efforts can be traced to the late nineteenth century in several parts of Asia. In temperate East Asia, the first significant advances were made by Japanese farmers and scientists when they developed relatively short-statured and fertili-ser-responsive cultivars. Known as the *rono* varieties, these belonged to the *japonica* class of rice and were widely cultivated in Japan as early as the 1890s. During the Japanese occupation of Taiwan in the early part of the twentieth century, Japanese scientists sought to adapt these varieties to the more tropical conditions of Taiwan. At the same time, researchers in tropical Asia were seeking more pro-ductive varieties of rice from the *indica* and *javanica* classes of rice. After World War II, the Food and Agriculture Organization of the United Nations (FAO) initiated a programme to cross *indica* rice with *japonicas* as a means of increasing rice yields, culminating in the formation of IRRI and the GR varieties of rice.

To Vaughan and Chang (1992), genetic narrowing in modern rice began early in the twentieth century. Development projects, population increases and forest clearing in Asia were the primary causes of the loss of wild and cultivated rice landraces. In the Mekong Delta, the replace-ment of traditional deep-water rice by irrigated rice occurred with drainage and irrigation schemes that were introduced during the French colonial period. On the other hand, Ford-Lloyd et al. (2009) argue based on their analysis of data of 33 years of rice land race collections, from 1962 to 1995, that they have not detected any sig-nificant reduction of actual genetic diversity of traditional rice land races in use by farmers. They assert that it is possible to conclude that genetic diversity in rice maintained in situ has continued to survive throughout South and Southeast Asia through their study period. Part of the reason for high prevalence of land races is that modern variety use is very limited in the low-productive rice lands, such as drought-prone and flood-prone environments; in these areas traditional rice varieties continue to be used.

Goodman (1995) reports that the major portion of the variability now found in maize developed before European contact (c. 1500), and several of the most widely grown races, including the commercially important Corn Belt dents, developed later. During the 'corn show era' in the nineteenth century US, farmers exhibited their open-pollinated varieties locally and emphasis was placed on uniformity and confor-mity to an 'ideal type'. By the early 1950s, essentially all of the maize grown in the Corn Belt was double-cross hybrid. After the late 1950s, more and more farmers in the US Corn Belt grew single-cross rather than double-cross hybrids. Because single-cross seed must be produced on an inbred line, this type of selection contributed to a marked loss of variability in US breeding materials. To Goodman, a countervailing influence during the past 25 years has been the emphasis by public researchers on development of improved maize populations.

Not all scientists agree about what constitutes genetic narrowing or precisely when such narrowing has occurred. For instance, in contradiction with Porceddu et al. (1988), Hawkes (1983) cites the introduction of Rht1 and Rht2 genes into western wheat breeding lines as an example of how diversity has been broadened by scientific plant breeders. The Japanese line Norin 10 carried the dwarfing genes from the landrace Daruma, believed to be of Korean origin. Similarly, the efforts to increase rice yields by crossing *japonica* and *indica* classes of rice extended the gene pool accessible to rice breeders. As these examples suggest, in modern agriculture, today's broadening of the genetic pool in a plant breeding programme may lead to a narrowing of the breadth of materials grown by farmers precisely because such innovations often produce varieties that are popular.

Genetic Diversity within Modern Varieties

Part of the concern for genetic narrowing is based on the perception that, with time, conventional plant breeding practices inevitably restrict the genetic base of modern varieties. The evidence from studies on the parentage of modern varieties of the major staples lends little support to this view (Witcombe, 1999). In an analysis of genealogies of 1709 modern rice varieties, Evenson and Gollin (1997) found that while a variety released in the 1960s had three landraces in its pedigree, more recent releases have 25 or more. The complexity of rice pedigrees, in terms of parental combinations, geographical origin and number of ancestors, has expanded over time. A similar pattern has been shown for about 800 wheat varieties released in the developing world since the 1960s (Smale, 1997). The average number of distinct landraces found in bread wheat pedigrees grew from around 20 in the mid-1960s to about 50 in 1990.

Skovmand and de Lacy (1999) analysed the distance among coefficients of parentage for a historical set of CIMMYT wheat varieties over the past four decades. Their results show a rate of increase in genealogical diversity that is positive, but decreases over time, with marked expansion in genealogies from 1950 to 1967 and gradual flattening through the 1990s. If progenitors were recycled and reused, the distance among them would decrease over time and the slope of the line would be negative. Kazi et al. (2013) provide evidence that bringing genes from wild relatives of wheat into breeding populations more recently has enhanced the gene pool and its utilisation for managing various biotic and abiotic stresses.

Smale (2000) points out that evidence from a number of studies does not support the pessimistic view that the genetic base of modern wheat varieties is restricted and tends to decline with the introduction of modern varieties. She argues that genealogical analysis shows a significant positive trend in the number of distinct land race ancestors in the pedigrees of over a thousand varieties of spring bread wheat released in the developing world since the start of the Green Revolution in 1966.

Less evidence is available worldwide on trends in the pedigrees or ancestry of maize varieties than for rice and wheat, in part because that information is confidential in an increasingly privatised industry. Following the epidemic of corn blight in the US crop in 1970, the National Research Council (1972) concluded that the genetic base of maize in the US was sufficiently narrow to justify concern. Duvick (1984) found that during the 10 years following the 1970 epidemic, breeders had broadened their germplasm pools.

Molecular markers, like genealogies, can be used to construct indicators of the latent diversity in a set of crop populations. Using molecular markers, Donini et al. (2005) compared changes in genetic diversity between 'old' (1930s) versus 'modern' (1990s) UK bread wheat varieties and concluded that there is no objective evidence to support the assertion that modern plant breeding has reduced the genetic diversity of UK wheat. Molecular evidence for a set of CIMMYT wheat varieties indicates that genetic distance has been maintained among major parents and popular varieties over the past 30 years. Since many of the varieties of spring bread wheat grown in the developing world have a combination of CIMMYT and locally bred materials in their ancestry (Heisey et al., 1999), these data represent a lower bound on actual genetic diversity. Furthermore, the genetic diversity that is accessible to conventional plant breeders today includes not only spring bread wheat, of course, but also wheat types with different growing habit, close relatives and wild grasses (Smith et al., 2015). Techniques of biotechnology may traverse the species barriers faced by conventional breeders (Moreta et al., 2015).

Green Revolution 2.0 and Crop Biodiversity

GR 2.0 is already beginning to take place, and it is happening in low-income countries as well as in emerging economies (Pingali, 2012). Low-income countries, many of them in sub-Saharan Africa, that have been bypassed by the Green Revolution, still face chronic hunger and poverty. They continue to be plagued by the age-old constraints to enhancing productivity growth, such as the lack of technology, poor market infrastructure, appropriate institutions and an enabling policy environment (Binswanger and McCalla, 2010). Emerging economies, including much of Asia where gains from the first GR were concentrated, are well on their way toward agricultural modernisation and structural transformation (Timmer, 2005). The challenge for agriculture in the emerging economies is to integrate smallholders into value chains, maintain their competitiveness and close the inter-regional income gap (Pingali, 2010).

Pingali (2012) argues that a confluence of factors has come together in recent years to generate renewed interest in agriculture and spur the early stages of GR 2.0. In the low-income countries, continued levels of food deficits and the reliance on food aid and food imports have reintroduced agriculture as an engine of growth on the policy agenda. African leaders have acknowledged the critical role of agriculture in their development process and that lack of investment in the sector would only leave them further behind. The CAADP[2] declaration of 2006 and resulting pledges by African Heads of State to increase agricultural investments demonstrated their commitment to improve the agriculture sector. There is also an increasing awareness of the detrimental impacts of climate change on food security, especially for tropical agriculture systems in low-income countries (Byerlee et al., 2009).

In the emerging economies, growing private sector interest in investing in the agricultural sector has created an agricultural renaissance (Pingali, 2010). Supermarkets are spreading rapidly across urban areas in emerging economies and are encouraging national and multi-national agro-business investments along the fresh produce value chains in these countries (Reardon and Minten, 2011). Consequently staple crop monoculture systems popularised by the Green Revolution are diversifying into high-value horticulture and livestock production. Despite these positive developments, inter-regional differences in productivity and poverty persist in many emerging economies. Rising demand for feed and biofuels, as well as technological advances in breeding for stress tolerance could result in a revitalisation of the marginal areas. The rapid rise of hybrid maize production in Eastern India is a case in point (Gulati and Dixon, 2008). Finally, at the global level, the food price crisis of 2008, sustained high prices, and more recent peaks observed in 2011 and 2012 have brought agriculture back onto the global and national agendas (FAO, 2011).

What Are the Implications for Crop Biodiversity?

As the Green Revolution 2.0 spreads to regions that have been bypassed by the original Green Revolution, familiar concerns about the consequence for sustaining crop biodiversity will emerge. In order to meet the unabated rise in demand for food due to growing populations and rising incomes, the GR 2.0 would need to enhance productivity both on the favourable lands as well as the more marginal production environments. Continued focus on yield-enhancing technical change is the primary mechanism for ensuring that lands will continue to be spared for non-agricultural uses, including for biodiversity conservation. Balmford et al. (2005) state that 'Conservationists should be as concerned about future agricultural yields as they are about population growth and rising per capita consumption.' Agricultural R&D can help in the quest for sustainable biodiversity conservation.

Rising incomes and the consequent decline in per capita consumption of staple cereals, such as rice and wheat, provide an opportunity for moving away from monoculture systems and toward more diversified cropping systems (Pingali, 2015). This would be particularly true in the favourable production environments given their better market connectivity and irrigation and power infrastructure. However, we may see the reverse for the less favourable environments, the movement toward monoculture systems, with the advent of improved stress tolerant varieties, especially when there are only a few successful ones. Pandey et al. (2015) point to the spread of 'mega' varieties, in other words single varieties of rice that cover large areas in South Asia. One such variety, 'Swarna', has spread widely throughout the rain-fed rice lands in India, to the extent of 30 per cent acreage in some Eastern Indian states. The successful spread of a few rain-fed varieties extend the concern about the narrowing of crop genetic diversity from the favourable environments to the unfavourable ones.

What about genetic diversity within varieties – will it rise or fall? The integration of cereal land races into modern breeding programmes could alleviate some of the risk of loss in genetic diversity within improved varieties (Smith et al., 2015). It could also lead to the incorporation of positive traits into new varieties or breeding populations for more sustainable agricultural production. In particular they have potential as sources of novel genes for disease and abiotic stress resistance, or for enhancing nutrient use efficiency and improving the nutritional quality of staple grains (Newton et al., 2010). Continued genetic improvement does not necessarily lead to loss of genetic diversity in areas where modern varieties dominate – especially when access to germplasm is relatively unrestricted and innovative plant breeding strategies may be employed. Access to diverse sources of germplasm, including land races and wild relatives, is therefore of great importance to the success of public and private breeding programmes and the supply of varieties in modern agriculture (Pingali and Smale, 2001).

What is the future of land races/traditional varieties? The coexistence of modern varieties and landraces of particularly crops may persist where market-based incentives exist. For example, in Asia, traditional varieties are generally of higher quality and fetch premium prices in the market. Thailand still grows low-yielding traditional rain-fed varieties extensively for the export market. Basmati rice production has expanded significantly in India and Pakistan, both for domestic as well as export markets. Traditional *japonica* rices have risen in popularity across East Asia and are sold at a substantial premium. Quinoa, a crop native to the Andean Mountains, has become very popular in the developed world due to its nutritional qualities. Once a neglected crop, it is now receiving a lot of attention from Andean farmers as an income growth opportunity (Massawe et al., 2016). Teff from Ethiopia has been making recent inroads into developed country diets. See Massawe et al. (2016) for a review of under utilised crops that have become or could become attractive to Western consumers due to their nutritive qualities.

Market-based incentives could play a major role in reviving the prospects for under utilised crops and ensuring their in situ conservation.

Conclusions

Agricultural intensification and the adoption of modern varieties of the
major staple crops led to the ubiquitous monoculture systems in the
favourable production environments across the developing world. The
lower productive rain-fed environments, on the other hand, continue to
maintain diversity of crops grown, such as traditional millets and root
crops. These environments have also sustained the cultivation of landraces of rice, wheat and maize. Narrowing of crop genetic diversity in
the GR areas has been averted to some extent by the replacement of the
first-generation modern varieties with second- and third-generation
varieties in more recent decades. The expansion in the numbers of
varieties available through crop-breeding programmes has reduced
the risk that intensive production systems would concentrate on
a few dominant varieties. Modern plant breeding has also helped
expand the genetic base of modern varieties by incorporating genes
from landraces and wild relatives of staple grains into the breeding
populations.

This paper argues that areas that have been bypassed by the original
GR are now witnessing intensification and agricultural productivity
growth. This GR 2.0 is being observed in parts of sub-Saharan Africa
as well as in the unfavourable environments of South Asia. Improved
varieties of sorghum, millet, cassava and tropical maize are being increasingly adopted by African smallholders. In South Asia, rice varieties that
are tolerant to drought and to flooding have made major inroads into the
stress prone environments that were bypassed by the original GR.

While the food security benefits of the GR 2.0 are obvious, there are
significant concerns about the consequences for crop biodiversity. The
spread of improved varieties of the traditional African crops could lead
to the encroachment of monoculture systems in areas where multi-crop
farming systems sustain diversity and landraces. In South Asia, the
spread of a few 'mega' varieties of rice that are stress tolerant could
lead to the risk of genetic narrowing in rain-fed environments where
multiple landraces are cultivated today. As GR 2.0 proceeds it would be
important to learn from original GR in terms of the appropriate
mechanisms to balance food security and crop biodiversity concerns.

Acknowledgements

Research support from Megan Witwer and helpful comments from Mathew Abraham are gratefully acknowledged.

Notes

1. This section builds on material presented in Pingali and Smale (2001).
2. The Comprehensive Africa Agriculture Development Programme (CAADP) is the agricultural program of the New Partnership for Africa's Development (NEPAD), an initiative of the African Union.

References

Alene, A. D., Abdoulaye, T., Rusike, J., Manyong, V. & Walker, T. S. 2015. The effectiveness of crop improvement programmes from the perspectives of varietal output and adoption: Cassava, cowpea, soybean and yam in sub-Saharan Africa and maize in West and Central Africa. In T. S. Walker & J. Alwang (Eds.), *Crop Improvement, Adoption, and Impact of improved varieties in Food Crops in Sub-Saharan Africa*. Wallingford, UK: CAB International.

Balmford, A., Green, R. E. & Scharlemann, J. P. W. 2005. Sparing land for nature: Exploring the potential impact of changes in agricultural yield on the area needed for crop production. *Global Change Biology*, 11(10): 1594–1605.

Bell, G. D. H. 1987. The history of wheat cultivation. In F. G. H. Lupton (Ed.), *Wheat Breeding: Its Scientific Basis*. London: Chapman & Hall.

Binswanger-Mkhize, H. & McCalla., A. F. 2010. The changing context and prospects for agricultural and rural development in Africa. In P. L. Pingali & R. E. Evenson (Eds.), *Handbook of Agricultural Economics*, Vol. 4, 4th ed.: 3571–3712. Oxford: Elsevier.

Birol, E., Villalba, E. & Smale, M. 2007. Farmer preferences for milpa diversity and genetically modified maize in Mexico: A latent class approach. IFPRI Discussion Paper 726. Washington, DC: The International Food Policy Research Institute.

Boserup, E. 1981. *Population and Technological Change: A Study of Long Term Change*. Chicago: Chicago University Press.

Brown, A. H., Clegg, M. T., Kahler, A. L. & Weir, B. S. (Eds.). 1990. *Plant Population Genetics, Breeding and Genetic Resources*. Sunderland, MA: Sinauer Associates.

Byerlee, D., de Janvry, A. & Sadoulet, E. 2009. Agriculture for development: Toward a new paradigm. *Annual Review of Resource Economics*, 1(1): 15–31.

Dalrymple, D. 1988. Changes in wheat varieties and yields in the United States, 1919–1984. *Agricultural History*, 62(4): 20–36.

Donini, P., Law, J., Koebner, R., Reeves, J. & Cooke, R. 2005. The impact of breeding on genetic diversity and erosion in bread wheat. *Plant Genetic Resources: Characteristics and Utilization*, 3: 391–399.

Duvick, D. N. 1984. Genetic diversity in major farm crops on the farm and in reserve. *Economic Botany*, 38(2): 161–178.

Evenson, R. E. & Gollin, D. 1997. Genetic resources, international organizations, and improvement in rice varieties. *Economic Development and Cultural Change*, 45(3): 471–500.

    2003. Assessing the impact of the Green Revolution, 1960 to 2000. *Science*, 300(5620): 758–762.

FAO. 2011. *The State of Food Insecurity in the World*. Rome: FAO.

Ford-Lloyd, B. V, Brar, D., Khush, G. S., Jackson, M. T. & Virk, P. S. 2009. Genetic erosion over time of rice landrace agrobiodiversity. *Plant Genetic Resources*, 7(02): 163–168.

Fu, Y. B. 2015. Understanding crop genetic diversity under modern plant breeding. *Theoretical and Applied Genetics*, 128(11): 2131–2142.

Fuglie, K. & Marder, J. 2015. The diffusion and impact of improved food crop varieties in sub-Saharan Africa. In T. S. Walker & J. Alwang (Eds.), *Crop Improvement, Adoption, and Impact of Improved Varieties in Food Crops in Sub-Saharan Africa*. Wallingford, UK: CAB International.

Goodman, M. M. 1995. The evolution of crop plants. In J. Smartt & N. Simmonds (Eds.), *Maize*: 193–202. New York: Wiley.

Gulati, A. & Dixon, J. 2008. *Maize in Asia: Changing Markets and Incentives*. New Delhi: Academic Foundation.

Hawkes, J. G. 1983. *The Diversity of Crop Plants*. Cambridge MA: Harvard University Press.

Hayami, Y. & Ruttan, V. W. 1985. *Agricultural Development*, 2nd ed. Baltimore: Johns Hopkins University Press.

Heisey, P. W. & Lantican, Dubin, H. J. 1999. Assessing the benefits of international wheat breeding research: An overview of the global wheat impacts study. In *CIMMYT 1998–99 World Wheat Facts and Trends. Global Wheat Research in a Changing World: Challenges and Achievements*. Mexico City: CIMMYT.

Kazi, G. A., Rasheed, A. & Mujeeb-Kazi, A. 2013. Biotic stress and crop improvement: A wheat focus around novel strategies. In R. K. Hakeem,

P. Ahmad & M. Ozturk (Eds.), *Crop Improvement: New Approaches and Modern Techniques*: 239–267. Boston: Springer.

Lupton, F. G. H. 1992. Wheat varieties cultivated in Europe. In F. G. H. Lupton (Ed.), *Changes in Varietal Distribution of Cereals in Central and Western Europe: Agroecological Atlas of Cereal Growing in Europe, Vol. 4*. Wageningen, Netherlands: Wageningen University.

Massawe, F., Mayes, M. & Cheng, A. 2016. Crop diversity: An unexploited treasure trove for food security. *Trends in Plant Science*, 21: 365–368.

Moreta, D. E., Mathur, P. N., van Zonneveld, M., Amaya, K., Arango, J., Selvaraj, M. G. & Dedicova, B. 2015. Current Issues in Cereal Crop Biodiversity. In J. Mukherjee (Ed.), *Biotechnological Applications of Biodiversity: Advances in Biochemical Engineering/Biotechnology*, vol. 147: 1–35. Berlin: Springer.

National Research Council. 1972. *Genetic Vulnerability of Major Crops*. Washington, DC: National Academy of Science.

Newton, A. C., Akar, T., Baresel, J. P., Bebeli, P. J., Bettencourt, E., Bladenopoulos, K. V, Czembor, J. H., Fasoula, D. A., Katsiotis, A., Koutis, K., Koutsika-Sotiriou, M., Kovacs, G., Larsson, H., Pinheiro de Carvalho, M. A. A., Rubiales, D., Russel, J., Dos Santos, T. M. M. & Vaz Patto, M. C. 2010. Cereal landraces for sustainable agriculture: A review. *Agronomy for Sustainable Development*, 30 (2): 237–269.

Pandey, S., Velasco, M. L. & Yamano, T. 2015. Scientific strength in rice improvement programmes, varietal outputs and adoption of improved varieties in South Asia. In T. S. Walker & J. Alwang (Eds.), *Crop Improvement, Adoption, and Impact of Improved Varieties in Food Crops in Sub-Saharan Africa*. CGIAR & CABI.

Pingali, P. 2010. Agriculture renaissance: Making 'agriculture for development' work in the 21st century. *Handbook of Agricultural Economics*, 4: 3867–3894.

2012. Green Revolution: Impacts, limits, and the path ahead. *Proceedings of the National Academy of Sciences*, 109(31): 12302–12308.

2015. Agricultural policy and nutrition outcomes – getting beyond the preoccupation with staple grains. *Food Security*, 7(3): 583–591.

Pingali, P. & Heisey, P. W. 2001. Cereal-crop productivity in developing countries: Past trends and future prospects. In J. M. Alston, P. G. Pardey & M. Taylor (Eds.), *Agricultural Science Policy*. Washington, DC: IFPRI & Johns Hopkins University Press.

Pingali, P. & Smale, M. 2001. Agriculture, industrialized. In *Encyclopedia of Biodiversity*, vol. 1: 85–97. New York: Academic Press.

Porceddu, E. C., Ceoloni, D. L., Tanzarella, O. A. & Scarascia, G. T. M. 1988. Genetic resources and plant breeding: Problems and prospects. In *The Plant Breeding International, Cambridge Special Lecture.* Cambridge: Institute of Plant Science Research.

Reardon, T. & Minten, B. 2011. Surprised by supermarkets: Diffusion of modern food retail in India. *Journal of Agribusiness in Developing and Emerging Economies*, 1(2): 134–161.

Skovmand, B. & DeLacy, I. 1999. Parentage of a historical set of CIMMYT wheats. In *Annual Meeting Abstracts*: 165. Madison, WI: American Society of Agronomy.

Smale, M. 1997. The Green Revolution and wheat genetic diversity: Some unfounded assumptions. *World Development*, 25(8): 1257–1269.

2000. Economic incentives for conserving crop genetic diversity on farms: Issues and evidence. Paper presented at the meetings of the International Agricultural Economics Association, Berlin.

Smith, S., Bubeck, D., Nelson, B., Stanek, J. & Gerke, J. 2015. Genetic diversity and modern plant breeding biotechnology. In R. M. Ahuja & M. S. Jain (Eds.), *Genetic Diversity and Erosion in Plants: Indicators and Prevention*: 55–88. Cham: Springer International.

Stevenson, J. R., Villoria, N., Byerlee, D., Kelley, T. & Maredia, M. 2013. Green Revolution research saved an estimated 18 to 27 million hectares from being brought into agricultural production. *Proceedings of the National Academy of Sciences*, 110(21): 8363–8368.

Timmer, C. P. 2005. Agriculture and pro-poor growth: An Asian perspective. Working Paper 63. Washington, DC: Centre for Global Development.

Vaughan, D. A. & Chang, T.-T. 1992. In situ conservation of rice genetic resources. *Economic Botany*, 46(4): 368–383.

Walker, T. S. & Alwang, J. (Eds.). 2015. *Crop Improvement, Adoption, and Impact of Improved Varieties in Food Crops in Sub-Saharan Africa.* Wallingford, UK: CAB International.

Witcombe, J. R. 1999. Does plant breeding lead to a loss of genetic diversity? In D. Wood & J. Lenne (Eds.), *Agrobiodiversity: Characterization, Utilization and Management*: 245–272. Wallingford, UK: CAB International.

7 | Population

The Current State and Future Prospects

JOHN BONGAARTS

World population size increased at a slow and uneven pace for centuries before the onset of the Industrial Revolution, and did not reach 1 billion until about 1800. The modern expansion of human numbers started then, but its pace was still modest for the next 150 years with the world total rising to 2.5 billion in 1950 . During the second half of the twentieth century, however, population growth rates accelerated to historically unprecedented levels, especially in Africa, Asia and Latin America. As a result, world population size nearly tripled to 7.3 billion by 2015. This ongoing population expansion is expected to continue for several more decades reaching 11.2 billion at the end of this century. The future addition of four billion more people to the planet will have wide-ranging and potentially adverse implications for human welfare and the natural environment.

This study consists of three parts. First, population trends for the world and its main regions will be summarised, including projections of population size, growth, fertility, mortality, urbanisation and age distribution. The second part summarises policy options in ageing societies. The third part discusses the role of responsible parenthood and declining fertility in improving human welfare in the developing world.

Population Trends

Population Size

Long-range trends in population size typically show a logistic pattern. For much of human history, population growth was absent or very slow. In the more recent past, waves of countries have gone through socio-economic and demographic transitions. Countries' population growth rates first accelerated, then declined, until population size levelled off at near its likely maximum. This process is referred to as the *demographic transition* which usually takes place over the course of

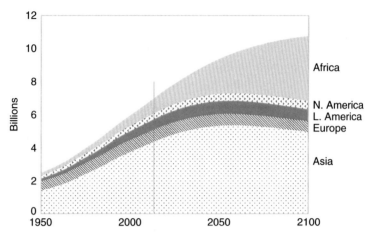

Figure 7.1 World population estimates and projections by region. Data from United Nations, Department of Economic and Social Affairs, Population Division (2015).

a century or more and is accompanied by a development process that transforms agricultural societies into industrial ones. Before the transition's onset, population growth fluctuated near zero as high birth rates more or less offset the high death rates typical of traditional agrarian societies that preceded the Industrial Revolution. After the completion of the transition, population growth was again near zero as birth and death rates both reached low levels. During the intervening transition period, population growth was positive as the death rate dropped before the birth rate. Over the course of the transition, population size of countries multiplied many times.

The first demographic transitions began in the early nineteenth century with declines in death rates in the now economically developed parts of the world (e.g., Europe, North America). Large declines in birth rates followed in the late nineteenth and early part of the twentieth centuries. The transitions in these countries are now more or less complete. Figure 7.1 and Table 7.1 present estimates of the population size of the world and major regions from 1950 to 2015 and projections made by the UN to 2100 (United Nations, Department of Economic and Social Affairs, Population Division, 2015). The population of the developed world (Europe, North America, Japan and Australia/New Zealand), which are referred to as the more developed countries, or MDCs, today stands

Table 7.1 *Population estimates (1950–2015) and projections (2015–2100), by region*

	Population (billions)			Ratio
	1950	2015	2100	2100/2015
Africa	0.23	1.19	4.39	3.70
Sub-Saharan	0.18	0.96	3.93	4.09
Asia	1.40	4.39	4.89	1.11
China	0.54	1.38	1.00	0.73
Latin America	0.17	0.63	0.72	1.14
Europe	0.55	0.74	0.65	0.87
Northern America	0.17	0.36	0.50	1.40
Less developed	1.72	6.10	9.94	1.63
More developed	0.81	1.25	1.28	1.02
World	2.53	7.35	11.21	1.53

Source. United Nations, Department of Economic and Social Affairs, Population Division (2015).

at 1.25 billion, up from 0.81 billion in 1950. The population of these countries is expected to remain virtually the same size over the remainder of this century as the continued population growth in North America offsets the declines expected in Europe and Japan. The MDCs are a shrinking part of the world population. In 1950 the MDCs represented 32 per cent of the world population; today this proportion stands at 17 per cent and by 2100 it is expected to be just 11 per cent.

The demographic transitions in Africa, Asia and Latin America (called the less developed countries or LDCs) started later and are still under way, but they are expected to end over the coming decades. Aside from the differences in timing between the more and less developed regions, the transitions in the LDCs have produced more rapid population growth rates in mid-transitions. In 2015 the population of the LDCs stood at 6.1 billion, representing the large majority of the world population of 7.3 billion. The population of Asia (4.4 billion) is much larger than that of Africa (1.2 billion) or Latin America (0.6 billion).

Since 1950, growth in LDCs has been very rapid with population size nearly quadrupling from 1.7 to 6.1 billion. Projections to 2100 see the LDCs adding a further 3.8 billion people (95 per cent of the projected world population growth). Populations in Asia, Latin America and North Africa are approaching the end of their transitions and will therefore experience only limited further growth. In contrast, the population of sub-Saharan Africa is expected to quadruple again by 2100 (from 0.96 to 3.93 billion). Fully 3 billion of the 4 billion future growth in the world population will therefore occur in sub-Saharan Africa, which is the region least prepared to meet the needs of their citizens (e.g., health clinics, infrastructure, school facilities) from an immense population increase over such a short period of time.

All population projections contain a degree of uncertainty. The UN has a consistent track record of making accurate projections. However, the further out the projections go into the future, the greater the likelihood that the assumptions underlying the projections will deviate from the eventual reality. The results presented in Table 7.1 and Figure 7.1 are for the medium – or most likely – projection variant, which assumes convergence of regional fertility levels to around two births per woman and continuing declines in mortality resulting in a global population of 11.2 billion by 2100. The uncertainty surrounding these median trajectories is summarised by the 95 per cent probability interval around this median. For example, there is a 95 per cent probability that the global population will be between 9.5 and 13.3 billion in 2100.

Population Growth Rate

The rate at which populations around the world are growing varies widely among regions and countries. As shown in Figure 7.2 in 2015 the highest growth rates were found in sub-Saharan Africa where rates exceed 3 per cent per year in a number of countries, while the lowest rates are negative in a number of East European and East Asian countries. Growth rates are highest in the least developed countries and near or below zero in the most developed countries. This is as expected because many LDCs have not yet reached the end of their demographic transitions, while most MDCs are post-transitional. A constant population growth rate of 3 per cent per year will result in a doubling of the population size about every 25 years.

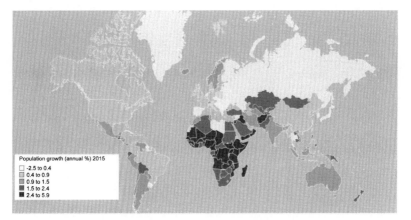

Figure 7.2 Population growth rate in 2015 (percentage per year). Data from World Development Indicators DataBank of the World Bank, http://databank .worldbank.org/data/source/world-development-indicators.

By definition a country's growth rate at a given point in time equals the birth rate minus the death rate plus (a usually small) net immigration rate. Birth and death rates are in turn largely determined by levels of fertility and mortality in the population. The projections of population size of the world and its major regions are driven by assumptions made about future trends in fertility and mortality which are discussed next.

Fertility

For most of human history before the Industrial Revolution, women did not deliberately regulate their fertility. As a result, average fertility was high, typically around six or seven births per woman, and women bore children throughout their reproductive lives. This high fertility was necessary to offset high mortality and to insure population survival.

Declines in fertility first began in the more developed countries in the nineteenth century as societies experienced rapid economic and social changes such as industrialisation, urbanisation, changing occupational structure, increased education and improved health care. These changes raised the cost of children (e.g., for education) and reduced their economic value (e.g., for labour and old age security), and couples

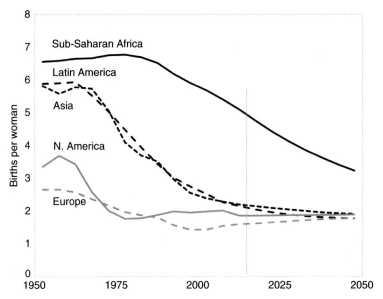

Figure 7.3 Fertility estimates and projections by region. Data from United Nations, Department of Economic and Social Affairs, Population Division (2015).

began to self-regulate family size. The declines in mortality that preceded declines in fertility were a precondition for fertility decline because parents needed to be assured that children would survive. The fertility transition in the MDCs was complete by the 1970s when fertility fell to around two births per woman.

The fertility transitions in the LDCs started later as shown in Figure 7.3 which presents estimates from 1950 to 2015 and projections to 2050 as measured by the total fertility rate (TFR), i.e., the average number of births over a woman's life time assuming current conditions. In the 1950s the TFRs in Asia, Latin America and across Africa were high and virtually stable at around six to seven births per woman on average. This high level of natural fertility was similar to the levels observed in the pre-transitional MDCs. In the late 1960s, rapid declines in fertility started nearly simultaneously in Asia and Latin America. In contrast, sub-Saharan Africa has experienced only limited reproductive change. As a result of these divergent past trends, fertility levels in 2010–2015 differed widely among regions from a high TFR of near five births per woman in Africa, to 2.2 in Asia and Latin America.

Average TFRs in Europe and North America reached relatively low levels in the early 1950s and (aside from a brief baby boom in the 1950s and early 1960s) has since declined to 1.9 in North America and to 1.6 in Europe. The decline in TFRs from six to just over two births per woman in Asia and Latin America in the past half-century has been very rapid by historical standards.

UN projections for fertility in the coming decades assume that TFRs will eventually stabilise at around two births per woman in all regions (see Figure 7.3). The TFRs in Asia and Latin America are now close to this level, but Africa's fertility transition is on a much slower trajectory. High fertility therefore remains the main driver of future population growth in Africa. In contrast, the already low TFRs of Europe and North America are expected to remain slightly below two births per woman and this is the main driver of population decline in a number of MDCs.

Mortality and Life Expectancy

Before the eighteenth century, mortality crises – epidemics, famines, wars – were frequent, average life expectancy was only about 30 years, and half of newborns failed to survive the first few years of life. One of the most notable achievements of modern industrial societies is the decline in preventable mortality resulting in the large rise in human longevity to about 80 years today.

The mortality transition started in Northern Europe early in the nineteenth century, and life expectancy rose to around 50 years by 1900. Several factors contributed to this improvement in longevity: public health measures reduced exposure to water- and food-borne diseases, better nutrition improved resistance to disease, and inoculation and vaccination prevented certain infectious diseases. Mortality decline accelerated after 1900 driven by a new set of factors: the institutional acceptance of the germ theory of disease led to measures to reduce exposure and transmission, and the development of antibiotics brought most infectious diseases under control. By the 1950s life expectancy in the most advanced countries had risen to 70 years and all but a few per cent of infants survived the first years of life. Today, life expectancy is 77 years in Europe and 80 years in North America. Infectious diseases are now rare and deaths are mostly due to chronic diseases among the old – for example, heart disease, cancer, diabetes.

Progress is being made in the treatment of these diseases and innovations in medicine, biotechnology and drug development will likely continue. Nevertheless, it is likely that future improvements in life expectancy will be less rapid than over the past century.

The mortality transition occurred later in the LDCs. Mortality declines were modest during the first half of the twentieth century and by the early 1950s life expectancy was only 38 years in Africa and 42 years in Asia (Figure 7.4). Latin America fared better with a life expectancy of 51 years. Over the past half-century mortality conditions in large parts of the developing world have improved rapidly due to rising incomes, improved nutrition levels, access to medical care and especially the implementation of public health measures and the availability of antibiotics and other drugs. Today, life expectancy in Latin America (75) and Asia (72) is similar to that of Europe in the 1970s. Africa still lags even though life expectancy has risen to 60 over the past half-century. Low incomes, lack of access to adequate health care and the still substantial burden of infectious diseases (including HIV/AIDS) are largely responsible.

Projections for life expectancy to 2100 assume continued improvements in all regions. The MDC trajectory is expected to reach near 90 years. Advances in life expectancy in the LDCs are expected to be more rapid than in the MDCs, thus slowly closing the gap between these regions.

Urbanisation

The development of agriculture and the domestication of plants and animals about 12,000 years BCE led to the growth of urban centres for trading surplus agricultural products, goods and services. Most people, however, continued to live in rural settings and engaged largely in subsistence agriculture for local consumption. The current era of rapid urbanisation began with the onset of the Industrial Revolution. Employment opportunities in the expanding manufacturing and service sectors were often located in towns and surplus labour from the rural areas moved to cities in search of jobs and a better life. Urban areas were also attractive because they provided higher incomes, better access to schools, health care, social services and cultural opportunities.

Driven by these multiple forces, urbanisation proceeded at a steady pace during the nineteenth and twentieth centuries in the MDCs, but

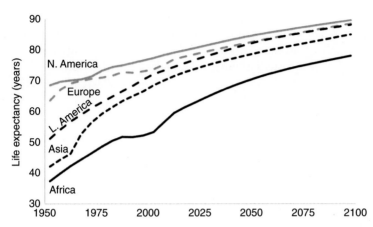

Figure 7.4 Life expectancy estimates and projections by region. Data from United Nations, Department of Economic and Social Affairs, Population Division (2015).

little changed in the rest of the world until the second half of the twentieth century. In 1950 the percentage of the world population living in urban areas reached 29 per cent, ranging from over 50 per cent in the MDCs, to just 15 per cent in Africa and Asia (United Nations, Department of Economic and Social Affairs, Population Division, 2014). Over the past half-century urbanisation has proceeded at a record pace with the world average reaching 54 per cent in 2014, and the urban proportions more than doubled in Africa and Asia. These trends are expected to continue in the coming decades with the urban proportion reaching 85 per cent in the MDCs. Africa and Asia remain less urban but nevertheless are expected to reach around 60 per cent by 2050. By the end of this century the global rural-to-urban transition should be nearly complete with a large majority of people living in urban areas.

In recent decades the combined effects of overall population growth and rising urbanisation produced extremely rapid growth in the size of urban populations of the less developed countries. This expansion has been difficult to absorb in the poorest countries where urban infrastructure has not kept pace with population growth, resulting in continuous traffic jams, lack of public transportation, clean water and sanitation and overcrowded schools and health facilities. The chronic paucity of housing has led to the explosive growth of slum areas where the poor and marginalised live in extremely difficult conditions with limited access to infrastructure and services.

The rapid expansion of urban areas has conversely contributed to a reduction in the growth of the rural population due to outmigration. In fact, the size of the rural population of the world is projected to remain stable for the next few decades, despite rural women typically having a higher TFR than urban women. This trend will reduce direct population pressures on some rural environments, but not those required to produce food for urban consumption. This trend also implies that a large majority of the 3.8 billion people expected to be added to the less developed world in future decades will end up in cities that are often poorly prepared to absorb this large influx of new inhabitants.

Population Ageing

Population ageing is a relatively new demographic phenomenon because for most of human history populations were young and lives were short. Population ageing is in part caused by increases in life expectancy which allows individuals to live to higher ages. But an even more important cause of population ageing is a decline in fertility. With fewer births, younger generations are smaller relative to older generations, thus raising the average age of the population. This ageing has important socio-economic consequences as discussed below.

The pattern of ageing can be examined by dividing the population into three age groups: the young (aged 0–14), the working-ages (15–64) and the old (65+). Figure 7.5 plots regional estimates of the proportions of the population in each of these age groups from 1950 to 2015 and projections to 2050. Differences between regions in 2015 are related to the stage of the demographic transition and in particular to levels and trends in fertility in recent decades. For example, Africa, which is still in mid-transition, has a much larger proportion under age 15 (41 per cent) than Europe (16 per cent). At the other end of the age spectrum the proportion aged 65+ ranges from 18 per cent in Europe to 3 per cent in Africa. These differences are largely explained by the higher level of fertility in the latter than in the former.

The main trend evident in Figure 7.5 is that the proportion of the old rises over time and the proportion of the young declines. In all regions except Africa the proportion of 65+ is expected to reach about

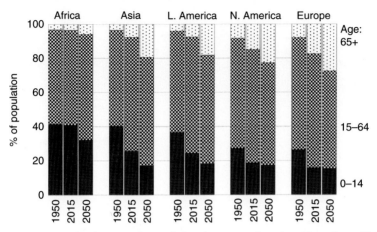

Figure 7.5 Distribution of population by age and region. Data from United Nations, Department of Economic and Social Affairs, Population Division (2015).

30 per cent in 2100. In some countries with low fertility and high life expectancy the proportion 65+ could reach over 35 per cent.

The young and the old tend not to be economically active and are therefore dependent on the working population for income, food, shelter, education, health care and social security. As a result, increases in the proportion of the population that is dependent has significant social and economic consequences. A simple indicator – called the age-dependency ratio (ADR) – summarises this. The ADR in a given year equals the ratio of the dependent population (those aged below 15 years and those aged 65 years and above) to the working-age population (aged 15–64). This ratio aims to measure how many 'dependents' there are for each person in the 'productive' age group. The ratio is rather crude because not every person below 15 or aged 65 and over is a dependent and not every person between ages 15 and 64 is productive, but it has been widely used to summarise trends in the age composition.

Over the course of a demographic transition, the ADR shows a characteristic pattern of change. Figure 7.6 presents this pattern for different regions from 1950 to 2015 and projections from 2015 to 2100. The figure does not capture the full transition for each region, because Europe and North America were already in their late demographic transition stage before 1950 and Africa is still early. However,

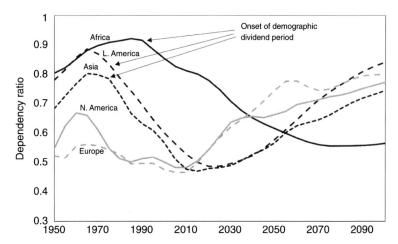

Figure 7.6 Age-dependency ratio estimates and projections by region. Data from United Nations, Department of Economic and Social Affairs, Population Division (2015).

the patterns for Asia and Latin America capture the critical central transition period. Early in the transition the ADR typically rises slightly, as improvements in health increase child survival and raise the number of young people. Next, the ADR falls sharply as declines in fertility reduce the proportion of the population under age 15. A few decades later the ADR rises again when the older population rises.

These fluctuations in the ADR over time have important economic consequences. The drop in the ADR in mid-transition (following the onset of the fertility decline) leads to a boost of GDP/capita growth rate. This effect is often referred to as the 'demographic dividend' (Bloom et al., 2003; Lee and Mason, 2006). Economic growth is stimulated by an increase in the size of the labour force relative to dependents and by increased savings, provided the right conditions are in place (e.g., investments in education and job creation). Asia and Latin America benefited from this decline in the ADR between 1970 and 2015. A study of the East Asian tiger economies concluded that fully a third of the rapid economic growth in these countries in the late twentieth century was due to their ability to harness the demographic dividend (Bloom and Williamson, 1998).

Toward the end of the transition the age structure turns economically unfavourable as the proportion of the population aged 65 and over rises. In Europe and North America the dependency ratio started rising around 2010 and is expected to rise substantially further over the next few decades. This trend is also evident in Asia and Latin America after 2025.

These trends in the ADR are sufficiently important in terms of socio-economic development that governments in countries with high fertility try to encourage the demographic dividend by lowering fertility and governments in MDCs try to minimise the effects of population ageing as discussed next.

Policy Options in Ageing Societies

The potential adverse effects of population ageing came to the attention of policy makers when TFRs in most MDCs dropped below two births per woman in the 1970s and 1980s. This trend was unexpected. The conventional wisdom, that TFRs at the end of the transition would stabilise at just above two (which would lead to a stable population size), proved to be wrong. Even a small deviation below this level leads to substantially more population ageing. In the 1990s the OECD and World Bank prepared influential reports calling for action to counteract the adverse effects from population ageing (World Bank, 1994; OECD, 1998).

The rapid ongoing and projected increase in the elderly population is of concern because it threatens the sustainability of public pension and health care systems. This is especially the case because most of these systems are pay-as-you-go, i.e., current benefits are paid for by contributions from current workers. As noted above, the proportion aged 65+ is projected to reach near one in three in the most rapidly ageing societies. This implies fewer than two persons between 15 and 65 for everyone aged 65 and above.

The first response of governments has been to make the pension and health care systems more sustainable. A wide range of measures are available, including reducing benefits, raising taxes or contributions, increasing the age at eligibility and reducing incentives for early retirement. Most MDCs have now implemented at least some of these adjustments. As a result, sustainability prospects have improved, but the situation remains highly precarious, especially in countries with the lowest fertility, e.g., Japan and Italy.

Since population ageing is in large part due to low levels of fertility, MDC governments also have strengthened their family policies. These policies were encouraged by the fact that a substantial proportion of women have fewer children than they want. This gap between actual and desired family size is largely the consequence of difficulties women face in combining childbearing with participation in the paid labour force. Family policies therefore implement measures to address this issue including subsidised childcare, reduced taxes for families with children and paid parental leave.

The effects of such policies on fertility have been relatively modest (up to a few tenths of a birth per woman) but even small increases in fertility lead to substantial reductions in population ageing. The scope and generosity of family policies differ widely between countries. The countries with the highest fertility in Europe (France, Netherlands and Scandinavia) have the most generous family policies.

Another demographic option to offset ageing is to allow higher levels of immigration. This option will not be discussed further here.

Responsible Parenthood

Responsible parenthood is a central concept in the teachings of the Catholic Church on marriage and the family. In a 1994 letter to the United Nations Saint John Paul II explained that responsible parenthood 'is not a question of unlimited procreation or lack of awareness of what is involved in rearing children, but rather the empowerment of couples to use their inviolable liberty wisely and responsibly, taking into account social and demographic realities as well as their own situation and legitimate desires' (Saint John Paul II, 1994). The letter further asks that more attention be given to 'securing for husband and wife the liberty to decide responsibly, free from all social or legal coercion, the number of children they will have and the spacing of their births'. During a recent visit to Asia, Pope Francis said: 'responsible parenthood requires that couples regulate the births of their children' (Pope Francis, 2015). The centrality of the couple as the decision-making unit regarding procreation is also noted in the Final Report of the Synod of Bishops *Relatio Finalis*: 'family planning fittingly takes place as the result of consensual dialogue between the spouses' (Synod of Bishops, 2015). These principles regarding the planning of family size and the spacing of births are widely shared in the international development community and, if universally accepted, would lead to many global health and development advances.

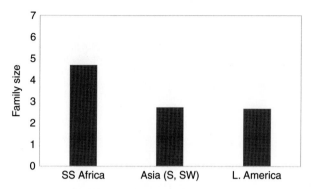

Figure 7.7 Ideal family size. Data from ICF International (2017).

Social scientists have undertaken extensive studies of the preferences of couples about their families. A few relevant findings from this research are provided below.

Preferences Regarding Family Size

In recent decades demographic and health surveys have been conducted in a majority of less developed countries (ICF International, 2017). In these surveys large numbers of women are asked a range of questions about childbearing and the health and well-being of their children. One question relates to the desired or ideal family size. Figure 7.7 gives the average desired family size reported by women in different regions of the less developed world. The desired size ranges from an average of 2.7 in Asia and Latin America to 4.7 in sub-Saharan Africa. These findings are consistent with the stages of the demographic transitions reached by these regions: Asia and Latin America are much further along in their transitions than sub-Saharan Africa. In more developed countries at the end of the transitions, women typically want two children.

Note that these desired family sizes are well short of the six to seven births women have when they do not regulate their fertility. In other words, in most countries women need only part of their reproductive years between ages 15 and 45 to achieve their desired family size. During the remaining years of their reproductive lives women would need to practice family planning to avoid unintended pregnancies.

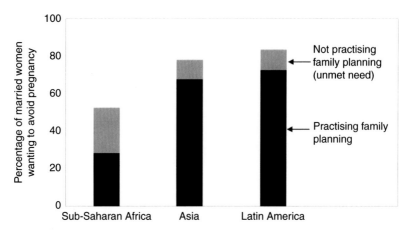

Figure 7.8 Percentage of married women wanting to avoid pregnancy, by family planning practice. Data from United Nations, Department of Economic and Social Affairs, Population Division (2016).

The Incomplete Implementation of Family Size Preferences

Given these findings on desired family size it is not surprising that large proportions of women in the developing world report not wanting to become pregnant at the present time.

This proportion varies among countries and regions. Generally, it is highest in countries with a low desired family size, and vice versa. Figure 7.8 provides estimates of the regional average proportions not wanting to become pregnant which range from 83 per cent in Latin America to 78 per cent in Asia and 53 per cent in sub-Saharan Africa.

Women who do not wish to become pregnant desire to regulate their fertility. However, the implementation of this desire is incomplete in all countries and substantial proportions of women wanting to avoid pregnancy report not practising family planning. These women are considered to have an *unmet need* for family planning and are at risk of experiencing unplanned pregnancies and related health complications (Casterline and Sinding, 2000). As shown in Figure 7.8, unmet need is much higher in sub-Saharan Africa than in Asia and Latin America. The UN estimates that 130 million married women in the developing world have an unmet need for family planning (United Nations, Department of Economic and Social Affairs, 2016).

Obstacles to Family Planning and Unplanned Pregnancies

Why do some women who wish to avoid pregnancy not practice family planning? Research on the causes of unmet need has identified a range of social, health and economic factors that pose barriers to women and men who desire to regulate their family size. These factors include lack of knowledge, lack of availability of methods, costs, health concerns, objections from family members and concerns about moral and social acceptability. These obstacles lead some women to forgo family planning despite their intention not to become pregnant.

Statistics on unplanned pregnancy outcomes in the less developed world in 2014 are presented in Table 7.2 (Singh et al., 2014). The total annual number of pregnancies in LDCs is estimated at 192 million, of which 74 million are unplanned (i.e., about two out of five).

Half of these unplanned pregnancies result in unplanned births (28 million) or miscarriages (9 million). About a quarter of all births in the less developed world are unplanned.

The remaining half of the unplanned pregnancies end in abortion (36 million) – the majority of which are unsafe. Unsafe abortion leads to around 22,000 maternal deaths per year and high levels of maternal morbidity.

These unplanned pregnancies, abortions and maternal deaths and injuries are most prevalent among poor, uneducated and rural women and could be averted if women with an unmet need practised family planning.

Assisting Couples to Be Responsible Parents

Many governments have developed services to assist women to implement their reproductive preferences. Research shows that these services are welcomed by women and men in countries at all stages of economic development. The best-documented demonstration of the demand for these services was provided by a large trial – the Family Planning and Health Services Project (FPHSP) – started in the late 1970s in Matlab, Bangladesh (Cleland et al., 1994). At that time Bangladesh was one of the poorest and most highly agricultural countries in the world, and there was widespread scepticism that family planning would be accepted in such a traditional society. The FPHSP divided the Matlab district (population of 173,000 in 1977) into intervention and control areas of approximately equal size. The control area received the same

Table 7.2 *Estimated number of planned and unplanned pregnancies in the developing world (in millions) in 2014 by outcome*

	Total no.	Births	Induced abortions	Miscarriages
All pregnancies	190	125	36	29
Planned pregnancies	116	97		19
Unplanned pregnancies	74	28	36	9
Percentage unplanned	39	23		

Source. Singh et al. (2014).

very limited services as the rest of the country, while in the intervention area comprehensive, voluntary, high-quality family planning and reproductive health services were provided. The impact of these services on reproductive behaviour is summarised in Figure 7.9. Within two years from the start of the project, the proportion of women practising family planning in the intervention area rose from less than 5 per cent to 33 per cent. In contrast, very little change occurred in the control area or in the rest of Bangladesh during the first few years.

A follow-up study in the Matlab district in the early 1990s measured family welfare outcomes including women's health, earnings and household assets, use of preventive health inputs, and effects on the health and schooling of the woman's children (Joshi and Schultz, 2013). The intervention area scored significantly better than the control area on many of these indicators of the welfare of women and their children, demonstrating how access to high-quality, voluntary family planning services can lead to multi-sectoral and multi-generational health and well-being benefits.

The Multi-Sectoral Impacts of Family Planning

When couples implement their own decisions about family size, their actions lead to a decline in fertility with a range of benefits:

- Women's empowerment: Women have greater freedom to determine the number and spacing of children and have more freedom to participate in the formal labour force and civic life;

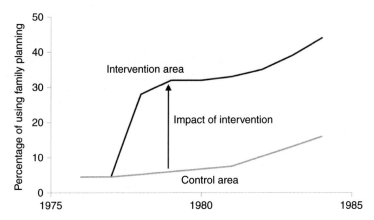

Figure 7.9 Trends in practice of family planning in Matlab, Bangladesh. Data from Cleland et al. (1994).

- Health: The reduction in unintended pregnancies and the wider spacing of pregnancies reduce maternal mortality and morbidity and improve infant and child survival and health;
- Economy: A decline in unplanned births reduces the ratio of dependents to workers, raises investment in human capital and leads to greater participation of women in the formal labour force. These trends are the cause of the demographic dividend (discussed earlier) which boosts GDP per capita and helps developing countries to accelerate poverty reduction;
- Government: Less pressure on education and health care sectors and on the country's infrastructure (e.g., transportation, communication, energy, water and sanitation);
- Environment: Reduced pressure on natural resources on which people's lives depend (fresh water, soil, forest, agriculture, energy, etc.) and reduces air, water and soil pollution; and
- Social/Political stability: With a slower-growing youth population there is less competition for jobs and fewer unemployed youth, thus making political environments more stable.

These wide-ranging benefits of investments in voluntary family planning programmes make them among the most cost effective development interventions available to governments and the international community.

Conclusion

Assisting couples to achieve their reproductive preferences is a compassionate act that promotes responsible parenthood and improves the lives of women, their children and their communities, especially among the poor and most vulnerable sections of societies. The resulting decline in unplanned births also enhances prospects for poverty reduction and moderates the increasingly harmful impact of human activities on the natural environment.

References

Bloom, D. E., Canning, D. & Sevilla, J. 2003. *The Demographic Dividend: A New Perspective on the Economic Consequences of Population Change.* Population Matters, a RAND Program of Policy-Relevant Research Communication. USA: RAND.

Bloom, D. & Williamson, J. 1998. Demographic transition and economic miracles in emerging Asia. *World Bank Economic Review*, 12: 419–456.

Casterline, J. B. & Sinding, S. W. 2000. Unmet need for family planning in developing countries and implications for population policy. *Population and Development Review*, 26: 691–723.

Cleland, J., Phillips, J. F., Amin, S. & Kamal, G. M. 1994. The determinants of reproductive change in Bangladesh: Success in a challenging environment. In *World Bank Regional and Sectoral Studies*. Washington, DC: The World Bank.

ICF International. 2017. *The DHS Program STATcompiler.* www.statcompiler.com.

Joshi, S. & Schultz, T. P. 2013. Family planning and women's and children's health: Long-term consequences of an outreach program in Matlab, Bangladesh. *Demography*, 50: 149–180.

Lee, R. & Mason, A. 2006. Back to basics: What is the demographic dividend? *Finance & Development*, 43: 16–17.

OECD. 1998. *Maintaining Prosperity in an Ageing Society.* Paris: OECD Publishing.

Pope Francis. 2015. *Post-Synodal Apostolic Exhortation Amoris Laetitia.* Vatican City: Vatican Press.

Saint John Paul II. 1994. *Letter to the Secretary General of the United Nations Organization on Population and Development.* Insegnamenti XVII/1.

Singh, S., Darroch, J. & Ashford, L. 2014. *Adding It Up: The Costs and Benefits of Investing in Sexual and Reproductive Health.* New York: Guttmacher Institute and UNFPA.

Synod of Bishops. 2015. The *Final Report* of the *Synod* of *Bishops* to the *Holy Father*, Pope Francis. www.vatican.va/roman_curia/synod/documents /rc_synod_doc_20151026_relazione-finale-xiv-assemblea_en.html.

United Nations, Department of Economic and Social Affairs, Population Division. 2014. *World Urbanization Prospects: The 2014 Revision.* New York: United Nations.

    2015. *World Population Prospects: The 2015 Revision, Key Findings and Advance Tables.* Working Paper No. ESA/P/WP.241. New York: United Nations.

    2016. *Model-Based Estimates and Projections of Family Planning Indicators 2016.* New York: United Nations.

World Bank. 1994. *Averting the Old Age Crisis: Policies to Protect the Old and Promote Growth (English).* A World Bank Policy Research Report. Washington, DC: World Bank.

8 | Game Over?
Drivers of Biological Extinction in Africa

CALESTOUS JUMA

Writing in his seminal essay in *Science* on 'The Historical Roots of Our Ecological Crisis' 50 years ago, Lynn White Jr said,

The greatest spiritual revolutionary in Western history, Saint Francis, proposed what he thought was an alternative Christian view of nature and man's relation to it: he tried to substitute the idea of the equality of all creatures, including man, for the idea of man's limitless rule of creation. He failed ... Since the roots of our trouble are so largely religious, the remedy must also be essentially religious, whether we call it that or not. We must rethink and refeel our nature and destiny. The profoundly religious, but heretical, sense of the ... Franciscans for the spiritual autonomy of all parts of nature may point a direction. I propose Francis as the patron saint of ecologists. (White, 1967: 1207)

When the article was published the population of sub-Saharan Africa was about 200 million. Now it is over 970 million. It is estimated to grow to 2.1 billion by 2050. This exponential growth, combined with limited economic opportunities, is hardly sustainable. Nearly 94,000 children will be added to Africa's population daily over the next 33 years. This will happen in a world that has less compassion for the poor. It will be a world in which industrialised countries will continue to defend their consumption patterns despite their global ecological impacts.

In the 1950s there were more than 500 endemic haplochromine cichlid fish species, with four endemic genera among them (Galis and Metz, 1998). This evolutionary marvel of the world has come under tremendous pressure from human activities, and many of the species are now extinct. Many of the diverse species were extirpated in just a decade.

This chapter argues that many of the drivers of species loss in Africa are unique to the continent and cannot be addressed by simply adopting lessons from other regions of the world. Demographic transitions and urbanisation in other parts of the world have helped to significantly increase income levels and reduce pressure on natural systems. Africa's case is exceptional. The demographic transition is too slow and occurs without the concomitant industrial development and rapid growth in agricultural productivity. The trends offer no discernible demographic or ecological dividends. To the contrary, they amplify the extinction of many species, many of which disappear before they have been documented. The drivers of species extinction are usually exponential and non-linear whereas conservation programmes tend to be linear and additive. They often have a narrow focus on protecting iconic species rather than on enacting policies to protect the wider ecosystems that support a range of species. The disappearance of these iconic species is a tragedy, but equally tragic is the extinction of other species as their habitats get lost or fragmented. Protected areas are reaching their limits as effective conservation measures, in part because many threatened species spend most of their time outside the boundaries of protected areas. Furthermore, in many countries, encroachment and internal degradation are reducing those areas. As such, a new approach is needed that aligns conservation efforts with the systems nature of the problem.

This chapter is divided into four sections. The first section outlines some of the key drivers of species loss in Africa. The next section explores the implications of Africa's exceptional demographic trends on species survival. The third section of the chapter uses the iconic examples of the cheetah, giraffe and grey parrot to illustrate the limits of current conservation approaches. The final section outlines conservation measures that reflect contemporary African conditions. The measures include the search for new conservation strategies, population management, technological innovation and sustainable development, with emphasis on agricultural intensification.

Trends and Drivers of Biodiversity Loss

Overview

Africa is a continent of misplaced perceptions. Most map projections of continents create a false impression of the actual size of the continent. The most common is the projection first presented by the Flemish cartographer Gerardus Mercator in 1569. The cylindrical map

Greenland vs. Africa

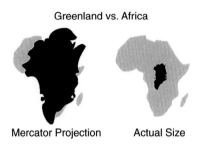

Mercator Projection   Actual Size

Figure 8.1 Maps of Africa and Greenland, showing that different map projections give very different impressions of their relative land areas. Image from Geoff Boeng, http://geoffboeing.com/. Used with permission.

projection became standard for nautical uses for its ability to show constant course lines (loxodromes or rhumb lines) as straight segments conserving the angles with meridians. This projection distorts the size of objects as the latitude increases from the equator to the poles. As a result, Africa is made to look much smaller than it actually is. This would normally not be an issue, but the projection is widely used and distorts people's perception of the true size of Africa (Figure 8.1).

   The continent and the surrounding islands occupy a vast region equal to the US (minus Alaska), China, India, Western Europe, Argentina and Great Britain combined. Put differently, it is three times the size of the US. It is this vastness and variations in ecological conditions that historically accounted for its incredible biodiversity. This large territory also explains the challenges associated with understanding the full taxonomic extent of biodiversity.

   Nearly 25 per cent of the world's 4700 mammal species live in Africa. The bulk of these are found in the eastern and southern savannahs. They include at least 79 species of antelope. There are more than 2000 species of birds in Africa, accounting for 20 per cent of the world total. Africa has more fish species (estimated at 2000) than any other continent (United Nations Environment Programme, 2010a). There are nearly 950 amphibian species. In fact, more reptile and amphibian species continue to be discovered. In the 1990s alone, discovery of new reptile and amphibian species in Madagascar alone increased their count by 18 per cent and 25 per cent, respectively (United Nations Environment Programme, 2010a). The mainland of Africa is home to between 40,000 and 60,000 plant species, with southern Africa alone having nearly 580 plant families and about 100,000 known species of insects, spiders and other arachnids (United Nations Environment Programme, 2010a).

These figures represent estimates of the vast biodiversity of the continent. They also do not adequately show the scale of the decline of biodiversity due to lack of information. It is estimated that nearly 120 plant species have gone extinct with another 1771 threatened.

Africa has a large proportion of the world's primate species (Figure 8.2). Worldwide, they 'occur in four regions – the Neotropics (171 species), mainland Africa (111 species), Madagascar (103 species) and Asia (119 species) – and are present naturally in 90 countries; however, two-thirds of all species occur in just four countries – Brazil, Madagascar, Indonesia and the Democratic Republic of the Congo' (Estrada et al., 2016: 1).

Africa has eight of the world's 34 biodiversity hotspots. These are defined as regions with at least 1500 endemic vascular plant species, about 0.5 per cent of the world's total. It must also have lost at least 70 per cent of its historical habitat (United Nations Environment Programme, 2010a). Madagascar, for example, is home to five bird families and five primate families that are found nowhere else on Earth. Its 72 lemur species and subspecies help to raise global conservation awareness. But 15 of them have gone extinct (United Nations Environment Programme, 2010b).

The statistics on the distribution of species in Africa give a glimpse into the magnitude of the challenge. The vastness of the continent provides opportunities for designing large conservation areas that can support a wide array of species. But this same vastness also makes it more challenging to have a detailed understanding of the distribution of species, especially given the low level of research capacity in the region. This reinforces the view that many species are being lost before they have had a chance to be documented.

Habitat Loss and Fragmentation

The loss and fragmentation of habitats is a leading driver of species loss in Africa. The key force in this process is deforestation (DeFries et al., 2010). The patterns of deforestation, however, differ considerably from trends in Asia and Latin America, where large-scale agriculture has played a key role in land use change. In Africa, two major factors drive deforestation. The first is the slow but steady expansion of

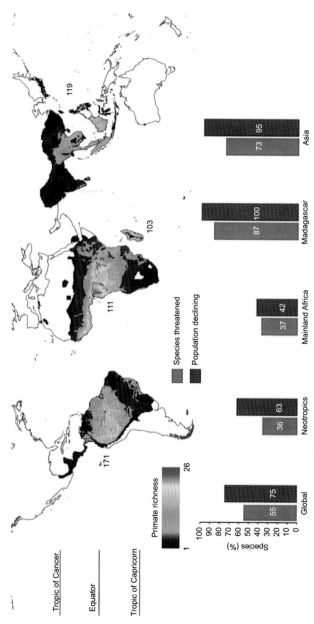

Figure 8.2 Global map of primate species richness. The numbers show the total number of primate species in that area. Bar charts show the proportion of primate species that are threatened with extinction and declining in each area, with the actual number of species given within each bar. Figure reproduced from Estrada et al. (2016) under a Creative Commons BY-NC 4.0 licence. (A black and white version of this figure will appear in some formats. For the colour version, please refer to the plate section.)

smallholder or subsistence agriculture. The second is the extraction of primary products such as wood fuel, timber and charcoal (Fisher, 2010). Generally 'people are poorer, the extractive sectors of economies are larger, and the climate is more arid' (Rudel, 2013: 5).

A recent study by Rudel (2013) shows that the 'most extensive clearing occurred in dry forest areas, so the countries with less dense forests and lots of arid lands unsuitable for agriculture experienced higher rates of deforestation. Consistent with Dutch disease theory, a large oil and gas sector and the large-scale importing of cereals tended to depress deforestation rates, but urbanisation accelerated forest clearing, perhaps because it generated increased demand for agricultural products. In the arid environments of the countries outside the Congo basin, the countries with the denser forests and most potential for rainfed agriculture saw the most deforestation. Population growth, wherever it occurred in these countries spurred deforestation' (Rudel, 2013: 4).

The growth of urban populations has helped to spur agricultural expansion in areas close to cities or with good transportation connections to cities. This is illustrated by the case of Kinshasa, whose growth contributed to expansion in smallholder agriculture 400 km to the north of the city along the Congo. The river facilitates shipping of foodstuffs downstream to Kinshasa (Rudel, 2013). The expansion of Kinshasa itself has been driven by income from raw material exports. It is one of those examples where commodity exports stimulate urban expansion, which in turn leads to growth in smallholder agriculture. It is the agricultural expansion that then directly leads to species loss.

There are, however, many regions of Africa that have experienced species loss over the centuries due to agricultural expansion independent of commodity exports. Take the case of forests in Madagascar, which are among the most biologically diverse in the world. Analysis of 'aerial photographs (c. 1953) and Landsat images (c. 1973, c. 1990 and c. 2000) indicates that forest cover decreased by almost 40 per cent from the 1950s to c. 2000, with a reduction in "core forest" >1 km from a non-forest edge of almost 80 per cent. This forest destruction and degradation threaten thousands of species with extinction' (Harper et al., 2007).

The traditional farming methods of slash-and-burn and the low levels of agricultural yield have put pressure on natural systems, leading to extensive habit loss and fragmentation. As Slingenberg et al. (2009)

point out, deforestation for 'large-scale permanent agriculture is, unlike small-scale agriculture, often practised using slash-and-burn techniques. Thousands of hectares of land have been deforested this way. The converted land supports agricultural growth and delivers large harvest for 3–4 years, but then excessive use of fertilisers is necessary to yield a minimum harvest and additional land is needed for agricultural purposes' (Slingenberg et al., 2009: 159). The main driving force for deforestation in Madagascar and other areas over the centuries has been agricultural expansion.

These patterns are replicated in many parts of the continent where the 'proximate causes of deforestation in Africa reflect the global pattern in order of importance with agricultural expansion as the main driver for deforestation with direct conversion of forest area to *small-scale permanent agriculture* accounting for approximately 60 per cent of the total deforestation and direct conversion of forest area to *large-scale permanent agriculture* accounting for another 10 per cent. However, also wood extraction and infrastructure play a significant role in deforestation in Africa' (Slingenberg et al., 2009: 156).

One of the emerging agricultural threats to biodiversity is the establishment of agro-industries such as oil palm production in tropical forest areas. So far the rate of expansion of oil palm production in Africa has been slow compared to Asia and Latin America (Vijay et al., 2016). However, an increasing number of countries with suitable habitats such as the Democratic Republic of the Congo are exploring how to expand such industries as part of their effort to diversify their economies. The main question is whether such investments can be pursued in a sustainable manner without contributing to species loss. So far much of the conservation attention has focused on the great apes (Ancrenaz et al., 2016). However, the focus on single species could lead to the neglect of other species that could be affected by the overall fragmentation and loss of habitats.

There are many factors that contribute to the fragmentation and loss of habitats in Africa, which is a key driver of species loss. Of the drivers, agricultural expansion remains a dominant force. This is mainly because of the combination of factors such as rapid population growth, limited economic opportunities in rural areas, and high urbanisation rates. Behind these trends are fundamental structural factors such as low levels of agricultural productivity and the slow pace of industrial growth in urban areas. It is unlikely that emerging trends in agricultural productivity increases and fertility reduction will occur fast enough to significantly reduce the ongoing impact of agriculture on habitat loss and fragmentation.

Invasive Alien Species

Invasive alien species are considered among the most significant sources of species extinction worldwide. Concern over alien invasive species is partly tied to the need to protect agricultural and forestry systems from foreign introductions that may have negative consequences. For this reason countries around the world have adopted phytosanitary measures aimed at restricting unauthorised importation of plants and animals. The larger challenge, however, has been about protecting the wider African environment from invasive species.

Ornamental species such as *Camara lantana*, which originated from South America, has taken root in Eastern and Central Africa as well as Madagascar. Its impact on native species extinction in these regions is not known. However, the plant produces chemicals that inhibit germination and root elongation in surrounding plants. It is also known to be toxic to cattle, dogs, goats, horses and sheep. Another ornamental alien species that is choking African water systems is water hyacinth (*Eichhornia crassipe*) from the Amazon basin. The plant has invaded most of the major African water bodies. It is reducing fish reservoirs, suffocating lakes and rivers and undermining local economies. Controlling it has been difficult because of the challenge of mechanical removal and the absence of natural enemies. Its impact on biodiversity is little known.

Many of the widely studied examples of invasive species were introduced accidentally. Some of those that have had well-documented impacts on African ecosystems were a result of deliberate release of other African species. One of the most dramatic examples of this was the introduction of Nile perch (*Lates niloticus*) into Lake Victoria (Ogutu-Ohwayo, 1990). The Uganda Game and Fisheries Department introduced the fish in the 1950s through a series of secretive efforts aimed at improving sport fishing and increasing fish production in the lake following overfishing of some of the commercially important species.

The premise of the programme was that most of the species of small fish were of little commercial value, and the economy of the lake would be improved if these species served as feed for Nile perch. This argument did not take into account the overall consequences for the lake's ecosystem or the livelihoods of millions of people around the lake that relied on those other species for their livelihoods. Opposition to the introduction by the East African Fisheries Research Organization did not carry sufficient political weight to stop the introduction (Pringle, 2005).

The sudden explosion of the Nile perch population and its impact on native species coincided with other changes in Lake Victoria. The decrease in haplochromine fish biomass was a result of 'changes in algal zooplankton composition, decreased water column transparency, and widespread hypoxia from increased eutrophication' (van Zwieten et al., 2016: 622). It was the complex interaction of external factors that led to the rapid explosion of Nile perch with devastating consequences for other species and local economies. The sudden rate at which this occurred makes it difficult to provide a precise assessment of the impact on species composition. The impact on native species was equally dramatic, mostly between 1975 and 1982. A community of hundreds of species collapsed over a very short period and led to dependence on three species: Nile perch, Nile tilapia (*Oreochromis niloticus*) and omena (*Rastrineobola argentea*) (Kaufman, 1992).

The ecological consequences of the introduction of Nile perch extended to terrestrial ecosystems. The flesh of the fish is oily and spoils quickly without refrigeration. Traditional sub-drying methods used for cichlids did not work with Nile perch. Smoking it resulted in more pressure on already diminished forests around Lake Victoria. Little is known about the loss of species associated with extensive deforestation to secure wood for smoking the fish.

When refrigeration facilities became available, they were used for storing fish for shipment to urban areas and not for local consumption. In addition to being sold in urban hotels, the fish was also exported to Europe and Israel. The imagery of a new export from Lake Victoria concealed a more disturbing local picture. First, the large fish destroyed nets used by local fishermen that had been designed for smaller fish. In addition, the small-scale subsistence fishery that focused on the native cornucopia took a severe beating, with most species simply disappearing from the marketplace (Kaufman, 1992: 849). Fishing Nile perch required heavier and more sophisticated equipment, which most local fishermen could not afford. Thus as fish biomass increased, so too did poverty and malnutrition among artisan fishermen.

The story of the impact of Nile perch introduction in Lake Victoria has been complicated by the resurgence of species that had been considered extinct. Part of this resurgence can be explained by overfishing of Nile perch and a return to coexistence with native species in some parts of Lake Victoria. But a more profound point here is that some of the debate may have arisen due to the lack of adequate taxonomic information of the species in the lake. As noted by Witte et al. (2007), until 'the 1970s, the fish fauna of Lake Victoria in East Africa was dominated by about 500 endemic haplochromine cichlid species, which comprised about 80 per cent of the demersal fish mass. The cichlids were extremely diverse ecologically; however, the small diversity in gross morphology and the presence of intra-specific variation made it difficult to distinguish among species' (Witte et al., 2007: 1146). This ignorance, confounded with knowledge uncertainty, suggests that extirpation may have occurred in many parts of the lake before the species were even known.

Illegal Hunting and Fishing

International efforts to regulate and reduce illegal hunting are some of the most visible features of the conservation movement. The focus on illegal hunting has more recently received more attention with studies showing that organised criminal syndicates are involved in trafficking wildlife. The total value of global environmental criminal activities was estimated to be at the high end of US$258 billion for 2016, of which illegal trade in wildlife accounted for up to US$23 billion (Nellemann et al., 2016). Illegal trade in large mammals from Africa such as elephants and rhinos has received most of the attention.

Much of the attention given to these species is linked to the fact they are also the symbols of protected areas and are part of different efforts to sustain trade in tourism. The pressure for trade in ivory and rhino horn is often in conflict with interests to conserve wildlife to support the tourist industry (Figure 8.3). These differences, for example, are reflected in tensions between Eastern African and Southern African countries in various international fora, especially under the Convention on International Trade in Endangered Species (CITES).

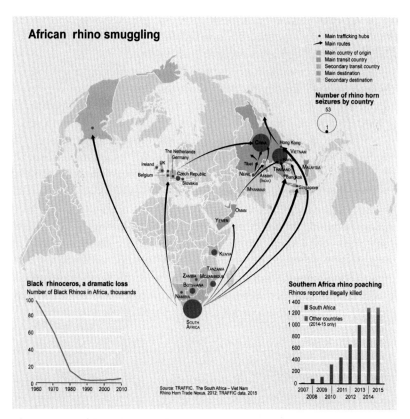

Figure 8.3 Illegal trafficking in wildlife and smuggling and poaching of rhinos. Map shows source countries, main smuggling routes and destination countries. Graphs show decline in black rhino numbers (1960–2010) and number of rhinos killed illegally (2007–2015). Reproduced from Nellemann et al. (2016). (A black and white version of this figure will appear in some formats. For the colour version, please refer to the plate section.)

The patterns of African international wildlife trade have shifted considerably in the last few decades. Historically, much of the trade was with the US and Europe, regions that also championed the existing international wildlife trade norms. More recently, Asian countries, particularly China, have become major destinations of wildlife products from Africa. This shift is associated with wider changes in Africa's trading patterns under which China has become the largest trading partner with the continent. China and other Asian countries, however, have not had a long tradition of regulating international trade. Recent efforts to bring China to the negotiating table appear to have yielded some diplomatic victories with the announcement that the country will stop local ivory trade by the end of 2017. It will do so by shutting down registered carving centres. It is not clear whether this will have an impact on illegal international trade as the bulk of it is conducted through the black market.

But behind these trade concerns lie more serious challenges related to the overall impact of hunting on ecosystem degradation and loss of species. The real issue is to understand the forces that make elephants, rhinos and other species susceptible to extinction. There is a growing body of literature showing that illegal hunting is causing trophic alterations in African forests in ways that increase pressure on a large number of species, most of which have not been documented. Recent studies, for example, show that hunters have access to all of Central African forests. Because of their activities, 'trophic webs are significantly disrupted in the region, with knock-on effects for other ecological functions, including seed dispersal and forest regeneration' (Abernethy et al., 2013: 1).

The hunting patterns in the forest have dramatically changed in character from traditional practices. A combination of the use of heavy weapons and an increase of access routes due to infrastructure and natural-resource exploitation have significantly increased the pace of the degradation of trophic webs (Thibault and Blaney, 2003). Ecological transect surveys show evidence of hunting such as 'snares, gun cartridges and hunting paths, which suggest that hunters are penetrating up to 40 km into the forest from the nearest access point such as roads and rivers' (Abernethy et al., 2013: 2). The problem is worsened by increasing expansion of road networks without complementary investment in regulation and conservation efforts (Wilkie et al., 2000). Between 2002 and 2011, for example, the forest elephant population in the region dropped by 62 per cent. Nearly 90 per cent of the carcasses found during surveys and by guard patrols in Central African protected areas in 2011 showed that they had been illegally killed (Abernethy et al., 2013).

Many of the species that are extirpated play important roles in dispersing seeds (Blake et al., 2009). The majority of the animals that are hunted for bushmeat are seed-dispersing frugivorous mammals. Their disappearance also leads to the loss of trees whose recruitment depends on them. The cascading effects extend to the species that depend on those trees. Without this function, forests become increasingly degraded leading to the loss of other species. Leopards, which sit at the apex of the food chain, have already been lost in areas where their prey is heavily hunted for bushmeat.

The Central African forest case illustrates the importance of taking a more inclusive and systemwide approach when examining the impact of illegal hunting on species extinction. The loss of iconic species such as elephants, rhinos and great apes are indicators of serious impacts of hunting on ecosystems that lead to unobservable loss of species but can be inferred from the degradation of trophic webs. Much of the loss also occurs outside protected areas, requiring a different approach to conservation (Chazdon et al., 2009).

This section has focused on terrestrial biodiversity in Africa. The same dynamics that affect terrestrial ecosystems also affect marine resources which are a foundation for the livelihoods of the majority of African nations. Out of Africa's 55 nations, 38 are coastal or small-island states. A large proportion of the population of these nations rely on marine resources for food and employment. Like in the case of terrestrial ecosystems, Africa's seas are the subject of extensive illegal fishing with emerging evidence of a decline in the diversity and distribution of fisheries. For example, a recent study estimates that 'illegal fishing in West Africa is responsible for a loss of over $2.3 billion US a year, of which only $13.8 million US/year (2016 baseline) are recovered through [monitoring, control and surveillance]' (Doumbouya et al., 2017: 7).

Changing Climate

Changing climate has added new uncertainties to Africa's biodiversity. Until recently the implications of changing climate for African biodiversity received little attention. The fact that the international community spent decades focusing on mitigation measures tended to downplay the potential impacts on biodiversity. Early attempts to bring adaptation measures to the global agenda did not receive the attention they deserved, especially from African perspectives.

There is considerable uncertainty over how changing climate might affect Africa's biodiversity. But there are also important lessons that can be learned from past experiences of the interactions between

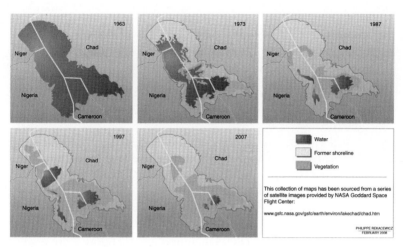

Figure 8.4 The change in area of Lake Chad between 1963 and 2007. Image from Philippe Rekacewicz, 2006, GRID-Arendal, www.grida.no/resources /5593.

drought, population growth and species loss. One of the most dramatic examples of ecosystem degradation in the last few decades was the shrinking of the surface area of Lake Chad, the sixth largest lake in the world (Figure 8.4; Coe and Foley, 2001).

The lake straddles the borders of Cameroon, Chad and Nigeria. It provides water for nearly 30 million people in the semi-arid Sahel region. Its overall basin is the largest endorheic basin in the world covering 2.5 million square km, or about 8 per cent of the African continent. From the early 1960s to the 1980s the lake shrunk from 22,000 square km to 300 square km (Gao et al., 2011).

Much has been written about the socio-economic impact of the crisis. But little of it shows the extent to which such a sudden loss of the coverage of the lake affected biological systems in general and species loss in particular. There are various accounts of fish species in the lake but not much else.

The main lesson from this case is that prolonged drought reduced the water flowing into the lake. The same drought and population growth pushed people in the catchment area to expand irrigation. This further reduced the flow of water into the lake.

In 1972, the lake split into two because of severe drought and its unique bathymetry. The two lakes were separated by a 40 km barrier

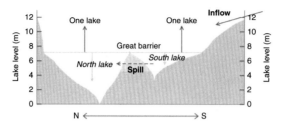

Figure 8.5 North–south cross section through the Lake Chad basin, showing how Lake Chad splits into two smaller lakes when the water level drops. Figure reproduced from Gao et al. (2011) under a Creative Commons BY-NC-SA 3.0 licence.

(Figure 8.5). The southern lake is shallower and therefore more susceptible to evaporation. To restore the lake level, enough water would need to flow into the southern lake to overflow the barrier and replenish the northern lake. But this has been compromised by drought and irrigation. Simulation studies have shown that the failure 'of the lake to merge back into a single lake following wetter conditions in the 1990s is the result of irrigation withdrawals – without irrigation, the lake would have merged in 1999, although it would have split again in 2004' (Gao et al., 2011: 6).

Little is known about the impact of the split on biodiversity in the lake. On the higher end, 179 fish species have been recorded in Lake Chad. Historical studies show that that fish species were less diverse in the northern part of the lake. Species reductions were observed during the period of the drought. After the split, for example, most of the *Synodontis* species disappeared in the northern lake. Their numbers were also later diminished in the southern lake. The drought also changes the composition of fish species by favouring marshy species that are adapted to surviving in low-water environments, low dissolved oxygen and high temperatures. The loss of fishing grounds had a dramatic impact on people with limited options for economic diversification. There is considerable land use conflict between fishermen, herders and farmers in the lake area (Sarch, 2001).

The cascading impact of the shrinking of the lake extends to terrestrial species in the region. Birds have been affected by the declining water levels. Examples of the impact include reductions in nesting sites for the endangered West African subspecies of the black-crowned crane

(*Balearica pavonina pavonina*) and inadequate availability of wintering grounds for the intercontinental migrant ruff (*Philomachus pugnax*).

The case of Lake Chad uses drought as a proxy for simulating the potential impact of changing climate on species extinction, especially in cases where such impacts are amplified by human activity such as an increase in water withdrawal to support agricultural activities. A growing body of evidence shows how over time warming climates are contributing to species loss in African lakes.

Historically, species extirpation has often been attributed to human activities. But in the case of Lake Tanganyika, Africa's deepest and oldest lake, a 1500-year palaeoecological record shows that the decline of fishery species and endemic molluscs began long before commercial fishing (Cohen et al., 2016). Palaeoclimate and instrumental records show sustained warming of Lake Tanganyika over the last 150 years. 'Late-20th century fish fossil abundances at two of three sites were lower than at any other time in the last millennium and fell in concert with reduced diatom abundance and warming water' (Cohen et al., 2016: 9563). As a result, the study shows that climate warming and intensifying stratification most likely reduced potential fishery production. This helps to explain the decline in fish catches.

Lake Chad offers important heuristics on what to expect. Drought alone was not a sufficient explanation for the shrinking of the lake. But the same drought combined with population growth led to the adoption of inefficient irrigation practices that compromised the replenishment of the lake. No viable options exist on restoring the lake, including proposals for inter-basin water diversion, which have turned out to be too expensive (Onuoha, 2008). Lake Tanganyika, on the other hand, provides evidence of the long-term implications of changing climate on species extinction.

Population Dynamics

The growth in our demand for resources is acknowledged as one of the drivers of species extinction. There is, however, a general tendency to view the impact of population growth through the lens of trends in the industrialised world where fertility rates are low and there has been a long history of decoupling between population growth and direct use

Table 8.1 *The population of the world and in major areas in 2015, 2030, 2050 and 2100*

Major area	Population (millions)			
	2015	2030	2050	2100
World	7349	8501	9725	11,213
Africa	1186	1679	2478	4387
Asia	4393	4923	5267	4889
Europe	738	734	707	646
Latin America and the Caribbean	634	721	784	721
Northern America	358	396	433	500
Oceania	39	47	57	71

Note. Population estimates made using the medium-variant projection.
Source. United Nations, Department of Economic and Social Affairs, Population Division (2015).

of natural resources. The situation in Africa is exceptional because of the low pace of the demographic transition and unique patterns of urbanisation that continue to exert pressure on natural resources in rural areas.

Demographic Transition

Africa's rapid population growth of 2.55 per cent per year is emerging as a key global policy theme. More than half (1.3 billion) of the 2.4 billion people added to the global population by 2050 will be in Africa. By 2050 Africa will be adding 42 million people per year, bringing the total population to 2.4 billion, double its current size (Table 8.1; United Nations, 2015). This is the equivalent of adding today's population size of Sudan to the continent annually. Africa alone will contribute nearly 54 per cent of the 2.37 billion population increase projected by 2050.

Africa has a relatively young population with a median age of 19.5 years, compared to a world median age of 29.5 years (Figure 8.6). There are major variations in the age structure of African countries. South Africa has the highest median age of 20 years while Niger is the lowest at 15.1 years. This age structure compounds the dependence

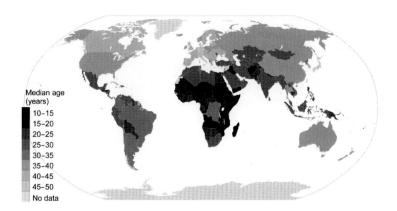

Figure 8.6 World median ages in 2017. Map by Sarah Welch from https://com mons.wikimedia.org/wiki/File:2017_world_map,_median_age_by_country.svg. Map made using data from https://esa.un.org/unpd/wpp/Download/Standard /Population/. Image shared under a Creative Commons BY-SA 4.0 licence.

problem, with a small section of the adult population being expected to support a large youth population with limited skills and employment opportunities to contribute to household income.

The persistence of dependence in the age structure is also reflected in leadership with the youngest continent having on average some of the oldest leaders. There are many factors that contribute to the persistence, but there is a clear pattern of a slow pace of political transition to younger leaders whose ideas, at least in theory, would be more aligned with the age structure. This point has ecological relevance because the ethical values that governed interactions with the environment in the past may not be relevant in the age of rapid ecological degradation.

Much of the policy concern about this rapid growth has been more on its future economic consequences and less on its current implications for species. The main area of interest in international policy circles has been whether this rapid growth will be accompanied by high rates of economic growth or demographic dividend that have historically been recorded in other regions of the world.

Under past scenarios, reductions in child mortality followed by a fall in fertility resulted in a bulge of working-age people and a relatively lower number of dependents. Where employment opportunities existed, high numbers of workers per capita spurred economic growth. Smaller families also allowed individuals and governments to invest in education and health, thereby improving overall labour productivity.

The labour productivity boost is reinforced by savings for retirement arising from increased life spans. The demographic transition also frees up women to join the labour force, thus expanding income opportunities for families. The full benefits from the transition usually arise from supportive government policies and the development of financial markets.

Contemporary Africa, except for a few countries, does not show signs of a demographic dividend. To the contrary, fertility and youth dependency rates are among the highest in the world. The result is 'higher poverty rates, smaller investments in children, lower labour productivity, high unemployment or underemployment, and the risk of political instability' (Canning et al., 2015: 1).

There is evidence of fertility declines in various African countries, especially in urban areas. But the shifts are not occurring fast enough to reduce unemployment. Unlike Asia, which relied on export-led strategies, African countries play an insignificant role in global industrial markets.

There are a number of immediate ecological implications of this scenario. First, African countries continue to depend heavily on agriculture, which accounts for 60 per cent of employment (AGRA, 2017). Much of this agriculture still relies on traditional farming practices that result in habitat loss and degradation. The impact is often more severe in semi-arid areas with fragile ecosystems. These regions have also historically been the habitats of much of Africa's biological diversity.

Second, protected areas have increasingly come under pressure from agricultural expansion as well as illegal hunting. Human settlements around protected areas are also limiting wildlife migration, resulting in land use conflicts.

In fact, much of the early post-colonial migration in countries such as Kenya was rural-rural migration. This pattern continues today in various regions due to limited urban employment opportunities. The problem is compounded by the prevalence of educational systems that hardly impart any new skills. Even if they did, the infrastructure needed to support rural industries is missing in most places.

The key policy challenge arising from this slow demographic transition is its short-term and long-term ecological implications. In the short term, the bulge is putting pressure on biological diversity and contributing to extinction. In the long term, the same pressure may undermine the prospects of a more sustainable transition with ecological dividends that could have arisen from reduced pressure on ecosystems.

Urbanisation

Africa is one of the fastest urbanising regions in the world. Under the classical scenario, this should lead to an ecological dividend as people leave rural areas, creating opportunities for conservation. Cities are meant to offer agglomeration efficiencies that reduce pressure on the countryside. The situation in much of Africa, however, tells a grimmer ecological story.

Other than the capital cities, most urbanisation occurs in smaller centres in rural areas with ready access to natural resources. Trade makes it possible to support the centres through food and bioenergy extracted from forests and woodlands.

There are, however, significant variations in how urbanisation affects deforestation across Africa. The variations are accounted for by the nature of national economies as well as the types of forest systems in the regions. As Rudel (2013) points out, deforestation 'rates tend to be higher in countries with little potential for rain-fed agriculture, less dense forests, small oil–mineral sectors, little reliance on imported cereals and more urbanised populations. Similar analyses of only countries with predominantly dry forests finds more rapid deforestation in dry forest countries with more potential for rain-fed agriculture, more dense forests and rapid population growth' (Rudel, 2013: 4).

Demographic transitions in other regions involved the movement of surplus labour arising from the growth of agricultural efficiency. This coincided with demand for labour in urban areas. Agricultural mechanisation also meant that some of those migrating to urban areas had basic skills that could be deployed in industry.

This is not the general pattern in Africa. Many of those migrating to urban areas are victims of agricultural stagnation or land degradation. Land subdivision among large families, for example, results in ownership of land parcels that are too small to support a family.

According to Lall et al. (2017) cities themselves are 'trapped in the production of non-tradables for local markets. As the African economies attain 60 per cent urbanisation, their share of manufacturing in GDP stays flat (or somewhat falling) at about 10 per cent. In contrast, the manufacturing share of the non-African economies rises from 10 per cent to nearly 20 per cent (falling back only when urbanisation exceeds 60 percent)' (Lall et al., 2017: 14). The cities are thus disconnected from the rest of the world, partly because of their low levels of manufacturing capabilities, poor infrastructure and lack of effective urban planning that generates economies of scale.

A large proportion of African cities are slum settlements. For example, nearly 60 per cent of Nairobi's 2.5 million people live in 200 slum settlements. Kibera, Africa's largest slum, has a population of 250,000 people. Lack of access to basic infrastructure, especially electricity, is one of the defining features of such slum areas. Access to 'electricity reaches only 16 percent of African citizens, compared to 41 percent in other developing countries. Average power consumption is 124 kilowatts per capita, or 10 percent of that in the rest of the world' (Freire et al., 2014: 15).

The bulk of the population in African cities relies on charcoal as a source of cooking energy. It is a major traded commodity that supports employment in sourcing areas. Much of this is produced using earth-mound kilns with a maximum conversion efficiency of 12 per cent. The IEA estimated that in 2012 about 36 million tonnes of charcoal were produced in Africa valued at US$11 billion. This figure is projected to rise to US$70 billion in 2040 (International Energy Agency, 2014). The charcoal business is so lucrative that in parts of Kenya and DRC organised groups control it and use the revenue to fund militias.

Little is known about the ecological impact of deforestation associated with charcoal production. Wood cultivation and kiln efficiency improvements are unlikely to keep up with the demand for charcoal arising from urban growth.

The prevalence of bushmeat consumption in urban areas is another example of the impact of Africa's urbanisation (Ripple et al., 2016). Both large and small towns in West and Southwest Africa are fuelling bush meat consumption. The demand is also driven by the emergence of cities whose growth is fuelled by raw material exports. Africa's largest bush meat market, for example, is in Angola. Livestock production in these areas has not kept pace with population growth and demand for bush meat has soared.

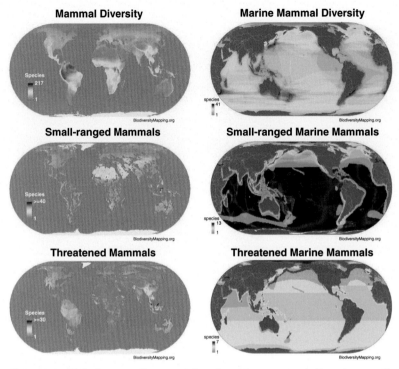

Figure 3.1 Global maps of terrestrial and marine mammal diversity, small-ranged mammal diversity, and numbers of threatened mammals (Jenkins et al., 2013; Jenkins and Van Houtan, 2016; Pimm et al., 2014). Maps from BiodiversityMapping.org, used with permission from Clinton Jenkins. Source of data used in terrestrial maps is IUCN, July 2013 update. Source of data used in marine maps is IUCN, August 2014 update. (A black and white version of this figure will appear in some formats.)

Figure 5.1 Denuded landscape of Iceland with two remnant soil pedestals (rofabards) that are about 2 m high, showing a landscape largely eroded of its soil. Photograph by Timothy Beach. (A black and white version of this figure will appear in some formats.)

Figure 5.2 Denuded landscape of Colombia's Northern Andes with a remnant soil pedestal that is about 1.5 m high, showing a landscape largely eroded of its soil. Photograph by Timothy Beach. (A black and white version of this figure will appear in some formats.)

Figure 5.3 Denuded badlands landscape of the Central Mexican Highlands with a remnant soil pedestal rising above the badlands. Photograph by Timothy Beach. (A black and white version of this figure will appear in some formats.)

Figure 5.4 The ancient Maya wetland field known as the Birds of Paradise, a form of landesque capital built as polycultural, intensive agroecosystems in the Maya Late Classic ca. 700 CE (Beach et al., 2009). Photograph by Dr Jon Lohse, 2004. Used with permission. (A black and white version of this figure will appear in some formats.)

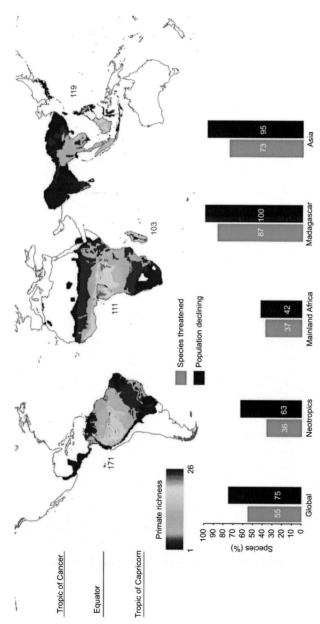

Figure 8.2 Global map of primate species richness. The numbers show the total number of primate species in that area. Bar charts show the proportion of primate species that are threatened with extinction and declining in each area, with the actual number of species given within each bar. Figure reproduced from Estrada et al. (2016) under a Creative Commons BY-NC 4.0 licence. (A black and white version of this figure will appear in some formats.)

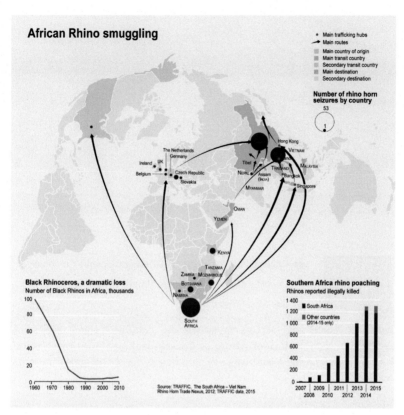

Figure 8.3 Illegal trafficking in wildlife and smuggling and poaching of rhinos. Map shows source countries, main smuggling routes and destination countries. Graphs show decline in black rhino numbers (1960–2010) and number of rhinos killed illegally (2007–2015). Reproduced from Nellemann et al. (2016). (A black and white version of this figure will appear in some formats.)

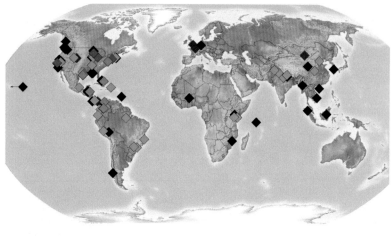

Figure 12.4 Sites and sectors in which the Natural Capital Project is mainstreaming the values of nature in decision-making. From the Natural Capital Project. (A black and white version of this figure will appear in some formats.)

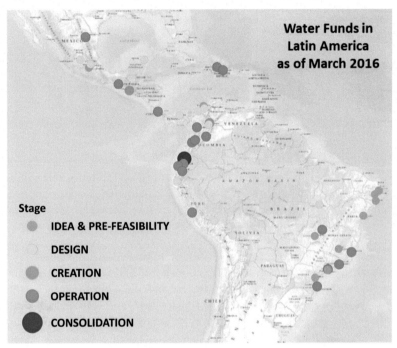

Figure 12.5 Water funds featured by stage of development (as of March 2016). Yellow and tan circles designate water funds that are in the process of scoping and creation, respectively; green and blue circles depict water funds that have been created, with a legal agreement among parties, at various degrees of maturity. Figure courtesy of the Latin American Water Funds Partnership Dashboard (March 2016) and The Nature Conservancy Internal Survey of Water Funds (December 2013). (A black and white version of this figure will appear in some formats.)

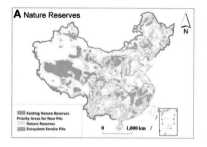

Figure 12.7A, China is in the process of implementing a comprehensive national park system. The delineations here distinguish nature reserves with a priority focus on biodiversity conservation and ecosystem service protected areas with biodiversity as a co-benefit. In the regions where ecosystem service protected areas are being delineated, intense competition for land leaves little or no scope for effective nature reserves without an ecosystem service justification – and investments to benefit private landholders. **B,** China's new system of Ecosystem Function Conservation Areas (EFCAs). As delineated by the Ministry of Environmental Protection and the Chinese Academy of Sciences, EFCAs span 49 per cent of China's land area. EFCAs have dual goals of securing biodiversity and ecosystem services and alleviating poverty. In this figure, flood mitigation in blue refers to that provided by wetlands; that provided by forest is encompassed by the areas shaded in green. Figure 12.7A from Xu et al. (2017). Figure 12.7B courtesy of Z. Ouyang, Research Center for Eco-Environmental Sciences, Chinese Academy of Sciences. (A black and white version of this figure will appear in some formats.)

One of the least studied features of urbanisation is the persistence of food tastes acquired in rural settings. Many of the slum settlements in urban Africa tend to include people from the same regions or ethnic groups. They bring to these communities their rural practices and often serve as markets for forest and agricultural products from their regions of origin. Recent conflicts in Angola forced local people to resort to bush meat. This created supply routes that go into the Congo. These are also the same routes that support illicit trade in ivory.

There is evidence that fertility rates are falling across Africa. They are dropping at a faster rate in urban areas. There has also been marked interest among African governments to improve urban infrastructure and expand access to electricity. Similarly, there are indications that agricultural productivity is rising in some parts of Africa, and the proportion of those engaged in agriculture is falling. The question is whether these changes will happen fast enough to help reduce pressure on natural ecosystems and deliver an ecological dividend. The exponential rate of population growth, the sudden impacts of many of the pressures, and the irreversible trends already in motion suggest that the prospects of an ecological dividend are quite slim for much of the continent.

Game Over? The Disappearance of Iconic Indicator Species

Much of the conservation effort across Africa has relied on highlighting the fate of iconic species, mostly large mammals such as elephants, to call for stricter protection of endangered species. The focus on individual species has historically been accompanied by efforts to maintain protected areas as a key method for reducing species loss. These two approaches have their validity, but today's situation calls for a different approach. The iconic species are important in their own right. Their loss is a tragedy. But what is worse is that the forces driving them to extinction are also affecting many other species that are being extirpated before they have even been studied.

The cases of the cheetah, giraffe and grey parrot illustrate the need to view such iconic species as indicators of a much larger challenge that requires a different conservation ethic. The focus on individual species and protected areas needs complementary measures that take into account the need to view conservation from a more systemic perspective and to acknowledge that today's ecological crisis is qualitatively different from the conditions that led to the creation of the national parks model. These examples also underscore the fact that the forces that lead to species extinction are exponential and non-linear but most conservation efforts tend to be incremental and hardly keep up with the pace of ecological degradation.

Cheetah

In a dramatic display of conflict between humans and wildlife in Africa in 2013, herders in Northeastern Kenya chased down and caught two cheetahs responsible for killing their goats. The men dutifully presented the cheetahs to wildlife authorities seeking compensation for their goats. Nowhere in the news was there a discussion of the underlying sources of the conflict, especially the loss and fragmentation of cheetah habitat or loss of prey due to human activity (Durant et al., 2017). Even more alarming is the lack of appreciation that the fate of the cheetah was linked to wider patterns of ecological change and species loss that hardly received public attention.

The world cheetah population is estimated to be 70,100 adults and adolescents across 33 populations in Africa and Asia. The bulk of the cheetah population is found in Africa, where they live in 30 fragmented populations confined to only 10 per cent of their historical distribution range (Figure 8.7). Much of this range (77 per cent) is unprotected land supporting nearly 67 per cent of the cheetah population (Durant et al., 2017). The cheetah is thus exposed to multiple human-induced threats that include 'prey loss caused by overhunting and bush meat harvesting, habitat loss and fragmentation, and illegal trade' (Durant et al., 2017: 2).

Much of the information available on the cheetah population is based on surveys carried out in protected areas. But since most of the cheetahs live outside such areas, the assessments provide limited overall information and declines are likely to go unnoticed. The challenge is compounded by the fact that cheetahs are elusive and wide-ranging.

In Zimbabwe, for example, cheetahs lost 63 per cent of their distributional range between 2007 and 2015, an annual decline of about 11 per cent. The cheetah population dropped by 85 per cent between 1999 and 2015 (Durant et al., 2017). This is an annual decline of 13 per cent. Much of this loss was due to land use changes in

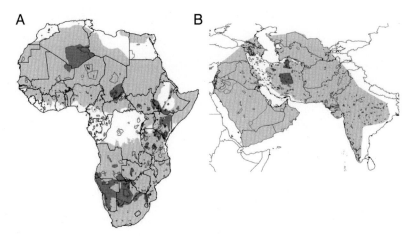

Figure 8.7 Cheetah distribution in, **A**, Africa and, **B**, Asia. Grey areas show the historical range of the cheetah, while darker areas show its current range. The boundaries of Protected Areas under IUCN categories I–IV are shown in grey. Figure from Durant et al. (2017), 'The global decline of cheetah *Acinonyx jubatus* and what it means for conservation', *Proceedings of the National Academy of Sciences*, 114(3): 528–533. Reproduced with permission.

unprotected areas. In other parts of Africa the range contraction is a result of changes in land tenure, land grabs, large-scale fencing and political conflict.

Overall, it is estimated that the cheetah range in Africa has contracted by 89 per cent, from 25.3 million square km to 2.7 million square km. The annual contraction rate is estimated at 2.26 per cent over the last 100 years (Durant et al., 2015). Today cheetahs only persist in 10 per cent of their historic range. They have been extirpated in their historical range in Cameroon, DRC, Ghana, Guinea, Ivory Coast, Mauritania, Nigeria, Senegal, Tunisia and Western Sahara.

Southern Africa is the home of the largest regional cheetah presence with a population of 4190 adults and adolescents in 10 subpopulations, of which the largest has 3940 individuals. Their range spans Botswana, Namibia, northern South Africa, southwestern Mozambique and southwestern Zambia. The estimate for Eastern Africa is 1960 and 440 for western, central and northern Africa (Figure 8.8; Durant et al., 2015).

Illegal international trade is adding more pressure on the cheetah. The main source of cubs for pet trade is Eastern Africa and the Horn

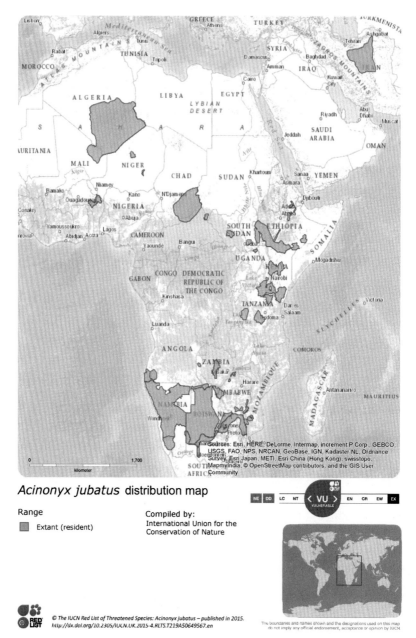

Acinonyx jubatus distribution map

Range

Extant (resident)

Compiled by:
International Union for the
Conservation of Nature

Figure 8.8 Distribution map of cheetah in Africa (Durant et al., 2015). Image copyright IUCN Red List of Threatened Species: *Acinonyx jubatus*. Reproduced with permission.

region, with the Gulf States being the main destination. Customs officials have reported up to 70 per cent of transit death. Some of the cheetahs come from conflict areas such as Somalia where criminal syndicates operate illegal trade in ivory and charcoal.

Giraffe

The rapid disappearance of the giraffe is an illustration of the critical conservation challenges facing Africa. Effective conservation measures require reliable knowledge about the status of a species, scale of the threats and confidence in institutional preparedness. In the case of the giraffe, the scale of the threats is only starting to unfold. This is compounded by the scientific discovery that there are in fact four giraffe species, not one. This reinforces the view that species are going extinct before they are documented. Taxonomic revisions also create operational uncertainty in the conservation community.

The giraffe stands out as one of the most iconic African animals. It is an emblem of the African savanna and woodlands. Its long neck inspires people to cross the limits of conventional thought. When Pliny the Elder (25–79 CE) encountered the ostrich for the first time, he proclaimed that the new creature must by a cross between a gnat and a giraffe. When the giraffe arrived in medieval China in 1413, it was considered to possess the characteristics of a cross between a horse and a dragon (or *quilin*). The reasons for the rise of the long neck were a puzzle for early evolutionists.

Giraffes have gone extinct in Burkina Faso, Eritrea, Guinea, Mali, Mauritania, Nigeria and Senegal. They inhabit 18 countries (Angola, Botswana, Cameroon, Central African Republic, DRC, Ethiopia, Kenya, Mozambique, Namibia, Niger, Somalia, South Africa, South Sudan, Tanzania, Uganda, Zambia and Zimbabwe) (Figure 8.9). They have been reintroduced in Malawi, Rwanda and Swaziland. The South African giraffe has been introduced in Senegal (Muller et al., 2016).

Giraffes now live in fragmented populations in non-continuous habitats ranging from woodland to desert regions. The fragmentation is reflected in the general decline in their sizes. The general threats to giraffes include habitat loss, conflict, illegal hunting and land use change. Overall, the giraffe population has dropped from 140,000 in the 1990s to less than 80,000 today (Woolston, 2016).

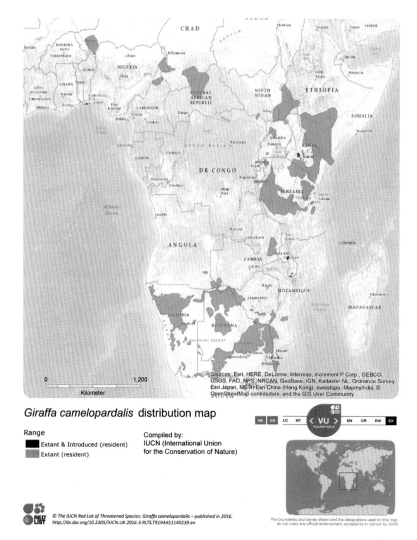

Giraffa camelopardalis distribution map

Figure 8.9 Distribution map of giraffe (Muller et al., 2016). Image copyright IUCN Red List of Threatened Species: *Giraffa camelopardalis*. Reproduced with permission.

The giraffe had been known to be one species with several subspecies based on their coat patterns and habitats. This formed the basis for assessing their population status and designing conservation strategies.

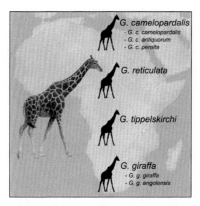

Figure 8.10 The four species of giraffe. Image from Fennessy et al. (2016), 'Multi-locus analyses revel four giraffe species instead of one', *Current Biology*, 26: 1. Reproduced with permission.

But recent genetic studies now show that there are four giraffe species rather than one (Figure 8.10). The study is based on the existence of four distinct lineages that do not interbreed in the wild. These genetic differences exist despite the giraffe's high mobility, which increases their chances of interbreeding. The study used 190 biopsies of giraffe skins to analyse their mitochondrial DNA. They were found to be distinct, suggesting that they were four different species.

As a result, the study recommends replacing the current species name, *Giraffa camelopardalis*, with four new ones. These are: the northern giraffe (*G. camelopardalis*) found in Eastern and Central Africa; the reticulated giraffe (*G. reticulata*) found in Kenya, Somalia and southern Ethiopia; Masai giraffe (*G. tippelskirchi*) found in Kenya, Tanzania and Zambia; and the southern giraffe (*G. giraffa*) in Botswana, Namibia and South Africa. This leaves out a subspecies, the Nubian giraffe (*G. camelopardalis camelopardalis*) of Ethiopia and South Sudan (Fennessy et al., 2016).

These findings and proposals have two major implications. First, they underscore the fact that we are losing large numbers of species before we have had a chance to identify them. This case suggests that the taxonomic work is larger that we imagined it. In addition to documenting new species, work is also needed to reassess some of the documented species. An example of this was the 2010 study that used DNA analysis to show that there were two species of African elephants:

savanna elephants (*Loxodonta africana*) and forest elephants (*Loxodonta cyclotis*).

The second implication is the realisation that the individual giraffe species are each under greater threat of extinction given their small numbers. This demands a change in conservation strategies, some of which may be resisted. In the case of the elephant it has been argued that splitting the species would lead to the neglect of hybrid elephants.

Grey Parrot

The catastrophic decline of the grey parrot (*Psittacus erithacus*) in Ghana over the last few decades illustrates how international trade, human population growth, local economic factors and habitat loss interact to drive species loss. Like the fate of other iconic indicator species, the case of the grey parrot provides a lens through which to examine the loss of many other species irrespective of their place in international trade.

The grey parrot is known for its long life span and remarkable ability to mimic human sound and interact with its owner. These attributes have made it an ideal pet that is traded globally. But these qualities have also made its survival vulnerable. The process of its decline has also exposed how other human-induced forces such as deforestation drive species loss.

Examining the demographic and economic context of Ghana is essential in understanding some of the pressure points that have influenced the decline of the grey parrot. Between 1970 and 2010 Ghana's population grew at an annual rate of 3 per cent, rising from 8.5 million to 24.2 million people. This growth occurred at a period of immense economic hardship for the country, which operated under the austerity programmes imposed by the World Bank and the International Monetary Fund.

The lack of industrial growth over the period led to heavy reliance on expansive agriculture and extractive forestry. The high population growth shortened fallow periods and increased demand for land. Forest cover, a critical habitat for the grey parrot, dropped from 74,480 square km in 1992 to 49,400 square km in 2000 (Annorbah et al., 2016).

The extensive felling of large trees to remove over-mature trees as part of the national forest management policy compounded the problem. Those same tall trees were where the grey parrot typically nested. It is not known how many other species were affected by these practices, but the impact on the grey parrot is an indication of the possible impacts.

The impact of logging on the grey parrot population extended beyond forest areas. About 70 per cent of the people interviewed reported that the parrot nested and roosted outside the forest. The parrot preferred to nest and roost in tall trees such as *Terminalia superba* and *Ceiba pentandra*, which are commercially important species (Annorbah et al., 2016). Over half of the timber harvested in Ghana in 1972–1992 occurred outside the forests. Farmers had no legal rights over trees on their land and were not compensated by licensed loggers for any damage caused to their crops during felling. The practice resulted in pre-emptive felling of large trees from farmlands by farmers outside forest areas (Ruf, 2011).

The historical distribution of the grey parrot covered much of Ghana's forest zone, estimated at 75,000 square km. This included 'the whole of Western and Central Regions of the country, nearly the whole of Ashanti Region as well as the semi-deciduous forest areas of the Brong-Ahafo Region, the western part of the Eastern Region, and parts of the Greater Accra Region' (Figure 8.11) (Annorbah et al., 2016: 85). The parrot also existed in the riparian forests of the northern region's savanna zone.

The combined impacts of trapping for trade and habitat loss have resulted in the loss of 90–99 per cent of the grey parrots in Ghana since 1992 (Annorbah et al., 2016). The population collapse drove trappers into other economic activities such as farming, while others switched to trapping other species or migrated to continue the practice in other countries.

The case of Ghana is not unique. There are signs that trade in the grey parrot from DRC to South Africa, which imports nearly 10,000 birds annually, is declining possibly due to population reduction and trade restrictions. The historical destination of the grey parrot was Europe, the US and the Middle East, but more recently China has been added to the export market (Birdlife International, 2017).

In conclusion, the reason that we are finally able to see the obvious loss of the tallest land mammal is because of the degradation of ecosystems and the loss of many other species. The fact that we can now pay attention to the fate of the cheetah, and even discover that it does not have the endurance of human runners despite being the fastest land

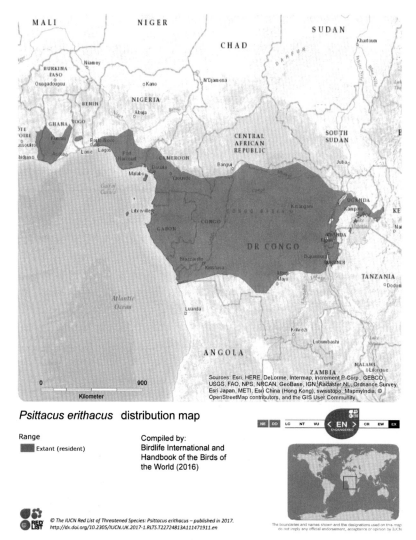

Psittacus erithacus distribution map

Range
■ Extant (resident)

Compiled by:
Birdlife International and
Handbook of the Birds of
the World (2016)

© *The IUCN Red List of Threatened Species: Psittacus erithacus – published in 2017.*
http://dx.doi.org/10.2305/IUCN.UK.2017-1.RLTS.T22724813A111471911.en

The boundaries and names shown and the designations used on this map
do not imply any official endorsement, acceptance or opinion by IUCN.

Figure 8.11 Distribution map of grey parrot (Birdlife International, 2017). Image copyright IUCN Red List of Threatened Species: *Psittacus erithacus*. Reproduced with permission.

mammal, is because its habitats have been destroyed and its prey depleted by human activity. The same is true of the grey parrot, whose habitats are being decimated and its numbers depleted by trappers for trade. Behind these iconic examples lie deeper concerns about the disappearance of species before they have even been documented. The species are special cases in their own right. But more importantly, their decline is a sign of a much deeper problem that demands a change in the way we think about the relationship between humans – especially those rendered vulnerable by economic forces – and other equally vulnerable species.

Options for Stemming Biological Extinction

In Search of New Conservation Approaches

Africa's species loss is usually lumped together with trends from other regions to create global overviews. But as this chapter shows, the African situation is exceptional in many respects and requires special consideration. It is possible that many of the proposals put forward to address species extinction in Africa can be applied to other regions of the world. Such convergence is likely, but it is not a reason to ignore the unique features of the African crisis and craft approaches that reflect its contemporary circumstances.

The first critical starting point is to question the underlying thinking behind Africa's conservation efforts. The fundamental thinking that Africa inherited in the nineteenth century was shaped largely by prevailing European worldviews. At its core lay ideas such as the supremacy of humans over other species, Cartesian ideas that supported the creation of isolated protection areas (PAs), and reductionist views that focus on individual species rather than ecosystems. The PAs are also largely national, and therefore the movement of wildlife is constrained by political boundaries. Protected areas that are based on these principles have not effectively protected species.

As the examples of the cheetah, giraffe and grey parrot show, no conservation programme can work well without taking into account the importance of spaces outside protected areas, which are critical to the survival of wildlife. The effectiveness of protected areas for forests in East Africa show mixed results (Pfeifer et al., 2012). According to a study by Pfeifer et al. (2012), 'the most successful PAs were National Parks, although only 26 out of 48 parks increased or maintained their forest area (i.e., *effective* parks). Forest reserves (*ineffective* parks, i.e., parks that lose forest from within boundaries: 204 out of 337), nature reserves (6 out of 12) and game parks (24 out of 26) were more likely to lose forest cover. Forest loss in buffer zones around PAs exceeded background forest loss, in some areas indicating leakage driven by *Effective National Parks'* (Pfeifer et al., 2012: 1).

New conservation approaches need to integrate humans and other species in ways that reflect the African context. The general expectation of low conflict between wildlife and humans was based on the assumption that species richness declined and human impacts rose with primary productivity. But as Balmford et al. (2001) showed, 'human population density is positively correlated with species richness of birds, mammals, snakes and amphibians. This association holds for widespread, narrowly endemic, and threatened species and looks set to persist in the face of foreseeable population growth' (Balmford et al., 2001: 2616).

These findings lead to the need for acknowledging that enlightened coexistence between humans and other species is possibly the best way to pursue a new approach to conservation. So far efforts to promote such coexistence have not worked well. This is partly because they were not designed to earn community trust, which is problematic given the history of conservation activities in Africa. A more inclusive philosophy that acknowledges the needs of both humans and wildlife must be developed.

The conservation challenges facing Africa transcend national boundaries. Until recently there were limited mechanisms for promoting transboundary efforts, except where each programme is negotiated by the participating countries. Today, Africa is negotiating new regional integration arrangements that allow countries to maintain their autonomy while being able to engage in trade across national boundaries. These negotiations are founded on the existence of eight Regional Economic Communities (RECs).The RECs have been designated by the African Union as the building blocs for economic integration. The RECs might offer Africa new opportunities to rethink how to design trans-boundary conservation measures, which are essential for species survival.

A regional conservation approach would also provide opportunities for governments to agree on large protected areas that could support wide-ranging wildlife or sites that require special protection. Some of these areas could be designated as public trusts because of their critical role in species survival. Many such areas, for example, the migration routes for wildebeest in Kenya and Tanzania, are threatened by habitat fragmentation and loss.

Population and Species Survival

There is ample evidence that Africa's exceptional population dynamics amplify the pressures on species. Africa has not demonstrated the kind of demographic transition that other regions of the world have gone through. In addition, its urbanisation trends do not necessarily relieve pressure on rural resources. In some cases, they even worsen the situation. There are, however, signs of reductions in fertility, mostly in urban areas. Emerging evidence also shows improvements in agricultural productivity, especially in those countries that have increased R&D funding over the last decade. These positive signs are not a reason to discount the need to address population growth. To the contrary, the evidence from urban areas suggests approaches for expanding programmes that manage population transitions in rural areas.

One of the critical features of African fertility trends has been the organisation of households as economic units with children providing a wide range of inputs from labour to care. Given the low level of the use of labour-saving technologies, children become a key component of the survival of families as economic units. High fertility rates were an essential strategy for ensuring that at least enough children would survive to sustain the family economy. But with advances and availability of medical care and cultural persistence, mortality rates have fallen while fertility rates, especially in rural areas, have remained high relative to other regions of the world.

There are, however, other factors that contribute to high fertility rates. As Dasgupta and Dasgupta (2017) point out, 'patrilineality, weak conjugal bonds, communal land tenure, and a strong kinship child support system have been broad characteristics of the region. They provide a powerful stimulus to fertility' (Dasgupta & Dasgupta, 2017: 416). These factors operate under conditions where women have limited rights over key assets such as land. They generally have diminished voices despite the fact that they carry the burden of raising families.

A faster demographic transition is important because of the income gains it confers to families. The benefits of the demographic dividend are directly reaped by families that delay the birth of the first child, optimise birth spacing and curtail the total number of births. These choices help to improve health, enhance work opportunities for women, raise the health and educational standards of children, and increase household incomes and savings (Canning et al., 2015). Policies that 'allow families to make informed decisions and provide the means to implement these decisions are critical. Gender equality is an important part of decision-making regarding family size because women bear most of the direct costs of childbearing. All of the policies for accelerating the transition are worthwhile regardless of the potential demographic dividend and independent of their effect on fertility. A healthier and better educated population with the ability to make choices about family structure is an inherent good' (Canning et al., 2015: 12).

Overall, 'policies in three key areas would help to accelerate the fertility transition and increase the demographic dividend: reductions in child mortality, increases in female education and improved access to comprehensive family planning services. Improvements in these three areas are desirable regardless of the potential economic payoffs, but they should receive even higher priority than they do today' (Canning et al., 2015: 32).

Such policies will not automatically result in a demographic dividend. Complementary economic policies that focus on industrial growth, agricultural improvement, skill enhancement and capital market development are essential for bridging the gap between the promise and realisation of the demographic dividend. In many cases, urgent measures need to be put in place to align educational institutions on contemporary and emerging market needs.

Similarly, new policies are necessary to help facilitate the sustainability transition needed to reduce species loss. Planning for overall economic development must take into account ecological considerations. So far policies aimed at promoting demographic transitions have been the preserve of national governments. Measures needed to promote species survival, however, are likely to involve groups of countries through the various RECs. It is at the regional level that African countries can best cater for more integrated conservation strategies.

One of the critical links between demographic transition and sustainability is the role of women. Promoting demographic transition entails acknowledging women's reproductive rights and their role in family planning. Most of Africa's agricultural production is carried out by women, which puts them at the frontline of ecological management. It is for this reason that programmes aiming at skills development should prioritise women. Failure to do so will not only compromise the question of demographic dividend, but it will also undermine efforts to promote measures aimed at species protection.

Environmental Monitoring and Systematics

Effective environmental management and species conservation are dependent on the quality of the data available. One of the limitations of African conservation efforts is the lack of reliable data on the distribution of species and ecological changes that influence species loss. In many cases the critical ecosystem linkages that support species survival are little understood. In fact, species loss is often used as an indicator of ecosystem disruptions. This method tends to rely on easily observable species and is hardly an effective tool for determining losses arising from subtle changes in the environment.

The field of systematics is generally underfunded in African countries. Large parts of Africa remain partially unexplored and their species distribution undocumented. Many of the international specimen collection and identification programmes that existed last century have also been compromised by the emergence of legal regimes that put biological resources under sovereign control. The need to derive development benefits from biological resources motivated African countries to push the stronger national control over their national resources.

But one of the consequences of some of the provisions of the United Nations Convention on Biological Diversity (CBD) was extended uncertainty over the status of biological material collected from those countries. The adoption of new rules for the international transfer of biological material came long after many collaborative research programmes had been stopped or scaled back. This also undermined interest in international partnerships in training young Africans in systematics.

Technological advancement, especially in the area of gene sequencing, has created new opportunities for African countries to join a new age of rapid systematics. The dramatic fall in the cost of genome sequencing has played a key role in low-cost identification of species. In the past, species identification was a laborious process that took years. Preliminary species identification work can be undertaken with portable sequencing devices that cost less than US$1000. The use of such devices can also help to motivate young people to take interest in systematics. But even where such possibilities exist, African governments are exploring ways to regulate gene sequencing, which would in turn undermine the prospects of renewing international partnerships in systematics.

Much of the cartographic information and data used for environmental planning and management in Africa are out of date. In addition, the existing knowledge base is being rendered obsolete by the same ecological changes that need to be addressed. The first step in seeking lasting solutions to the problem is to conduct real time monitoring of ecological trends. This will involve leveraging the power of emerging Earth observing technologies, especially satellites (Waswa and Juma, 2012).

Part of the slow adoption of satellite technology is the perception that space technology is too expensive. The popular and false image of the technology is derived from the last century, when the space programmes were too expensive for emerging countries. This perception has persisted despite the dramatic fall in costs of developing such programmes. African countries can now establish start-up space programmes with about US$300 million. The costs could be shared by neighbouring countries. The East African Community, for example, could have one regional space programme instead of five separate ones.

More countries around the world are starting to focus on small satellites, which are easier to build and launch in modular constellations. This is also making it possible for students in South Africa to participate in the design of small satellites and the accompanying scientific experiments.

The other major concern is that the few space initiatives that exist in Africa focus more on turnkey projects. Instead, they should stress building the requisite human capacity needed to rise up the space ladder. The best place to build such capacity is in universities, not in secretive departments in government ministries.

The life span of a satellite is about 10 years. Countries that do not invest in continuous training quickly see their ground facilities rendered obsolete by technological change. A space programme only functions effectively when it is supported by a strong human resource foundation on the ground.

The future of environmental monitoring is being transformed by the increased use of emerging technologies such as civilian drones, digital imaging and moisture sensors. The changing climate offers Africa yet another reason to leverage the drones to complement satellite technology. Increasing the installation of weather stations across Africa would provide additional support for environmental monitoring. The land mass of sub-Saharan Africa is 35 times that of Texas (Sara Menker, Gro Intelligence, New York, personal communication). Yet the two have nearly the same number of weather stations.

The long-term contribution of such efforts lies in building strong institutions of higher learning attached to major infrastructure projects. Such universities can then work with networks of technical institutes and high schools to broaden the base for competence in environmental management. The adoption of such technologies will also increase options for citizen engagement in environmental monitoring and enforcement.

Innovation and Economic Transformation

One of the most salient features of Africa's development history has been the low level of technological innovation and industrial growth. Reliance on raw material extraction still remains the dominant development model. This has direct and indirect impacts on the fate of species. The direct impacts arise from human activities such as agricultural expansion and logging. Indirect effects are driven by urbanisation patterns that have no ecological dividend.

This is the background against which African leaders have in recent years been stressing the importation of science, technology and innovation in long-term economic transformation. One example is the African Union's decision to adopt the 10-year Science, Technology and Innovation in Africa Strategy (STISA-2024). The strategy seeks to reposition African countries as technology-driven economies, away from a supplier of raw materials for the global economy.

One of the transitional approaches advocated by African countries is to add value to their natural resources. Policymakers hope that by adding value to exports they can capture more financial returns from their commodities. At the moment, most of the benefits go to nations that process the commodities for the re-export market. For example, in 2014 Africa exported $2.4 billion of coffee. Germany, which is not a producer but a processor, re-exported nearly $3.8 billion worth of coffee worldwide. The standard response to the disparity is to call on Africa to add value to its coffee.

Value addition, however, should not be the primary model for industrial transformation. There is little evidence to support the view that countries industrialise by adding value to their raw materials.

Rather, the causality runs in the opposite direction. Countries add value to raw materials because they already have the requisite technological capacity to do so (Ville and Wicken, 2013). Africa's traditional focus on its minerals has caused it to lag far behind in such efforts.

There is a common perception that industrialised countries advanced mainly because they exploited low-cost natural resources from their colonies. Developing countries then conclude that they too can industrialise and grow by adding value to their natural resources. The evidence from countries such as Australia, Canada and the US does not support the claim (Power, 2002). Commodity booms are often a result of policy incentives, improvements in exploration technology, and investment in resource-related public research (David and Wright, 1997).

African countries have the benefit of being latecomers. Unlike its predecessors, Africa has access to a much wider range of technologies that can serve as platforms for industrial learning. These technologies cover fields such as electronics, digital technologies, genetics, synthetic biology and new materials. Harnessing these technologies requires building among the youth an ethic of innovation that is driven by learning and not extraction.

A critical entry point for creating the learning that cultures need for rapid economic transformation lies in making educational systems more relevant to contemporary needs. The reforms must stress practical approaches to problem-solving, which should include addressing ecological challenges. But more importantly, fields such as engineering need to have priority in order to expand productive opportunities for the youth (Juma, 2016a).

The challenge for Africa is not just to industrialise, but to do so upon an ethical foundation that includes a strong emphasis on conservation. It is only by pursuing such an approach that Africa can avoid the environmental damage caused around the world by industrial development. Technological leapfrogging strategies are likely to backfire if they are not guided by the need to make the sustainability transition. This logic applies to all economic sectors, especially agriculture, given the role of the sector in species loss.

Agricultural Intensification

Agriculture will continue to play a major role in Africa's economic transformation. The manner in which the sector is developed will have significant implications for species survival. A recent study by van Ittersum et al. (2016) shows that sub-Saharan Africa is unlikely to meet its cereal needs under current productivity growth rates without major cropland expansion and food imports (van Ittersum et al., 2016). The study assessed trends in Burkina Faso, Ghana, Mali, Niger, Nigeria, Ethiopia, Kenya, Tanzania, Uganda and Zambia.

It focused on whether self-sufficiency can be achieved in five main cereals (maize, millet, rice, sorghum and wheat) by 2050. The 10 countries account for 54 per cent of Africa's total population and 58 per cent of the arable land area. The article shows 'that although yield gap closure on existing cropland and a large acceleration in yield growth rates are essential to achieve cereal self-sufficiency, they are most likely not sufficient. For instance, increasing maize yields from the approximately 20 per cent of yield potential in 2010 to 50 per cent by 2050 implies a doubling of annual yield increases compared with the past decades. Even then, cereal areas must increase by more than 80 per cent to realise self-sufficiency in the 10 countries' (van Ittersum et al., 2016: 14968).

Achieving self-sufficiency will entail closing the yield gap, increasing cropping intensity and expanding irrigated land areas in suitable regions. Pursuing these sustainable intensification options will involve considerable private and public investment in research and development. But even more importantly, it must be guided by specific policy measures that reduce its ecological impact. Leveraging emerging technologies needs to be accompanied by a wide range of institutional innovations that help to align agricultural expansion with ecological considerations.

Efforts to find alternative livelihoods for people relying on direct utilisation of natural resources such as bushmeat hunting show little evidence of success. A study of 64 such projects in Central Africa shows that many projects are 'funded through small, short-term grants, and are struggling to meet their objectives with the available time, funding and capacity' (Wicander and Coad, 2015: 4). The projects are mostly managed by non-governmental organisations focusing on small localities. Their impact is largely negligible despite their efforts to involve local communities.

The way forward will involve major efforts to make African agriculture more knowledge-intensive and entrepreneurial (Juma, 2015). There are a number of measures that can help achieve this objective.

These include harnessing emerging technologies, investing in research and development, strengthening technical education, expanding rural infrastructure and promoting regional trade. These measures must be pursued with sustainability objectives in mind.

Africa is seeking to expand its agriculture at a time when it has access to a wide range of emerging technologies that can help to facilitate the adoption of sustainable intensification practices. Technologies such as transgenic crops, satellites, drones and sensors can be deployed to provide critical information on weather and moisture that could assist in optimising the use of water. Drones are already being used in countries such as Nigeria to carry out surveys to determine the most optimal regions for crop production. Other technologies such as mobile phones are already being adapted to a wide range of agricultural uses and will become critical tools in the creation of a new agricultural extension system throughout the continent. Further adaptations in smartphones, for example, will turn them into mobile labs supporting activities such as plant disease identification and nutrient testing.

Transgenic crops have been a subject of considerable controversy in Africa. The debates have made it difficult to consider each application on its own merit and to identify those that can contribute to agricultural intensification by reducing the amount of land used in production, cutting back on the use of insecticides, and reducing the need for tillage. One of the arguments against transgenic crops is that they lead to monoculture, which is detrimental to biodiversity. The use of monoculture, however, is a choice of farming system, not the method used to confer certain traits to crops. Monocultures are common in crops that do not use transgenic crops. Advances in gene editing are also ushering in new techniques that could achieve the same goals without the transfer of genes across species.

A more pressing challenge, however, is increasing R&D expenditures not only for plant breeding but also for adapting existing technologies to local conditions. Closely related to this point is the need to provide training programmes that prepare young people for modern farming methods both in rural and urban areas. This will require reforms in existing educational institutions to make them more practical and experiential. Currently, many agriculture departments in Africa still train students for non-existent government positions. The challenge is to reform curricula so that they can focus on sustainable agribusiness.

The prevalence of subsistence agriculture in much of Africa is a result of poor infrastructure, especially energy, transportation and irrigation. Investment in such infrastructure will not only facilitate sustainable intensification with the appropriate support, but it will be easier for farmers to increase their incomes through local and regional trade. Only about 4 per cent of African agriculture is irrigated, whereas the share is 45 per cent in Asia and 18 per cent worldwide. A growing number of African countries are already taking advantage of emerging technologies to adopt solar irrigation. This is just one example by which new technologies could help in redesigning rural infrastructure so that it meets sustainability requirements.

Agricultural trade among African countries is vital to sustaining agriculture. In 2013 only 17 per cent of the food imported by African countries came from within the continent. Regional trade in agricultural produce could help countries decide on regional specialisation, which would help them avoid attempting to fulfil their food needs without the benefits of economies of scale and sustainable intensification.

The establishment of the Tripartite Free Trade Area in 2015 created a market of more than 300 million people in 26 countries valued at US$1.5 trillion. Africa is currently negotiating a Continental Free Trade Area that will cover a billion people in 54 countries with a combined GDP of over US$3.5 trillion. Agriculture could be one of the key beneficiaries of this market. In addition to incorporating produce, the market will also provide opportunities for trade in agricultural technology and services. Technologies and services for sustainable intensification could be part of this market.

Conclusions

Africa's biological diversity is at an inflection point. Over the last five decades the continent has been pursuing economic strategies that in theory could foster rapid economic growth and help reduce pressure on natural systems. Much of the concern over the fate of Africa's biological diversity has been based largely on relying on past trends in relationships between population growth and natural habitats. However, evidence shows the exceptional nature of key drivers of ecological changes such as demographic change and urbanisation. The impact of population on the environment is not just driven by the sheer growth in human numbers, but by their amplification effects.

Unlike in other regions of the world, Africa's population growth has not been accompanied by industrialisation and improvements in agricultural productivity. Urban centres are largely populated by poor people with limited access to modern infrastructure such as electricity. Large proportions of urban dwellers rely on the extraction of wood fuel as well as diverse sources of nutrition – including bush meat – which lead to species extirpation. The low levels of agricultural productivity are associated with farming methods that lead to habitat loss and fragmentation.

There are, however, indications that fertility rates are starting to decline, especially in urban areas. Emerging evidence also shows that agricultural productivity is rising, especially in countries that have increased their agricultural research funding. Overall, these positive trends are too slow to deliver the kind of changes needed to reduce pressures on species survival. Additional measures are needed to facilitate economic transformation in ways that are sustainable.

Urgent measures are needed to facilitate the demographic transition, an essential starting point for sustainable development. Policies that promote reproductive rights and family planning are needed for sustainable development. But such policies will not be enough to reduce species loss unless they are accompanied by new approaches that focus on the need to integrate conservation with economic activity. Some of these policies could take advantage of the growing emphasis on regional integration in Africa by creating trans-boundary wildlife conservation programmes.

The way forward entails the construction of a new ethic that acknowledges the importance of coexistence between humans and other species. Such a new ethic will also involve massive ecological education, legal change and institutional adjustments which take into account the exceptional nature of the African setting. The desirability and benefits of such innovation will not be sufficient to guarantee their adoption. There will be many incumbent forces that will stand in the way of such efforts. Additional time and energy will need to be invested in addressing the sources of resistance to change (Juma, 2016b). Much of this work will involve close partnerships between government, academia, the private sector, civil society and private individuals. Achieving this fast enough to stall the pace of species loss will require leaders and governance systems at all levels to champion a new contract between humans and nature, the kind of approach foreshadowed by Saint Francis.

References

Abernethy, K. A., Coad, L., Taylor, G., Lee, M. E. & Maisels, F. 2013. Extent and ecological consequences of hunting in Central African rainforests in the twenty-first century. *Philosophical Transactions of the Royal Society B: Biological Sciences*, 368(1625). DOI:10.1098/rstb.2012.0303.

AGRA. 2017. *Africa Agriculture Status Report: The Business of Smallholder Agriculture in Sub-Saharan Africa* (Issue 5). Nairobi, Kenya: Alliance for a Green Revolution in Africa (AGRA).

Ancrenaz, M., Meijaard, E., Wich, S. & Simery, J. 2016. *Palm Oil Paradox: Sustainable Solutions to Save the Great Apes.* Nairobi: UN Environmental Programme.

Annorbah, N. N. D., Collar, N. J. & Marsden, S. J. 2016. Trade and habitat change virtually eliminate the Grey Parrot *Psittacus erithacus* from Ghana. *Ibis*, 158(1): 82–91.

Balmford, A., Moore, J. L., Brooks, T., Burgess, N., Hansen, L. A., Williams, P. & Rahbek, C. 2001. Conservation conflicts across Africa. *Science*, 291(5513): 2616–2619.

BirdLife International. 2017. Psittacus erithacus. *The IUCN Red List of Threatened Species 2016.* e.T22724813A94879563. https://doi.org/10.2305/IUCN.UK.2018-2.RLTS.T22724813A129879439.en.

Blake, S., Deem, S. L., Mossimbo, E., Maisels, F. & Walsh, P. 2009. Forest elephants: Tree planters of the Congo. *Biotropica*, 41: 459–468.

Canning, D., Raja, S. & Yazbeck, A. S. 2015. *Africa's Demographic Transition: Dividend or Disaster?* Washington, DC: World Bank.

Chazdon, R. L., Harvey, C. A., Komar, O., Griffith, D. M., Ferguson, B. G., Martínez-Ramos, M., Morales, H., Nigh, R., Soto-Pinto, L., Van Breugel, M. & Philpott, S. M. 2009. Beyond reserves: A research agenda for conserving biodiversity in human-modified tropical landscapes. *Biotropica*, 41: 142–153.

Coe, M. T. & Foley, J. A. 2001. Human and natural impacts on the water resources of the Lake Chad basin. *Journal of Geophysical Research*, 106 (D4): 3349–3356.

Cohen, A. S., Gergurich, E. L., Kraemer, B. M., McGlue, M. M., McIntyre, P. B., Russell, J. M., Simmons, J. D. & Swarzenski, P. W. 2016. Climate warming reduces fish production and benthic habitat in Lake Tanganyika, one of the most biodiverse freshwater ecosystems. *Proceedings of the National Academy of Sciences*, 113(34): 9563–9568.

Dasgupta, A. & Dasgupta, P. 2017. Socially embedded preferences, environmental externalities, and reproductive rights. *Population and Development Review*, 43: 405–441.

David, P. A. & Wright, G. 1997. Increasing returns and the genesis of American resource abundance. *Industrial and Corporate Change*, 6 (2): 203–245.

DeFries, R. S., Rudel, T., Uriarte, M. & Hansen, M. 2010. Deforestation driven by urban population growth and agricultural trade in the twenty-first century. *Nature Geoscience*, 3: 178–181.

Doumbouya, A., Camara, O. T., Mamie, Josephus, Intchama, J. F., Jarra, A., Ceesay, S., Guèye, A., Ndiaye, D., Beibous, E., Padilla, A. & Belhaviv, D. 2017. Assessing the effectiveness of monitoring control and surveillance of illegal fishing: The case of West Africa. *Frontiers in Marine Science*, 4(50). doi:10.3389/fmars.2017.00050.

Durant, S. M., Mitchell, N., Groom, R., Pettorelli, N., Ipavec, A., Jacobson, A. P., Woodroffe, R., Böhm, M., Hunter, L. T. B., Becker, M. S., Broekhuis, F., Bashir, S., Andresen, L., Aschenborn, O., Beddiaf, M., Belbachir, F., Belbachir-Bazi, A., Berbash, A., Machado, I. B. D., Breitenmoser, C., Chege, M., Cilliers, D., Davies-Mostert, H., Dickman, A. J., Ezekiel, F., Farhadinia, M. S., Funston, P., Henschel, P., Horgan, J., de Iongh, H. H., Jowkar, H., Klein, R., Lindsey, P. A., Marker, L., Marnewick, K., Melzheimer, J., Merkle, J., M'Soka, J., Msuha, M., O'Neill, H., Parker, M., Purchase, G., Sahailou, S., Saidu, Y., Samna, A., Schmidt-Kuntzel, A., Selebatso, E., Sogbohossou, E. A., Soultan, A., Stone, E., van der Meer, E., van Vuuren, R., Wykstra, M. & Young-Overton, K. 2017. The global decline of cheetah *Acinonyx jubatus* and what it means for conservation. *Proceedings of the National Academy of Sciences*, 114(3): 528–533.

Durant, S., Mitchell, N., Ipavec, A. & Groom, R. 2015. Acinonyx jubatus. *The IUCN Red List of Threatened Species 2015*. e.T219A50649567. https://doi.org/10.2305/IUCN.UK.2015-4.RLTS.T219A50649567.en.

Estrada, A., Garber, P. A., Rylands, A. B., Roos, C., Fernandez-Duque, E., Di Fiore, A., Nekaris, K. A.-I., Nijman, V., Heymann, E. W., Lambert, J. E., Rovero, F., Barellis, C., Setchell, J. M., Gillespie, T. R., Mittermeier, R. A., Arregoitia, L. V., de Guinea, M., Gouveia, S., Dobrovolski, R., Shanee, S., Shanee, N., Boyle, S. A., Fuentes, A., MacKinnon, K. C., Amato, K. R., Meyer, A. L. S., Wich, S., Sussman, R. W., Pan, R., Kone, I. & Li, B. 2016. Impending extinction crisis of the world's primates: Why primates matter. *Science Advances*, 3(1), e1600946.

Fennessy, J., Bidon, T., Reuss, F., Kumar, V., Elkan, P., Nilsson, M. A., Vamberger, M., Fritz, U. & Janke, A. 2016. Multi-locus analyses reveal four giraffe species instead of one. *Current Biology*, 26(18): 2543–2549.

Fisher, B. 2010. African exception to drivers of deforestation. *Nature Geoscience*, 3: 375–376.

Freire, M. E., Lall, S. & Leipziger, D. 2014. *Africa's Urbanization: Challenges and Opportunities.* Working Paper Number 7. Washington, DC: The Growth Dialogue.

Galis, F. & Metz, J. A. J. 1998. Why are there so many cichlid species? *Trends in Ecology and Evolution*, 13(1): 1–2.

Gao, H., Bohn, T. J., Podest, E., McDonald, K. C. & Lettenmaier, D. P. 2011. On the causes of the shrinking of Lake Chad. *Environmental Research Letters*, 6: 034021.

Harper, G. J., Steininger, M. K., Tucker, C. J., Joun, D. & Hawkins, F. 2007. Fifty years of deforestation and forest fragmentation in Madagascar. *Environmental Conservation*, 34(4): 325–333.

International Energy Agency. 2014. *Africa Energy Outlook.* Paris: International Energy Agency.

Juma, C. 2015. *The New Harvest: Agricultural Innovation in Africa.* New York: Oxford University Press.

2016a. *Education, Research, and Innovation in Africa: Forging Strategic Linkages for Economic Transformation.* Discussion Paper 2016–01. Cambridge, MA: Harvard Kennedy School.

2016b. *Innovation and Its Enemies: Why People Resist New Technologies.* New York: Oxford University Press.

Kaufman, L. 1992. Catastrophic change in species-rich freshwater ecosystems. *BioScience*, 42(11): 846–858.

Lall, S. V., Henderson, J. V. & Venables, A. J. 2017. *Africa's Cities: Opening Doors to the World.* Washington, DC: World Bank.

Muller, Z., Bercovitch, F., Brand, R., Brown, D., Brown, M., Bolger, D., Carter, K., Deacon, F., Doherty, J. B., Fennessy, J., Fennessy, S., Hussein, A. A., Lee, D., Marais, A., Strauss, M., Tutchings, A. & Wube, T. 2016. Giraffa camelopardalis. *The IUCN Red List of Threatened Species 2016*: e.T9194A109326950. https://doi.org/10.2305/IUCN.UK.2016-3.RLTS.T9194A136266699.en.

Nellemann, C., Henriksen, R., Kreilhuber, A., Steward, D., Kotsovou, M., Raxter, P., Mrema, E. & Barrat, S. (Eds.). 2016. *The Rise of Environmental Crime – A Growing Threat To Natural Resources Peace, Development and Security.* Nairobi, Kenya: United Nations Environment Programme.

Ogutu-Ohwayo, R. 1990. The decline of the native fishes of Lakes Victoria and Kyoga (East Africa) and the impact of introduced species, especially the Nile perch, *Lates niloticus*, and the Nile tilapia, *Oreochromis niloticus*. *Environmental Biology of Fishes*, 27(2): 81–96.

Onuoha, F. C. 2008. Saving Africa's shrinking lakes through inter-basin water transfer: Reflections on the Lake Chad Replenishment Project. *Nigerian Journal of International Affairs*, 34: 65–84.

Pfeifer, M., Burgess, N. D., Swetnam, R. D., Platts, P. J., Willcock, S. & Marchant, R. 2012. Protected areas: Mixed success in conserving East Africa's evergreen forests. *PLoS One*, 7(6): e39337.

Power, T. M. 2002. *Digging for Development? A Historical Look at Mining and Economic Development*. Boston: Oxfam America.

Pringle, R. M. 2005. The origins of the Nile perch in Lake Victoria. *BioScience*, 55(9): 780–787.

Ripple, W. J., Abernethy, K., Betts, M. B., Chapron, G., Dirzo, R., Galetti, M., Levi, T., Lindsey, P. A., Macdonald, D. W., Machovina, B., Newsome, T. M., Peres, C. A., Wallach, A. D., Wolf, C. & Young, H. 2016. Bushmeat hunting and extinction risk to the world's mammals. *Royal Society Open Science*, 3: 160498.

Rudel, T. K. 2013. The national determinants of deforestation in sub-Saharan Africa. *Philosophical Transactions of the Royal Society B*, 368: 20120405.

Ruf, F. O. 2011. The myth of complex cocoa agroforests: The case of Ghana. *Human Ecology*, 39(3): 373–388.

Sarch, M. T. 2001. Fishing and farming at Lake Chad: Institutions for access to natural resources. *Journal of Environmental Management*, 62: 185–199.

Slingenberg, A., Braat, L., van der Windt, H., Eichler, L. & Turner, K. 2009. *Study on Understanding the Causes of Biodiversity Loss and the Policy Assessment Framework*. Rotterdam, The Netherlands: ECORYS Research and Consulting.

Thibault, M. & Blaney S. 2003. The oil industry as an underlying factor in the bushmeat crisis in Central Africa. *Conservation Biology*, 17: 1807–0813.

United Nations, Department of Economic and Social Affairs, Population Division. 2015. *World Population Prospects: The 2015 Revision, Key Findings and Advance Tables*. Working Paper No. ESA/P/WP.241. New York: United Nations.

United Nations Environment Programme. 2010a. *Africa: Atlas of Our Changing Environment*. Nairobi, Kenya: United Nations Environment Programme.

2010b. *State of Biodiversity in Africa*. Nairobi, Kenya: United Nations Environment Programme.

van Ittersum, M. K., van Bussel, L. G. J., Wolf, J., Grassini, P., van Wart, J., Guilpart, N., Claessens, L., de Groot, H., Wiebe, K., Mason-D'Croz, D., Yang, H., Boogaard, H., van Oort, P. A. J., van Loon, M. P., Saito, K., Adimo, O., Adjei-Nsiah, A., Agali, A., Bala, A., Chikowo, R., Kaizzi, K., Kouressy, M., Makoi, J. H. J. R., Ouattara, K., Tesfaye, K. & Cassman, K. G. 2016. Can sub-Saharan

Africa feed itself? *Proceedings of the National Academy of Sciences*, 113(52): 14964–14969.

van Zwieten, P. A. M., Kolding, J., Plank, M. J., Hecky, R., Bridgeman, T. B., MacIntyre, S., Seehausen, O. & Silsbei, G. M. 2016. The Nile perch invasion in Lake Victoria: Cause or consequence of the haplochromine decline. *Canadian Journal of Fisheries and Aquatic Sciences*, 73(4): 622–643.

Vijay, V., Pimm, S. L., Jenkins, C. N. & Smith, S. J. 2016. The impacts of oil palm on recent deforestation and biodiversity loss. *PLoS One*, 11(7): e0159668.

Ville, S. & Wicken, O. 2013. The dynamics of resource-based economic development: Evidence from Australia and Norway. *Industrial and Corporate Change*, 22(5): 1341–1371.

Waswa, P. & Juma, C. 2012. Establishing a space sector for sustainable development in Kenya. *International Journal of Technology and Globalisation*, 6(1/2): 152–169.

White, Jr. L. 1967. The historical roots of our ecologic crisis. *Science*, 155 (3767): 1207.

Wicander, S. & Coad, L. 2015. *Learning Our Lessons: A Review of Alternative Livelihood Projects in Central Africa*. Gland, Switzerland: IUCN.

Wilkie, D., Shaw, E., Rotberg, F., Morelli, G. & Auzel, P. 2000. Roads, development, and conservation in the Congo Basin. *Conservation Biology*, 14: 1614–1622.

Witte, F., Wanink, J. H. & Kishe-Machumu, M. 2007. Species distinction and the biodiversity crisis in Lake Victoria. *Transactions of the American Fisheries Society*, 136(4): 1146–1159.

Woolston, C. 2016. DNA reveals four giraffe species. *Nature*, 537: 290.

9 | Why We're in the Sixth Great Extinction and What It Means to Humanity

PARTHA S. DASGUPTA AND PAUL R. EHRLICH

The annihilation of biological diversity is one of the most severe human-induced global environmental problems. Species and populations are being driven to extinction every year at so high a rate, that Earth's assemblage of plants and animals is now well into a sixth mass extinction episode.[1] The most recent Living Planet Index has estimated that wildlife abundance on the planet dropped by some 60 per cent between 1970 and 2012 (WWF, 2016). The richest biota the world has ever seen is disappearing in the blink of an eye from the perspective of geological time. And humanity is busily making it worse.

Why Preserve Biodiversity?

One reason humanity should care about the destruction of biodiversity is that it leads to the deterioration of ecosystem services upon which civilisation is utterly dependent (Daily, 1997; Ehrlich and Ehrlich, 1981; Holdren and Ehrlich, 1974). These services include preserving and regenerating soil, fixing nitrogen and carbon, pollinating crops, recycling nutrients, controlling floods, filtering pollutants, maintaining a genetic library, operating the hydrological cycle, controlling pests and disease vectors, maintaining the gaseous composition of the atmosphere, and providing cultural, intellectual, spiritual and aesthetic inspiration. Enumerating those services indicates how deeply intertwined are the problems of improving the welfare of humanity (Arrow et al., 2014). Most of these ecosystem services cannot be replaced by artificial means. The few that can will incur extraordinary costs. It is far better to avoid destroying the services that nature provides for free, than to incur massive costs for replacements that will never be complete. Moreover, it is the poor of the world who are most directly dependent upon ecosystem services (Dasgupta, 1993; Kumar, 2012; ten Brink et al., 2012). Contemporary industrial activities, including industrial agriculture, usually have devastating impacts on local ecosystem services that are essential to the lives of poor, rural and forest communities in developing countries. The economic benefits of those industrial works rarely filter back to the victims.

Research over the past two decades has drawn increasing attention to the diversity of microorganisms crucial to our lives (Montgomery and Biklé, 2015). That includes the microbiomes of soil and those involved in industry (what professor Andrew Beattie[2] calls 'production biodiversity') and the microbiomes of human bodies.

Ethics and Conservation

The arguments above focus on pragmatic reasons to maintain biodiversity. There are profound ethical reasons also. Below we identify the causes behind the ongoing sixth great extinction, the first in 66 million years. Whatever created this miraculous collection of life, it is morally reprehensible for humans to destroy it in the pursuit of unnecessary adornments and obscene wealth. Pope Francis (2015) has given expression to this in his magisterial Encyclical:

Each year sees the disappearance of thousands of plant and animal species which we will never know, which our children will never see, because they have been lost for ever. The great majority become extinct for reasons related to human activity. Because of us, thousands of species will no longer give glory to God by their very existence, nor convey their message to us. We have no such right.

Causes of the Destruction of Biodiversity: Habitat Destruction

Some of the proximal causes of the extinction process that is now destroying the life-forms that share Earth with *Homo sapiens* – the only known living beings in the universe – are obvious. The first is habitat destruction and its near synonym, 'land use change'. Natural ecosystems are converted by human activities into grazing lands, tree plantations, croplands, roads, railroads, airports and cities. Natural ecosystems are cut down, ploughed under, poisoned and paved over. All organisms depend on an appropriate environment to persist; a coral reef for many kinds of animals, a tropical forest for many others, a human body for some kinds of microbes. Few creatures can survive in ploughed fields or on pavement. With some 40 per cent of Earth's land in crops and pasture[3] and another 2 per cent paved or built over, and with *every* habitat changing in temperature and polluted by synthetic toxic chemicals, it is not hard to see why many plants and animals are in trouble – especially in view of the projected increase in human pressure on the biosphere. Toxification of the planet's ecosystems and the organisms within them is pervasive, with air and water transport of contaminants to the most remote landscapes in the world. Scientists have even found persistent organic pollutants in the crustaceans six miles under the sea in the bottom of the Marianas Trench.[4] The expanding human enterprise is relentlessly converting forests, wetlands and grasslands into farmland, which destroys local biodiversity. Habitats are undergoing change today of a rapidity not seen in 66 million years, since the last mass extinction event that killed off all the dinosaurs (except for birds).

Total destruction of an environment is not necessary to push plants and animals to extinction. Cutting roads through tropical forests may make some of the resulting fragments too small to support populations of various animals, and cause microclimate changes, the consequent drying extending well inside the forest edge, thus destroying populations of plants and the animals dependent on them (Harper et al., 2007). Even the moving around of species can lethally alter the habitats of native organisms. In lakes, rivers and oceans, silting, rising temperatures, increasing acidification, chemical pollution, plastic debris, fish nets and heavy ship traffic can amount to habitat destruction for organisms as diverse as plankton, river dolphins, marine plankton with calcified shells like foraminifera, and corals. The loss of coral reefs will be especially disastrous because of the rich array of other organisms they support. At concentrations in the water column of fewer than 100 parts per trillion, a common ingredient of sunscreens can initiate coral bleaching.[5]

Causes of the Destruction of Biodiversity: Overharvesting

A second cause of biodiversity destruction is harvesting renewable natural resources like plant and animal populations at rates that exceed their regenerative capacity. Examples that are frequently cited are disappearing megafauna; overharvesting has reduced such iconic animals as gorillas, rhinos, elephants and whales to a relatively few remnant groups. Some 99 per cent of African elephants have been destroyed by *Homo sapiens* (Safina, 2015). We exterminated all of the mammoths and mastodons before people settled and developed a global ivory trade that persists to this day. Many species of endangered animals such as various pangolins, mammals whose skin is covered by keratin scales, are threatened because of oriental (largely Chinese) demand for their meat and scales (thought by some to have medicinal value) (Xu et al., 2016). Sharks and swordfish are also endangered by overfishing, and the main reason why great whales are so scarce now compared to the eighteenth century was the Western demand for whale oil in the nineteenth. It is not only animals that suffer overharvesting – so do cacti, where populations can be extirpated by removing them from nature for planting in gardens, indoor decoration, medical, recreational and religious use (Robbins, 2003).

Resources and Pollutants

To identify the proximal causes behind the Sixth Extinction with habitat destruction and overharvesting is to model the biosphere as a renewable natural resource. However, the underlying model covers pollution as well (application of pesticides; contemporary carbon emissions into the atmosphere; and so on). Pollutants reduce the capacity of the sink into which they are discharged. The way to conceptualise pollution economically is to view it as the depreciation of a sink. The latter is a capital asset. As examples: acid rains damage forests; carbon emissions into the atmosphere trap heat; industrial seepage and discharge reduce water quality in streams and underground reservoirs; sulphur emissions corrode structures and harm human health; and so on. The damage inflicted on each type of asset (buildings, forests, the atmosphere, fisheries, human health) should be interpreted as depreciation. In the case of natural resources, depreciation amounts to the difference between the rate at which they are harvested and their regenerative rate; in the case of pollutants, the relevant depreciation is the difference between the rate at which they are discharged into the sink and the rate at which the sink is able to recover, in quality or quantity. The task in either case is to estimate those depreciations. It follows that the analytical structures of resource management problems and pollution management problems are the same. Roughly speaking, 'resources' are 'goods', while 'pollutants' (the degrader of resources) are 'bads'. Pollution is the reverse of conservation.

Causes of the Destruction of Biodiversity: The Irony of Agriculture

That conversion to agriculture is so destructive to habitats is ironic, since agriculture is deeply dependent on biodiversity and the ecosystem services it delivers, from the soil microbes that recycle nutrients that nourish crops to surrounding vegetation that regulates the hydrological cycle. For example, coffee farms in Costa Rica do much better if natural forest is left unmolested nearby. The forest provides habitat for bees that pollinate the coffee, adding substantial value to the crop (Ricketts et al., 2004). Farms commonly destroy habitat for birds, bats, frogs, predacious insects and other enemies of crop pests, and to replace these natural pest controlling ecosystem services industrial farming operations spread deadly poisons far and wide. As a result, pesticides now affect populations of animals from pole to pole. Polar bears suffer from production of food in California (Sonne, 2010). Honey bees that originated in southern Asia now pollinate crops around the world, but they and native bee species are threatened by the worldwide use of neonicotinoid pesticides (Goulson, 2013; Goulson et al., 2015). The application of pesticides and land use change are elements in the pollination crisis humanity has begun to experience. 'Wild pollinators are in decline, and managed honeybees cannot compensate for their loss' (Tylianakis, 2013). Wild schemes to produce artificial drones to replace bees in pollination are appearing in the news, but they are far too expensive to take to scale. Artificial fertilisers devastate the micro-organisms and invertebrates that help give soil its fertility, and ploughing helps overtax critical soil resources (Montgomery and Biklé, 2015).

Agriculture is far from the only source of chemical pollution that assaults biodiversity. A dazzling array of novel synthetic organic compounds, including hormone disrupting chemicals with impacts on the reproductive biology of people and other vertebrates (Maffini et al., 2006), has been and continues to be released into the environment so rapidly that the releases outpace other well-known agents of global change (Bernhardt et al., 2017). Persistent organic pollutants such as DDT and PCBs now coat the massive amounts of tiny plastic pellets accumulating in the oceans, are then carried on them into the food chains that support ocean life and lead to human beings (Rios et al., 2007). Industrial extraction of ores from the Earth's crust spreads heavy metals and other naturally occurring toxins widely, bringing them into contact with organisms, including people, that have not evolved defences against them.

Climate Disruption and Other Causes

One of the most serious assaults on biodiversity obviously is the discharge of large quantities of carbon dioxide and other greenhouse gases into the atmosphere. The climate disruption it causes is, of course, a threat to organisms with tight requirements of temperature regimes within which they can survive. Thermal limits on animal distributions are well known but poorly understood (Sunday et al., 2012), and heating itself can be trouble for plants (Heskel et al., 2016). Historically plants and animals have long been known to migrate in response to changing climates, or gradually to evolve new tolerances, or to go extinct (Dorf, 1955). Today's situation is unique, with substantial human barriers to migration and rates of change sufficiently rapid to prevent evolution in situ for organisms whose generation times are in years. Furthermore, in addition to heating the oceans, humanity is, as noted above, also acidifying them. Sea level rise caused by ocean warming will eventually flood huge areas of coastal land, thus further threatening terrestrial biodiversity, including ourselves. Climate warming also is not independent of global pollution problems. Among other things it increases the release of toxic pollutants trapped in ice or sediments (Obbard et al., 2014).

Besides spreading toxic chemicals globally, humanity is also changing the distributions of organisms, sometimes to the disadvantage of members of the recipient ecosystems. While adding to the diversity of a local site, invasive species, by forcing natives to extinction, may reduce global diversity (Crowl et al., 2008). Some cases are dramatic. The transfer of a European fungal pathogen to North America, perhaps by spelunkers, has devastated American bat populations (Warnecke et al., 2012), lessening the ecosystem service of controlling crop pests and disease vectors. Spreading fungal diseases now pose a serious threat to biodiversity (including *Homo sapiens*) (Fisher et al., 2012), having already participated in a wave of amphibian extinctions (Phillott et al., 2013; Rowley et al., 2007).

One possible cause of major destruction of biodiversity is nuclear war. Even a small war would likely damage global civilisation hugely (Toon et al., 2007). Conventional warfare also often harms biodiversity (Hanson et al., 2009), but ironically can sometimes help protect it by making overexploitation more difficult (McNeely, 2003). That, of course, in no way reduces the need for humanity to give up battle as an instrument of policy.

In sum, the driving force of extinction, the ultimate cause of the current sixth mass extinction crisis is much too high a level of aggregate consumption.[6] Biodiversity is a critical (and much neglected) part of humanity's natural capital, which civilisation is rapidly depleting (Ceballos et al., 2015a, 2015b; Pimm et al., 2014). Such degradation of a natural resource base (destruction of native populations of flora and fauna) affects the volume of production. It has been found in experiments in field stations that species-rich plots yield greater bio-mass than species-poor ones, which would indicate that the total productivity of an assemblage of species is greater than the sum of the productivities of any individual species grown in isolation. This reflects a form of synergy (Tilman et al., 2001). Loss of species richness not only affects the quality of ecosystem services, but also challenges the system's resilience which is its capacity to absorb disturbances without undergoing fundamental changes in its functional characteristics. Thus diversity itself may contribute to preservation of natural capital in the long run, and extinctions can compromise the ability of capital to be restocked after calamity. As with other natural resources, humanity is now living on its capital rather than the interest from that capital (Klare, 2012). The need to dangerously degrade our living capital stock is one of the surest signs of expansion of the human enterprise, overconsumption by the rich, and approaching collapse (Ehrlich and Ehrlich, 2013).

The Biosphere in the Anthropocene

We measure humanity's impact on the biosphere, and thus on biodiversity, in terms of the demands we make on it, both as a source of goods and services and as a repository of the waste we produce. Those demands can be measured in terms of the volume and composition of our economic activities. GDP is the most commonly used index of those activities. A large GDP signals a large demand on the biosphere, a small GDP in turn signals a small demand.

Studying biogeochemical signatures over the past 11,000 years has provided a sketch of the human-induced evolution of soil nitrogen and phosphorus inventories (more specifically of polyaromatic hydrocarbons, polychlorinated biphenyls and pesticide residues) in sediments and ice (Waters et al., 2016). The authors reported a sharp increase in the middle of the twentieth century in the inventories. Their work shows that the now-famous figure of the 'hockey stick' (Mann, 2012) that characterises time series of atmospheric carbon emission also characterises a broad class of geochemical signatures, and signal a sharp increase in the rate of deterioration of Earth's life-support system. It has been proposed (Waters et al., 2016) that the mid-twentieth century should be regarded as the time we entered the era now widely named the Anthropocene. Not coincidentally, it roughly corresponds with the rapid expansion of the sixth mass extinction event.

These readings are consistent with macroeconomic statistics. World population in 1950 was 2.5 billion and global GDP was a bit over 7.5 trillion international dollars (at 2015 prices). The average person in the world was poor, with an annual income of a bit over 3000 international dollars. Since then the world has prospered materially beyond recognition. Life expectancy at birth has risen from a global average of 49 years to 71 years, population has increased to 7.5 billion and world output of final goods and services (global GDP) is now 110 trillion international dollars, meaning that per capita global income is about 15,000 international dollars. The proportion of the world's population in absolute poverty (regarded by the World Bank to be below 1.9 international dollars a day) has fallen so dramatically (it is now just over 10 per cent of the world's population, down from about 50 per cent in 1980 but still, disgracefully, some 750 million individuals in a world replete with rich people), that enthusiasts predict that within a generation the blight will have been eliminated (Jamison et al., 2013). Set against those achievements, however, is that the 15-fold increase in global output over a 65-year period reflects not only the stresses to the Earth system in general and biodiversity in particular that we have just reviewed, but also that humanity's demands from the biosphere have for some time exceeded its capacity to supply them.

But demand cannot exceed supply indefinitely. Translated into the language of equity, humanity's enormous success in recent decades is very likely to have been a down payment for future failure. The trade-off is between living standards today and living standards in the future. Our immediate success in raising the average standard of living has created a conflict between us and our descendants. Nevertheless, contemporary success receives the far greater hearing in public discourse. If you worry about environmental degradation, you will be told that nature does not represent much more than 5 per cent of global wealth (a figure derived from the share of agricultural income in global output at market prices) and that natural capital can be so shifted round in the contemporary world, that dwindling supplies in one place can be met by imports from another. Intellectuals and commentators use the terms 'globalisation' and 'flat Earth' to imply that location does not matter. The view emphasises the prospects offered by trade and investment and says if they are not enough, technological progress can be relied upon to solve the problems arising from environmental degradation. Today Malthus, the 'pessimistic parson', is seen as a 'false prophet', remaining as wrong as ever (*The Economist*, 15 May 2008), and books celebrating humanity's achievements read as breathless expressions of triumphalism.[7]

The reason the intergenerational conflict we have identified here is not widely appreciated is that it remains hidden. And it remains hidden because it has become customary to interpret success as economic success, and economic success as growth in GDP. The notion of sustainable development in the Brundtland Commission Report was designed to reflect a balancing of the interests of the present and future generations. Economic progress should therefore mean growth in what we may loosely call a society's 'productive capacity'. GDP does not reflect productive capacity. It instead measures the magnitude of economic activity at a point in time (a year usually), estimated at market prices; whereas productive capacity points to an economy's portfolio of assets. GDP is a flow, whereas assets are stocks. An economy's portfolio of assets reflects its capacity to produce goods and services, now and in the future.

The assets in question include not only manufactured capital (roads, buildings, machines) and human capital (health and education), but also living natural capital (pollinators enriching human diets, enemies of crop pests keeping humanity able to practice high-yield agriculture, songbirds giving us pleasure, wetland plants purifying water and reducing flooding, life-rich estuaries playing nurseries to oceanic food fishes, forests sequestering dangerous carbon dioxide, grasslands supporting game herds, vegetation guarding water sources allowing us to produce crops, microorganisms in soil nourishing crops; more broadly the composition of the biosphere).

The social worth of an economy's stock of capital assets is its wealth. It can be shown that wealth reflects an economy's productive capacity (Dasgupta, 2004). When environmental degradation exceeds the accumulation of manufactured and human capital, wealth declines. Normative economics tells us that the indicator we should deploy for assessing the sustainability of human development is the magnitude and distribution of the wealth of nations relative to their population size (Arrow et al., 2012), not the per capita GDP of nations, nor the Human Development Index of nations.[8] Intergenerational well-being is shaped by the balance humanity strikes between population size and the portfolio of productive assets. Wealth and its distribution, relative to population size, is a measure of that balance.

GDP is incapable of saying much about future possibilities because of the qualifier 'gross', which signals that the depreciation of assets, especially degradation of the biosphere, is ignored. Nevertheless, GDP has assumed such prominence in public discourse today, that if someone mentions 'economic growth', we know they mean growth in GDP. Governments today regard GDP growth to be above all else on their list of objectives. The mainstream media extol it and the public succumb to it. That could be why it has become customary to regard an economy whose GDP is large as wealthy.

But that is to make a mistake. Because GDP is a flow (so many dollars worth of the flow of goods and services in a year), whereas wealth is a stock (so many dollars worth of assets, period), it could be that a country produces lots of goods and services by running down its assets. Lack of depreciation in national accounts of natural resources in general, and of biodiversity in particular reflects this error. In classic work depreciation of timber supplies was analysed but not that of non-timber forest products (Repetto, 1989), which might include defaunation (Dirzo et al., 2014), another depreciation of biodiversity. In that case GDP and wealth would be pointing in opposite directions. GDP could rise over a period of time even as the economy's wealth declines. But that could not go on forever, any more than one can continually write ever larger checks without paying attention to the balance in the account. With a dwindling and deteriorating stock of natural capital, even GDP would eventually have to take a beating. GDP growth would not be sustainable. Indeed, a return to sustainability could be very difficult, since unlike manufactured and human capital, natural capital (especially biodiversity) can be extremely difficult to restock. That GDP does not include the depreciation of capital explains why the phrase 'Green GDP' is a misnomer and why to call for indefinite GDP growth and to demand sustainable development at the same time is to seek two incompatible objectives.

Global Ecological Footprint as a Basis for Estimating Sustainable Consumption

In a review of the state of the Earth's life-support system, WWF (2012) reported that in the early years of this century, humanity's demand for ecological services exceeded by 50 per cent the rate at which the biosphere is able to supply those services to us. The figure is based on the idea of a 'global ecological footprint', which is the surface area of biologically productive land and sea needed to supply the resources a human population consumes (food, fibres, wood, water) and to assimilate the waste it produces (materials, chemicals, gases). The Global Footprint Network (GFN) regularly updates their estimates of the global ecological footprint.[9] A footprint in excess of 1 means meeting the demand for ecological services requires depleting capital. GFN's most recent estimate is a footprint of a bit over 1.6. Sustainable development would require that the footprint over time must on average equal 1.

The greatest contributors to the ecological footprint overshoot, and thus to the demise of our living companions and supporters, are the OECD countries (a club of rich nations). Estimating national footprints poses enormous conceptual and practical difficulties (among other things owing to imports and exports of goods and services). And without notional prices to guide us, it is not possible to estimate the value of the future environmental impact of an average new birth. But for the global economy the matter is less opaque. That is because errors in measuring national footprints that arise on account of trade in goods and services cancel in the aggregate.

Assuming that the global ecological footprint is 1.6, we may conclude that to maintain the global average living standard at the prevailing distribution of income, we would need 1.6 Earths. No doubt estimates of the global ecological footprint are crude. Moreover, in contrast to estimates of such development indicators as GDP, population size, life expectancy and literacy, which are made by a multitude of national and global institutions, we are obliged here to rely on the estimates of a solitary research group. But that group relies on estimates of many factors made by numerous other groups, including United Nations agencies, the US government and other governments as well as many NGOs. Those estimates are often not included in economic analyses. In any case, that there is an overshoot (ecological footprint in excess of 1) is entirely consistent with a wide range of evidence on the state of the biosphere, some of which we have reviewed above. As the figures are the only aggregated ones on offer, we make use of them.[10]

We assume for simplicity that demand from the biosphere is proportional to income. Global income in 2015 was approximately 110 trillion international dollars. With current technologies and under contemporary institutional arrangements, a footprint of 1 would require that global income be approximately 70 trillion international dollars (110 trillion/1.6 international dollars). To put it in the crudest of terms, 70 trillion international dollars represent today the outer limit to global economic activity if the biosphere is to be protected against further damage. We make use of this figure subsequently when estimating what could be done to achieve that without undue stress to the global community.

Externalities as Drivers of the Human Predicament

Previously we noted that habitat destruction and overharvesting have been and continue to be the main proximal causes of biodiversity loss. Being proximal, they cry out for explanation. How can it be, it may be asked, that humanity has chosen to drive the global socio-ecological system toward destruction? An easy answer is myopia (more generally, greed), or more charitably, irresponsible behaviour. We eschew that line of thought here because there are deeper reasons. We argue below that people can be thoughtful and considerate and try to behave responsibly and yet fail hopelessly as a collective at protecting the biosphere for the future.

Processes driving the balance between population size and the portfolio of assets we hold harbour externalities, which are the unaccounted for consequences for others of actions taken by one or more persons. The qualifier 'unaccounted for' means that the consequences in question follow without prior engagement with those who are affected.

The way we have formulated the notion of externalities could appear ineffective. One could argue that our actions inevitably have consequences for future generations, but that they by the nature of things cannot engage with us. In fact future people engage with us constantly, albeit indirectly. Parents care about their children and know that they in turn will care about their children. By recursion, thoughtful parents take the well-being of their descendants into account when choosing the rates at which they save for their children and invest in them. Intergenerational engagement would be imperfect if parents choose without adequate concern for their children (e.g., if they discount the future well-being of their children at overly high rates). Externalities across the generations would be rampant in that case. As just mentioned, we ignore that line of analysis here. Here we study systematic reasons why choices made even by thoughtful parents do not reflect adequate engagement with *other people's* descendants. As they are symptoms of institutional failure, externalities cannot be substantially reduced without considered collective action. That is why responsible parenthood and consumption decisions at the individual level can nevertheless result in collective failure.

There are two broad categories of externalities of significance here. One consists of the consequences of household consumption and reproduction that work through those components of the biosphere to which access is free; that is, 'open-access resources', or, more simply 'the commons'. That is the familiar variety of externalities, much noted and studied by environmental economists (e.g., Baumol and Oates, 1975). Institutional failures in this class of externalities arise from an absence of appropriate property rights to nature's goods and services, many supplied by biodiversity. By property rights we mean not only private rights, but communitarian and public rights too. One reason rights over natural capital are difficult to define, let alone enforce, is that nature is constantly on the move (the wind blows, particulates diffuse, rivers flow, fish swim, birds and insects fly and even earthworms are known to travel undetected). No person can contain the atmosphere he or she befouls. That means the price paid by someone for environmental services (that is the private cost) is less than the cost borne by all (that is the social cost). In cases involving the global commons, such as the atmosphere as a sink for our carbon emissions, the damage an individual suffers from her own emissions is negligible even though the damage to all from the climate change that is triggered from everyone's emission is large and positive. From the collective point of view there is excessive use of a part of humanity's natural capital – the atmosphere as a carbon sink. The externalities that our use of open-access resources give rise to are adverse.

The other category of externalities has been less recognised in the literature. It arises because our consumption choices and our desire for parenthood are both to some extent influenced by attention to others. No doubt a single household cannot much influence others, but the aggregate effect of all households on one another is not negligible. And they are unaccounted for.

In his contribution to this symposium, John Bongaarts addresses regional and global population projections, and considers women's reproductive rights and the extent to which their responsible desires continue not to be met. Here we concentrate on consumption.

Consumption in the Rich World

The World Bank in its World Development Indicators 2016 reports that the 1.4 billion people living in its list of high-income countries enjoy a per capita income of 40,700 international dollars. Thus, the richest 19 per cent of the world's population consume over 51 per cent of world income (57 trillion/110 trillion). Continuing to assume that humanity's impact on the biosphere is proportional to income, 51 per cent of that impact can be attributed to 19 per cent of world population. If the UN's Sustainable Development Goals are to be met, consumption patterns in these countries have to alter substantially.

Consumption behaviour is influenced both by our urge to compete with others (Veblen's 'conspicuous consumption') and by our innate desire to conform. Each is a reflection of socially embedded consumption preferences for goods and services. As both drivers give rise to consumption externalities, the psychological cost to a person of a collective reduction in consumption is likely to be far less than what it would be if she were to reduce consumption unilaterally. The aggregate cost could even be negative, especially if the working poor were less poor relative to the working rich, as the former are far greater in number.

An analysis of one set of global surveys of 'stated happiness' and their relationship with household incomes has revealed that in countries where per capita income is in excess of 20,000 international dollars, additional income is not statistically related to greater reported happiness (Layard, 2011).[11] Imagine that the 1.4 billion people in today's high-income countries were to reduce their average consumption (or income) to 20,000 international dollars. The drop of 20,700 international dollars (40,700 – 20,000 international) per person in a population of 1.4 billion adds up to a total of 31 trillion international dollars (Dasgupta and Dasgupta, 2017). Other things being equal, world income would then be 79 (i.e., 110 – 31) trillion international dollars, a figure for global economic activity that is not far above the 70 trillion international dollars we obtained as a crude estimate for sustainable global income with present technology under contemporary social institutions.

A further route to sustainable dependence on the biosphere is technological progress. The thought here is that with the right kind of technological progress humanity could increase aggregate economic activity without exceeding the biosphere's capability to supply goods and services. Economic historians of the Industrial Revolution point to the role institutions have played in providing incentives to create the technological innovations that have been responsible for reducing natural resource constraints.[12] But we can be sanguine about the character of technological advances only if the biosphere is priced appropriately. Entrepreneurs economise on the expensive factors of production, not the cheap ones. So long as nature's goods and services remain under-priced, technological advances can be expected to be rapacious in their use. Moreover, technological advances that are patently good can have side-effects that are not benign. The ability to use fossil-based energy at large scales has transformed lives for the better, but it has created the unintended consequence of global climate change. Bull-dozers and chain-saws enable people to deforest land at rates that would have been unimaginable 250 years ago, and modern fishing technology devastates large swathes of sea beds in a manner unthinkable in the past. If technological progress is our hope, it has to come allied with elimination of environmental externalities.

Conclusion: The Ultimate Drivers of Destruction

The short-range solutions to the problem of preserving biodiversity are many, and dealt with extensively in the literature of conservation biology (Sodhi and Ehrlich, 2010). But these will all prove to no avail unless the basic drivers of extermination – policies seeking economic growth at any cost, overconsumption by the rich and failure to redistribute – are addressed. Collectively addressing these are possibly the greatest challenges civilisation has ever faced.

Acknowledgements

We thank Aisha Dasgupta, Anne Ehrlich and Pete Myers for helpful comments.

Notes

1. See, e.g., Ehrlich and Ehrlich (1981), Wilson (1992), Pimm et al. (2014) and Ceballos et al. (2015, 2017). Kolbert (2014) provides an excellent non-technical account.
2. http://mahb.stanford.edu/blog/dont-overlook-whats-underfoot/.
3. http://bit.ly/1p6fvzJ.
4. http://go.nature.com/29gRisU.
5. http://bit.ly/2lyoLqu.
6. There is also one especially dangerous human activity that threatens all of biodiversity. It is the promotion of 'de-extinction', the idea that molecular biology will allow humanity to simply recreate extinct organisms from DNA samples. Even if the molecular job could be done (it cannot), the scale of the problem and the steady attrition of habitats into which to release the products make the idea less than silly (Beattie and Ehrlich, 2013; Ehrlich, 2014). The financial resources that would be required to take this approach to scale are mind-boggling, and the opportunity costs of using those finances for this as opposed to realistic conservation efforts are simply unacceptable. The big danger here is moral hazard – that talk and laboratory experimentation with de-extinction will allow people to care less about the biological holocaust now under way. 'Why should we care about tigers – if they are driven to extinction, molecular biologists will simply recreate them?'
7. See, e.g., Micklethwait and Wooldridge (2000), Ridley (2010), Deaton (2013), Lomborg (2013) and Norberg (2016).

8. The latter index was proposed by UNDP (1990) and has been revised and updated by the organisation ever since.
9. For pioneering work on the idea of ecological footprints, see Rees and Wakernagel (1994) and Rees (2001, 2006). See also Kitzes et al. (2008).
10. The quantitative estimates that follow are taken from Dasgupta and Dasgupta (2017).
11. Twenty thousand international dollars is the per capita income in Mauritius, a widely admired country.
12. Landes (1998) is the classic on the subject.

References

Arrow, K. J., Dasgupta, P., Goulder, L. H., Mumford, K. J. & Oleson, K. 2012. Sustainability and the measurement of wealth. *Environment and Development Economics*, 17(3): 317–353.

Arrow, K. J., Ehrlich, P. R. & Levin, S. A. 2014. Some perspectives on linked ecosystems and socioeconomic systems. In S. Barret, K.-G. Mäler & E. S. Maskin (Eds.), *Environment and Development Economics: Essays in Honour of Sir Partha Dasgupta*: 95–119. Oxford: Oxford University Press.

Barnosky, A. D., Matzke, N., Tomiya, S., Wogan, G. O. U., Swartz, B., Quental, T. B., Marshall, C., McGuire, J. L., Lindsey, E. L., Maguire, K. C., Mersey, B. & Ferrer, E. A. 2011. Has the Earth's sixth mass extinction already arrived? *Nature*, 471(7336): 51–57.

Baumol, W. J. & Oates, W. E. 1975. *The Theory of Environmental Policy*. Englewood Cliffs, NJ: Prentice Hall.

Beattie, A. & Ehrlich, P. R. 2013. *De-extinction: Moral Hazard Writ Large*. MAHB Blog November 14. https://mahb.stanford.edu/blog/deextinction/.

Bernhardt, E. S., Rosi, E. J. & Gessner, M. O. 2017. Synthetic chemicals as agents of global change. *Frontiers in Ecology and the Environment*, 15 (2): 84–90.

Brandt, L. J., Aroniadis, O. C., Mellow, M., Kanatzar, A., Kelly, C., Park, T., Stollman, N., Rohlke, F. & Surawicz, C. 2012. Long-term follow-up of colonoscopic fecal microbiota transplant for recurrent *Clostridium difficile* infection. *American Journal of Gastroenterology*, 107(7): 1079–1087.

Ceballos, G., Ehrlich, P. R., Barnosky, A. D., García, A., Pringle, R. M. & Palmer, T. M. 2015b. Accelerated modern human-induced species losses: Entering the sixth mass extinction. *Science Advances*, 1(5), e1400253.

Ceballos, G., Ehrlich, P. R. & Dirzo, R. 2017. Biological annihilation via the ongoing sixth mass extinction signaled by vertebrate population losses and declines. *Proceedings of the National Academy of Sciences*, 114 (30): E6089–E6096.

Ceballos, G., Ehrlich, A. H. & Ehrlich, P. R. 2015a. *The Annihilation of Nature: Human Extinction of Birds and Mammals*. Baltimore: Johns Hopkins University Press.

Crowl, T. A., Crist, T. O., Parmenter, R. R., Belovsky, G. & Lugo, A. E. 2008. The spread of invasive species and infectious disease as drivers of ecosystem change. *Frontiers in Ecology and the Environment*, 6(5): 238–246.

Daily, G. C. (Ed.). 1997. *Nature's Services*. Washington, DC: Island Press.

Dasgupta, P. 1993. *An Inquiry into Well-Being and Destitution*. Oxford: Clarendon Press.

2004. *Human Well-Being and the Natural Environment*. Oxford: Oxford University Press.

2007. *Economics: A Very Short Introduction*. Oxford: Oxford University Press.

Dasgupta, A. & Dasgupta, P. 2017. Socially embedded preferences, environmental externalities, and reproductive rights. *Population and Development Review*, 43(3): 405–441.

Deaton, A. 2013. *The Great Escape: Health, Wealth, and the Origins of Inequality*. Princeton, NJ: Princeton University Press.

Dirzo, R., Young, H. S., Galetti, M., Ceballos, G., Isaac, N. J. B. & Collen, B. 2014. Defaunation in the Anthropocene. *Science*, 345(6195): 401–406.

Dorf, E. 1955. Plants and the geologic time scale. *Geological Society of America Special Papers*, 62: 575–592.

Ehrlich P. R. 2014. The case against de-extinction: It's a fascinating but dumb idea. *Yale Environment 360*. http://bit.ly/1gAIuJF.

Ehrlich, P. & Ehrlich, A. 1981. *Extinction: The Causes and Consequences of the Disappearance of Species*. New York: Random House.

2013. Can a collapse of global civilization be avoided? Proceedings of the Royal Society B – Biological Sciences, 280(1754): 20122845. https://doi.org/10.1098/rspb.2012.2845.

Ehrlich P. R. & Harte, J. 2015. Food security requires a new revolution. *International Journal of Environmental Studies*. https://doi.org/10.1080/00207233.2015.1067468:1-13.

Fisher, M. C., Henk, D. A., Briggs, C. J., Brownstein, J. S., Madoff, L. C., McCraw, S. L., Gurr & S. J. 2012. Emerging fungal threats to animal, plant and ecosystem health. *Nature*, 484: 186–194.

Goulson, D. 2013. Review: An overview of the environmental risks posed by neonicotinoid insecticides. *Journal of Applied Ecology*, 50(4): 977–987.

Goulson, D., Nicholls, E., Botias, C. & Rotheray, E. L. 2015. Bee declines driven by combined stress from parasites, pesticides, and lack of flowers. *Science*, 347(6229): 1255957.

Hanson, T., Brooks, T. M., Da Fonseca, G. A. B., Hoffmann, M., Lamoreux, J. F., Machlis, G., Mittermeier, C. G., Mittermeier, R. A. & John, D. P. 2009. Warfare in biodiversity hotspots. *Conservation Biology*, 23(3): 578–587.

Harper, G. J., Steininger, M. K., Tucker, C. J., Juhn, D. & Hawkins, F. 2007. Fifty years of deforestation and forest fragmentation in Madagascar. *Environmental Conservation*, 34(4): 325–333.

Heskel, M. A., O'Sullivan, O. S., Reich, P. B., Tjoelker, M. G., Weerasinghe, L. K., Penillard, A., Egerton, J. J. G., Creek, D., Bloomfield, K. J., Xiang, J., Sinca, F., Stangl, Z. R., Martinez-de la Torre, A., Griffin, K. L., Huntingford, C., Hurry, V., Meir, P., Turnbull, M. H. & Atkin, O. K. 2016. Convergence in the temperature response of leaf respiration across biomes and plant functional types. *Proceedings of the National Academy of Sciences of the United States of America*, 113(14): 3832–3837.

Holdren, J. P. & Ehrlich, P. R. 1974. Human population and global environment. *American Scientist*, 62(3): 282–292.

Jamison, D. T., Summers, L. H., Alleyne, G., Arrow, K. J., Berkley, S., Binagwaho, A., Bustreo, F., Evans, D., Feachem, R. G. A., Frenk, J., Ghosh, G., Goldie, S. J., Guo, Y., Gupta, S., Horton, R., Kruk, M. E., Mahmoud, A., Mohohlo, L. K., Ncube, M., Pablos-Mendez, A., Reddy, K. S., Saxenian, H., Soucat, A., Ulltveit-Moe, K. U. & Yamey, G. 2013. Global health 2035: A world converging within a generation. *The Lancet*, 382(9908): 1898–1955.

Kitzes, J., Wackernagel, M., Loh, J., Peller, A., Goldfinger, S., Cheng, D. & Tea, K. 2008. Shrink and share: Humanity's present and future ecological footprint. *Philosophical Transactions of the Royal Society B-Biological Sciences*, 363(1491): 467–475.

Klare, M. T. 2012. *The Race for What's Left: The Global Scramble for the World's Last Resources*. New York: Macmillan.

Kolbert, E. 2014. *The Sixth Extinction: An Unnatural History*. New York: Henry Holt.

Kumar, P. (Ed.). 2012. *The Economics of Ecosystems and Biodiversity: Ecological and Economic Foundations*. London: Earthscan.

Landes, D. S. 1998. *The Wealth and Poverty of Nations: Why Are Some So Rich and Others So Poor*. New York: Norton.

Layard, R. 2011. *Happiness: Lessons from a New Science*. London: Penguin UK.

Le, T. X. & Munekage, Y. 2004. Residues of selected antibiotics in water and mud from shrimp ponds in mangrove areas in Viet Nam. *Marine Pollution Bulletin*, 49(11–12): 922–929.

Lomborg, B. (Ed.). 2013. *How Much Have Global Problems Cost the World? A Scoreboard from 1900 to 2050*. Cambridge: Cambridge University Press.

Maffini, M. V., Rubin, B. S., Sonnenschein, C. & Soto, A. M. 2006. Endocrine disruptors and reproductive health: The case of bisphenol-A. *Molecular and Cellular Endocrinology*, 254: 179–186.

Maisels, F., Strindberg, S., Blake, S., Wittemyer, G., Hart, J., Williamson, E. A., Aba'a, R., Abitsi, G., Ambahe, R. D., Amsini, F., Bakabana, P. C., Hicks, T. C., Bayogo, R. E., Bechem, M., Beyers, R. L., Bezangoye, A. N., Boundja, P., Bout, N., Akou, M. E., Bene, L. B., Fosso, B., Greengrass, E., Grossmann, F., Ikamba-Nkulu, C., Ilambu, O., Inogwabini, B. I., Iyenguet, F., Kiminou, F., Kokangoye, M., Kujirakwinja, D., Latour, S., Liengola, I., Mackaya, Q., Madidi, J., Madzoke, B., Makoumbou, C., Malanda, G. A., Malonga, R., Mbani, O., Mbendzo, V. A., Ambassa, E., Ekinde, A., Mihindou, Y., Morgan, B. J., Motsaba, P., Moukala, G., Mounguengui, A., Mowawa, B. S., Ndzai, C., Nixon, S., Nkumu, P., Nzolani, F., Pintea, L., Plumptre, A., Rainey, H., de Semboli, B. B., Serckx, A., Stokes, E., Turkalo, A., Vanleeuwe, H., Vosper, A. & Warren, Y. 2013. Devastating decline of forest elephants in Central Africa. *PLoS One*, 8(3): e59469.

Mann, M. E. 2012. *The Hockey Stick and the Climate Wars: Dispatches from the Front Lines*. New York: Columbia University Press.

McNeely, J. A. 2003. Biodiversity, war, and tropical forests. *Journal of Sustainable Forestry*, 16: 1–20.

Micklethwait, J. & Wooldridge, A. 2000. *A Future Perfect: The Challenge and Promise of Globalization*. New York: Random House.

Montgomery, D. R. & Biklé, A. 2015. *The Hidden Half of Nature: The Microbial Roots of Life and Health*. New York: Norton.

Norberg, J. 2016. *Progress: Ten Reasons to Look Forward to the Future*. London: One World.

Obbard, R. W., Sadri, S., Wong, Y. Q., Khitun, A. A., Baker, I. & Thompson, R. C. 2014. Global warming releases microplastic legacy frozen in Arctic Sea ice. *Earth's Future*, 2(6): 315–320.

Phillott, A. D., Grogan, L. F., Cashins, S. D., McDonald, K. R., Berger, L. & Skerratt, L. F. 2013. Chytridiomycosis and seasonal mortality of tropical stream-associated frogs 15 years after introduction of *Batrachochytrium dendrobatidis*. *Conservation Biology*, 27(5): 1058–1068.

Pimm, S. L., Jenkins, C. N., Abell, R., Brooks, T. M., Gittleman, J. L., Joppa, L. N., Raven, P. H., Roberts, C. M. & Sexton, J. O. 2014. The biodiversity of species and their rates of extinction, distribution, and protection. *Science*, 344(6187): 1246752.

Pope Francis. 2015. *Laudato Si': On Care for Our Common Home* [Encyclical]. Vatican City, Italy: Vatican Press. http://w2.vatican.va/content/francesco/en/encyclicals/documents/papa-francesco_20150524_enciclica-laudato-si.html.

Rees, W. E. 2001. Ecological footprint, concept of. In S. A. Levin (Ed.), *Encyclopedia of Biodiversity*, vol. 2. New York: Academic Press.

2006. Ecological footprints and biocapacity: Essential elements in sustainability assessment. In J. Dewulf & H. V. Langenhove (Eds.), *Renewable-Based Technology: Sustainability Assessment*. Chichester, UK: John Wiley.

Rees, W. E. & Wackernagel, M. 1994. Ecological footprints and appropriated carrying capacity: Measuring the natural capital requirements of the human economy. In A. M. Jansson, M. Hammer, C. Folke & R. Costanza (Eds.), *Investing in Natural Capital: The Ecological Economics Appropriate for Sustainability*. Washington, DC: Island Press.

Repetto, R, Magrath, W., Wells, M., Beer, C. & Rossini, F. 1989. *Wasting Assets: Natural Resources and the National Income Accounts*. Washington, DC: World Resources Institute.

Ricketts, T. H., Daily, G. C., Ehrlich, P. R. & Michener, C. D. 2004. Economic value of tropical forest to coffee production. *Proceedings of the National Academy of Sciences of the United States of America*, 101 (34): 12579–12582.

Ridley, M. 2010. *The Rational Optimist: How Prosperity Evolves*. London: 4th Estate.

Rios, L. M., Moore, C. & Jones, P. R. 2007. Persistent organic pollutants carried by synthetic polymers in the ocean environment. *Marine Pollution Bulletin*, 54(8): 1230–1237.

Robbins, C. S. 2003. *Prickly Trade: Trade and Conservation of Chihuahuan Desert Cacti*. Washington, DC: TRAFFIC North America, WWF.

Rowley, J. J. L., Chan, S. K. F., Tang, W. S., Speare, R., Skerratt, L. F., Alford, R. A., Cheung, K. S., Ho, C. Y. & Campbell, R. 2007. Survey for the amphibian chytrid *Batrachochytrium dendrobatidis* in Hong Kong in native amphibians and in the international amphibian trade. *Diseases of Aquatic Organisms*, 78(2): 87–95.

Safina, C. 2015. *Beyond Words: What Animals Think and Feel*. New York: Henry Holt.

Sodhi, N. S. & Ehrlich, P. R. (Eds.). 2010. *Conservation Biology for All*. Oxford: Oxford University Press.

Sonne, C. 2010. Health effects from long-range transported contaminants in Arctic top predators: An integrated review based on studies of polar bears and relevant model species. *Environment International*, 36(5): 461–491.

Sunday, J. M., Bates, A. E. & Dulvy, N. K. 2012. Thermal tolerance and the global redistribution of animals. *Nature Climate Change*, 2(9): 686–690.

ten Brink, P., Mazza, L., Badura, T., Kettunen, M. & Withana, S. 2012. *Nature and Its Role in the Transition to a Green Economy.* www .teebweb.org/publication/nature-and-its-role-in-a-green-economy/ A T EEB report.

Tilman, D., Reich, P. B., Knops, J., Wedin, D., Mielke, T. & Lehman, C. 2001. Diversity and productivity in a long-term grassland experiment. *Science*, 294(5543): 843–845.

Toon, O. B., Robock, A., Turco, R. P., Bardeen, C., Oman, L. & Stenchikov, G. L. 2007. Nuclear war – Consequences of regional-scale nuclear conflicts. *Science*, 315(5816): 1224–1225.

Tylianakis, J. M. 2013. The global plight of pollinators. *Science*, 339(6127): 1532–1533.

United Nations Development Programme (UNDP), 1990. *Human Development Report 1990: Concept and Measurement of Human Development Technical Report.* New York: UNDP.

Warnecke, L., Turner, J. M., Bollinger, T. K., Lorch, J. M., Misra, V., Cryan, P. M., Wibbelt, G., Blehert, D. S. & Willis, C. K. R. 2012. Inoculation of bats with European *Geomyces destructans* supports the novel pathogen hypothesis for the origin of white-nose syndrome. *Proceedings of the National Academy of Sciences of the United States of America*, 109(18): 6999–7003.

Waters, C. N., Zalasiewicz, J., Summerhayes, C., Barnosky, A. D., Poirier, C., Gałuszka, A., Cearreta, A., Edgeworth, M., Ellis, E. C., Ellis, M., Jeandel, C., Leinfelder, R., McNeill, J. R., Richter, D. D., Steffen, W., Syvitski, J., Vidas, D., Wagreich, M., Williams, M., An, Z. S., Grinevald, J., Odada, E., Oreskes, N. & Wolfe, A. P. 2016. The Anthropocene is functionally and stratigraphically distinct from the Holocene. *Science*, 351(6269): aad2622.

Wilson, E. O. 1992. *The Diversity of Life.* Cambridge, MA: Harvard University Press.

Wittemyer, G., Northrup, J. M., Blanc, J., Douglas-Hamilton, I., Omondi, P. & Burnham, K. P. 2014. Illegal killing for ivory drives global decline in African elephants. *Proceedings of the National Academy of Sciences of the United States of America*, 111(36): 13117–13121.

WWF. 2008. *Living Planet Report 2008*. Gland, Switzerland: World Wildlife Fund.

2012. *Living Planet Report 2012*. Gland, Switzerland: World Wildlife Fund.

2016. *Living Planet Report 2016*. Gland, Switzerland: World Wildlife Fund.

Xu, L., Guan, J., Lau, W. & Xiao, Y. 2016. *An Overview of Pangolin Trade in China*. Cambridge: TRAFFIC, WWF & WILDAID.

Zoomers, A. 2010. Globalisation and the foreignisation of space: seven processes driving the current global land grab. *Journal of Peasant Studies*, 37(2): 429–447.

10 | The Consequences of Biodiversity Loss for Human Well-Being

CHARLES PERRINGS AND ANN KINZIG

Biodiversity Change and Human Well-Being

Biodiversity is frequently thought of as synonymous with species diversity in wild lands, and biodiversity loss is frequently thought of as synonymous with the extinction of wild species. But biodiversity is much more than species diversity in wild lands, and biodiversity loss is much more than species extinction. Biodiversity is the variety of species used in both the production and consumption of goods and services. Examples include the ornamental plants, birds and animals that people use to enrich their lives, the variety of foods they use to enrich their diet, the mix of biofuels or biofibres used to support productive activities. It includes the genetic diversity of cultivated crops, of crop pests, of wild crop relatives, of weedy species. It includes the range of biotic disease agents that affect human, animal and plant health, and the species used to control disease such as traditional medicinal plants and the plants used as the source of modern pharmaceuticals. The biotechnology sector is as dependent on genetic and species diversity as agriculture, forestry or wild capture fisheries. Biodiversity change does encompass a dramatic increase in the rate at which species are going extinct (Hoffmann et al., 2010; Secretariat of the Convention on Biological Diversity, 2010). But it also encompasses an even more dramatic transformation of terrestrial and marine ecosystems fuelled by land use and land cover change. It includes the simplification of agroecosystems, production forests, wild capture fisheries and aquaculture, resulting in the increased abundance of crops, livestock, and farmed fish stocks, and the suppression of crop and livestock competitors, predators, pests and pathogens (Millennium Ecosystem Assessment, 2005a).

The last century has seen more change in all these facets of biodiversity than the preceding millennium, all of which impact human well-

285

being. Sometimes such impacts are captured in market prices. Diseases of commercial crops, for example, almost always result in an increase in their cost of production, and so the cost to the consumer. Sometimes they are not. The extirpation or local extinction of a songbird is unlikely to trigger a change in prices. It turns out that if we are judging how much biodiversity change is warranted by the benefits conferred on humanity, this distinction matters. Changes that are directly reflected in market prices attract our attention. Changes that have no direct effect on market prices are often ignored. In this paper we ask what can be said about the welfare implications of anthropogenic change – both increases and decreases – in the diversity of genes, species and ecosystems. To do this, we discuss why people have altered their environment in such dramatic ways, and what they might have missed in the process.

Our starting point is the concept of ecosystem services, popularised by the Millennium Assessment (Millennium Ecosystem Assessment, 2005b). This concept gives us a way of characterising the interests that people have in their environment. Ecosystem services are the flow of benefits (or costs) obtained from ecosystems. Many are managed through the control people exercise over ecosystem structures and processes. Production of most foods, fuels and fibres, for example, involves the transformation of natural ecosystems, and their distribution involves market transactions between producers and consumers. The marketed products of agriculture, aquaculture, forestry and fisheries are private goods – said to be both 'rival' and 'exclusive' in consumption. They are rival in the sense that their consumption by one person precludes their consumption by others (two people can't eat the same apple). They are exclusive in the sense that their ownership by one person confers the right to exclude others (the person who purchases an apple is able to deny others access to that apple). These properties give individual producers and consumers of foods, fuels and fibres secure rights over the capturable benefits they offer, and hence a strong interest in their production and consumption (and protection). Many of the incidental effects of agriculture, aquaculture, forestry and fisheries are neither rival nor exclusive. The depletion and fragmentation of habitats, the offsite pollution of air, soil and water, and the genetic effects of pesticide applications, all affect other people and other species. Moreover, their impacts on one person or one species do not diminish their impacts on other people or other species. They are public goods (or bads) generated through market transactions, but external to those transactions.

Many of the environmental consequences of productive activities have similar properties. The storm protection offered by coastal mangroves, for example, depends on the combined activities of many independent land users, none of which can be excluded from the benefits it offers. Moreover, the protection enjoyed by one land user has no implications for the protection enjoyed by others. Where the benefits that storm protection offers can be capitalised into the value of land or other privately owned assets, they are directly priced. Where they cannot – on public lands, for example – they will be unpriced. There will be no market signal of the value of protection.

Agriculture is one example of an activity that has yielded substantial private benefits to humankind, but only at the public cost of reducing or otherwise altering biodiversity. While the benefits of agricultural production are recorded faithfully in national income and product accounts, the biodiversity costs are not. There are many other activities that similarly yield benefits at some biodiversity cost. Aside from agriculture, industrial activity, infrastructural development and urbanisation, all involve the conversion of habitat to alternative uses, and so lead to the loss of the species that occupied the converted habitat. Industrial development frequently has offsite effects involving the pollution of air, water and soils that reduce the abundance or richness of species in affected areas. The development of roads, railways, power transmission corridors and canals also fragments the habitats through which they pass, with similar effects on species richness and abundance. Urban development typically transforms existing habitat, sometimes leaving fragments intact, but always introducing new communities of microorganisms, insects, plants and animals. In some cases, the biodiversity in urban systems is much greater than the biodiversity in the habitats displaced by urban development. This is almost always true of microorganisms, but is frequently true of plants as well (Crane and Kinzig, 2005). In others, little is added beyond the human commensals and micro-and macro-parasites that accompany dense human populations.

By contrast, conservation is an activity that focuses first and foremost on the preservation of biodiversity for the public good. It involves not just the designation and implementation of protected areas in existing wilderness areas, but the restoration of degraded ecosystems,

the design and implementation of conservation-compatible development projects, and the establishment of a regulatory framework
designed to limit the impact of other activities on biodiversity outside
protected areas. The earliest protected areas were hunting reserves, and
many modern wildlife sanctuaries and national parks have their origin
in such reserves. In the last century, the focus has switched to the
protection of wilderness areas of outstanding natural beauty, and landscapes of special cultural significance. In the US, much of the impetus
came from the conservation-minded president Theodore Roosevelt.
Across the world, however, the designation of protected areas has
followed a similar pattern, focusing on landscapes of special significance, reserves dedicated to the protection of mega-vertebrates, or sites
of special scientific interest. Around 15 per cent of the worlds land area
and 4 per cent of the global oceans are now protected. Although a much
smaller proportion of the oceans is protected as of now, the rate at
which new sea areas within national jurisdiction are being brought
under some form of protection is much greater than on land. In the
period since the Caracas Action Plan, protected national waters have
increased by more than 130 per cent (UNEP-WCMC and IUCN,
2016).

In Latin America, and Eastern, Southeastern and Western Asia, the
selection of new areas for protection increasingly targets densely populated areas having high 'conservation value'. These 'biodiversity hotspots' (Myers, 1988) are areas characterised by high levels of
endemism, on the one hand, and high levels of anthropogenic stress,
on the other. Just as the growth of agriculture in pursuit of privately
capturable benefits has had a (public) external cost, so the growth of
protected areas has a (private) external cost – to the people who lose
access to the resources involved. And just as neglect of the public
external costs of agriculture can result in too much biodiversity loss,
so neglect of the private external costs of protection can result in too
much conservation. The two cases are not, however, symmetric.

Since most of the gains from agriculture are private, while most of the
external costs are public, the default outcome has been neglect of the
public costs. Farmers have had little incentive to take account of their
effect on biodiversity. Since most of the gains from conservation are
public, however, while most of the external costs are private, the
default outcome has been underprovision of the public good. Those
displaced by protected areas have had an incentive to oppose them.

Those asked to fund protected areas have had an incentive to free ride on the efforts of others.

The same asymmetry affects all activities that contribute to biodiversity loss. While the gains offered by those activities warrant some biodiversity loss, no one has a private incentive to ask how much. Nor do they have an incentive to limit their activity in the absence of regulations that force such action. The protection of human, animal and plant health warrants some reduction in the abundance of viruses, bacteria and fungi. The production of foods, fuels and fibres warrants some reduction in the abundance of plant pests and predators. That is not the problem. It is the unwarranted, ill-considered loss of biodiversity as an external effect of production and consumption decisions that is the problem.

In this paper we consider the impact of unwarranted biodiversity loss or change on human well-being. To do this we first discuss the effect of biodiversity loss (change) on ecosystem functioning, and the delivery of ecosystem services. We then consider which services are most likely to be neglected in the decisions people make, and why those services matter.

Unwarranted Biodiversity Change as a Consequence of Poverty, Parochialism and Myopia

The Millennium Ecosystem Assessment identified four broad types of ecosystem services. The first, the provisioning services, involve the production of foods, fuels, fibres, genetic material, water and so on. They all involve the consumptive use of ecosystems. The second, the cultural services, include the non-consumptive benefits that people get from their environment, such as recreation, aesthetic satisfaction, inspiration, information, spiritual meaning and the importance of place. The third, the regulating services, comprise the buffering functions of the environment. They include the mitigation of a wide range of natural and anthropogenic environmental risks, including storms, flooding, drought and disease. They also include the assimilation of pollutants of one kind or another. The fourth, the supporting services, comprise basic ecosystem processes such as photosynthesis, nutrient cycling, soil formation and so on. The first (provisioning) is generally well served by markets; cultural services are partially served by markets. The last two are not. These unmarketed services are also often the services that most depend on the diversity of species in an ecosystem, and that are most likely to be public in nature. The external effects of production and consumption decisions are accordingly most likely to impact these services.

Our central point is there are very good reasons why people should behave in ways that cause a loss of biodiversity. The need to produce food, to generate a safe living environment or to combat disease can all be expected to lead to a loss of biodiversity. But at the same time, the concerns that lead people to simplify agroecosystems, to exclude predators, or to control disease vectors have consequences for human well-being over greater areas and on longer time scales than most people are able to consider. This is true of all of us. But poverty can exacerbate this problem. Poor households understandably discount the impacts on others of the activities they undertake merely to survive. Similarly, poor countries are unable to invest in resources and regulations that might reduce unwarranted impacts of human activities, even if they wanted to. Parochialism and myopia are often understandable products of poverty.

The Brundtland Report (WCED, 1987) argued that there existed a causal connection between environmental change and poverty both within and between generations. A large literature has subsequently examined the empirical relation between per capita income (GDP or GNP) and environmental change. What it shows is that the relation between changes in income and changes in the environment are complex, involving feedback effects in both directions. The consensus view by the time the Millennium Assessment began its work was that although poverty alleviation did not necessarily enhance environmental quality, and could increase stress on the environment, environmental protection generally benefited the poor (Markandya, 2001).

The evidence since then is more mixed. The linkages between poverty and environmental change are often indirect – working through, for example, changes in fertility rates. Where people's access to assets is uncertain, and their expectations of secure future income are low, their response is often to have more children. This can increase pressure on the environment, further compromising future income, resulting in a positive feedback between poverty, fertility and environmental change (Dasgupta, 2001). While growth in the demand for food in high-income countries has generally stimulated the intensification of agriculture (greater yields on existing lands), in low-income countries it has frequently led to extensive growth (clearing of new habitat for agriculture). More mouths to feed has meant more people farming more land. In cases where traditional land tenure and resource access regimes prevail, and where credit markets are poorly developed, increasing demand for food can only be met by land clearance (International Assessment of Agricultural Knowledge, Science and Technology for Development, 2008).

Most people in the least developed countries still live in rural areas, and still make a living from agriculture. In the poorest countries, more than 75 per cent of the population earn a living from agriculture.[1] In many of these countries rural population growth rates are still positive and, in some Sub-Saharan African countries (specifically in Benin, Burkina Faso, Burundi, Eritrea, Guinea-Bissau, Mauritania and Uganda) are still increasing (World Bank, 2013).

Poverty alleviation in such cases necessitates agricultural growth – whether extensive or intensive. For poverty alleviation to benefit biodiversity intensive growth is required. Where it reduces the rate of land conversion, for example, intensification reduces habitat loss (Bruinsma, 2009; Foley, 2005; Foley et al., 2011; Godfray et al., 2010; Sachs et al., 2009). Initiatives designed to promote crop improvements and integrated pest management are accordingly argued to offer positive conservation externalities (Pretty et al., 2011).

The evidence from sub-Saharan Africa shows that extensive agricultural growth is the primary driver behind biodiversity loss. The extensive growth of agriculture over the last 50 years is strongly and positively related to the threat faced by endemic species. In the long run, intensification has the opposite effect. It reduces the incentive for poorer farmers to convert forests, savannas and grasslands to crop production (Perrings and Halkos, 2015). On shorter timescales, however, extensive growth and intensive growth are equally damaging. Aside from habitat loss, nutrient runoff and the application of insecticides and fungicides that are prevalent in intensive agriculture have negative impacts on wild plants (Firbank et al., 2008; Geiger et al., 2010), as well as indirect impacts via effects on pollinators (Kremen et al., 2002; Potts et al., 2010), and pest predators (Zhao et al., 2015). Expansion of the area committed to agriculture reduces habitat, and with it both species richness and abundance. The introduction of roads (and development along roads) to connect production to markets leads to the fragmentation of habitat.

The question is how much habitat (and hence biodiversity) loss is warranted. The answer depends on the balance between the costs of the biodiversity lost through habitat conversion and the benefits of income growth among the rural poor. The costs of biodiversity loss occur at many scales. The conservation of the genetic diversity on which all future evolution depends, for example, is a public good at the global scale, as is the control of emerging infectious diseases that have the potential to become pandemic. But the conservation of species that have totemic, cultural or spiritual significance to particular groups is a public good at the scale of those groups only. Similarly, the ecosystem services supported by biodiversity provide benefits at many different scales. Pollination services tend to be quite localised. Watershed protection, on the other hand, can extend from extremely small scales to regions involving several countries.

At both local and global levels, the public good nature of biodiversity conservation implies that, if left to the market, there will be too little conservation effort. People will take some account of the biodiversity costs of their activities, but not enough. They will acknowledge the costs that fall on them, but not on others. This is true at all scales – from households to nations. Biodiversity loss that affects ecosystem services benefiting future generations or people other than kith and kin will be neglected.

Myopia and parochialism have many causes. Just as the resurgent nationalism of the post-recession years is marked by an unwillingness to acknowledge the international environmental consequences of local production and consumption, so the adoption of corporate approaches to accountability is marked by a reluctance to take a long view of the public good. Our concern in this paper is with the role of poverty as a driver of both myopia and parochialism. There are three elements to this.

The first element is the relation between poverty and information on the broader and longer-term consequences of biodiversity change. Poor resource users might well have a good understanding of the local ecological consequences of their actions gained through observation (Berkes et al., 2000), but could not be expected to have the kind of understanding of systemwide consequences that can only be gained from a science-based education. In sub-Saharan Africa, for example, although primary school enrolment rates have been rising rapidly, nearly one-quarter of all young people have never attended primary school, and nearly three-quarters have never attended secondary school (Preece, 2006).

The second element is the rate at which households discount the future. Building on a long-standing observation that discount rates depend on income (Fisher, 1930), it has been found that increasing poverty causes people to discount the longer-term consequences of their decisions more heavily (Chavas, 2002; Perrings, 1989). It is difficult to care much about tomorrow when one is in dire straits today. This in turn discourages investment in conservation and environmental enhancement. Perversely, it can induce the poor to run down environmental assets in ways that undermine their own future security.

The third element is the relation between poverty and the weight people attach to their impact on those outside their immediate community. Two manifestations of this are the weakness of the social capital to which the poor have access (Cleaver, 2005), and its limited reach (Collier, 2002). The poor may well have strong connections with their neighbours, but less time and fewer resources to connect with those outside their immediate community.

A common consequence of this is that changes caused by the independent decisions of rural households in many parts of the world have impacts that are largely unknown, and largely ignored. What are they?

The Costs of Unwarranted Loss and Change

We have argued that the value of biodiversity – the composition of species – derives from the complementarity and substitutability between species in the supply of ecosystem services over a range of environmental conditions. Biodiversity has a portfolio effect on the risks attached the supply of ecosystem services. Species have functional traits that enable them to execute the ecological functions that underpin particular services. Individual species may be near-perfect functional substitutes for other species only if they share a full set of traits with those other species (Naeem, 1998). Species are also related through ecological interactions – trophic relationships, competition, parasitism, facilitation and so on – that make them more or less complementary in executing ecological functions (Thébault and Loreau, 2006). Their value depends on their substitutability and complementarity in the delivery of valuable services. Value is not an inherent property of either individual species or species richness, but reflects the fact that people are willing to pay (either monetarily or in other ways) for the services biodiversity yields.

What people are willing to pay depends partly on the characteristics of individual species, functional groups of species and so on, and partly on people's preferences, institutions, culture and technology. But it also depends on the distribution of income and wealth. The rich are able to pay more for ecosystem services than the poor. This biases the relative value of the many ecosystem services supported by biodiversity in favour of those preferred by the rich.

Much effort has gone into estimating the aggregate willingness to pay of different communities for the benefits of ecosystem services (Heal et al., 2005). These benefits can include both use (eating food, hiking) and non-use (valuing preservation of an endangered species) values. The timing of use is also important. This is partly because consumption in the future is less valuable to people than consumption today, and partly because the future is uncertain. But ecosystem services of species that are not important today might be important in the future. It follows that today's biodiversity also has an *option value* (in the sense that it might contain a cure for future diseases, the biological control of future pests or the basis for a new technology) (Goeschl and Swanson, 2003; Simpson et al., 1996). So the option value of biodiversity conservation is equivalent to an insurance premium against future pests or diseases (Baumgärtner, 2007; Quaas and Baumgärtner, 2007).

We note, in passing, that none of this connects with the notion that species have intrinsic value. Intrinsic value is irrelevant to decision-making. This is not to say that ethics and aesthetics are unimportant. They are major factors in the value of species for some people. So too are religious convictions, cultural traditions and social norms. The non-use values identified by economists include the value of assuring the continued existence of species, not only for the enjoyment of the valuer, but also for the benefit of future generations, of people elsewhere on the planet, and of other species. It is the willingness of people to commit resources toward some end that enables us to derive the value of the ecosystem components needed to meet that end. This is ultimately constrained by the availability of resources, i.e., willingness to pay is ultimately constrained by ability to pay.

The environmental impacts of local land use decisions, but neglected by local land users, typically affect risks at different scales. We take just two examples. The first involves the risks posed by the emergence and dispersal of pests and pathogens through the extensive growth of agriculture. The conversion of wild habitat to pasture or crop production is not only a driver of local biodiversity loss, but also a source of species introductions across the wider system. While the potential costs this imposes on producers elsewhere are substantial, they are not part of the local land users' calculus. For the reasons we have described above, the poor (understandably) ignore this risk more than the rich. This includes the effects of government capacities to secure the public good.

The opening of new markets or trade routes has resulted in the introduction of new species either as the object of trade or, more frequently, as the unintended consequence of trade. The growth in the volume of trade along existing routes has increased the frequency with which new introductions are repeated, and hence the probability that an introduced species will establish and spread (Cassey et al., 2004; Semmens et al., 2004). Indeed, the volume and direction of trade turn out to be good empirical predictors of species dispersal (Costello et al., 2007; Levine et al., 2003).

The costs of species dispersal include both direct and indirect effects. Direct effects include the impacts of pests and disease outbreaks in agricultural systems generally. One (dated) estimate of the damage caused by species dispersal put it at 53 per cent of agricultural GDP in the US, but at 96 per cent of agricultural GDP in South Africa, and 112 per cent of agricultural GDP in Brazil (Pimentel et al., 2001). The indirect effects have not been evaluated but include, for example, the loss of native species over a wide range of ecosystems (Daszak et al., 2000). This in turn affects the capacity of ecosystems to deliver the services that underpin much economic activity, and to absorb anthropogenic and environmental stresses and shocks without losing resilience (Kinzig et al., 2002; Loreau et al., 2002; Naeem et al., 2009).

Potentially much larger are the costs of infectious diseases of humans. Most such diseases are zoonotic, and have their origin at the interface between wildlands and farmlands. Although the burden of infectious diseases falls primarily on the people in the developing world, pandemics such as HIV-AIDS, SARS or highly pathogenic avian flu, affect the well-being of people everywhere. For SARS, for example, the global cost of a single outbreak was estimated to be as much as US$50 billion (Beutels et al., 2009; Gupta et al., 2005). The

World Bank estimates that a severe influenza pandemic could cost $3 trillion – nearly 5 per cent of GDP (World Bank, 2012). Globally, total health expenditures accounted for just under 10 per cent of GDP in 2014 (World Bank, 2017). The range of expenditures is very wide – from 1.5 per cent of GDP in East Timor to 17.1 per cent in the US. This reflects disparities in income and priorities rather than disparities in health. The first Global Burden of Disease survey showed that sub-Saharan Africa and India experienced 21·4 per cent and 20·9 per cent of the burden of disease, respectively, but accounted for only 0·7 per cent and 1·0 per cent of health expenditures. The established market economies, on the other hand, accounted for 7·2 per cent of the burden of disease but 87·3 per cent of health expenditures (Murray and Lopez, 1997). Nor has the position changed much since then. Emerging infectious diseases that have their origins in cross-species contact at the interface between farmlands and wildlands in poor countries may impose the highest cost in rich countries.

Our second example involves the cumulative risks of biodiversity loss in agroecosystems. In these systems, the species with the greatest impact on human well-being are cultivated plants. The raw material for all modern varieties are landraces – traditionally cultivated plants that are morphologically distinct, have some genetic integrity but are also genetically variable and dynamic, and have distinctive properties in terms of yield, date of maturity, pest and disease resistance and so on. The traits of many landraces have been bred into modern cultivars offering a range of benefits in terms of productivity, pest and disease resistance and drought tolerance. The modern cultivars are also genetically stable. The conservation problem in these developments lies in the widespread adoption of improved seeds. The more that farmers adopt the modern varieties, the less effort is made to maintain landraces and wild crop relatives that may provide important future genetic options. Indeed, genetic erosion of crops has been mostly associated with the introduction of modern cultivars (van de Wouw et al., 2010).

The conservation of land races and crop wild relatives lies in their dynamic nature. If in situ populations of land races and crop wild relatives are able to evolve under climatic or other selection pressure, they may develop traits that are helpful to future plant breeding efforts (Food and Agriculture Organization, 2010). Ex situ collections can provide valuable insurance against extinction in place, but they cannot substitute for this property of land races and wild crop relatives. Wild crop relatives are particularly problematic, since they have fallen into the cracks between ex situ conservation of domesticated crops in collections and in situ conservation of endangered wild species in protected areas (Food and Agriculture Organization, 2010).[2]

The genetic engineering of modern cultivars may be opening some new options for seed producers, but the disappearance of landraces and wild crop relatives at a time of rapid environmental change is closing down many more. A reduction in the genetic diversity of landraces and wild crop relatives is reducing the resilience of agroecosystems, and hence the capacity to adapt the production of foods, fuels and fibres to future environmental stresses – climate change among them. In the language of ecosystem services, the role of landraces and wild crop relatives in regulating production risks over time has been compromised. At the same time, the increasingly widespread adoption of a small number of modern varieties has potentially increased the spatial correlation of risk across agroecosystems. The more widespread is the adoption of common cultivars, the greater is the potential for simultaneous crop failures across the system (Smale et al., 2008).

What to Do?

Many of the poorest people in the world have a natural interest in biodiversity – in the species needed to support production of foods, fuels and fibres, in the availability of medicines (old and new), in landscapes that have totemic or cultural significance, in the regulation of water flows, microclimate, pests and pathogens. They have a farmer's interest in predators, weeds and diseases, a hunter's interest in wildlife, a gatherer's interest in honey and fruits. These interests are not necessarily served by traditional conservation practices. Decades of evidence on the effectiveness of integrated conservation and development projects has shown how difficult it is to reconcile protected area-based conservation with the development aspirations of a growing rural population (Adams et al., 2004; Wells et al., 2004).

The most urgent and important objective in many countries is poverty alleviation, not traditional biodiversity conservation. For the rural poor, the only reasonable road to poverty alleviation is agriculture. If the Global North believes that the cost of biodiversity loss caused by the extensive growth of agriculture in poor countries is unacceptably high, then it should invest in development options that conserve natural assets of global importance, and that involve less collateral damage to other species. There is little evidence that appeals based on biological notions of conservation value have had much effect on the governments of rich countries in the past. Aside from the arguments most frequently invoked by conservation biologists, however, there are two utilitarian reasons to believe that global investment in the economic development of the poorest countries in the world would offer benefits both in terms of the conservation of endangered endemic species, and in terms of our global capacity to navigate the risks of environmental change.

First, as the One Health approach indicates, human, animal and plant health are closely interconnected across space and over time. As the experience of HIV-AIDS, SARS, MERS, Nipah Virus, Zika and many other zoonotic epidemics has shown, human health in the richest countries is tightly connected to contact between livestock and wildlife in the poorest countries. The 2014 West African Ebola outbreak prompted a review of the effectiveness of current efforts to manage global health, along with calls for the establishment of stronger global mechanisms for the governance of the health risks of trade and travel, and increased global investment in epidemic and pandemic response capability (Gates, 2015). The World Bank estimates that if the international community invested $3.4 billion annually in improved global pandemic detection and response, it could generate annual benefits to the global community of $30 billion (depending upon how many pandemics were averted) (World Bank, 2012). It is reasonable to see investment in measures that reduce the risks of cross-species contacts in the same way.

Second, we have argued that all of humanity has a strong interest in the in situ conservation of the genetic material in landraces and wild crop relatives that are currently being lost as farmers switch to modern varieties. The ever-widening range of pharmaceutical, industrial and consumer products that incorporate genetic material from other species suggests that global interest in the in situ conservation of genetically dynamic material extends well beyond foods, fuels and fibres. But even if we were only concerned with our capacity to feed ourselves as environmental conditions change, there is a strong case for strengthening farmers' incentives to conserve plant genetic material – and many of the most important landraces are found in the poorer countries of the world.

At the international level, farmers' rights are recognised through the Convention on Biological Diversity (CBD) (United Nations, 1993) and the International Treaty on Plant Genetic Resources for Food and Agriculture (Plant Treaty; 2009). Both instruments leave authority over genetic resources with national governments. The CBD focuses on the conservation and sustainable use of wild-living species and the fair and equitable sharing of the benefits arising out of their utilisation, while the Plant Treaty focuses on the conservation and sustainable use of plant genetic resources for food and agriculture and the fair and equitable sharing of the benefits arising out of their use. Landraces clearly fall under the Plant Treaty. While wild crop relatives are in principle covered by the CBD, in practice they tend to fall between the two stools.

Both treaties aim to protect a global public good – the genetic resources needed to manage environmental change in an uncertain future. But both also force interventions through bilateral or multilateral agreements between national governments. There are, however, other options. Direct investment by the Gates Foundation, or by non-governmental organisations such as The Nature Conservancy or Conservation International, illustrate one option. Payments for ecosystem services are another. Such schemes offer a mechanism for civil society to invest in the common wealth of humankind. They may not be effective mechanisms for poverty alleviation (Kinzig et al., 2011), but they can potentially convert global willingness to pay for the conservation of plant genetic material into direct incentives to farmers (Perrings, 2014).

What is needed to secure the global public interest in conservation is a global effort to secure the environmentally sustainable development of the world's poorest economies. Biodiversity conservation is one among many potential global benefits of a development strategy that focuses on the poorest countries, and that specifically takes the environmental consequences of alternative investment options into account. The pervasiveness of 'win-win' narratives for simultaneous biodiversity protection and poverty alleviation (Sachs et al., 2009) – whether through creation of protected areas or introduction of payment for ecosystem services schemes – means that needed protections both for biodiversity and for people are often overlooked, or added only later in an ad hoc and often inefficient manner, after harms have already been experienced. There are also good examples of what not to do. Large-scale land acquisition (LaSLA) is the phenomenon of multi-national companies and/or foreign governments, sometimes in collaboration with national-level wealthy investors, leasing or purchasing significant tracts of land in developing countries for the purposes of producing food or biofuels for export. Although LaSLA is argued to spur investment, to develop rural infrastructure and to build capacity in local populations, the evidence suggests that more common outcomes are the disenfranchisement and loss of livelihood of local people.

There is little evidence that economic growth will, by and of itself, reduce the threat to valuable functional groups of species. There is, however, evidence that development programmes can be devised that both improve living standards and mitigate the biodiversity risks of extensive agricultural growth. Some components of such programmes are quite familiar: intensification of agriculture, development of employment opportunities in non-agricultural sectors, extension of education and training opportunities, strengthening of credit markets, establishment of secure property rights and so on. Others are less so: land use/investment zones to complement protected areas, separation of agricultural production zones from wild habitat, extension of property rights to include genetic material, institutional reforms to regulate common-pool resources, development of incentives to resource users to undertake activities that serve the global public good (public-private environmental partnerships).

To conclude, we draw attention to the significant social justice issues associated both with unwarranted biodiversity loss and with efforts to protect biodiversity, or mitigate loss. For one thing, the poor (at household, community and national scales) are more dependent on natural resources than are the rich, and thus more likely to suffer the negative consequences of *unwarranted* biodiversity loss. For another, the poor are less likely to have the rights – or the capacity to exercise those rights – to be represented in decisions about how local biodiversity is to be managed. That means decisions being taken are more likely to reflect the interests of the rich and powerful – either within the nation or those who are foreign nationals. Since we have already seen that the poor and rich can have very different interests in how biodiversity is to be managed, this can undermine the often already precarious livelihoods of the poor. Furthermore, when the national or global community is willing to compensate the local community for biodiversity management that favours the broader interests, the poor may be overlooked in that compensation if they lack property rights or representation.

In a provocative paper on climate change, Schelling (1997) argued that the best climate change strategy for poor nations was to develop their economies. Although this would inevitably lead to an *increase* in greenhouse gas emissions, and so would be worse from a global perspective, each poor country would be better off because they would have reduced their reliance on the natural-resource base (Schelling, 1997). We have drawn attention to something quite similar in the case of biodiversity. In the 'rich' nations of the world, agriculture's share in GDP averages about 5 per cent, while in the poor nations of the world it averages about 25 per cent. And in these poor nations, nearly 70 per cent of the population resides in rural areas, and is directly dependent on both marketed and non-marketed natural resources for survival (Dasgupta, 2007). A survey of rural communities in 24 developing countries found that 'environmental income' (income derived from uncultivated forest and non-forest products) delivered, on average, 28 per cent of total household income (Angelsen et al., 2014). One implication of this is that any *unwarranted* degradation in biodiversity is going to disproportionately affect the poor – both at the household and national level. A second is that if the economic development of poor countries reduces the number of people directly dependent on natural resources, it will also reduce stress on biodiversity.

Our central point is that some loss of biodiversity to advance human well-being is undoubtedly warranted, though the decisions of the rich and poor as to how much and what types of biodiversity could productively be eliminated will differ. Since the poor often lack property rights or are otherwise disenfranchised from decision-making, the world risks biodiversity outcomes that reflect the desires of the rich more than they do the poor. But this also creates a space for negotiation between the rich and the poor. This can (and does) include government-to-government or intergovernmental organisation-to-government negotiated conservation and development projects, but it can also include private and/or non-governmental initiatives. At a time when many national governments are pulling back from established international commitments, and are becoming more isolationist and protectionist, this may be the space in which the global public interest is best protected.

Notes

1. This group of countries includes Afghanistan, Bhutan, Burkina Faso, Burundi, Cambodia, Eritrea, Ethiopia, Kenya, Lao People's Dem Rep, Lesotho, Malawi, Micronesia, Fed States, Nepal, Niger, Papua New Guinea, Rwanda, Samoa, Solomon Islands, Sri Lanka, Tajikistan, Trinidad and Tobago and Uganda.
2. In situ conservation priorities for wild relatives include: in Africa, finger millet (*Eleusine spp.*), pearl millet (*Pennisetum spp.*), garden pea (*Pisum spp.*) and cowpea (*Vigna spp.*); in the Americas, barley (*Hordeum spp.*), sweet potato (*Ipomoea spp.*), cassava (*Manihot spp.*), potato (*Solanum spp.*) and maize (*Zea spp.*); in Asia and the Pacific, wild rice (*Oryza spp.*) and the cultivated banana/plantain (*Musa spp.*); and in the Near East, the garden pea (*Pisum spp.*), wheat (*Triticum spp.* and *Aegilops spp.*), barley (*Hordeum spontaneum* and *H. bulbosum*), faba bean (*Vicia spp.*), chickpea (*Cicer spp.*), alfalfa (*Medicago spp.*), clover (*Trifolium spp.*), pistachio (*Pistacia spp.*) and stone fruits (*Prunus spp.*) (Maxted and Kell, 2009).

References

Adams, W. M., Aveling, R., Brockington, D., Dickson, B., Elliott, J., Hutton, J., Roe, D., Vira, B. & Wolmer, W. 2004. Biodiversity conservation and the eradication of poverty. *Science*, 306(5699): 1146–1149.

Angelsen, A., Jagger, P., Babigumira, R., Belcher, B., Hogarth, N. J., Bauch, S., Börner, J., Smith-Hall, C. & Wunder, S. 2014. Environmental income and rural livelihoods: A global-comparative analysis. *World Development*, 64: S12–S28.

Baumgärtner, S. 2007. The insurance value of biodiversity in the provision of ecosystem services. *Natural Resources Modeling*, 20: 87–127.

Berkes, F., Colding, J. & Folke, C. 2000. Rediscovery of traditional ecological knowledge as adaptive management. *Ecological Applications*, 10(5): 1251–1262.

Beutels, P., Jia, N., Zhou, Q., Smith, R., Cao, W. & de Vlas, S. 2009. The economic impact of SARS in Beijing, China. *Tropical Medicine and International Health*, 14(November): 85–91.

Bruinsma, J. 2009. By how much do land, water and crop yields need to increase by 2050? Paper presented at How to Feed the World in 2050, Rome.

Cassey, P., Blackburn, T. M., Russel, G. J., Jones, K. E. & Lockwood, J. L. 2004. Influences on the transport and establishment of exotic bird species: An analysis of the parrots (Psittaciformes) of the world. *Global Change Biology*, 10: 417–426.

Chavas, J.-P. a. M. D. 2002. On the valuation of uncertainty in welfare analysis. *American Journal of Agricultural Economics*, 84(1): 23–38.

Cleaver, F. 2005. The inequality of social capital and the reproduction of chronic poverty. *World Development*, 33(6): 893–906.

Collier, P. 2002. Social capital and poverty: A microeconomic perspective. In R. Puttnam, C. Grootaert & T. Van Bastelaer (Eds.), *The Role of Social Capital in Development: An Empirical Assessment*: 19–41. Cambridge: Cambridge University Press. https://doi.org/10.1017/CBO9780511492600.003.

Costello, C., Springborn, M., McAusland, C. & Solow, A. 2007. Unintended biological invasions: Does risk vary by trading partner? *Journal of Environmental Economics and Management*, 54(3): 262–276.

Crane, P. & Kinzig, A. 2005. Nature in the metropolis. *Science*, 308(5726): 1225.

Dasgupta, P. 2001. *Human Well-Being and the Natural Environment*. Oxford: Oxford University Press.

2007. Nature and the economy. *Journal of Applied Ecology*, 44: 475–487.

Daszak, P., Cunningham, A. A. & Hyatt, A. D. 2000. Wildlife ecology: Emerging infectious diseases of wildlife – threats to biodiversity and human health. *Science*, 287(5452): 443–449.

Firbank, L. G., Petit, S., Smart, S., Blain, A. & Fuller, R. J. 2008. Assessing the impacts of agricultural intensification on biodiversity: A British perspective. *Philosophical Transactions of the Royal Society of London B: Biological Sciences*, 363(1492): 777–787.

Fisher, I. 1930. *The Theory of Interest*. New York: Macmillan.

Foley, J. A. 2005. Global consequences of land use. *Science*, 309: 570–574.

Foley, J. A., Ramankutty, N., Brauman, K. A., Cassidy, E. S., Gerber, J. S., Johnston, M., Mueller, N. D., O'Connell, C., Ray, D. K., West, P. C., Balzer, C., Bennett, E. M., Carpenter, S. R., Hill, J., Monfreda, C., Polasky, S., Rockström, J., Sheehan, J., Siebert, S., Tilman, D. & Zaks, D. P. M. 2011. Solutions for a cultivated planet. *Nature*, 478 (7369): 337–342.

Food and Agriculture Organization. 2010. *The Second Report on the State of the World's Plant Genetic Resources for Food and Agriculture*. Rome: FAO.

Gates, B. 2015. The next epidemic – lessons from Ebola. *New England Journal of Medicine*, 372(15): 1381–1384.

Geiger, F., Bengtsson, J., Berendse, F., Weisser, W. W., Emmerson, M., Morales, M. B., Ceryngier, P., Liira, J., Tscharntke, T., Winqvist, C.,

Eggers, S., Bommarco, R., Pärt, T., Bretagnolle, V., Plantegenest, M., Clement, L. W., Dennis, C., Palmer, C., Oñate, J. J., Guerrero, I., Hawro, V., Aavik, T., Thies, C., Flohre, A., Hänke, S., Fischer, C., Goedhart, P. W. & Inchausti, P. 2010. Persistent negative effects of pesticides on biodiversity and biological control potential on European farmland. *Basic and Applied Ecology*, 11(2): 97–105.

Godfray, H. C. J., Beddington, J. R., Crute, I. R., Haddad, L., Lawrence, D., Muir, J. F., Pretty, J., Robinson, S., Thomas, S. M. & Toulmin, C. 2010. Food security: The challenge of feeding 9 billion people. *Science*, 327 (5967): 812–818.

Goeschl, T. & Swanson, T. 2003. Pests, plagues, and patents. *Journal of the European Economic Association*, 1(2–3): 561–575.

Gupta, A. G., Moyer, C. A. & Stern, D. T. 2005. The economic impact of quarantine: SARS in Toronto as a case study. *Journal of Infection*, 50 (5): 386–393.

Heal, G. M., Barbier, E. B., Boyle, K. J., Covich, A. P., Gloss, S. P., Hershner, C. H., Hoehn, J. P., Pringle, C. M., Polasky, S., Segerson, K. & Shrader-Frechette, K. 2005. *Valuing Ecosystem Services: Toward Better Environmental Decision Making*. Washington, DC: National Academies Press.

Hoffmann, M., Hilton-Taylor, C., Angulo, A., Böhm, M., Brooks, T. M., Butchart, S. H. M., Carpenter, K. E., Chanson, J., Collen, B., Cox, N. A., Darwall, W. R. T., Dulvy, N. K., Harrison, L. R., Katariya, V., Pollock, C. M., Quader, S., Richman, N. I., Rodrigues, A. S. L., Tognelli, M. F., Vié, J.-C., Aguiar, J. M., Allen, D. J., Allen, G. R., Amori, G., Ananjeva, N. B., Andreone, F., Andrew, P., Ortiz, A. L. A., Baillie, J. E. M., Baldi, R., Bell, B. D., Biju, S. D., Bird, J. P., Black-Decima, P., Blanc, J. J., Bolaños, F., Bolivar -G., W., Burfield, I. J., Burton, J. A., Capper, D. R., Castro, F., Catullo, G., Cavanagh, R. D., Channing, A., Chao, N. L., Chenery, A. M., Chiozza, F., Clausnitzer, V., Collar, N. J., Collett, L. C., Collette, B. B., Fernandez, C. F. C., Craig, M. T., Crosby, M. J., Cumberlidge, N., Cuttelod, A., Derocher, A. E., Diesmos, A. C., Donaldson, J. S., Duckworth, J. W., Dutson, G., Dutta, S. K., Emslie, R. H., Farjon, A., Fowler, S., Freyhof, J., Garshelis, D. L., Gerlach, J., Gower, D. J., Grant, T. D., Hammerson, G. A., Harris, R. B., Heaney, L. R., Hedges, S. B., Hero, J.-M., Hughes, B., Hussain, S. A., Icochea M., J., Inger, R. F., Ishii, N., Iskandar, D. T., Jenkins, R. K. B., Kaneko, Y., Kottelat, M., Kovacs, K. M., Kuzmin, S. L., La Marca, E., Lamoreux, J. F., Lau, M. W. N., Lavilla, E. O., Leus, K., Lewison, R. L., Lichtenstein, G., Livingstone, S. R., Lukoschek, V., Mallon, D. P., McGowan, P. J. K., McIvor, A., Moehlman, P. D., Molur, S., Alonso, A. M. o., Musick, J. A.,

Nowell, K., Nussbaum, R. A., Olech, W., Orlov, N. L., Papenfuss, T. J., Parra-Olea, G., Perrin, W. F., Polidoro, B. A., Pourkazemi, M., Racey, P. A., Ragle, J. S., Ram, M., Rathbun, G., Reynolds, R. P., Rhodin, A. G. J., Richards, S. J., Rodriguez, L. O., Ron, S. R., Rondinini, C., Rylands, A. B., Sadovy de Mitcheson, Y., Sanciangco, J. C., Sanders, K. L., Santos-Barrera, G., Schipper, J., Self-Sullivan, C., Shi, Y., Shoemaker, A., Short, F. T., Sillero-Zubiri, C., Silvano, D. b. L., Smith, K. G., Smith, A. T., Snoeks, J., Stattersfield, A. J., Symes, A. J., Taber, A. B., Talukdar, B. K., Temple, H. J., Timmins, R., Tobias, J. A., Tsytsulina, K., Tweddle, D., Ubeda, C., Valenti, S. V., Paul van Dijk, P., Veiga, L. M., Veloso, A., Wege, D. C., Wilkinson, M., Williamson, E. A., Xie, F., Young, B. E., Akçakaya, H. R., Bennun, L., Blackburn, T. M., Boitani, L., Dublin, H. T., da Fonseca, G. A. B., Gascon, C., Lacher, T. E., Mace, G. M., Mainka, S. A., McNeely, J. A., Mittermeier, R. A., Reid, G. M., Rodriguez, J. P., Rosenberg, A. A., Samways, M. J., Smart, J., Stein, B. A. & Stuart, S. N. 2010. The impact of conservation on the status of the world's vertebrates. *Science*, 330(6010): 1503–1509.

International Assessment of Agricultural Knowledge Science and Technology for Development. 2008. *Agriculture at a Crossroads: Synthesis Report*. Washington, DC: Island Press.

Kinzig, A. P., Pacala, S. & Tilman, D. (Eds.). 2002. *Functional Consequences of Biodiversity: Empirical Progress and Theoretical Extensions*. Princeton, NJ: Princeton University Press.

Kinzig, A. P., Perrings, C., Chapin, F. S., III, Polasky, S., Smith, V. K., Tilman, D. & Turner, B. L., II. 2011. Sustainability: Paying for ecosystem services–promise and peril. *Science*, 334(6056): 603–604.

Kremen, C., Williams, N. M. & Thorp, R. W. 2002. Crop pollination from native bees at risk from agricultural intensification. *Proceedings of the National Academy of Sciences of the United States of America*, 99(26): 16812–16816.

Levine, J. M., Vila, M., D'Antonio, C. M., Dukes, J. S., Grigulis, K. & Lavorel, S. 2003. Mechanisms underlying the impacts of exotic plant invasions. *Proceedings of the Royal Society of London, Series B, Biological Sciences*, 270(1517): 775–781.

Loreau, M., Naeem, S. & Inchausti, P. 2002. *Biodiversity and Ecosystem Functioning: Synthesis and Perspectives*. Oxford: Oxford University Press.

Markandya, A. 2001. *Poverty Alleviation and Sustainable Development Implications for the Management of Natural Capital*. Washington, DC: World Bank.

Maxted, N. & Kell, S. P. 2009. *Establishment of a Global Network for the In Situ Conservation of Crop Wild Relatives: Status and Needs*. Rome: FAO Commission on Genetic Resources for Food and Agriculture.

Millennium Ecosystem Assessment. 2005a. *Ecosystems and Human Well-Being: Biodiversity Synthesis.* Washington, DC: World Resources Institute.
  2005b. *Ecosystems and Human Well-Being: General Synthesis.* Washington, DC: Island Press.
Murray, C. J. L. & Lopez, A. D. 1997. Global mortality, disability, and the contribution of risk factors: Global Burden of Disease Study. *The Lancet,* 349: 1436–1442.
Myers, N. 1988. Threatened biotas: 'Hot spots' in tropical forests. *Environmentalist,* 8(3): 187–208.
Naeem, S. 1998. Species redundancy and ecosystem reliability. *Conservation Biology,* 12: 39–45.
Naeem, S., Bunker, D., Hector, A., Loreau, M. & Perrings, C. (Eds.). 2009. *Biodiversity, Ecosystem Functioning, and Human Wellbeing: An Ecological and Economic Perspective.* Oxford: Oxford University Press.
Perrings, C. 1989. An optimal path to extinction – poverty and resource degradation in the open agrarian economy. *Journal of Development Economics,* 30(1): 1–24.
  2014. *Our Uncommon Heritage: Biodiversity, Ecosystem Services and Human Wellbeing.* Cambridge: Cambridge University Press.
Perrings, C. & Halkos, G. 2015. Agriculture and the threat to biodiversity in sub-Saharan Africa. *Environmental Research Letters,* 10(9): 095015.
Pimentel, D., McNair, S., Janecka, S., Wightman, J., Simmonds, C., O'Connell, C., Wong, E., Russel, L., Zern, C., Aquino, T. & Tsomondo, T. 2001. Economic and environmental threats of alien plant, animal and microbe invasions. *Agriculture, Ecosystems and Environment,* 84: 1–20.
Potts, S. G., Biesmeijer, J. C., Kremen, C., Neumann, P., Schweiger, O. & Kunin, W. E. 2010. Global pollinator declines: Trends, impacts and drivers. *Trends in Ecology & Evolution,* 25(6): 345–353.
Preece, J. 2006. Widening participation for social justice: Poverty and access to education. In A. Oduaran & H. S. Bhola (Eds.), *Widening Access to Education as Social Justice*: 113–126. Dordrecht: Springer Netherlands.
Pretty, J., Toulmin, C. & Williams, S. 2011. Sustainable intensification in African agriculture. *International Journal of Agricultural Sustainability,* 9(1): 5–24.
Quaas, M. & Baumgärtner, S. 2007. Natural vs. financial insurance in the management of public good ecosystems. *Ecological Economics,* 65(2): 397–406.

Sachs, J. D., Baillie, J. E. M., Sutherland, W. J., Armsworth, P. R., Ash, N., Beddington, J., Blackburn, T. M., Collen, B., Gardiner, B., Gaston, K. J., Godfray, H. C. J., Green, R. E., Harvey, P. H., House, B., Knapp, S., Kumpel, N. F., Macdonald, D. W., Mace, G. M., Mallet, J., Matthews, A., May, R. M., Petchey, O., Purvis, A., Roe, D., Safi, K., Turner, K., Walpole, M., Watson, R. & Jones, K. E. 2009. Biodiversity conservation and the Millennium Development Goals. *Science*, 325 (5947): 1502–1503.

Schelling, T. C. 1997. The cost of combating global warming: Facing the tradeoffs. *Foreign Affairs*, 76(6): 8–14.

Secretariat of the Convention on Biological Diversity. 2010. *Global Biodiversity Outlook 3*. Montréal: Convention on Biological Diversity.

Semmens, B. X., Buhle, E. R., Salomon, A. K. & Pattengill-Semmens, C. V. 2004. A hotspot of non-native marine fishes: Evidence for the aquarium trade as an invasion pathway. *Marine Ecology Progress Series*, 266: 239–244.

Simpson, R. D., Sedjo, R. A. & Reid, J. W. 1996. Valuing biodiversity for use in pharmaceutical research. *Journal of Political Economy*, 104(1): 163–185.

Smale, M., Hazell, P., Hodgkin, T. & Fowler, C. 2008. Do we have an adequate global strategy for securing the biodiversity of major food crops? *Agrobiodiversity Conservation and Economic Development*, 10: 40.

Thébault, E. & Loreau, M. 2006. The relationship between biodiversity and ecosystem functioning in food webs. *Ecological Research*, 21: 17–25.

UNEP-WCMC and IUCN. 2016. *Protected Planet Report 2016*. Cambridge: UNEP-WCMC and IUCN.

United Nations. 1993. *Convention on Biological Diversity*. New York: United Nations.

van de Wouw, M., Kik, C., van Hintum, T., van Treuren, R. & Visser, B. 2010. Genetic erosion in crops: Concept, research results and challenges. *Plant Genetic Resources*, 8(1): 1–15.

WCED. 1987. *Report of the World Commission on Environment and Development: Our Common Future*. Oxford: Oxford University Press.

Wells, M. P., McShane, T. O., Dublin, H. T., O'Connor, S. & Redford, K. H. 2004. The future of integrated conservation and development projects: Building on what works. In T. O. McShane & M. P. Wells (Eds.), *Getting Biodiversity Projects to Work: Towards More Effective Conservation and Development*: 397–422. New York: Columbia University Press.

World Bank. 2012. *People, Pathogens and Our Planet: The Economics of One Health.* Washington, DC: World Bank.

    2013. *World Data Bank: Health Nutrition and Population Statistics,* vol. 2013. Washington, DC: World Bank.

    2017. *Health Expenditure, Total (% of GDP),* vol. 2017. Washington, DC: World Bank.

Zhao, Z.-H., Hui, C., He, D.-H. & Li, B.-L. 2015. Effects of agricultural intensification on ability of natural enemies to control aphids. *Scientific Reports,* 5: 8024.

11 | *Terra Incognita*
In Search of the Disconnect
MATHIS WACKERNAGEL

One Perspective: The Significance of a Finite Planet for Human Development

Natural scientists start from the assumption that people and their economies exist physically. Therefore, without resource security – without continued access to the materials needed to feed and power human economies, these economies lose their ability to operate. Opportunities erode (Rockström et al., 2009; Steffen et al., 2015). Financial resources can be employed to compensate for local lack of resources, as these financial resources can access physical resources elsewhere, as long as those 'elsewheres' have extra resource capacity. However, global over-use adds pressure to resource competition, as made apparent in the prominent example of climate change which is driven by emissions from fossil fuel use and from land use change. To comply with the goal set by the Paris Climate Agreement, humanity would need to have left the fossil fuel age well before 2050 (Figueres et al., 2017; Rockström et al., 2017).[1] Alternatively, if humanity will not have left that era, the associated climate risks may feed instead into increased economic and social uncertainty and volatility as more people face more direct impacts (such as heat waves, droughts, floods) or indirect resource constraints (such as less steady food production, increased migration). In an unprepared world, it will therefore become increasingly difficult to improve, or even maintain, human development achievements and prosperity.

Another Perspective: Resource Security Is Overplayed

The majority of economic advisors and strategists for governments around the world discount the significance of the material underpinnings of economies. Consider this: rating agencies like S&P and Moody's, or economic rankings like the competitiveness report of the World

Economic Forum barely include resource security in their analyses (WEF, 2017a, 2018a). Analysts behind such studies consider resources as a minor economic parameter. Yes, resource costs, such as fossil fuels, can have an effect, but in their view, particularly renewable resources are negligible, with agriculture in high-income countries making up less than 3 per cent of those countries' GDP. The key drivers of national competitiveness, according to their view, are the quality of the workforce, the institutional set-ups and a country's macroeconomic stability, not their resource situation. Therefore, countries must primarily focus on fomenting a positive economic climate. The ability to adapt and to find technological alternatives in order to overcome resource shortages, should they come up, is the best insurance for resource security. Resource policies that are too specific would be inefficient and limit potential solutions. Also, higher incomes by themselves provide more benefit as they typically help societies afford a cleaner environment.

Terra Incognita

Both views cannot be simultaneously correct yet they coexist. Both are even touted to be 'knowledge-based' and 'data driven'. Both are backed up not only by academic studies, but by entire journals and scientific disciplines.

A reflection of this confusion is captured by the contrast between the World Economic Forum's annual risk report and its competitiveness report. For the risk report, the World Economic Forum surveys CEOs and other prominent leaders on the global risks they perceive. The ranking of the top five risks in terms of either 'imminence' or 'impact' vary from year to year (even though most of the risks have decades long half-lives). Their risk report for 2017 (WEF, 2017b) states that six out of the top 10 risks are environmental (if we include water crises in the environmental camp), two are military (nuclear and cyber), one is social (large-scale involuntary migration which could well have resource scarcity roots), and finally, just one is technical (cyber fraud). The 2018 report (WEF, 2018b) identifies 7 environmentally related risks among the top 10. In contrast, the World Economic Forum's annual competitiveness reports (WEF, 2017a, 2018a) endeavour to evaluate how well countries are set up to economically succeed. They claim to evaluate the 'set of institutions, policies, and factors that determine a country's productivity which in turn sets the level of prosperity that the country can achieve'. The reports use 114 indicators grouped into 12 pillars to evaluate countries. Yet none of these indicators address any environmental, resource or climate aspects, in spite of the significance of environmental risks identified by CEOs in the same organisation's equally prominent risk report. Coincidentally, both the risk and the competitiveness report are produced by the same World Economic Forum department 'Global Competitiveness and Risks Team' and both are endorsed by the Chair of the Forum.

The World Economic Forum is not alone. Examples abound:

- Switzerland's government, while committed to the Paris Agreement, is also advocating to increase its national highway fund, when personal transport is the portion of carbon emissions that Switzerland has been least able to contain, let alone reduce. The voting population resoundingly supported this commitment to a larger national highway fund.[2]
- Marrakesh opened a new airport wing, which opened just prior to the arrival of the ministers coming to Climate COP22, doubling the airport's capacity.[3]
- The airport of Vienna plans to double its flight capacity by adding another runway. Most of Vienna's political and business community favours the construction of this runway. Initially, the Federal Administrative Court rejected the permit to expand on environmental grounds: doubling the flight capacity contradicts the Paris Agreement (by 2030, CO_2 emissions should be halved, not doubled). But the Austrian Constitutional Court overturned this judgement in June 2017.[4]
- The current US administration is banking on expanding the US fossil energy infrastructure as a driver for increasing economic activities.[5]

Where exactly is the disconnect between these incompatible views, both of which are motivated by finding strategies to keep economies strong and healthy? This zone of incompatibility and contradiction is the 'terra incognita' we desperately need to explore. Finding this land of true knowledge and understanding is what humanity's future depends on.

What We Do Know: The Significance of Our Physical Foundation

By 2050, the world population is expected to reach 9.8 billion people, with 70 per cent living in urban areas, according to the Population

Reference Bureau (2017). These urban areas will house an ever larger segment of the world's lowest-income populations. In addition, there will be even more stress on rural areas providing for those cities.

The most rapidly expanding cities lack the financial resources to adequately accommodate their expansion. Yet, even the inadequate expansion and operation of urban infrastructure created to serve more people could require significant amounts of additional resources. Inadequacy may lead to even less resource effective urban solutions, increasing, rather than decreasing, cities' resource dependence. It will make these cities more vulnerable, most likely hurting low-income populations overproportionally. This trend becomes challenging at a time when current human demands for resources and energy already significantly exceed what planet Earth can renew, and fossil fuel use will need to be phased out within a few decades.

Therefore, without resolving this contradiction not only intellectually but also in practice, the world will be faced with increasing risks of climate change and resource constraints.

By emphasising resource constraints, or inversely, the need for resource security, Global Footprint Network argues that ultimately the most limiting material factor for life, including human life, is nature's ability to renew. Even the amount of fossil fuel on this planet is not most limiting, because what we lack is enough capacity to absorb the CO_2 emissions, not the amount underground.

Given these vastly separate, mutually inconsistent views on the significance of natural capital for the human enterprise, three key questions emerge:

1 Is it possible to map the resource dependence of the human economy and compare it to what the planet's natural capital can provide?
2 How can such a metric be used to explore under which conditions such a dependence affects humanity's ability to end poverty and secure long-term prosperity?
3 And finally, how does such a metric help manage human dependence on natural capital, particularly in those conditions where excessive resource dependence is starting to erode humanity's ability to end poverty and secure long-term prosperity?

This paper answers the first question and outlines how the second and third questions could be explored. It builds on Global Footprint Network's endeavours which aim at making apparent, through biophysical resource accounting, the nature and significance of resource security. Through these resource accounts, the organisation seeks to help people and government administrations document resource dependence, set goals and manage and monitor progress.

Mapping the Path to the Terra Incognita with the Footprint

The 'Ecological Footprint', or 'Footprint' for short, was developed as a resource accounting tool to map how much nature there is to support life, and to contrast this with how much people use (Wackernagel and Rees, 1996).

On the demand side, the Footprint adds up all the biologically productive area needed to regenerate everything people demand from nature. These are all the things that compete for biologically productive areas: fruits and vegetables, fish, timber, fibre and absorption of carbon dioxide from fossil fuel burning, space for buildings and roads. This area can then be compared to the productive areas available globally or locally – this is what we call biocapacity (Wackernagel et al., 2018a, 2018b).

As fossil fuel is phased out – as anticipated in most imaginable scenarios – biocapacity will not only have to feed people, but it will also have to help replace fossil fuel. Also, fossil fuel underground is not limited by how much is underground, but by how much of the carbon waste the biosphere can cope with. Therefore, mapping an economy's material dependence on biocapacity provides an overarching view on that economy's material dependence. This approach allows us to track the critical resources and waste streams, including CO_2.

Currently there are 1.7 hectares of ecologically productive space per person on the planet. This corresponds to about one-quarter of the planetary surface, since the rest is deserts, steep mountains, deep oceans or icefields. We express all these areas, both for biocapacity and Ecological Footprint, in global hectares, which are explained in more detail below. Essentially, these global hectares are biologically productive hectares with world average productivity. Global hectares therefore are the measurement unit, or the accounting 'currency', in Ecological Footprint analysis.

This information on biocapacity and human demand on that biocapacity (i.e., the Ecological Footprint) is critical if one believes that economies that want to be resilient and successful need to find ways to operate and provide for thriving lives within the budget of nature. This means the goal for 2050 becomes: *How can populations, on a worldwide average, get to a 1 global hectare Footprint per person?* This contrasts with world average Footprints of currently 2.8 global hectares; or current European Footprint averages of 5–7 gha per person.

Why one global hectare per person? With a higher population in the future, possibly 9 to 10 billion by 2050, and the global commitments to live up to the Aichi Targets for biodiversity conservation, the currently available 1.7 gha per person is reduced to one global hectare per person. If we followed E. O. Wilson's proposition of sharing the planet's bounties to only use 50 per cent of it for human activities, including its domesticated animals and crops, and if the other 50 per cent is left for wild species, this would provide the population at its current size with half of the 1.7 gha per person, i.e., 0.85 gha for each current resident of this planet (Wilson, 2016). In other words, one global hectare per person is still an overly generous allocation, which does not meet the population growth plus E. O. Wilson's Half-Earth target.

How Ecological Footprint Accounting Works

Ecological Footprint accounting is driven by one key question: *How much of the biosphere's (or any region's) regenerative capacity does any human activity demand?* Or more specifically: How much of the planet's (or a region's) regenerative capacity[6] does a defined activity demand in order to provide all the ecosystem services that are competing for mutually exclusive space? These services include provision of all the resources that the population consumes and absorption of that population's waste, using prevailing technology and management practice (Wackernagel and Rees, 1996; Wackernagel et al., 2002, 2018a, 2018b). The ability of ecosystems to provide for these resources and services – its renewable capacity – is the 'biocapacity' that can accommodate the Ecological Footprints.

As financial 'profit and loss' statements track both 'expenditure' and 'income', or balance sheets document 'assets' and 'liabilities', Ecological Footprint accounts also have two sides; demand on biocapacity (Footprint) against availability of biocapacity. Both Footprint and biocapacity can be calculated at global, national, local and individual levels, in the very same way financial accounts can be scaled to different entities.

Biocapacity is shorthand for biological capacity, which is the ability of any ecosystem – hence the whole biosphere – to produce useful ecosystem services for humans. This includes regeneration of biological materials and absorption of wastes generated by humans. Biocapacity is not fixed. It represents the regeneration of natural, renewable resources and waste absorption services that can be used by humanity in a given year. The abundance and productivity of natural capital changes each year.[7] For instance, natural disasters, such as forest and crop pests and landslides, or human-induced degradation such as deforestation, soil loss, climatic impacts or acidification can reduce biocapacity. On the other hand, careful agricultural and forestry management can also magnify biocapacity over long time periods.

It is possible, as with money, to run a Footprint that is larger than the biocapacity one controls.[8] Countries that have a larger Footprint than the country's territorial biocapacity, run, what we call, an ecological deficit. Three mechanisms allow for such a deficit:

- Net-importing biocapacity from elsewhere;
- Using the global commons (such as in the case of fishing international waters or emitting greenhouse gases into the global atmosphere); and
- Overusing one's own territorial biocapacity.

Obviously, for the world as a whole, only the last option is available, since there is no elsewhere that can compensate overuse (the planet is largely materially contained). The overuse of these and other renewable resources is called 'overshoot'. It occurs, for example, when people:

- catch more fish than fishing grounds can regenerate, and then fisheries eventually collapse;
- harvest more timber than forests can regrow, and then they advance deforestation;
- emit more CO_2 than the biosphere can absorb, CO_2 accumulates in the atmosphere, and then they contribute to global warming.

The Ecological Footprint compares these demands against regeneration, and aggregates across all of the planet's surface areas that provide regeneration.

Ecological Footprint accounting is based on two basic accounting principles:

1 *Additivity*: Given that human life competes for biologically productive surfaces, these surface areas can be added up. The Ecological
 Footprint (or Footprint) therefore adds up all human demands on
 nature that compete for biologically productive space: providing
 biological resources, accommodating urban infrastructure or
 absorbing excess carbon from fossil fuel burning. (Surfaces that
 serve multiple human demands are counted only once.) The
 Footprint then becomes comparable to the available biologically
 productive space (biocapacity).

2 *Equivalence*: Since not every biologically productive surface area is
 of equal productivity, areas are scaled proportionally to their biological productivity. Therefore, the measurement unit for Ecological
 Footprint accounting, global hectares, are biologically productive
 hectares with world average productivity. Ideally, if there were no
 data and measurement limitations, hectares should be compared in
 terms of their 'potential NPP' or more precisely the Net Primary
 Productivity the piece of land or ocean area could provide without
 any human intervention. This represents the underlying potential of
 each particular surface area. Since this data does not exist, Global
 Footprint Network's National Footprint Accounts, for instance, use
 'agricultural potential', which is based on FAO's GAEZ maps, as
 a proxy. This points to the fact that there is an ideal definition of
 Ecological Footprint accounting, and that the practice cannot
 always reach the ideal due to data constraints.

Therefore, the mathematical logic behind the accounts becomes
simple: area demanded is calculated by turning the formula for yield
on its head. Since yield is defined as

$$\text{Yield} = \frac{\text{Amount per year}}{\text{Area occupied}}$$

It follows that

$$\text{Area occupied} = \frac{\text{Amount per year}}{\text{Yield}}$$

Applying the second accounting principle of equivalency, rather than
expressing the area results in hectares, each hectare is adjusted for its
respective biocapacity. These adjusted hectares are called *global*

hectares. These global hectares are defined as biologically productive hectares with world average bioproductivity. They are the standard measurement units for both the Ecological Footprint and biocapacity. One global hectare worth of any area is (in theory) inherently able to produce a similar amount of biomass regeneration.[9] It is a 'similar' amount, because different hectares across the world do not provide identical kinds and amounts of biomass – potential Net Primary Productivity (pNPP) would ideally be taken as a common yardstick. However, since such data is not available globally, consistently and reliably, the execution of such an estimate for relative productivity of hectares is simplified (Borucke et al., 2013).

Even though hectares vary across biomes and host vastly different plant communities – from tropical to boreal, from wet to dry – Ecological Footprint accounting compares them based on what they are able to provide. In practical terms, National Footprint Accounts do this by using both equivalence factors based on relative agricultural potential of different area types even though ideally relative potential NPP (pNPP) should be used, and yield factors that compare areas within the same area types using data on each area's relative productivity for meat, cereals, timber or carbon sequestration capacity (Borucke et al., 2013).

Ecological Footprint accounts attempt to track all competing demands for biologically productive surfaces. These demands include regenerating harvested renewable resources and absorbing wastes generated by human processes, as well as accommodating urban infrastructure and roads. Still UN data limitations prevent national calculations from capturing all resource flows. Particularly on the waste side, current accounts only include CO_2 emissions from burning fossil fuel.

Demand on nature, i.e., the Ecological Footprint, is categorised into six different area types: cropland, grazing land, forest products, carbon footprint, built-up land and fishing grounds (see Figure 11.1). Biocapacity is categorised by only five categories, since forestland is used both for two mutually exclusive demands: sequestering the carbon footprint and regenerating forest products. Forests require long-term protection from harvest in order to serve as effective and lasting carbon sequestration. Current national accounts do not distinguish between, or identify, which portions of forests are under such protection.

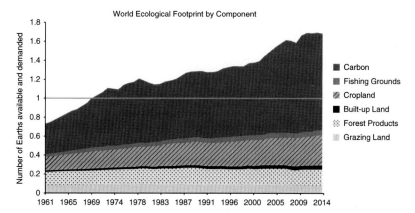

Figure 11.1 Humanity's Ecological Footprint, 1961–2014. This graph shows the ratio between human demand and the Earth's biocapacity, and the components of the human demand, from 1961 to 2014. In other words, the footprint in this figure is not expressed in global hectares but in number of planets. It does not imply that biocapacity does not change over time – just that the number of planets available has been constant, even though the planet itself has changed over the time period. From Global Footprint Network (2018).

Global Footprint Network's most recent national and global accounts – its National Footprint Accounts (Global Footprint Network, 2018) – show that, in 2014 (the most recent year for which UN data is available) humanity continued to be in overshoot,[10] demanding over 68 per cent more than what the biosphere renewed in that year.

Given these accounts, many material aspects of the human economy can be mapped. For instance, each country's demand versus biocapacity can be traced over time (see www.footprintnetwork.org/maps for overarching trends, and http://data.footprintnetwork.org for all the components as well). Through multi-regional input–output assessments, Global Footprint Network overlays the analyses and estimates the resource intensity of each country's sectors (about 57 sectors), as well as how the various consumption activities contribute to the overall Ecological Footprint (in about 35 categories) (Ewing et al., 2012; Galli et al., 2012), based on Purdue University's GTAP input–output tables (Aguiar et al., 2016).

Another application is to extract the various factors that make up the overall demand of people. For instance, one can compare how per

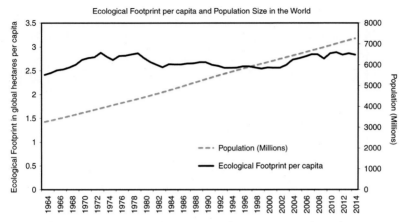

Figure 11.2 Humanity's population size and per person Ecological Footprint, 1964–2014. This graph shows in black the population trend and in grey the per person Ecological Footprint averaged across all people, from 1964 to 2014. The population more than doubled, while the per person demand on nature stayed relatively constant. This means efficiency increase compensated for increase in consumption. In other words, they are getting more use per person out of this same demand (e.g., more efficient lightbulbs, better insulated houses). From Global Footprint Network (2018).

person Footprints change over time as compared to population size. To compare global hectares over time, they are calculated by estimating how many current global hectares it would take to provide for the resource basket of past consumption. This makes comparisons of Footprints over time more meaningful.

Figure 11.2 shows the population and Ecological Footprint per person trends for the world. Figure 11.3 shows the same trends for the current low-income countries (as classified by the World Bank). The figures demonstrate that for the world, the per capita Ecological Footprint has only increased slightly, slower than the population that has nearly doubled. For the low-income countries, the per person Footprint has even declined, while the population size nearly quadrupled.

Should These Numbers Be Trusted?

Providing a framework for measuring is one thing. But can the Footprint and biocapacity results be trusted?

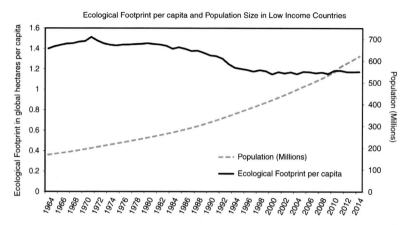

Figure 11.3 Population size of current low-income countries over time, and their per person Ecological Footprint, 1964–2014. This graph shows in black the population trend and in grey the per person Ecological Footprint averaged across all people in low-income countries, from 1964 to 2014. The population nearly quadrupled in those countries, with their Ecological Footprint per person declining 23 per cent from the peak. From a human health and development perspective, this decline is particularly troubling given that the Ecological Footprint per person in these countries is already at a very low level. Also note that in these countries, the footprint per unit of cereal and animal protein is typically higher than the world average because they need speciality cereals for marginal land areas and because animals are kept as savings, leading to a high ratio between feed and fodder input to animal product output. From Global Footprint Network (2018).

If we accept that the Footprint's question is relevant, then the first issue to contend with is whether this question is expressed as a testable, falsifiable, research question. 'Is humanity taking more from the planet than the planet can renew?' does become testable. By adding up all the areas needed to renew what people demand, and then comparing that area with the biologically productive areas that exist, this question can be empirically explored.

But how do we know that the numbers current Ecological Footprint accounts generate can be trusted? The method is widely published and documented in detail on the Global Footprint Network website. This means others can replicate the calculation, particularly given that Global Footprint Network calculations nearly exclusively use publicly available UN datasets. In addition to academic review, Global

Footprint Network has encouraged national government institutes to review and verify the accounts. Such reviews had various benefits, including prompting improvements. Mostly though, these studies focused on verifying the results. The first verification by a national government was in Switzerland (von Stokar et al., 2006). The French had a number of independent reviews,[11] including one by the statistical office of their Ministry of Environment (SOeS, 2010). The latter office replicated the French Ecological Footprint calculations on their own and recreated the 1961-present time series for each year with 1–3 per cent difference to the Global Footprint Network results.

Carbon assessments, or research via planetary boundaries also confirm our results.

Still, with more available or updated data, results have changed. And every year, Global Footprint Network recalculates the entire time series using the most updated approach. There is no change in methodology per se, just better execution or more accurate input data. One major improvement of the last years was to carefully review and update the newest carbon sequestration capability of forests, based on the latest data used by IPCC (Mancini et al., 2016). We also did this review in response to criticism that our conversion factors for the carbon footprint were not sufficiently solid. After the review, we found that the average carbon sequestration was about 20 per cent lower than what we estimated with older data. In other words, the carbon footprint for the same amount of carbon increased by about 20 per cent. Also note that this was not a methodological change. Rather it was a more accurate assessment of conversion factors based on improved data. While this 20 per cent change was a large shift, other methods have even larger ones (Coyle, 2014). GDP for instance, given different inflation rates and shifts in estimates can fluctuate even more. Furthermore, for instance, the IMF and World Bank figures on countries' GDP do not match, even though both institutions are located just one block from each other.

Yes, Global Footprint Network would be the first to acknowledge that the current national assessments are far from perfect. Yet Global Footprint Network is able to replicate them annually, with little deviance for most countries. (At the same time, Global Footprint Network is in the process of developing an academic network, supported by one academic host centre, that could in the near future take over the National Footprint Accounts and make them fully independent of Global Footprint Network – this would increase their independence, academic accessibility and hopefully lead to a faster pace of improvement and development.)

Still the numbers the National Footprint Accounts produce could be criticised on two other grounds. One criticism is that there might be other results available that give a more accurate, reliable account of how much nature we have and how much we use. I do not know of any at this point that are able to answer this question. I also want to emphasise here that I as well as everybody at Global Footprint Network would welcome such results, because the question is too important to be left to just one set of accounts.

The other reason could be that even though these current Ecological Footprint results are the best ones available, and even though they seem replicable, they may still be too weak for use in decision-making. In other words, humanity would be better off not having them at all. While we recognise that our results are almost certainly not perfectly accurate, all past testing suggests that the results represent a reasonable picture of the size of a country's or humanity's material metabolism, and most likely underestimate ecological deficits as Footprints are not fully complete (and hence underestimated), while productivity may be inflated because in current accounts (for lack of data) nothing is deducted for overused groundwater or soil depletion.

What Do the Numbers Mean?

While I attempted to make the case here that it is possible, with reasonable accuracy, to map the resource dependence of the human economy and compare it to what the planet's, or each nation's natural capital can renew, this paper has not addressed the other two questions:

1 How can such a metric be used to explore under which conditions such a dependence affects humanity's ability to end poverty and secure long-term prosperity? and
2 How does such a metric help manage human dependence on natural capital, particularly in those conditions where excessive resource dependence is starting to erode humanity's ability to end poverty and secure long-term prosperity?

These questions need to be answered through joint inquiries – for instance between Global Footprint Network and other institutions who have an interest in understanding these relationships. Unilateral answers from Global Footprint Network alone would not convince. A joint inquiry has to help participants with differing perspectives come to their own conclusions.

The process for such inquiries that Global Footprint Network suggests in its collaboration with national governments and other decision-making bodies follows the 'VIA' approach (verification, interpretation, application) – *via* being the Latin word for 'path'. This approach is a sequence of three logical steps.

Verification

The inquiry starts with the question: Are the result numbers a sufficiently accurate representation of the current situation? Before any interpretation or discussion, a common understanding needs to be generated about the validity and accuracy of the analysis. To achieve this, a variety of researchers and government agencies (as representatives of the ultimate clients) need to test and verify National Footprint Accounts results against national data and other relevant assessments they may have available. This is why Global Footprint Network has pursued verifications with national government agencies since its inception.[12] So far over 12 have been completed. Verification is fundamental. Otherwise, no consensus can be built. Obviously, before trusting the results, it does not make sense to invite interpretations of them.

Interpretation

Once there is a solid common recognition that the results are an adequate description of the reality this accounting system intends to portray, including a joint agreement of what the accounts try to measure, how accurate they are, and what their limitations are, only then does it make sense to start interpreting the results. A key question to consider might be: What do these trends mean for the competitiveness and sustainable development of a country or city? How do various stakeholders see these trends shape their country's or city's economic performance, and that of their trade partners – particularly considering the possibility of entering into increased global competition for resource access and emission rights? What might the implications be for strategies in order to make them more likely to produce the expected results? Only once there is some minimum level of common agreement on what makes the country's or city's development plan more effective and more likely to succeed, does it make sense to apply the tool in decision-making. Such an inquiry could be run in a Chatham House style closed door workshops with key stakeholders.

Application

Once a country has been able to generate a solid, common interpretation of the results, then the conversation can start to translate into implementation. Only then does it make sense to identify what coherent set of actions would be needed that could address the revealed issues. What are the pathways forward, and how should this information affect the decision-making of the country or city? How can options be evaluated? And how do such evaluations enable more successful economic long-term strategies?

How Footprint Accounting Adds Value to the Climate Debate

Given the current prominence of the climate debate, it may be helpful to point out how a biocapacity or Footprint analysis adds value (rather than distracting attention).

Currently, 60 per cent of humanity's Footprint is carbon emissions from fossil fuel use, up from 43 per cent in 1961, a time when the total Ecological Footprint was only one-third of today's (Global Footprint Network, 2018).[13]

The carbon footprint represents the biocapacity needed to neutralise all the excess CO_2. Some biocapacity is allocated for such purposes, for instance through UNDP's REDD+ programme, but overall the amount allocated is much less than is the amount necessary to sequester all the CO_2. In fact, given the amount of current emissions, sequestration alone is not a viable option to make humanity carbon neutral. There is just not enough biocapacity on the planet for this level of sequestration. In addition, some of the biocapacity is needed for producing humanity's food.

150 years ago, humanity's carbon footprint was close to zero.[14] And the Paris Agreement would require a carbon footprint of zero before 2050 (Figueres et al., 2017). This might indicate that just focusing on carbon, rather than the entire human demand on the biosphere, may

suffice, or help focus our attention on the portion that is most dynamic and needs particular attention, particularly since carbon emissions have become a dominant concern of the current environmental discussion.

For this reason, let me explain how the Ecological Footprint contributes to addressing and contextualising climate risks, and adds value, even if carbon emissions were our only environmental concern.

Primarily, Ecological Footprint accounting adds value (if one believes in the significance of resource security) by measuring and communicating the relationships between resource security and lasting human development. Ecological Footprint accounting complements and strengthens the rationale for climate action in at least four ways.

1 *Easy, intuitive and transparent.* Ecological Footprint accounts confirm reduction requirements consistent with the Paris Agreement's 2°C or 1.5°C goal, complementing the more complex, dynamic and less testable climate models. *With basic, widely understood and easily testable scientific principles, the accounts can be understood and audited by anyone with basic science education.* (Climate models are needed to estimate the remaining carbon budget; Ecological Footprint accounting complements them by revealing the steady-state availability of renewable capacity.) Anybody can add up the various areal demands of our resource demand. Global Footprint Network uses the global accounts to determine the level of global overshoot. This result can easily be expressed as a ratio between human demand and Earth ecosystems' regeneration – which is currently at 171 per cent for 2018, now-casting the latest National Footprint Accounts results to 2018 (Global Footprint Network, 2018). And that ratio can be translated into a date: Earth Overshoot Day, or the date by which humanity's demand on nature has exceeded what Earth can regenerate for the year (365/ 171 per cent = the 213th day in the year or August 1 for 2018). Translating overshoot into a date seems to resonate with many people and generates enormous amounts of media attention.[15] It also helps to explain the contribution of solutions toward shifting the date.[16]

2 *Ecosystem productivity as a core resource.* The focus on ecosystem productivity (or biocapacity, as expressed in Footprint accounting) becomes a primary concern once we acknowledge commitment to

a societal transition from fossil fuel to renewable energy sources. Economies will therefore rely primarily on what ecosystems can provide for their physical inputs, plus that energy which is not in competition for bioproductive land such as photovoltaics in deserts. This latter includes PV on biologically non- or low-productive areas (which Wolfgang Pekny calls 'photocapacity') or windmills offshore. Without cheap energy, it might be difficult to maintain high agricultural yields, and the demand for fuel wood may go up, both potentially increasing demand on land. If humanity should continue to use fossil fuels beyond the carbon budget, the ensuing climatic changes would most likely reduce the planet's biocapacity, making it even more difficult to run the economy in the future.

3 *Connecting land and atmosphere.* The National Footprint Accounts are consistent with the Paris Agreement's call for focusing on net-emissions. The focus on net-emissions recognises the fundamental link between the atmosphere and the biosphere. It is not only about additional carbon emissions, but also about how much of the carbon can be sequestered, by biological, technical or other means. This opens up broader opportunities for mitigation. Biocapacity is a safe and natural way to get rid of excess carbon. In contrast, there are many geoengineering ideas but no meaningful governance mechanism to keep carbon safely stocked away for the long-run.

4 *Emphasis on self-interest.* By putting the climate challenge into the context of biocapacity, the resource security perspective (and its link to an economy's self-interest to be resource secure) becomes more obvious, possibly helping to overcome the common misperception that climate change is an inevitable 'tragedy of the commons'. Rather, as is becoming evident by looking at the world from a biocapacity perspective, addressing resource security and climate change in all our investment choices enables the development of successful, resilient economies. In other words, the Ecological Footprint allows policy makers and researchers to enter the climate debate through the adaptation door, making clear which actions enable an economy to perform well now and in the future. The co-benefits of such adaptation, particularly by making an economy or a city less resource dependent so it can operate well in the future, is obviously mitigation. The main difference is that mitigation was not used as the opening argument, while still resulting in large mitigation benefits. Starting from the mitigation angle feeds more into the

tragedy of the commons perception and can discourage vast and fast action as the actor's direct benefit is not seen.

Conclusion

Our planet is finite, yet our ability to innovate and to look ahead is not. Possibilities are indeed infinite, and will continue to be, if we embrace physical reality and make sure humanity's resource dependence can be met by this planet.

Sustainable production technologies, efficiency and urban planning solutions exist to successfully drive radical reductions in humanity's resource dependence (agricultural transformations, photovoltaic energy, smart grids, compact cities). Many of these possibilities, if managed well, are even economically superior to conventional solutions and can also provide for a higher quality of life (Hawken et al., 2017; McKinsey & Company, 2009).

If we do not measure what we treasure, we put our treasures at risk. Measures based on clearly defined, observable concepts using reliable data collection make those metrics trustworthy. Because of the transparency, such measures invite others to participate in the collective inquiry and test them. Without trust, collective action is unlikely to succeed. Trusted, transparent accounts, that are relevant to large numbers of people, help transcend particular views or perspectives, and provide common ground for exploring how to get to 'terra incognita'. Humanity cannot afford this severe knowledge gap identified at the outset of this paper. Once we can eliminate the intellectual disconnect between those seemingly irreconcilable perspectives about resource security and economic success, effective action becomes possible.

All entities that treasure a resilient, prosperous future will benefit from robust measurement tools that can map their dependence on nature. These tools become a navigational aid through the new territories we will inevitably have to explore, whether or not we rapidly move out of net carbon emissions. Each pathway will be a different territory, but both will need good measurement tools to navigate. On the first pathway, such metrics can be used to drive well-being while simultaneously reducing their Ecological Footprint. The motivation is simple: economies that can do this will have a promising future.

Notes

1. See also www.mcc-berlin.net/en/research/co2-budget.html.
2. The referendum was held on 12 February 2017, www.nzz.ch/schweiz
   /abstimmungen/abstimmung-vom-12-februar-auf-einen-blick-ld.131731.
3. For more information, consult https://en.wikipedia.org/wiki
   /Marrakesh_Menara_Airport.
4. Brief discussions in English can be found here: www.viennaairport.com
   /en/company/flughafen_wien_ag/third_runway_project or https://phys
   .org/news/2017-06-climate-halt-vienna-runway-court.html.
5. An example of this position is displayed on the White House's website:
   www.whitehouse.gov/america-first-energy.
6. A more precise way is to define it as the potential of the planet's surface
   to provide net primary productivity.
7. Sometimes, results are presented in terms of 'number of planets'. This is
   equivalent to showing the ratio between humanity's Footprint and the
   planet's biocapacity.
8. This is similar to the possibility that people can spend more money
   than they earn. But the consequence is reduced assets or increased
   liabilities.
9. Note that the number of global hectares, as well as their respective
   biocapacity changes every year – similar to currencies that change
   value over time. Similar to financial currency, one can distinguish
   nominal from constant global hectares. When depicting time trends,
   they are typically shown in constant global hectares, indexed against the
   latest year (Borucke et al., 2013).
10. Ecological overshoot occurs when a population's demand on an
    ecosystem exceeds the capacity of that ecosystem to regenerate the
    resources it consumes and to absorb its wastes (see also Catton,
    1982).
11. France has conducted a number of reviews of the Ecological Footprint as
    a step toward considering it for adoption as a national sustainability
    indicator. The first review, initiated by France's Economic, Social and
    Environmental Council, examined the general assumptions of the
    Ecological Footprint and other sustainability indicators. It was
    released in May 2009 (CES, 2009). The second report, completed in
    2010, is the above mentioned SOeS (2010) report. The third report
    focused on alternatives to GDP and contained a significant section on
    the Ecological Footprint. It was a report commissioned by then
    president Sarkozy and lead by Stiglitz et al. (2009). The latter report
    contained a number of misconceptions such as claiming that (1) the
    Ecological Footprint is anti-trade (it is not – it is just a descriptor of

resource flow), or (2) that it is wrong to compare a country's Ecological Footprint to the country's biocapacity (while in reality Ecological Footprint accounting does not prescribe what the Ecological Footprint should be compared to, and also emphasising that comparison to one's own biocapacity is as meaningful as farmers wanting to know how big their respective farms are).

12. Examples are available here: www.footprintnetwork.org/reviews.
13. The open data platform at http://data.footprintnetwork.org gives direct access to all the countries' results.
14. See, e.g., https://ourfiniteworld.com/2012/03/12/world-energy -consumption-since-1820-in-charts/.
15. In 2016, Earth Overshoot Day generated over 1.9 billion media impressions. Key media stories are displayed here: www .overshootday.org/newsroom/media-coverage-2016. In 2017, it made front page news in many European newspapers and TV outlets, some of which are listed here: www.overshootday.org/newsroom/media -coverage/.
16. www.overshootday.org/solutions/ summarises opportunities for solutions in terms of days they would push Earth Overshoot Day into the future. They are based on a McKinsey & Company (2009) study and on Project Drawdown (Hawken et al., 2017).

References

Aguiar, A., Narayanan, B. & McDougall, R. 2016. An overview of the GTAP 9 data base. *Journal of Global Economic Analysis*, 1(1): 181–208.

Borucke, M., Moore, D., Cranston, G., Gracey, K., Iha, K., Larson, J., Lazarus, E., Morales, J. C., Wackernagel, M. & Galli, A. 2013. Accounting for demand and supply of the Biosphere's regenerative capacity: The National Footprint Accounts' underlying methodology and framework. *Ecological Indicators*, 24: 518–533.

Catton, W. R. 1982. *Overshoot: The Ecological Basis of Revolutionary Change*. Champaign: University of Illinois Press.

CES Conseil Economique Social et Environnemental. 2009. *Les indicateurs du développement durable et l'empreinte écologique*. Avis présenté par Philippe Le Clézio. Les éditions des journaux officiels, 15. NOR: CES X09000115V, p. 62.

Coyle, D. 2014. *GDP: A Brief but Affectionate History*. Princeton, NJ: Princeton University Press.

Ewing, B. R., Hawkins, T. R., Wiedmann, T. O., Galli, A., Ercin, A. E., Weinzettel, J. & Steen-Olsen, K. 2012. Integrating ecological and water footprint accounting in a multi-regional input–output framework. *Ecological Indicators*, 23: 1–8.

Figueres, C., Schellnhuber, H. J., Whiteman, G., Rockström, J., Hobley, A. & Rahmstorf, S. 2017. Three years to safeguard our climate. *Nature*, 546: 593–595.

Galli, A., Weinzettel, J., Cranston, G. & Ercin, A. E. 2012. A footprint family extended MRIO model to support Europe's transition to a one planet economy. *Science of the Total Environment*, 461–462: 813–818.

Global Footprint Network. 2018. *National Footprint Accounts 2018*. http://data.footprintnetwork.org/.

Hawken, P. (Ed.). 2017. *Drawdown: The Most Comprehensive Plan Ever Proposed to Reverse Global Warming*. London: Penguin Books. www.drawdown.org.

Mancini, M. S., Galli, A., Niccolucci, V., Lin, D., Bastianoni, S., Wackernagel, M. & Marchettini, N. 2016. Ecological Footprint: Refining the carbon footprint calculation. *Ecological Indicators*, 61: 390–403.

McKinsey & Company. 2009. *Pathways to a Low-Carbon Economy, Version 2 of the Global Greenhouse Gas Abatement Cost Curve*. www.mckinsey.com/business-functions/sustainability-and-resource-productivity/our-insights/pathways-to-a-low-carbon-economy.

Population Reference Bureau. 2017. *World Population Data Sheet 2017*. Washington, DC: Population Reference Bureau. www.prb.org/2017-world-population-data-sheet/.

Rockström, J., Gaffney, O., Rogelj, J., Meinshausen, M., Nakicenovic, N. & Schellnhuber, H. J. 2017. A roadmap for rapid decarbonization. *Science*, 355(6331): 1269–1271.

Rockström, J., Steffen, W., Noone, K., Rersson, A., Chappin, F. S. I., Lambin, E., Lenton, T. M., Scheffer, M., Folke, C., Schellnhuber, H. J., Nykvist, B., De Wit, C. A., Hughes, T., Van Der Leeuw, S., Rodhe, H., Sornlin, S., Snyder, P., Constanza, R., Svedin, U., Falkenmark, M., Karberg, L., Corell, R. W., Fabry, V. J., Hansen, J., Walker, B., Liverman, D., Richardson, K., Crutzen, P. & Foley, J. 2009. A safe operating space for humanity. *Nature*, 461: 472–475.

Steffen, W., Richardson, K., Rockström, J., Cornell, S. E., Fetzer, I., Bennett, E. M., Biggs, R. Carpenter, S. R., de Vries, W., de Wit, C. A., Folke, C., Gerten, D., Heinke, J., Mace, G. M., Persson, L. M., Ramanathan, V., Reyers, B. & Sörlin, S. 2015. Planetary boundaries: Guiding human development on a changing planet. *Science*, 347(6223): 1259855.

Stiglitz, J. E., Sen, A. & Fitoussi, J. P. 2009. *Report by the Commission on the Measurement of Economic Performance and Social Progress*. Commission on the Measurement of Economic Performance and

Social Progress. http://library.bsl.org.au/jspui/bitstream/1/1267/1/Mea
surement_of_economic_performance_and_social_progress.pdf.

SOeS. 2010. *An expert examination of the Ecological Footprint. Extract
from final report.* Études & documents: No 16, January. www
.statistiques.developpement-durable.gouv.fr/fileadmin/documents/Prod
uits_editoriaux/Publications/Etudes_et_documents/2010/An_expert_e
xamination_of_the_Ecological_Footprint_03.pdf.

von Stokar, T., Steinemann, M. & Rüegge, B. 2006. *Ecological Footprint of
Switzerland.* Technical Report, INFRAS, Neuchâtel. www
.bfs.admin.ch/bfs/de/home/statistiken/nachhaltige-entwicklung/oekolo
gischer-fussabdruck.assetdetail.500264.html.

Wackernagel, M., Galli, A., Hanscom, L., Lin, D., Mailhes, L. &
Drummond, T. 2018a. Ecological Footprint accounts: Principles.
In S. Bell & S. Morse (Eds.), *Routledge Handbook of
Sustainability Indicators*: 244–264. Oxford: Routledge
International Handbooks.

2018b. Ecological Footprint accounts: Criticisms and applications. In
S. Bell & S. Morse (Eds.), *Routledge Handbook of Sustainability
Indicators*: 521–539. Oxford: Routledge International Handbooks.

Wackernagel, M. & Rees, W. E. 1996. *Our Ecological Footprint: Reducing
Human Impact on the Earth.* Gabriola Island, BC: New Society.

Wackernagel, M., Schulz, N. B., Deumling, D., Linares, A. C., Jenkins, M.,
Kapos, V., Monfreda, C., Loh, J., Myers, N., Norgaard, R. &
Randers, J. 2002. Tracking the ecological overshoot of the human
economy. *Proceedings of the National Academy of Sciences,* 99(14):
9266–9271.

Wilson, E. O. 2016. *Half-Earth: Our Planet's Fight for Life.* New York:
Liveright.

World Economic Forum. 2017a. *The Global Competitiveness Report
2016–2017.* Geneva: WEF.

2017b. *The Global Risks Report 2017.* 12th ed. Geneva: WEF.

2018a. *The Global Competitiveness Report 2017–2018.* Geneva: WEF.

2018b. *The Global Risks Report 2018.* 13th ed. Geneva: WEF.

12 | *How Do We Stem Biodiversity Loss?*

GRETCHEN C. DAILY AND STEPHEN
POLASKY

There are three pathways to wisdom.
The first is through contemplation, and that is the noblest.
The second is through imitation, and that is the easiest.
The third is through experience, and that is the bitterest.   Confucius

Efforts to value and protect 'natural capital' – Earth's lands, waters, and biodiversity and the stream of benefits that flow from it – have emerged over the past decade in many arenas that formerly seemed far removed from matters of ecology and conservation. For example, several large multi-national corporations have teamed up with conservation organisations to incorporate the values of nature into corporate operations (e.g., Dow Chemical Corporation and The Nature Conservancy, Coca Cola and World Wildlife Fund, Unilever and the Natural Capital Project). The World Bank initiated the Wealth Accounting and Valuation of Ecosystem Services (WAVES) programme. Governments worldwide have established the Intergovernmental Science-Policy Platform on Biodiversity and Ecosystem Services (IPBES). These, and many other initiatives, make clear that many people now recognise the vital importance of nature for human well-being.

Globally, 'natural capital' now appears in society's thinking about agriculture, water, energy, health, fisheries, forestry, mining, cities and the infrastructure supporting these and other vast sectors – and it is increasingly evident in the ways communities, corporations, governments and other institutions frame decisions (e.g., Goldstein et al., 2012; Kiesecker et al., 2010; Levy et al., 2012; Li et al., 2005; Ministry of Environmental Protection of China & Chinese Academy of Sciences, 2008; Ouyang, 2007; Ouyang et al., 2016; Rapidel et al., 2011). In particular, there is growing demand for rigorous approaches that integrate the values of natural capital into major development decisions, in order to reverse the degradation of Earth's life-support systems and enhance human well-being.

Within the conservation community, the idea that ecosystems are a vital science and policy focus for securing human well-being has also taken root. But some conservationists, motivated to protect nature for nature's sake, are uneasy about embracing a more human-centred conservation. The evolution of the dominant motivation for conservation involving combinations of nature for nature's sake and nature for people (Figure 12.1) has been nicely captured by Georgina Mace (2014). From an earlier orientation of nature for nature's sake and conservation as protecting nature from people (1960s–1990s), conservation has swung toward an orientation highlighting natural capital and links to human well-being in the 2000s (nature for people). More recently, there has been a synthesis bringing together elements of both views, in which people and nature are interconnected in a social-ecological system. In an interconnected system, it is difficult to separate what is good for people and what is good for nature. Conservation of nature is good for people and nature.

Moreover, with humanity's great power to destroy life should also come the recognition of humanity's responsibility to protect life in all its varied forms. The motivation for doing so arises from both ethical considerations about duties to other species and our own current and future well-being.

Now marks a key moment for the communities working on this grand challenge. While much has been learned, the planet remains besieged by massive degradation and growing threats of catastrophic change. To date, creative yet highly dispersed innovation has shown glimpses of what is possible, but has not successfully stopped the loss of biodiversity or ecosystem degradation. How can we help channel and magnify the energy of this movement into large-scale, durable, improved outcomes for nature and people?

A wide range of strategies is needed. After a bit of background, we will focus our brief remarks on meeting and cultivating further demand from decision makers now. This requires rapid advances on four science and policy frontiers: (1) *fundamental understanding* of biodiversity, ecosystem services, human well-being, and their interlinkages in biophysical, economic, social, institutional and governance domains; (2) *practical, science-based tools*, for characterising the magnitude, distribution and value of ecosystem services supplied by human-dominated and natural ecosystems, tailored initially for use in highest-leverage decisions; (3) *inspiring demonstrations* in diverse regions and sectors globally that integrate the values of ecosystem services into influential decisions; and (4) *engaging leaders and building*

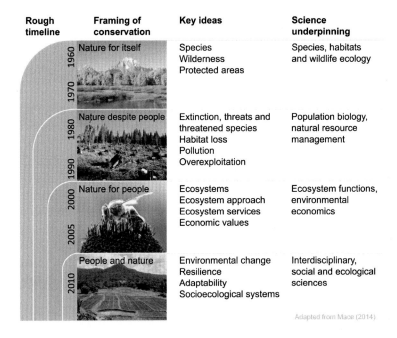

Rough timeline	Framing of conservation	Key ideas	Science underpinning
1960 1970	Nature for itself	Species Wilderness Protected areas	Species, habitats and wildlife ecology
1980 1990	Nature despite people	Extinction, threats and threatened species Habitat loss Pollution Overexploitation	Population biology, natural resource management
2000 2005	Nature for people	Ecosystems Ecosystem approach Ecosystem services Economic values	Ecosystem functions, environmental economics
2010	People and nature	Environmental change Resilience Adaptability Socioecological systems	Interdisciplinary, social and ecological sciences

Adapted from Mace (2014)

Figure 12.1 Evolving views of nature and conservation. Table text and design from Mace (2014), 'Whose conservation?', *Science*, 345: 1558–1560. Reprinted with permission from AAAS. Images in table from FreeImages .com. Authors (top to bottom): Jack Sanders, Petr Kovar, Danijel Juricev and Fintan Boyle.

capacity to *scale up these models of success* to achieve transformative, lasting change. We take a close look at two real-world examples of how these advances are unfolding, in Latin America and China.

Background

Living Natural Capital

The world's ecosystems – Earth's lands, waters and the myriad types of organisms embedded within them – can be seen as a stock of living natural capital, vital to human well-being and worthy of the greatest care. If properly managed, they yield a stream of 'ecosystem services' that sustain and fulfil human life. These include the *production of goods*, such as seafood, crops, timber and many industrial products, a familiar part of the economy. Second, the services also include less visible *life-support processes*, such as water purification, pest control, crop pollination, flood control and climate stabilisation. Third, they include *life-fulfilling conditions*, such as the beauty and uniqueness in nature that spawn deep cultural attachments to place, and that improve aspects of cognitive function and emotional well-being. Fourth, ecosystem services include the *preservation of options and resilience*, such as those embodied in biological diversity, from genetic to ecosystem levels.

Framing ecosystems as natural capital assets is a way of incorporating human impacts and dependence on nature into mainstream decision-making. It is a way of making biodiversity – despite its mystery and complexity – tangible and actionable in mainstream decision-making. This framing shows starkly that – relative to other forms of capital (physical, financial, human and social forms) – living natural capital is poorly understood, scarcely monitored, and in many important cases undergoing rapid degradation and depletion (Balmford et al., 2002; Daily et al., 2000; Dasgupta, 2001, 2010; National Research Council, 2005). Often its importance is widely appreciated only upon loss, such as in the wake of Hurricane Katrina or the Asian Tsunami.

Including the value of ecosystem services in the decisions of governments, corporations, traditional cultures and individuals is designed to broaden our understanding of the roles nature plays in our lives and the reasons – including the moral imperative – for conserving it (e.g., Daily and Ellison, 2002; Ehrenfeld, 1988; Leopold, 1949; Norton, 1987; Rolston, 2000).

The Scope for Conservation in Human-Dominated Countryside

We tend to think of the scope for – and value of – biodiversity conservation as being primarily in designated protected areas. Yet rural lands, especially in the tropical forest biome, hold the greatest potential to sustain or lose biodiversity into the future. A recent synthesis of 25 years of work in Costa Rica documents tremendous potential to sustain biodiversity in human-dominated countryside, at least over the medium term. This is crucial because there is very little scope for establishing new protected areas in most countries worldwide.

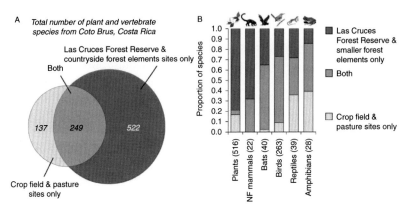

Figure 12.2 There is great potential to secure biodiversity in human-dominated countryside across much of the world. Of the 908 species recorded in a well-studied system in the canton of Coto Brus, Costa Rica, the majority inhabit small (0.05–100 ha) forest elements as well as crop fields and pastures. From Mendenhall et al. (2016).

The synthesis reports on a region with a wide range of land covers, from extensive forest (e.g., La Amistad International Peace Park, the largest protected area in Central America) to relatively intensive cropland. Systematic surveys have focused on understory plants, non-flying mammals, bats, birds, reptiles and amphibians. Using data from 67,737 observations of 908 species (all thought to be native to the area), the findings show, firstly, that fine-scale mapping of tree cover predicts biodiversity (within a taxon-specific radius of 30–70 m) about a point in the landscape. Secondly, nearly 50 per cent of the tree cover in the study region is embedded in countryside forest elements, small (typically 0.05–100 ha) clusters or strips of trees on private property. Herein lies the conservation opportunity, if private and societal incentives can be aligned.

Thirdly, taxonomic groups have affiliations with all habitat types, including crop fields & pastures (to which only 15 per cent of species are restricted), though some taxa depend heavily on forest (57 per cent of species are restricted to forest elements) (Figure 12.2). In fact, many individual species use multiple habitat types, across the spectrum from human-dominated to relatively natural (Figure 12.3). These findings are supported by 90 study comparisons by other research teams across Latin America. They provide a guide to investments in tropical forest biodiversity.

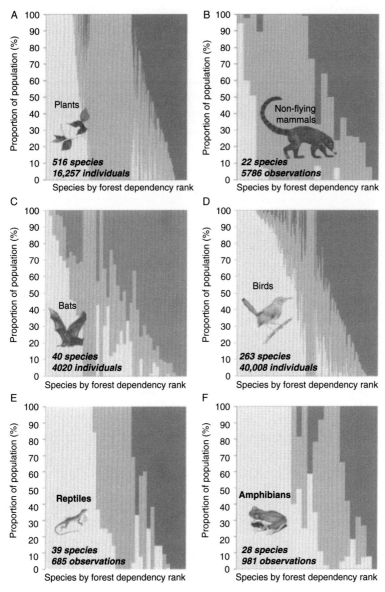

Figure 12.3 Most species native to Costa Rica use multiple habitat types along the spectrum from human-dominated agriculture to native forest. Plots A–F show changes in abundances for each species across different habitats for 908 species. A total of 67,737 individual plants and animals were recorded in sites distributed across three broad categories: (1) Las Cruces Forest Reserve (dark grey), (2) countryside forest elements (mid-grey) and (3) crop fields and pastures (light grey). The forest-dependency rank ranges from forest avoidance to forest dependence and was determined by comparing relative abundance in the Las Cruces Forest Reserve (dark grey) with that in crop fields and pastures (light grey). From Mendenhall et al. (2016).

The Opportunity to Mainstream Nature into Decision-Making Today

Mainstreaming biodiversity and ecosystem services into everyday decisions requires a systematic method for characterising their value, and the change in value resulting from alternative choices. Unlike traditional economic goods where market prices can be used as a proxy for value, there is no market price for most of the values of nature and other methods for estimating a value must be used (MA, 2005; Mäler et al., 2008; National Research Council, 2005). Mainstreaming also requires policy or institutional reforms so that decision makers realise the full costs and benefits of their actions. As noted by Guerry et al. (2015): 'There is a fundamental asymmetry at the heart of economic systems that rewards short-term production and consumption of marketed commodities at the expense of stewardship of natural capital necessary for human well-being in the long term.' Providing positive incentives for stewardship, or negative incentives for destructive actions, is needed to fix this asymmetry.

What makes it thinkable that mainstreaming is now possible? Four big advances of the last decade offer promise that mainstreaming ecosystem service values into decisions is within reach. First, the Millennium Ecosystem Assessment represented a visionary step in global science – it was the first comprehensive assessment of the status and trends of the world's biodiversity and major ecosystem services. The key finding of this assessment was that two-thirds of the world's ecosystem services were declining, a finding that captured the attention of world leaders (MA, 2005).

Second, the science of ecosystem functions and processes has made huge advances, so that we can now model (albeit with uncertainty) the impacts of management decisions and activities across landscapes and seascapes on biodiversity and ecosystem processes. Ecological science has also become adept at spatially explicit modelling, essential for mapping ecosystem services and their distribution to people (e.g., Bennett et al., 2009; Chan et al., 2006; Goldstein et al., 2012; Guerry et al., 2012; Harrison et al., 2010; Nelson et al., 2009; Ouyang et al., 2016; Rokityanskiy et al., 2007).

Third, economic valuation methods have been applied to the spatial provision of ecosystem services to estimate the monetary value of benefits and the distribution of those benefits to different segments of society (Bateman et al., 2013; Naidoo and Ricketts, 2006; National Research Council, 2005). In addition, qualitative and quantitative methods from other fields are now being applied to gain better understanding of the psychological, social and cultural importance of biodiversity and ecosystem services, and of shared values that people hold together (e.g., Bratman et al., 2012; Daniel et al., 2012; Kenter et al., 2014; MA, 2005; US EPA, 2009).

Lastly, experiments in payments for ecosystem services, in ecosystem-based management, and in regional-level and national-level planning give us the empirical data to evaluate approaches to valuing ecosystem services and incorporating values into decision-making (Barbier et al., 2008; Ouyang et al., 2016; Pagiola and Platais, 2007; Wunder et al., 2008; Zheng et al., 2013). There is a growing recognition that bundling together of ecosystem services and explicit attention to trade-offs will both better inform decisions, and help diverse stakeholders to appreciate the perspectives of others (e.g., Bennett et al., 2009; Boody et al., 2005; Egoh et al., 2008; Goldstein et al., 2012).

Meeting the Challenge

A Strategy

Our urgent challenge today is to build on this foundation and move from ideas to action on a broad scale (Carpenter et al., 2006, 2009; Daily et al., 2009; Guerry et al., 2015). Doing so requires understanding the production of services from landscapes and seascapes, together with their biodiversity and human activities; quantifying service flows, from producers to beneficiaries, across space, social class, economic sector and time; understanding the decision-making processes of individuals, communities, governments and corporations; integrating research with institutional design and policy implementation; and crafting policy interventions that provide incentives for stewardship with flexibility for learning and improvement. Each of these alone is a complex and difficult task; together they form a daunting but critically important agenda for collaboration.

The Natural Capital Project is an international partnership, founded in 2006 to help meet this challenge (www.naturalcapitalproject.org). The vision of the Natural Capital Project (NatCap) is a world in which people, governments and corporations recognise the values of nature in supporting human well-being, and routinely incorporate them into policy, finance and management decisions. NatCap aims to transform the way people think about nature and drive open a path to green growth, improving the well-being of both people and Earth's life-support systems. In the face of poverty and inequity, and turbulent change erupting across the world in climate, demographic, economic and other key realms, it is critical to act now, co-developing solutions with influential partners across the world and educating the next generation of leaders.

NatCap is focused on making three major advances that together will help transform how businesses, governments and individuals interact with nature:

1 The first advance is in co-developing interdisciplinary knowledge, packaged into practical tools and approaches, for incorporating natural capital values into planning and policy. This work is accelerating in institutions globally, and involves greatly increasing the interaction between researchers and real-world generators and users of knowledge.

In support of such work, NatCap has developed InVEST, a family of tools for Integrated Valuation of Ecosystem Services and Trade-offs (Table 12.1). InVEST helps decision makers visualise the impacts of potential policies – identifying trade-offs and compatibilities between environmental, economic and social benefits – by modelling and mapping the delivery, distribution and economic value of ecosystem services under alternative scenarios (Sharp et al., 2016). These models were co-developed with hundreds of researchers, practitioners and managers. InVEST is free and designed for data available anywhere, globally.

These tools mark a start but by no means a complete answer, with much remaining scope for innovation and improvement. Yet they are already making an impact, having been used in over 160 countries, with active users in c. 80 countries – and some countries, like China, having adopted them officially in development and conservation planning (Ouyang et al., 2016; Xu et al., 2017).

2 The second advance is in implementing new knowledge, tools and approaches in major resource decisions, in replicable and scalable

Table 12.1 *The Natural Capital Platform includes InVEST software models and many of the data layers to support them for biodiversity and 18 classes of ecosystem services*

Marine 'blue' carbon sequestration	Land-based carbon sequestration	Habitat for biodiversity
Wave energy	Nutrient filtration	Scenic quality
Offshore wind energy	Erosion control	Recreation & tourism
Protection from storms	Water supply	Habitat risk analysis
Protection from sea level rise	Crop production	Urban services (15 services under development)
Marine fisheries (wild and farmed)	Crop pollination	Mental health (under development)

models of success. Working with over 200 partners around the world, NatCap is integrating the diverse values of natural capital into major resource policies and decisions (Figure 12.4).

These demonstrations range from: informing the infrastructure development strategies of major development banks and private investors, in transportation and other key sectors; to working with indigenous communities in strategic planning of land and ocean resource uses to balance conflicting values; to working with corporations to quantify the risks and opportunities of alternative resource development options. The approach has informed decisions relating to spatial planning, payment for ecosystem services, climate adaptation planning, impact assessments for permitting and mitigation, corporate risk mitigation, marine and coastal development, and habitat restoration (Ruckelshaus et al., 2015). InVEST is designed to balance scientific complexity and pragmatic needs, and can be run with free public data.

3 The third advance is in engaging leaders and practitioners in key institutions to create The Natural Capital Platform to magnify the impact of these successes, build capacity, and forge lasting, transformative change. The focus is on developing tools for mainstreaming natural capital systemically, across high-leverage decision contexts, where there is strength and commitment among necessary leading partners to demonstrate and accelerate meaningful change.

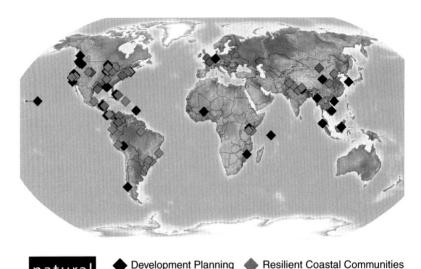

	Development Planning		Resilient Coastal Communities
natural capital PROJECT	Livable Cities		Standards for Private Sector
	Securing Freshwater		2018 G. VERUTES

Figure 12.4 Sites and sectors in which the Natural Capital Project is mainstreaming the values of nature in decision-making. From the Natural Capital Project. (A black and white version of this figure will appear in some formats. For the colour version, please refer to the plate section.)

Real-World Demonstrations

A great number and diversity of efforts to implement the ecosystem services framework have emerged worldwide over the past decade. Individually, most of these efforts are small and idiosyncratic. But collectively, they represent a powerful shift in the focus of conservation organisations and governments (primarily) toward a more inclusive, integrated and effective set of strategies. Taken together, these efforts span the globe and target a full suite of ecosystem services, including carbon sequestration, water supply, flood control, biodiversity conservation and enhancement of scenic beauty (and associated recreation/ tourism values).

Many local or regional efforts focus on a single service that stands out as sufficiently important, from economic and political perspectives, to protect it. Under the institutional umbrella created for the focal service it is possible that other services may be at least partially protected. Beginning in the late 1990s, larger-scale investment in natural capital for water flow regulation in China – and for a broad suite of ecosystem services in Costa Rica – set pioneering examples that are now being adapted elsewhere and scaled up.

Next, we briefly describe two contrasting models, at different scales and in different kinds of social-ecological systems. In each case, there is an acute or looming crisis, innovative leadership and an experiment under way in pursuit of dual goals: securing natural capital and human well-being.

Water for Cities in Latin America and Beyond

In the mid-1990s, New York City made one of the first and most famous investments in ecosystem service provision in recent history. The city invested about US$1.5 billion in a variety of watershed protection activities to improve drinking water quality for 10 million users rather than spending the estimated US$6–8 billion needed (excluding annual operating and maintenance costs) for building a new filtration plant. This seminal example is widely cited as evidence of the business case for investing in natural capital (Daily and Ellison, 2002).

Now the New York City investment is one of many such experiments under way. With rapidly growing urban populations, expanding natural-resource extraction in upstream watersheds, and climate change, water security for cities is a growing concern for governments, corporations and other stakeholders globally. The source watersheds serving cities are now the target of a range of creative policy and finance mechanisms that link beneficiaries to suppliers through a payment system.

Water funds are a finance mechanism through which downstream water consumers and other parties (e.g., conservation and human development organisations, public entities) pay for upstream changes in land cover and use in order to achieve certain objectives. In biophysical terms, the objectives typically include maintenance or enhancement of: water quality; regular water flows (for dry-season supply and flood control); groundwater recharge; terrestrial and aquatic biodiversity; and well-being in upstream human communities. Other services are also anticipated, such as carbon storage and sequestration, crop pollination, and pest control (Goldman-Benner et al., 2012). Water fund objectives may also include sustainable improvements in human livelihoods and well-being.

There is now a major effort under way, supported by The Nature Conservancy, the World Bank, the Inter-American Development Bank and FEMSA (a major bottling company) to replicate and standardise these funds in terms of design, implementation and monitoring, across more than 40 major cities throughout Latin America. Analysis is focused on predicting the relative feasibility and payoff of potential land use/cover changes, such as conservation and restoration in head-waters, on steep slopes and in riparian areas; and shifting to more sustainable pastoral and cropping practices. InVEST has been tailored for use in this decision context, to predict where and which potential activities would yield the greatest societal return-on-investment (the decision-support system is called Resource Investment Optimisation System, RIOS).

Fondo Agua por la Vida y la Sostenibilidad, one of the recently established water funds, demonstrates the diversity of water users that are becoming engaged in these funds and the kinds of watershed management changes these funds motivate. Formally established in the Cauca Valley, Colombia in 2009, this water fund is supported by the region's sugar cane grower's association (PROCAÑA), the sugar pro-ducers' association (ASOCAÑA), 16 local watershed and river man-agement groups, The Nature Conservancy and a Colombian peace and justice non-government organisation. Many of these entities began working together as far back as 20 years ago, and the water fund is seen as building upon and strengthening these vital relationships.

Each member of the water fund voluntarily pays a self-determined amount into the fund that is then jointly managed by the members to improve landscape and river condition over 3900 square kilometres. The aim is to strengthen the financing in the future. For now, members in this fund have committed to contributing US$10 million over five years to be invested in five kinds of management changes: protection of native vegetation, restoration of denuded lands, enrichment of degraded forests, fencing of rangelands and implementation of best practices combining trees, pasture and livestock. The fund also invests in farmer training (agroforestry systems, cattle management), environ-mental education in schools, strengthening local community organisa-tions and setting up 'food security modules' – essentially home gardens, with a diversity of crops, chickens and other production. The invest-ments target the dual goals of improving upstream livelihoods as well as downstream water security.

Investments will be targeted across landscapes to yield the highest return, using RIOS, subject to stakeholder preferences for security and equity. A great deal of stakeholder input feeds into the analysis of options. The fund is starting a monitoring programme designed to ensure that these investments lead to measurable improvements in water quality for approximately 1 million water users downstream, as well as significant improvements in terrestrial and freshwater biodiversity.

Since the official establishment of the first water fund in Quito, Ecuador, in 2006, the model has spread rapidly (Figure 12.5). The Nature Conservancy is exploring establishing the first funds in Africa. The effort is focused on developing standards – in the biophysical modelling (through RIOS), financing, governance and monitoring – that can be sensibly applied in contrasting conditions, but that guide the process and incorporate lessons as they are learned.

Water funds are an inspiring example of rapid advances in all areas of the three-part strategy laid out above. Today they are still at an early and vulnerable stage. With care, one could envision the emergence of flexible yet durable institutions that help guide growth of cities and management of the natural capital they depend on, more broadly.

China's Land Use and Human Development Planning

The ecosystem service investments being made in China today are breath-taking in their goals, scale, duration and innovation. Following massive droughts and flooding in 1997–1998, China implemented several national forestry and conservation initiatives, into which investments exceeded 700 billion yuan (about US$100 billion) over 2000–2010 (Liu et al., 2008; Zhang et al., 2000). The larger and older of these initiatives, the Sloping Land Conversion Program (SLCP), involves 120 million farmers directly and is being rigorously evaluated to improve its design and efficacy (e.g., Ren et al., 2018).

These initiatives all have dual goals: to secure critical natural capital through targeted investments across landscapes and to alleviate poverty through targeted wealth transfers from coastal provinces to inland regions where many ecosystem services originate. The investments are focused on forests and grasslands, to help secure people from flooding,

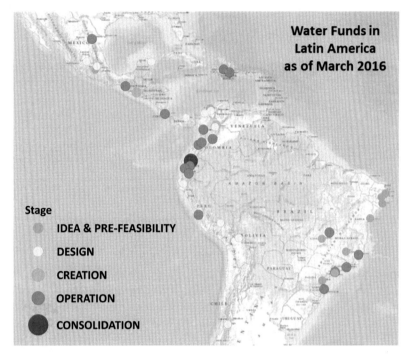

Figure 12.5 Water funds featured by stage of development (as of March 2016). Small grey and white circles designate water funds that are in the process of scoping and creation, respectively; medium and large circles depict water funds that have been created, with a legal agreement among parties, at various degrees of maturity. Figure courtesy of the Latin American Water Funds Partnership Dashboard (March 2016) and The Nature Conservancy Internal Survey of Water Funds (December 2013). (A black and white version of this figure will appear in some formats. For the colour version, please refer to the plate section.)

improve drinking and irrigation water supply, maintain efficient hydropower production, protect biodiversity, stabilise climate, reduce sand storms and soil loss, and foster more sustainable farming and other aspects of human well-being (Daily et al., 2013). In addition, the government aims to change the economic structure in rural areas to increase local household income while simultaneously making local households' patterns of land utilisation and agricultural production more sustainable (Li et al., 2011; Liu et al., 2008).

Evaluation of the SLCP shows significant achievement of the bio-physical goals, with remarkably rapid land conversion in the desired directions. For example, by the end of 2006, the SLCP had converted c. 9 million ha of cropland into forest / grassland and had afforested c. 12 million ha of barren land. Village level field measurements have shown not only that the payments for ecosystem services have altered land use patterns, but in turn soil erosion has been decreased in some areas by as much as 68 per cent (Cao et al., 2009).

Overall social impacts of the programmes are mixed, and depend on the details of the financial incentives and property rights (Cao et al., 2009; Liu et al., 2008). In some places, payment levels and types are leading to improvements in economic measures of well-being, whereas in others payments were not sufficient to compensate for loss of income from shifting livelihoods (Liu et al., 2008). In addition, in some places where participation in the SLCP has significant positive impacts upon household income, it has not yet transferred labour toward non-farming activities as the government wished (Li et al., 2011). Payments are now being adjusted to improve success in achieving goals of poverty alleviation and growth of new economic sectors in rural areas (Ren et al., 2018).

China also stands out in strengthening the scientific foundation supporting these public policies. This is illustrated in the development of a first National Ecosystem Assessment, spanning a wide range of ecosystems, services and spatial scales, over the past decade (2000–2010). The first step was to classify land cover for the whole of China, for 2000, 2005 and 2010, based on satellite imagery (e.g., Landsat TM data at 30 x 30m resolution). The next stages of work involved characterising the composition and structure of ecosystems and their changes over the assessment decade. The final stage involved characterising levels and types of ecosystem services, and changes therein across China and the assessment decade, using InVEST (Figure 12.6). This important effort showcases state-of-the-art technical approaches relevant to other nations undertaking such assessments (Ouyang et al., 2016). The effort provides critical analysis to decision makers (e.g., Perrings et al., 2011).

In evaluating ecosystem service provision over 2000–2010, a key finding was that all examined services improved – thanks to China's conservation policies – apart from habitat provision for biodiversity. This is prompting the central government to propose a new national park system, with two types of parks – one focused primarily on biodiversity conservation and the other focused primarily on provision

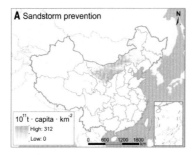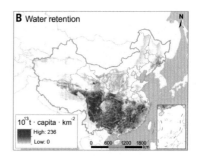

Figure 12.6 Two examples of the spatial pattern of ecosystem service provision weighted by number of people affected, here showing (for 2010) **A**, sandstorm prevention (supply in each location weighted by the downwind population, 10^{11} t · capita · km^{-2}), and **B**, water retention (in each location weighted by downstream urban population, 10^{13} t · capita · km^{-2}). From Ouyang et al. (2016), 'Improvements in ecosystem services from investments in natural capital in China', *Science*, 352: 1455–1459. Reprinted with permission from AAAS.

of priority ecosystem services (with biodiversity conservation as a co-benefit) (Figure 12.7A).

Perhaps most ambitiously, China is establishing a new network of 'ecosystem function conservation areas' (EFCAs) (Ministry of Environmental Protection of China & Chinese Academy of Sciences, 2008) (Figure 12.7B). The network now spans 49 per cent of the country; the exact delineation and implementation is now being defined using InVEST together with a broad set of biophysical and social science tools and approaches.

EFCAs are a way of zoning land, so as to focus conservation and restoration in places with the highest return-on-investment for public benefit, to halt and reverse degradation of vital ecosystems and their services. The zoning is also meant to focus high-impact human activities in places where they will do least damage. The design and implementation of EFCAs involves assessments from local to national scales. At the national scale, the priority services are conservation of soil and water resources, flood protection, biodiversity and sand storm protection (Ehrlich et al., 2012; Ouyang, 2007).

EFCAs are also a way of focusing poverty alleviation efforts in places where the stakes are highest, both for local residents and for beneficiaries of ecosystem services living farther away. Implementing EFCAs

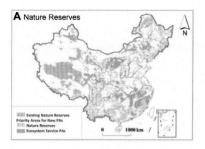

Figure 12.7 A, China is in the process of implementing a comprehensive national park system. The delineations here distinguish nature reserves with a priority focus on biodiversity conservation and ecosystem service protected areas with biodiversity as a co-benefit. In the regions where ecosystem service protected areas are being delineated, intense competition for land leaves little or no scope for effective nature reserves without an ecosystem service justification – and investments to benefit private landholders. **B,** China's new system of Ecosystem Function Conservation Areas (EFCAs). As delineated by the Ministry of Environmental Protection and the Chinese Academy of Sciences, EFCAs span 49 per cent of China's land area. EFCAs have dual goals of securing biodiversity and ecosystem services and alleviating poverty. Figure 12.7A from Xu et al. (2017). Figure 12.7B courtesy of Z. Ouyang, Research Center for Eco-Environmental Sciences, Chinese Academy of Sciences. (A black and white version of this figure will appear in some formats. For the colour version, please refer to the plate section.)

involves compensation mechanisms, whereby regional beneficiaries – of, for example, water purification and sand storm control in Beijing – invest in the transformation to more sustainable livelihoods and durable improvements in well-being among the landholders producing the services (e.g., Zheng et al., 2013).

While these initiatives represent a massive scientific and policy undertaking, they are very young and there is still little understanding of the local costs of implementation, or their effects on poor and vulnerable populations. The EFCA model represents a new paradigm for integrating conservation and human development, but for this policy innovation to have wide applicability and success, it will be important to assess and improve local livelihoods (e.g., Li et al., 2011, 2012; Liang et al., 2012). This need points to the science and policy frontiers before us.

Pushing the frontiers further, in March 2014, the State Council called for development of a new metric for tracking natural capital – the Gross Ecosystem Product (GEP), the total value of ecosystem goods and services. The Natural Capital Project is helping to design this metric, to be reported alongside Gross Domestic Product (GDP). The aim of GEP accounting is to help reveal the contribution of ecosystems to human development; reveal the ecological connections among regions (e.g., between suppliers and consumers of flood control and other ecosystem services); inform appropriate compensation from consumers to suppliers; serve as a performance metric for government officials; and otherwise inform government policy and investment. GEP accounting is now being demonstrated in pilot cities, counties and provinces.

The current and potential future impacts of ecosystem service investments in China are enormous, both within the country and globally, perhaps most importantly in lessons on making the investments needed in natural capital and human well-being everywhere. This is seen as a vital matter of national security, and national leaders now speak of 'China's dream' as becoming 'the ecological civilisation of the twenty-first century'.

Conclusion

Mainstreaming natural capital into decisions is a long-term proposition, requiring co-evolving advances in knowledge, social institutions and culture. Certainly no single effort will be sufficient to achieve this. But each can contribute to the theory of change (Bradach et al., 2008) laid out here, with its three key elements: co-development of new tools and approaches; real-world demonstrations; and engaging leaders.

First, governments, businesses and individuals must find it easy to integrate ecosystem services and natural capital into their decisions, and the methods for doing so must be transparent, credible and predictable. In many cases, sectors of society are open to the concepts of ecosystem services and natural capital, but simply do not know how to use them in a tangible way.

Second, there need to be examples of projects or enterprises that – as a result of properly valuing ecosystem services and natural capital – end up with improved decisions, institutions and human well-being. These examples both test our knowledge against real-world problems, but also produce compelling stories of how an ecosystem services approach made a difference.

Lastly, these examples of success must have visibility and charisma, to draw political and thought leaders to them and thereby trigger much broader awareness. This is where the lessons of a set of examples can be mainstreamed into the myriad decisions – by businesses, governments, farmers and banks – that are made every year and that impact our natural and social world. This is where the impact of scattered projects can be magnified into worldwide change.

None of these steps is complicated, and this theory of change does not require a brilliant and novel strategy. In fact, all three ingredients appear within striking distance. The environmental and human development movement has a much bigger and more diverse and powerful community behind it now than ever before. Co-development of knowledge with knowledge users is beginning to provide tools and methods that will reduce the transaction costs. There are enough policy experiments under way that compelling examples of natural capital stewardship enhancing human well-being are already forthcoming – the first step in an iterative process between basic science and application to real-world problems. Science alone cannot change the world, but science plus the vision and action of leaders can.

Acknowledgements

We are deeply grateful to the many collaborators and partners whose insight, trust and commitment make this work possible. And we appreciate tremendously the heroic efforts of the workshop organisers, Professor Partha Dasgupta, Professor Peter Raven, Chancellor Marcelo Sánchez Sorondo and the Pontifical Academy of Social Sciences and the Pontifical Academy of Sciences.

References

Balmford, A., Bruner, A., Cooper, P., Costanza, R., Farber, S., Green, R. E., Jenkins, M., Jefferiss, P., Jessamy, V., Madden, J., Munro, K., Myers, N., Naeem, S., Paavola, J., Rayment, M., Rosendo, S., Roughgarden, J., Trumper, K. & Turner, R. K. 2002. Economic reasons for conserving wild nature. *Science*, 297(5583): 950–953.

Barbier, E. B., Koch, E. W., Silliman, B. R., Hacker, S. D., Wolanski, E., Primavera, J., Granek, E. F., Polasky, S., Aswani, S., Cramer, L. A., Stoms, D. M., Kennedy, C. J., Bael, D., Kappel, C. V., Perillo, G. M. E. & Reed, D. J. 2008. Coastal ecosystem-based management with nonlinear ecological functions and values. *Science*, 319(5861): 321–323.

Bateman, I. J., Harwood, A. R., Mace, G. M., Watson, R. T., Abson, D. J., Andrews, B., Binner, A., Crowe, A., Day, B. H., Dugdale, S., Fezzi, C., Foden, J., Hadley, D., Haines-Young, R., Hulme, M., Kontoleon, A., Lovett, A. A., Munday, P., Pascual, U., Paterson, J., Perino, G., Sen, A., Siriwardena, G., van Soest, D. & Termansen, M. 2013. Bringing ecosystem services into economic decision-making: Land use in the United Kingdom. *Science*, 341(6141): 45–50.

Bennett, E. M., Peterson, G. D. & Gordon, L. J. 2009. Understanding relationships among multiple ecosystem services. *Ecology Letters*, 12 (12): 1394–1404.

Boody, G., Vondracek, B., Andow, D. A., Krinke, M., Westra, J., Zimmerman, J. & Welle, P. 2005. Multifunctional agriculture in the United States. *BioScience*, 55(1): 27–38.

Bradach, J. L., Tierney, T. J. & Stone, N. 2008. Delivering on the promise of nonprofits. *Harvard Business Review*, December: 88–97.

Bratman, G. N., Hamilton, J. P. & Daily, G. C. 2012. The impacts of nature experience on human cognitive function and mental health. *Annals of the New York Academy of Sciences*, 1249(1): 118–136.

Cao, S., Zhong, B., Yue, H., Zeng, H. & Zeng, J. 2009. Development and testing of a sustainable environmental restoration policy on eradicating the poverty trap in China's Changting County. *Proceedings of the National Academy of Sciences*, 106(26): 10712–10716.

Carpenter, S. R., DeFries, R., Dietz, T., Mooney, H. A., Polasky, S., Reid, W. V. & Scholes, R. J. 2006. Millennium ecosystem assessment: Research needs. *Science*, 314: 257–258.

Carpenter, S. R., Mooney, H. A., Agard, J., Capistrano, D., DeFries, R. S., Díaz, S., Dietz, T., Duraiappah, A. K., Oteng-Yeboah, A. & Pereira, H. M. 2009. Science for managing ecosystem services: Beyond the Millennium Ecosystem Assessment. *Proceedings of the National Academy of Sciences*, 106(5): 1305–1312.

Chan, K. M., Shaw, M. R., Cameron, D. R., Underwood, E. C. & Daily, G. C. 2006. Conservation planning for ecosystem services. *PLoS Biology*, 4(11): e379.

Daily, G. C. & Ellison, K. 2002. *The New Economy of Nature: The Quest to Make Conservation Profitable*. Washington, DC: Island Press.

Daily, G. C., Ouyang, Z., Zheng, H., Li, S., Wang, Y., Feldman, M., Kareiva, P., Polasky, S. & Ruckelshaus, M. 2013. Securing natural capital and human well-being: Innovation and impact in China. *Acta Ecologica Sinica*, 33(3): 677–685.

Daily, G. C., Polasky, S., Goldstein, J., Kareiva, P. M., Mooney, H. A., Pejchar, L., Ricketts, T. H., Salzman, J. & Shallenberger, R. 2009. Ecosystem services in decision making: Time to deliver. *Frontiers in Ecology and the Environment*, 7(1): 21–28.

Daily, G. C., Söderqvist, T., Aniyar, S., Arrow, K., Dasgupta, P., Ehrlich, P. R., Folke, C., Jansson, A.-M., Jansson, B.-O., Kautsky, N., Levin, S., Lubchenco, J., Mäler, J.-G., Simpson, D., Starrett, D., Tilman, D. & Walker, B. 2000. The value of nature and the nature of value. *Science*, 289(5478): 395–396.

Daniel, T. C., Muhar, A., Arnberger, A., Aznar, O., Boyd, J. W., Chan, K. M., Costanza, R., Elmqvist, T., Flint, C. G. & Gobster, P. H. 2012. Contributions of cultural services to the ecosystem services agenda. *Proceedings of the National Academy of Sciences*, 109(23): 8812–8819.

Dasgupta, P. 2001. *Human Well-Being and the Natural Environment*. Oxford: Oxford University Press.

    2010. Nature's role in sustaining economic development. *Philosophical Transactions of the Royal Society of London B: Biological Sciences*, 365 (1537): 5–11.

Egoh, B., Reyers, B., Rouget, M., Richardson, D. M., Le Maitre, D. C. & van Jaarsveld, A. S. 2008. Mapping ecosystem services for planning and management. *Agriculture, Ecosystems & Environment*, 127(1–2): 135–140.

Ehrenfeld, D. 1988. Why put a value on biodiversity? In E. O. Wilson (Ed.), *Biodiversity*. Washington, DC: National Academies Press.

Ehrlich, P. R., Kareiva, P. M. & Daily, G. C. 2012. Securing natural capital and expanding equity to rescale civilization. *Nature*, 486: 68–73

Goldman-Benner, R. L., Benitez, S., Boucher, T., Calvache, A., Daily, G. C., Kareiva, P., Kroeger, T. & Ramos, A. 2012. Water funds and payments for ecosystem services: Practice learns from theory and theory can learn from practice. *Oryx*, 46(1): 55–63.

Goldstein, J. H., Caldarone, G., Duarte, T. K., Ennaanay, D., Hannahs, N., Mendoza, G., Polasky, S., Wolny, S. & Daily, G. C. 2012. Integrating ecosystem-service tradeoffs into land-use decisions. *Proceedings of the National Academy of Sciences*, 109(19): 7565–7570.

Guerry, A. D., Polasky, S., Lubchenco, J., Chaplin-Kramer, R., Daily, G. C., Griffin, R., Ruckelshaus, M., Bateman, I. J., Duraiappah, A., Elmqvist, T., Feldman, M. W., Folke, C., Hoekstra, J., Kareiva, P., Keeler, B., Li, S., McKenzie, E., Ouyang, Z., Reyers, B., Ricketts, T., Rockström, J., Tallis, H. & Vira, B. 2015. Natural capital and ecosystem services informing decisions: From promise to practice. *Proceedings of the National Academy of Sciences*, 112(24): 7348–7355.

Guerry, A. D., Ruckelshaus, M. H., Arkema, K. K., Bernhardt, J. R., Guannel, G., Kim, C. K., Marsik, M., Papenfus, M., Toft, J. E., Verutes, G., Wood, S., Beck, M., Chan, F., Chan, K., Gelfenbaum, G., Gold, B.,Halpern, B., Labiosa, W., Lester, S., Levin, P., McField, M., Pinsky, M., Plummer, M., Polasky, S., Ruggiero, P., Sutherland, D., Tallis, H., Day, A. & Spencer, J. 2012. Modeling benefits from nature: Using ecosystem services to inform coastal and marine spatial planning. *International Journal of Biodiversity Science, Ecosystem Services & Management*, 8(1–2): 107–121.

Harrison, J. A., Bouwman, A., Mayorga, E. & Seitzinger, S. 2010. Magnitudes and sources of dissolved inorganic phosphorus inputs to surface fresh waters and the coastal zone: A new global model. *Global Biogeochemical Cycles*, 24: 271–279.

Kenter, J., Reed, M., Everard, M., Irvine, K., O'Brien, L., Molloy, C., Brady, E., Bryce, R., Christie, M., Church, A., Cooper, N., Davies, A., Hockley, N., Fazey, I., Jobstvogt, N. Molloy, C., Orchard-Webb, J., Ravenscroft, N., Ryan, M. & Watson, V. 2014. *Shared, Plural and Cultural Values: A Handbook for Decision-Makers*. Cambridge: UNEP-WCMC.

Kiesecker, J. M., Copeland, H., Pocewicz, A. & McKenney, B. 2010. Development by design: Blending landscape-level planning with the mitigation hierarchy. *Frontiers in Ecology and the Environment*, 8(5): 261–266.

Leopold, A. 1949. *A Sand County Almanac*. Oxford: Oxford University Press.

Levy, K., Daily, G. C. & Myers, S. S. 2012. Human health as an ecosystem service: A conceptual framework. In J. C. Ingram, C. Fumbaitis el Rio & A. DeClerck (Eds.), *Integrating Ecology and Poverty Reduction*: 231–251. New York: Springer.

Li, C., Li, S., Feldman, M. W., Daily, G. C. & Li, J. 2012. Does out-migration reshape rural households' livelihood capitals in the source communities? Recent evidence from Western China. *Asian and Pacific Migration Journal*, 21(1): 1–30.

Li, F., Wang, R., Paulussen, J. & Liu, X. 2005. Comprehensive concept planning of urban greening based on ecological principles: A case study in Beijing, China. *Landscape and Urban Planning*, 72(4): 325–336.

Li, J., Feldman, M. W., Li, S. & Daily, G. C. 2011. Rural household income and inequality under the Sloping Land Conversion Program in western China. *Proceedings of the National Academy of Sciences*, 108(19): 7721–7726.

Liang, Y., Li, S., Feldman, M. W. & Daily, G. C. 2012. Does household composition matter? The impact of the Grain for Green Program on rural livelihoods in China. *Ecological Economics*, 75: 152–160.

Liu, J., Li, S., Ouyang, Z., Tam, C. & Chen, X. 2008. Ecological and socioeconomic effects of China's policies for ecosystem services. *Proceedings of the National Academy of Sciences*, 105(28): 9477–9482.

Mace, G. M. 2014. Whose conservation? *Science*, 345(6204): 1558–1560.

Mäler, K.-G., Aniyar, S. & Jansson, Å. 2008. Accounting for ecosystem services as a way to understand the requirements for sustainable development. *Proceedings of the National Academy of Sciences*, 105 (28): 9501–9506.

Mendenhall, C. D., Shields-Estrada, A., Krishnaswami, A. J. & Daily, G. C. 2016. Quantifying and sustaining biodiversity in tropical agricultural landscapes. *Proceedings of the National Academy of Sciences*, 113(51): 14544–14551.

Millennium Ecosystem Assessment. 2005. *Ecosystems and Human Well-Being: The Assessment Series (Four Volumes and Summary)*. Washington, DC: Island Press.

Ministry of Environmental Protection of China & Chinese Academy of Sciences. 2008. National Ecosystem Service Zoning in China. Beijing.

Naidoo, R. & Ricketts, T. H. 2006. Mapping the economic costs and benefits of conservation. *PLoS Biology*, 4(11): e360.

National Research Council. 2005. *Valuing Ecosystem Services: Toward Better Environmental Decision-Making*. Washington, DC: National Academies Press.

Nelson, E., Mendoza, G., Regetz, J., Polasky, S., Tallis, H., Cameron, D., Chan, K., Daily, G. C., Goldstein, J., Kareiva, P. M., Lonsdorf, E., Naidoo, R., Ricketts, T. H. & Shaw, M. R. 2009. Modeling multiple ecosystem services, biodiversity conservation, commodity production, and tradeoffs at landscape scales. *Frontiers in Ecology and the Environment*, 7(1): 4–11.

Norton, B. G. 1987. *Why Preserve Natural Variety?* Princeton, NJ: Princeton University Press.

Ouyang, Z. Y. 2007. *Ecological Construction and Sustainable Development*. Beijing: Science Press.

Ouyang, Z., Zheng, H., Xiao, Y., Polasky, S., Liu, J., Xu, W., Wang, Q., Zhang, L., Xiao, Y., Rao, E., Jiang, L., Lu, F., Wang, X., Yang, G., Gong, S., Wu, B., Zeng, Y., Yang, W. & Daily, G. C. 2016. Improvements in ecosystem services from investments in natural capital in China. *Science*, 352(6292): 1455–1459.

Pagiola, S. & Platais, G. 2007. *Payments for Environmental Services: From Theory to Practice*. Washington, DC: World Bank.

Perrings, C., Duraiappah, A., Larigauderie, A. & Mooney, H. A. 2011. The biodiversity and ecosystem services science-policy interface. *Science*, 331(6021): 1139–1140.

Rapidel, B., Declerck, F., Le Coq, J.-F. & Beer, J. (Eds.). 2011. *Ecosystem Services from Agriculture and Agroforestry: Measurement and Payment*. London: Earthscan.

Ren, L., Li, J., Li, C., Li, S. & Daily, G. 2018. Does poverty matter in payment for ecosystem services program? Participation in the New Stage Sloping Land Conversion Program. *Sustainability*, 10(6): 1888.

Rokityanskiy, D., Benítez, P. C., Kraxner, F., McCallum, I., Obersteiner, M., Rametsteiner, E. & Yamagata, Y. 2007. Geographically explicit global modeling of land-use change, carbon sequestration, and biomass supply. *Technological Forecasting and Social Change*, 74(7): 1057–1082.

Rolston, H., III. 2000. The land ethic at the turn of the millennium. *Biodiversity & Conservation*, 9(8): 1045–1058.

Ruckelshaus, M., McKenzie, E., Tallis, H., Guerry, A., Daily, G. C., Kareiva, P., Polasky, S., Ricketts, T., Bhagabati, N., Wood, S. A. & Bernhardt, J. 2015. Notes from the field: Lessons learned from using ecosystem service approaches to inform real-world decisions. *Ecological Economics*, 115: 11–21.

Sharp, R., Tallis, H., Ricketts, T., Guerry, A., Wood, S., Chaplin-Kramer, R., Nelson, E., Ennaanay, D., Wolny, S., Olwero, N., Vigerstol, K., Pennington, D., Mendoza, G., Aukema, J., Foster, J., Forrest, J., Cameron, D., Arkema, K., Lonsdorf, E., Kennedy, C., Verutes, G., Kim, C. K., Guannel, G., Papenfus, M., Toft, J., Marsik, M., Bernhardt, J., Griffin, R., Glowinski, K., Chaumont, N., Perelman, A., Lacayo, M., Mandle, L., Hamel, P., Vogl, A. L., Rogers, L. & Bierbower, W. 2016. *InVEST 3.3.3 User's Guide*. Stanford, CA: The Natural Capital Project.

US EPA. 2009. *Valuing the Protection of Ecological Systems and Services*. EPA-SAB-09-012. Washington, DC: US EPA.

US EPA Science Advisory Board. 2009. *Valuing the Protection of Ecological Systems and Services*. EPA-SSAB-09-012. Washington, DC: US EPA.

Wunder, S., Engel, S. & Pagiola, S. 2008. Taking stock: A comparative analysis of payments for environmental services programs in developed and developing countries. *Ecological Economics*, 65(4): 834–852.

Xu, W., Xiao, Y., Zhang, J., Yang, W., Zhang, L., Hull, V., Wang, Z., Zheng, H., Liu, J., Polasky, S., Jiang, L., Xiao, Y., Shi, X., Rao, E., Lu, F., Wang, X., Daily, G. C. & Ouyang, Z. 2017. Strengthening protected areas for biodiversity and ecosystem services in China. *Proceedings of the National Academy of Sciences of the United States of America*, 114(7): 1601–1606.

Zhang, P., Shao, G., Zhao, G., Le Master, D. C., Parker, G. R., Dunning, J. B., Jr. & Li, Q. 2000. China's forest policy for the 21st century. *Science*, 288(5474): 2135–2136.

Zheng, H., Robinson, B. E., Liang, Y.-C., Polasky, S., Ma, D.-C., Wang, F.-C., Ruckelshaus, M., Ouyang, Z.-Y. & Daily, G. C. 2013. Benefits, costs, and livelihood implications of a regional Payment for Ecosystem Service program. *Proceedings of the National Academy of Sciences*, 110 (41): 16681–16686.

13 | Can Smart Villages Help to Stem Biodiversity Loss?

BRIAN HEAP, JOHN HOLMES AND BERNIE JONES

Urban areas generate 80 per cent of global GDP (CBD, 1992; Ammann, 2016; Gressel, 2007) and no country has developed without urbanisation, according to Paul Collier (Dobbs et al., 2012; Collier, 2015). Just 2 per cent of the world's population was urbanised in 1800; the figure passed 50 per cent by 2008, and on current trends it will reach 60 per cent by 2030. Virtually all this urban future growth will take place in developing countries, emulating Western Europe and North America, so that by 2025 it is estimated that 235 million households earning more than US$20,000 pa ppp will live in cities in the emerging economies, compared to 210 million in cities in the developed regions (Department for Business, Innovation and Skills, 2013). Cities are able to harness economies of scale and specialisation through the economies of agglomeration, but they consume 75 per cent of the world's energy and are responsible for up to 70 per cent of global greenhouse gases (GHGs) (Satterthwaite, 2008).

With the focus on smart cities and the global conversion process of land use away from natural capital and toward human-selected capital (Swanson, 1999), much greater attention needs to be given to the 46 per cent of the world's population that lives in rural communities. About 1.1 billion people (mostly rural dwellers) live off-grid without access to electricity, 2.5 billion live in households that depend primarily on an agricultural-based economy and 70 per cent of the global poor live in the countryside (Collier, 2008). In India, the 2011 census data show that around 833 million people (69 per cent of the population) lived in rural areas, compared to 377 million people (31 per cent), in urban areas. By 2050 it is projected that the population of India will be 1.6 billion and the urban figure will jump to about 800 million. This implies that a similar number of people will continue to live in villages.

There is a pressing need to convert these villages in India and elsewhere in the developing world into smart villages thereby respecting the UN principle – 'leave no one behind' (UNA-UK, 2015). This will help to ensure the development of entire countries, and in particular rural areas which is where biodiversity can be found and needs to be maintained. The living conditions and prospects of rural populations will remain a key global concern for decades to come. Growth in rural economies will be a major factor in the overall economic growth of developing countries and will play a central role in achieving the Sustainable Development Goals.

A lack of affordable energy access is one of the deprivations of the global poor. Multiple causes of poverty range from the impact of the discovery and exploitation of natural resources that leads to an under-investment in local agricultural activities, inadequate access to international markets by landlocked countries, national and international conflict, and poor governance (UN-UK, 2015; McFarland et al., 2015; Leonard and Haddad, 2008). These poverty traps (Collier, 2015) have roots, though not exclusively so, in the global North where the insatiable demand for resources such as oil and minerals makes the natural resource trap so potent, and where agricultural protectionism and perverse subsidies deny the poor opportunities for which they would otherwise have competitive advantages (Satterthwaite, 2008; Collier, 2008).

A grand vision is needed to tackle these challenges, and one that originates in the Global South (Collier, 2008). The vison should ensure that consequent interventions do not imperil the remarkable biodiversity that we still enjoy and consign it to what has been called an 'evolutionary dustbin' (Swanson, 1999). 'Smart villages' are a necessary analogue of 'smart cities' – providing a grand vision that would help to preserve biodiversity because of its value and long-term benefits, elements that are normally never as powerful as the immediate need for survival of the bottom billion.

The Smart Villages Initiative

The concept of the smart village is that affordable modern energy access in the form of sustainable renewable energy, when appropriately integrated with other development initiatives, can act as a catalyst for development – education, health, food security, environment, productive enterprises and participatory democracy. This in turn supports further improvements in modern energy access, ensuring sustainable electricity supplies to meet rural needs and the availability of clean and

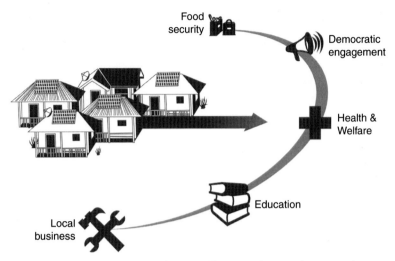

Figure 13.1 Holistic concept of smart villages (Holmes and van Gevelt, 2015). From https://e4sv.org/about-us/what-are-smart-villages/.

efficient appliances for cooking, communication, irrigation, food processing, etc. As such, energy access can provide a much-needed driver for sustainable economic development, social justice and the mitigation of risks for a major, but neglected, sector of the world's economy in reversing the direct and potentially damaging impact of energy poverty in the rural environment (Figure 13.1; Holmes and van Gevelt, 2015).

In recent years, the concept of energy poverty has resurfaced in international and national public policy discussions (Pereira et al., 2011). Between 1.5 and 3 billion individuals in the world today are defined as energy poor – 'people who live on less than US$1.15 per day and have no access to reliable, safe and efficient energy for cooking, lighting, space heating and mechanical power … [and] who rely upon harmful energy like biomass-generated fire for their cooking and heating' (Guruswamy, 2011). Energy poverty is most severe among rural communities living off the grid in developing countries and it has negative effects on the environment, health, education, productivity and the quality of life of villagers.

The Smart Villages Initiative (www.e4sv.org) has been set up to support energy access for development and the establishment of smart villages. It brings together frontline players in the Global South – entrepreneurs, scientists and engineers, villagers, rural poor,

NGOs, financiers, civil society, development and environmental organisations, sociologists, economists, policymakers and regulators – who are engaged in off-grid rural communities in order to identify the barriers to progress, and how they can be overcome. The focus is on off-grid villages where local energy solutions are cheaper than national electricity grid extension, and a key aim is to identify the framework conditions necessary to foster entrepreneurial initiatives that ensure that governments and donor funding achieve maximum leverage of private sector investment. An underlying premise is that activities to enable energy access need to be integrated with other development initiatives, taking a holistic and community level approach, to maximise social benefit and sustainable environmental development (Guriswamy, 2011; Van Gevelt et al., 2016; Lorentz Biopanel Statement, 2016).

Renewable sources of energy can play a key role in enabling many of the basic services that are required in 'off-grid' communities, as seen in the spectacular growth of solar home systems in East Africa. An 80 per cent fall in the cost of solar panels since 2010, major improvements in the efficiency of domestic appliances, and innovative 'pay-as-you-go' business models have been key factors in this success.

The nature of the energy escalator illustrated in Table 13.1 stresses the fact that energy access should not be limited to attaining the most basic level of services as fossil fuels can be progressively replaced by renewable energy sources or by hybrid combinations. Compared with fossil energy, renewable energy for smart villages is sustainable, local and less polluting in terms of greenhouse gas emissions and therefore it will help to mitigate climate change, one of the key threats to biodiversity. Globally, renewable electricity generation is rapidly increasing, and by the end of 2015 it was enough to supply an estimated 23.7 per cent of global electricity (the major part of which was hydropower). Renewable energy has therefore become a mainstream energy source and this has been signalled in the United Nations General Assembly's adoption of a dedicated Sustainable Development Goal – SDG7 (UN-UK, 2015).

In the Smart Villages Initiative we consider how energy-poor people depend on, and affect, biodiversity and ecosystem services and functions, and some of the practical ways by which smart villages could help to stem the threats to biodiversity losses in rural communities, which are largely of humanity's making. Many of these losses are caused by

Table 13.1 *Smart villages and the energy escalator*

Technology	Generation capacity (kW)	Energy sources	Services available	Estimated economic cost per household
Pico-power systems	0.001–0.01	Hydro, wind, solar	Lighting, radio communication reception, two-way mobile communication	US$10–100
Stand-alone home systems	0.01–1	Hydro, wind, solar	Same as above plus additional lighting and communication, television, fans, limited motive and heat power	US$75–1000
Mini-grids	1–1000	Hydro, wind, solar, biomass; diesel; hybrid combinations	Same as above plus enhanced motive and heat power, and ability to power community-based services	Medium to large capital cost, low marginal cost to end user
Regional grid connection	1000–1,000,000	Gas, hydro, wind, solar PV, biomass	Assuming high quality of connection, same as above up to a full range of electric power appliances, commercial and industrial applications	Medium to large capital cost, low marginal cost to end user

Source. Holmes and van Gevelt (2015).

unsustainable agricultural practices, land and forest degradation and the erosion of genetic resources in different regions of the world.

Stemming Biodiversity Losses Arising from Energy Demands

Agroforestry helps to reduce biodiversity loss by providing a protective tree cover and a habitat for a diversity of flora and fauna (Chavan et al., 2016). But with three billion people in the world using direct energy in the form of wood and agricultural waste for cooking and heating, deforestation and biomass can destroy biodiversity and ecosystem functions (BEF) and services (BES), prolong poverty, accelerate climate change and expose people to emerging infectious diseases – many of which have been traced to tropical rainforests and specifically to freshwater aquatic systems. For many of the estimated 33 million smallholder farmers in sub-Saharan Africa (and the estimated 570 million worldwide), deforestation has become a widespread solution to their needs; but they remain largely uneducated about its effects on the ecosystems on which they rely and the global impacts on humanity (FAO, 2012; Morris et al., 2016; WWF, 2016a). Smart villages help to stem biodiversity loss by mitigating these anthropogenic impacts on forests.

Deforestation

There are many reasons for deforestation, including large-scale agriculture for international commodities (e.g., soybean, oil palm particularly in S E Asia), logging and mining. About 130 m hectares of forests rich in biological diversity and home to many terrestrial species of animals, plants and insects have been lost since 1990, an area almost equivalent in size to South Africa, so that the global intact forest landscape has been reduced by 7.2 per cent since 2000 (Potapov et al., 2017). The threat is likely to continue with further deforestation from illegal logging, forest degradation, fire and pollution, to which is added the challenge of climate change (FAO, 2015). Effective conservation policies will need to create incentives for efficient resource management and the recycling of water and nutrients (Kline et al., 2017).

Smart villages recognise the critical importance of forests for sustainable landscape management and for the development of a country's low carbon energy strategy. The UN Framework Convention on

Climate Change and its programmes of Reducing Emissions from Deforestation and Forest Degradation (REDD+) have the broad intent to help developing countries to value healthy forests as one of the largest stores of carbon. Through information and communication technologies (ICT, radio, telephony, computers, Internet) smart villages will be advised about a country's REDD+ strategy or action plan, the voluntary forest monitoring systems to conserve and restore healthy forests, and results-based payments schemes for reductions in forest emissions (WWF, 2016b).

A Payment for Ecosystem Services (PES) used to transfer money to individual farmers has the objective of incentivising biodiversity conservation, sustainable resource management and the provision of ecological services. In Mexico, a study from 2004 to 2009 showed a 40–51 per cent mitigation of forest cover losses compared to what would have happened in the absence of a PES programme. However, the greatest impacts were observed in the areas with lower risks of deforestation rather than in areas at high risk, and overall the programme was more effective at achieving environmental goals than benefiting the socioe-conomic status of the areas. Similar schemes have been tested with user-financed PES, in which funding comes from the users of the ecosystem service being provided, and government-financed PES where funding comes from a third party. User-financed programmes were found to be better targeted to local conditions and needs, and better monitored than government-financed schemes (Wundera et al., 2008). Any promising signs of forest conservation are therefore welcome and results over the last five years in Africa show the highest annual increase in the area of forest for conservation while Europe, North and Central America reported the lowest compared to previous reporting periods. The increase reported by Asia for 2010–2015 was lower than that reported for 2000–2010 but higher than the increase reported in the 1990s (Kline et al., 2017).

For smart villages, confirmation of the critical importance of biodiversity conservation comes from recent studies of forests in 44 countries that show a positive and consistent relationship exists between tree diversity and ecosystem productivity; a 10 per cent loss in biodiversity leads to a 3 per cent loss in productivity (Liang et al., 2016). Furthermore, the economic value of maintaining biodiversity for the purpose of forest productivity is fivefold greater than the cost of conservation, with clear implications for the biodiversity-productivity relationships in off-grid villages with their dependence on biomass.

Biomass

Nearly 40 per cent of the world's population rely on solid biomass as it is the world's fourth largest energy resource for heat, burning and cooking (138 exajoules of primary energy). In sub-Saharan Africa (excluding South Africa) over 80 per cent of the total energy supply for heating, cooking and processing of agricultural produce is derived from biomass such as fuelwood and agricultural residues. In Latin America the figure is somewhat less (40 per cent) but in other regions it is about 60 per cent. Calculations show the vital role of biomass consumption in the economic growth of sub-Saharan countries; a 1 per cent increase in biomass production can lead to an increase in GDP of up to 1.8 per cent compared with a 1 per cent increase in a country's openness to trade leading to a 0.3 per cent increase in GDP, and a 1 per cent increase in population to a 0.7 per cent increase in GDP (Ozturk and Bilgili, 2015). However, although about two-thirds of households in the least developed countries (LDCs) depend on biomass and charcoal for cooking purposes, it is responsible for causing respiratory illness and the deaths of 4.3 million per year, primarily among women and children.

Biodiversity loss affects the production of biomass and essential services such as water, nutrients and light (biodiversity and ecosystem services, BES). The transformation of a diverse plant stand into a monoculture can also influence biodiversity and ecosystem functions (BEF) and reduce plant biomass (Cardinale et al., 2012). Therefore, biomass harvesting and usage in LDCs are an issue when conducted in unsustainable ways because they affect ecosystem functioning (Heap, 2016a; SCOPE 2015). Smart villages seek to produce and use biomass in ways that are sustainable and renewable, that do not deplete resources, and that utilise it efficiently. Technologies for the clean and efficient use of biomass for cooking and heating in households can make major improvements to the lives of women living in off-grid villages (Smart Villages Initiative, 2015a).

Different forms of biomass exist, ranging from woody and cellulosic biomass (grasses, trees, and some agricultural and forestry wastes) for combustion to produce heat and electricity; sugar-rich crops (sugar cane, sugar beet) for fermentation to produce ethanol and the leftover biofuel (bagasse) in the case of sugar cane; oil seeds (rape seed, soy, sunflower, palm oil) for pressing and biodiesel production; sorghum and cassava for ethanol production; to Jatropha, peanuts and palm oil for biodiesel. Biomass also originates from the food supply chain, such as animal wastes, crop and forest residues (Heap, 2016a; SCOPE, 2015). India, with over 600,000 villages and a substantial biomass energy sector, has the potential to produce about 17,000 MW of electricity from surplus agro-residues and a further 5000 MW if the sugar mills switch over to modern techniques of co-generation. This projection is part of India's ambitious programme to source nearly 60 per cent of its electricity capacity from non-fossil fuels by 2017.

Biomass usage in LDCs includes the provision of direct energy in households. It can be in the form of energy carriers such as briquettes for heating and cooking that use agricultural waste like sugarcane, which saves cutting down trees. Biomass may fuel combined heat and power plants through anaerobic digestion processes, or may be converted to liquid biofuel in commercial production plants. The non-governmental organisation Energy4Impact (2016) identifies the importance of biomass along with other generation technologies such as solar PV, hydro and renewable-diesel hybrids for developing mini-grids in rural communities. Energy4Impact supports developers to overcome financial obstacles and facilitate site selections, equity provision and market analysis to ensure that the new energy supply has the most powerful impact possible. Working with rural communities the aim is to develop mini-grids, though few have been economically successful in Africa to date. African countries and Brazil are frequently identified as the two regions with the greatest capacity for biomass production. Smart villages adopt novel crop and forestry systems that are sustainable, reduce unsustainable deforestation and make more effective use of innovations in renewable energy technologies (SCOPE, 2015).

Cookstoves

Substantial reductions in fuel wood requirements in smart villages from the adoption of clean and efficient cookstoves, together with sustainable management of forests, can make a useful contribution to reducing deforestation and biodiversity loss, and to climate change mitigation. Impacts are likely to be location specific and more effective in arid areas than in greener areas like Southeast Asia. Increasing attention is being given to the deployment of clean cooking technologies. The Global Alliance for Clean Cookstoves hosted by the UN Foundation is a public-private partnership that aims to spur the adoption of clean cookstoves and fuels in 100 million households by 2020 (Global Alliance for Clean Cookstoves, 2016).

A Smart Villages Initiative workshop held in Myanmar, with inputs from Indonesia, Laos, Cambodia and the Philippines, focused on the design and dissemination of improved cookstoves in South East Asia (Smart Villages Initiative, 2015b). The annual consumption rate of fuelwood in Myanmar is about 2.5 tonnes per household, and increasing fuelwood requirements present a significant challenge to the sustainability of forest resources. The Ministry of Environmental Conservation and Forestry aims to reduce the total biomass energy consumption from its current 76 per cent of total annual energy consumption to 58 per cent by 2020 and to 46 per cent by 2030. It also aims to supply 25 per cent of fuelwood needs through forest plantations and reforestation, and to distribute new designs of cookstoves which are up to 40 per cent more efficient than traditional open-fire cooking or self-made stoves. This can result in up to one tonne of fuelwood being saved per rural household per year, while the use of novel forestry systems reduces soil degradation and combats pests and diseases. A similar initiative has been launched in Indonesia with the support of the World Bank with the aim to ensure universal access to clean cookstoves by 2030 (Smart Villages Initiative, 2015b).

In the Indawgyi Lake area of Kachin State in Myanmar, where biomass dependence is extremely high, the majority of the firewood comes from the felling of mature Dipterocarp trees, thus threatening local forest biodiversity. Unlike in most other areas, men collect the firewood and women are responsible for cooking. Focus groups were organised to understand local requirements for improved cookstoves, which led to the development of the Indawgyi Stove. The stove has a constant flow of air and uses less fuel than traditional cookstoves. It can be constructed from locally available materials and the design can be modified to meet the requirements of different households. The Smart Villages Initiative was welcomed by George Dura of the European Union Delegation at Myanmar, as reduced deforestation helps to combat climate change in a country that ranks as the second most vulnerable in the world to climate change and where communities

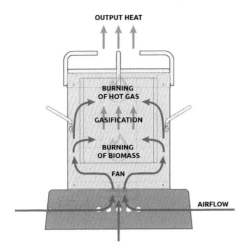

Figure 13.2 Efficient cooking stoves save fuel and biomass and reduce smoke inhalation (Vianello et al., 2016). Image of biomass cookstove courtesy of Reuben Walker, African Clean Energy, www.africancleanenergy.com/.

are often poorly equipped to deal with extreme climate events (Smart Villages Initiative, 2015b).

Envirofit, a producer of modern cookstoves, claims to have saved over the past decade US$179 million in fuel costs from 1.3 million stoves, created 2500 direct and indirect jobs, conserved 52 million trees and prevented 22 million tonnes of carbon dioxide emissions. African Clean Energy (ACE) is the producer of the ACE 1 solar biomass energy system that reduces smoke emissions to low levels and provides clean cooking with a range of biomass fuels, as well as offering solar electricity for mobile phone charging and LED lighting (Figure 13.2).

The rate of progress in disseminating improved cookstoves has been slow and is considered to be a rather neglected issue. This is an important omission given that cooking accounts for the major part of energy consumption in the rural areas of many developing countries with all its implications for biodiversity loss and human health.

The Biomass Dilemma

Over 20 million tonnes of charcoal are consumed annually in Africa and this is expected to increase to 46 million tonnes by 2030, driven by sustained population growth, rapid urbanisation and lack of practical and affordable alternatives. When comparing price and energy content at the point of use against other alternatives, charcoal may outcompete most on several fronts, though the rationale for choosing energy sources at the household level is influenced by context, price, energy content, ash content, smoke and fumes, available cooking appliance, type of food to be prepared and time of preparation.

Experience in Kenya shows that advising a village against charcoal production in the interest of stemming biodiversity loss will probably fail (Barasa, 2015). Charcoal is one of the most important energy sources on the African continent and its production provides employment in rural communities, with more than 65 per cent of all households in urban areas of East Africa using it as part of their energy mix. Any alternative to charcoal comes up against a societal structure that involves traditional forms of household energy provision for cooking and living, embedded patterns of rural employment for charcoal production, and a livelihood influenced by shadowy interests along the value-chain of charcoal for the urban market.

No one aspires to be a charcoal producer as it is a low-paid, physically intense and health-threatening undertaking, often done as a last-resort coping mechanism. But, as Barasa says, 'a "top-down" techno-utopian solution could advance modern and alternative sources to charcoal ... but (it) has to be matched by a "bottom-up" social transformation that generates employment and viable income alternatives for (charcoal) producers' (Barasa, 2015). The message is that replacing charcoal as a productive enterprise will require a smart village to produce real livelihood alternatives and economic development to divert people from practices that are deeply embedded in rural structures even if they harm biodiversity and the environment.

Stemming Losses Arising from Agricultural Practices

Biodiversity in agriculture means not only the supply of a variety of foods for consumers but also the creation of environments that support healthy populations of microbes, insects and small animals (Fahrig et al., 2015). During the past 50 years, while land has been lost to urbanisation, agriculture has led to loss through soil degradation, desertification, erosion, overgrazing, salt accumulation and pollution. Managed as opposed to natural habitats where there is little human intervention, have often resulted in agricultural practices that produced major biodiversity loss. This has occurred with the ever-increasing demand for food, feed and fibre products. However, the picture is complex since in some instances (e.g., adult hoverflies, farmland bird diversity) conventional agriculture can generate more biodiversity than organic farming depending on the scale of the landscape (Gabriel et al., 2010). Smart villages take advantage of the many advances in agronomy to produce food in a sustainable manner, create productive enterprises that are linked to market opportunities, and are enabled by appropriate responsible policies that internalise externalities and reward the stemming of biodiversity loss in managed habitats (Dasgupta, 2001; Ehrlich and Harte, 2015).

Reducing the Impacts of Agricultural Practices

Agricultural expansion in developing countries has been associated with an 8 per cent decline in the world's natural forest cover, and habitat loss in tropical regions with their high biological diversity is a particular concern (UNEP, 1997). More needs to be learned about the dynamics of loss of habitats in relation to individual species as more diverse communities are more productive when they contain key species that have a large influence on productivity. A 21–40 per cent loss of species can reduce plant production by 5–10 per cent, similar to the effects of climate warming. When higher levels of extinction occur (41–60 per cent) the effects rival those of acidification and nutrient pollution (Sole and Montoya, 2006; Hooper et al., 2012). Such extinctions alter key services important to the productivity and sustainability of Earth's ecosystems, and it has been estimated that an increase of species extinction rates by 1000 times could have occurred in the last 300 years, comparable in magnitude to one of the five big extinction events (Lawton and May, 1994). At last, steps are being taken by multinational organisations that recognise these risks and a coherent set of principles will be launched in order to safeguard commitments to areas of 'no deforestation' (HCSA, 2016).

Smart villages address the challenge of agriculture's impact on biodiversity by a holistic approach similar to that advocated by WWF (2012), involving renewable (clean) energy, technologies that monitor environmental indicators such as water quality, soil conditions and landscape changes, and sustainable productive enterprises that create an income stream and facilitate sustainable development. Productive enterprises in smart villages are essential. In locations in India, farmers, fishermen and food processing businesses can kick-start cooperative ventures using the energy sources of biomass, solar and wind power, and hydropower, and they adopt the use of non-lead batteries to facilitate energy storage. Agro-businesses expand through improved solar energy-based irrigation systems, agro-processing and refrigeration and biogas systems and mini-grid power for milling rice and maize. Harvest losses are reduced and post-harvesting processing facilitated. Where heating and cooling systems can be provided, added-value from agricultural products can be gained through food preparation, processing, extraction, refining and preserving. Modern information and communication technologies (ICT) enable farmers to be informed about best practices and market opportunities for the sale of products.

A prototype of the smart villages concept is found at Chhotkei, Odisha, India, a small remote village 160 km from the state capital, Bhubaneswar, and situated amidst rich natural resources but previously without electricity. The primary livelihood is rain-fed paddy cultivation once a year, but the village has now been supplied with a 30 kW solar-powered Smart Nanogrid^{TM} to meet the energy demands of 140 households, 20 streetlights, a temple and three community centres. The renewable energy supplies microenterprises such as poultry, stitching, puffed-rice machines, provision stores, refrigerators, oil mills, welding machines, and irrigation and enables value addition to agriculture. Power is supplied throughout the village by underground electrical cables to minimise losses. Fibre optic cables are used for communication purposes, and a Smart Nanogrid^{TM} controls metering, billing and payment, as well as alerts to 'cut off' if unpaid. Smart Nanogrid^{TM} ICT supports tele-medicine, tele-education, smart agriculture and water management (Figure 13.3A) (SunMoksha, 2015).

Sustainable Intensification

'Growing more from less' is the rallying cry for increased food production (Royal Society, 2009; Godfray et al., 2010) whereby each hectare of land will need ideally to feed five people by 2050, compared to just two people in 1960, using less water and with reduced biodiversity loss. Whereas in the past the primary solution has been to bring more land

Figure 13.3 A, Solar-powered village at Chhotkei, Odisha, India (SunMoksha, 2015). Photograph courtesy of Ashok Das, SunMoksha, https://youtu.be/eED xZK0bXgc. **B,** Tatu Rajabu of Mitonto village, Kijota ward, Tanzania, harvested 15 kg of pearl millet grain from a 50 g small pack of seed (Seward, 2015). Photograph courtesy of Paul Seward, http://fipsafrica.org/. **C,** ICT training in Long Lamai, Sarawak, Borneo, Malaysia. Photograph by Tariq Zaman (Zaman, 2016). **D,** Solar pumps for irrigation in smart villages developed by Gram Oorja, India. Photograph courtesy of Anshuman Lath, Gram Oorja, 2015, http://gramoorja.in/.

into production or to take a greater supply of fish, such options are no longer straightforward as little additional land suitable for agriculture remains in many regions and several fisheries have been diminished. Increased cropping intensity by growing a greater number of crops each year on the same land and sustainable expansion of irrigated areas will be necessary.

A different approach would be to close the yield gap, since the best yields from cereal crops grown under optimal conditions are far greater than those typically obtained by farmers. Wheat yields in the UK were 2.8t/ha in 1948 and 8t/ha in 2016 with best yields of 10–12 t/ha limited only by water availability. The yield gap measured locally or by crop simulation models can be as great as 50–60 per cent in some countries in Africa and c. 20–25 per cent in Asia and South America, while yields for maize, rice, wheat and soybean in a third of areas studied have either not improved or stagnated (Ray et al., 2012). (A yield gap of about 20 per cent also occurs between conventional compared to organic crop yields (de Ponti et al., 2012). Questions remain, however, about closing the yield gap of crops in sub-Saharan Africa and whether it can be done sustainably without the negative externalities frequently associated with the conventional methods of increased production – land erosion, eutrophication of water courses and soil degradation (Pradhan et al., 2015; van Ittersum et al., 2016).

Investment in agricultural R&D in the developing countries is problematic as it has relied almost entirely on publicly funded research and global partnerships, such as the Consultative Group for International Agricultural Research (CGIAR), unlike the situation in high-income countries which are relatively well supported by the private sector. Investment strategies to close the yield gap do exist as they provide important opportunities for crop breeders and practitioners familiar with modern agronomic and managerial improvements, and for the conservation of genetic resources in genebanks such as the Crop Genebank Knowledge Base.

A key development for smart villages will be local solutions. For example, *Brachiaria,* a high-quality, drought-resistant native forage grass grown in East Africa, has a high crude protein and a low fibre content which leads to less methane gas produced for each unit of livestock product such as milk or meat. It withstands dry seasons of three to six months, and when fed to cattle increases milk production by 40 per cent (González et al., 2016). Smart villages also use better managerial measures, such as the extension service provided by the Science and Technology Backyard platform developed in China that empowers smallholder farmers by agricultural scientists living among them and alerting them to relevant research findings. The increases in the five-year average yield of wheat and maize have been from 67.9 per cent to 97.0 per cent of attainable levels locally, and from 62.8 per cent to 79.6 per cent of attainable yields countywide (Zhang et al., 2016).

Pioneering work by Seward (2015) at FIPS-Africa, a not-for-profit company working in Kenya, Tanzania and Mozambique, also demonstrates how simple local solutions can improve the status and performance of large numbers of poor smallholder farmers who live off-grid and below the poverty line. Self-employed Village-based Advisors (VBAs) selected by the villagers themselves teach good agricultural practice and business skills to generate enough income to sustain their advisory role. The 'Small Pack/Whole Village' method provides a seed pack of 25–100 g of an improved crop variety and fertiliser for every farmer. Farmers invariably return to the VBA to purchase larger quantities of seed, and maize crop productivity increases from one to four tonnes/ha within one year (Figure 13.3B). Other offers include improved seeds for the most important cereal, legume, root and tuber, banana (vegetative propagation), vegetable and fruit tree crops, and dietary protein obtained from improved livestock breeds and indigenous chickens protected against Newcastle disease by a thermostable vaccine. Future partnerships with seed and fertiliser companies plan to improve the livelihoods of 350,000 smallholder farmer families. The FIPS model enables smallholder farmers in Africa to quickly and sustainably become food secure on existing land through simple methodologies of sustainable intensification (Seward, 2015).

'Hi-tech' approaches to sustainable intensification can raise crop productivity and nutritional quality by the application of accelerated plant breeding gained from knowledge of plant genomes and the use of key marker genes to aid selection by local farmers. Future technologies may pave the way by the transfer of the high-productivity C4 photosynthetic pathway found in maize and putting it into rice, or by photoprotection from specific gene transfer that gives greater yields of leaves, stems and roots by up to 20 per cent (Kromdijk et al., 2016). These options are still at an early stage of development and beyond the reach of poor off-grid smallholder farmers, who are among the most disadvantaged in the world, but they reflect the aggressive intent of plant breeders and companies to tackle the challenges that lie ahead to improve the sustainable intensification of food production. Doubts remain about whether closing the yield gap alone will suffice to meet the demands of food security in sub-Saharan Africa (Pradhan et al., 2015; van Ittersum et al., 2016), and they provide a stark warning that if this cannot be done the tensions between increased agricultural productivity, sustainable intensification and biodiversity losses could be aggravated by a massive expansion of cropland and expensive cereal importations with detrimental effects on any smart village initiatives (UN, 1987; FAO, 2010; van Ittersum et al., 2016).

Energy for Agriculture

Affordable energy from renewable sources and access to ICT in the forms of radio, telephony, tablets and the Internet have the potential to make villages smart and help develop a much-needed second Green Revolution among smallholder farmers. New solar pumps (Ghosh and Agrawal, 2015) that make irrigation easier and more efficient align with government policies in countries such as India and Ethiopia to improve small-scale irrigation. They emit no carbon, contribute to more sustainable agricultural practices, and with appropriate business models can boost small-scale irrigation development by saving water, reducing costs and managing natural resources more sustainably. Solar pumps can be used for drip irrigation, household micro-irrigation and domestic use, and solar drying of crops enables threshing, milling, sorting and grading.

These solar technologies do not require high investment, gain better price returns and, crucially, lead to youth employment. The overall caveat is that solar-sourced equipment must be serviced and maintained, the lack of training being a common source of setback in the use of renewable energy technologies. Smart villages also use biosensors for soil fertility monitoring to reduce fertiliser usage and decrease not only energy inputs but environmental impacts. They also adopt precision farming methods that become feasible with drones, satellites and on-farm computer-aided technologies, providing greater accuracy and timing of applications of seeds or fertilisers.

Integrated food–energy systems (IFES) make more efficient use of cropping and agro-forestry systems through links with livestock and fish production (Bogdanski et al., 2010a, 2010b). On-farm synergies arise from the use of by-products such as crop residues, animal wastes and food waste that help to generate energy with little effect on BES. IFES in smart villages lend themselves to being scaled up so that anaerobic digesters for biogas production and neighbouring farms form clusters that invest in the construction of mini-grids. However, specific case studies are scarce and the idea of integrating different farming practices has not gained wide appeal; the more crops and procedures that have to be managed and for which farmers require a greater range of management skills, the greater the losses of economies of scale (El Bassam, 2010; Bogdanski, 2012). Looking ahead, however, the agricultural engineering company New Holland has developed the concept of the 'Energy Independent Farm' that would use renewable electricity generated on-site to produce hydrogen fuel for tractors, trucks and transportation (Rodriguez, 2011; Bogdanski, 2012).

Rimbunan Kaseh, located to the northeast of Kuala Lumpur, Malaysia, is one of numerous village communities in S E Asia that exemplify many of the features of IFES. Its integrated production system of agricultural crops, aquaculture and livestock production uses water in aquaculture where highly valued species of fish are reared. It is then recycled to irrigate crops through an energy efficient hydroponic system that ensures plants receive precisely the level of water and nourishment required. Agricultural waste is mulched to use as poultry feed and to create fish food for aquaculture. Villagers experienced significant improvements in their quality of life, with household income supplemented by up to US$500 per month, largely due to the production of high-value crops such as golden melon and jade perch fish. ICT-enabled integration of the village into global value chains means that these high-value products reach Singaporean supermarket shelves (Smart Villages Initiative, 2015c).

Biofuels

Unsurprisingly, much attention has been given to crop production for biofuels and its effect on biodiversity. Currently biofuels provide about 3 per cent of the world's transportation fuels, a figure that could possibly increase to about 30 per cent by 2050. Targets for biofuel blending for transportation fuels range from 5–27 per cent in different countries, with Brazil having already attained the higher figure (SCOPE, 2015). Biogas is another energy source of growing importance, being a mixture of methane and carbon dioxide produced by the anaerobic digestion of organic waste including manure, landfill organics or dried and ensiled grass. Expanding energy biomass plantations into the natural landscape obviously brings the risk of direct biodiversity loss due to habitat destruction and fragmentation, or agricultural practices that lead to environmental damage (Ozturk, 2016; Dale et al., 2014). An additional caveat concerns the unregulated production of biofuels without full life-cycle analyses of the threats to biodiversity and food security.

Land taken up for non-food use means that crops and farmland will be removed from food production, and land used outside a feedstock's production area will need to be replaced by the supply of the original commodity, creating an indirect land use change (iLUC). Rebound effects will occur where the replacement of fossil fuels reduces demand, lowers their prices and leads to higher fuel consumption and a consequent increase in greenhouse gases (GHG) emissions. Soil nutrient depletion may also occur if carbon is not returned to the soil (Heap, 2016a).

Notwithstanding these perceived drawbacks, smart villages may use perennial grassy crops or short rotation coppicing as a second-generation feedstock compared with annual crops. They can reduce pesticide and net fertiliser use and provide a greater animal biodiversity as habitats are improved and natural ecosystems functions restored. Accounting procedures of land use, land use change and forestry (LULUCF) will need to be applied to determine the efficacy of these procedures if adopted in smart villages (EASAC, 2017). Biofuel facilities can also be designated to absorb surpluses if 'flex crops' are grown that serve food, feed and fuel markets. They absorb surpluses according to the circumstances of supply and demand, thereby helping to dampen commodity volatility (Kline et al., 2017).

Other forms of distributed energy for smart villages come from pooling sorghum crops from groups of smallholder farmers, and the greater use of agricultural residues (SCOPE, 2015). The benefits need to flow to the village rather than a distant corporation in order to raise rural incomes and offset rising food prices. Terrat, a Maasai village located in the Manyara region of Tanzania (Hurley-Depret, 2016), produces biodiesel from Jatropha and croton. The village was at a crossroads with residents increasingly vulnerable to the pressures of globalisation. Terrat inhabitants, including village elders such as Martin Saning'o, developed the Institute for Orkonerei Pastoralists Advancement (IOPA) to create opportunities initially through a local radio station for community-driven economic empowerment. Processing surplus milk to make higher-value dairy products such as cheese, yogurt, butter and ghee was discussed and, with the help of a Dutch family foundation, a company was founded, and milk processing units purchased. IOPA obtained three generators of 300 kW total capacity to run on locally produced biofuel. Milk processing has become a successful economic activity with daily production of up to 2000 litres per day, and export of processed dairy products to niche national and regional markets. Although the initiative has not been without its tensions with the Tanzanian government, training opportunities for women, employment opportunities for young people and distributed biofuel production from locally managed feedstocks have been achieved.

Education

Energy access in smart villages makes ICT into a realistic vehicle for the expansion of education in rural communities, depending on the distance from urban centres. Mobile phones and the Internet become key linkages between researchers, extension agents and farmers (mostly women) raising awareness of best practices, environmental issues and market prospects. They reduce the information asymmetries faced by small and marginal farmers, help to deal with some of the weaknesses of traditional agricultural extension services, and provide weather forecasts, local language training and advice about sustainable self-financing business models. In India, ICRISAT's GreenPHABLET (Dileepkumar, 2014) empowers women by providing farm education and market intelligence, and routes to conventional modes of learning about child health, women's health, nutrition, prevention and cure of common ailments, and employment opportunities. Therefore, the provision of material for smallholder farmers through ICT about the benefits of BES and the impact of their farming systems underpin strategies to stem biodiversity losses (CISL, 2016).

Tariq Zaman of the University of Sarawak, Malaysia, speaks of indigenous communities who transmit knowledge from one generation to another (Zaman, 2016). 'There is so much to learn from indigenous communities,' he says, 'especially in matters pertaining to stewardship of the earth and community empowerment.' Long Lamai where he works is a Penan village in the Malaysian Borneo, eight hours on rough logging roads and an hour of hiking through the dense rainforest from the nearest town. It is a very lively, gender and generation balanced village of approximately 598 individuals and 116 households situated next to the river and consisting of individual (long) houses on poles, surrounded by the rainforest. People live a subsistence agrarian lifestyle with everyone depending on the jungle as a source of food. Electricity generated through mini-hydro and solar photovoltaic systems makes it one of the most advanced Penan communities, having adopted ICT into economic, social, institutional and environmental activities. Its telecentre provides full internet connection and Wi-Fi within the village, and its mobile tower gives access to the outside world and, with external partners for educational purposes, marketing of touristic activities and the preservation of indigenous knowledge. Zaman writes of the need for support from the public and private sectors – 'a smart village can only be created and maintained if the villagers make smart decisions . . . residents have worked hard to carve out a village and preserve (its) intimate relationship with the environment and jungle . . . they seek to gain sovereignty of resources (energy, income, and information) in a way that supports long-term community resilience' (Figure 13.3C).

Livestock

Livestock farming is the world's largest land use sector, utilising around 60 per cent of the global biomass harvest, and is one of the fastest-growing sectors in the agricultural industry. It will be driven in future by the projected increase in the human population and an expansion of a middle class that demand dietary upgrading and can afford a meat-based diet. In developing countries mixed farming systems produce the bulk of animal-derived products: 75 per cent of milk and 60 per cent of meat. Smart villages improve the efficiency of livestock rearing by increasing the amount of animal product (by weight) produced per unit of emission by improvements in nutrition (Canales, 2017). Overall, burgeoning livestock production with its contributions to pollution and GHG emissions (14.5 per cent) provides a major challenge to BES.

Feed for poultry can account for 60–80 per cent of the total cost of inputs, together with increasing demands on land availability and water resources (Robinson and Pozzi, 2011; Weindl et al., 2015; Freese, 2016). Public health consequences exist because livestock are the source of approximately 75 per cent of newly emerging infectious diseases (Gebreyes et al., 2014). The spread of infectious zoonotic and non-zoonotic diseases, such as H5N1 avian influenza panzootic and the pandemic (H1N1) influenza A crisis, demonstrate the magnitude of the problem.

Smart villages take advantage of livestock vaccination schemes because they bring benefits to livestock health, productivity and available household expenditure on childhood education and food purchase

(Marsh et al., 2016). They also facilitate business opportunities for more than half of the bottom billion farmers who keep livestock in rural areas, but these are the people who risk being squeezed out of the sector if land grabs for large-scale production systems become dominant.

Other opportunities in smart villages come from aquaculture, because almost one-sixth of all animal protein consumed on the planet comes from fish. With the increase in demand for animal protein, aquaculture represents a significant source of improved livelihoods. But the same stresses of densification and yield improvement will occur with fish as with livestock, and therefore efforts to improve the genetic stock of fish and to preserve biodiversity will necessarily have to be strengthened. To date only 18 out of the 400 species of cultured fish have been subject to significant genetic improvement programmes (Canales and Jones, 2016).

Several elements discussed in this section on stemming biodiversity losses from agricultural practices are being addressed in entrepreneurial prototypes of smart villages that are being developed in India. Gram Oorja (2015), not unlike Chhotkei, Odisha mentioned previously, consists of a comprehensive enterprise established by four young entrepreneurs who realised that renewable energy could have a significant role in enhancing rural livelihoods. The aim was to establish smart villages that fulfil the electricity, cooking fuel and water needs of tribal communities in remote off-grid regions using solar PV micro-grids, biogas-based cooking grids and solar pumps for irrigation. Operational and financial stability is achieved through an effective metering and tariff mechanism. Micro-grids support productive enterprises such as a flour mill, rice huller, water pumps, and education and health institutions (Figure 13.3D). Biogas cooking stoves reduce the burden on women for firewood collection, and increase time for the family, produce cottage industries and reduce the burden on forests. Where cattle are present in villages the availability of cow dung enables biogas production.

Improving Biodiversity

Overexploitation of genetic resources is perceived as a continuing threat to biodiversity, though a meta-analysis of 44 published papers demonstrated that no substantial reduction in the regional diversity of crop varieties released by plant breeders has taken place in more developed countries. A significant reduction of 6 per cent in diversity in the 1960s as compared with the diversity in the 1950s was observed, but after the 1960s and 1970s, breeders have been able to again increase the diversity in released varieties. Similarly, growers of garden beans, garlic, lettuce, peppers, squash and tomatoes had many more choices in 2004 than they did in 1903, though growers of beets, cabbage, radishes and turnips had vastly fewer choices (van de Wouw et al., 2010; Heald and Chapman, 2011).

Agroecology

Employing methods close to nature has many attractions for smart villages and they have options to improve BES by the adoption of conservation agriculture with minimum disturbance of the soil, using crop remains to protect the soil and planting a variety of crops to achieve biodiversity rather than monoculture production systems. Conservation agriculture makes greater use of natural fertilisers in view of the paucity of nitrogen fertilisers in several LDCs, though many African countries have been slow adopters suggesting small-holder farming is undergoing a slow evolution rather than a revolution. Research into 'push–pull' or 'stimulo-deterrent diversion-ary' strategies exploits natural semiochemicals that repel insect pests from the crop ('push') and attract them into trap crops like *Desmodium* spp., which in turn produce a nitrogen fertiliser through their nodular activity (Figure 13.4). The strategy increases yields of maize substantially in areas of Kenya where stem borer and parasitic *Striga* are prevalent pests. It makes soil more fertile through nitrogen fixation, gives natural mulching, better biomass and erosion control, and provides high-value animal fodder for improved milk production, all achieved without any chemical burden (Hassanali et al., 2008; Khan et al., 2008).

Agroecology is less well authenticated or developed as an agriculture production system and technologies such as 'push–pull' may have limited geographical spread, but advantages accrue from multiple applications of rhizobia nitrogen-fixing bacteria and mycorrhizal fungi that greatly enhance the ability of roots to extract various nutrients from the soil. Neither the bacteria nor the fungi can survive without the host plant that in return supplies oxygen

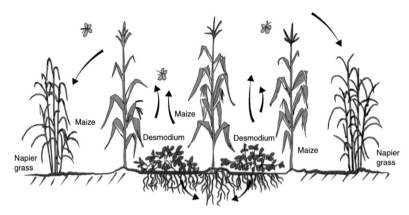

Figure 13.4 'Push–pull' inter-cropping where natural chemicals from Napier grass pull in moths to lay eggs; natural chemicals from *Desmodium* repel moths (push) (Hassanali et al., 2008). Figure from Pickett et al. (2014), used under a Creative Commons BY 3.0 licence.

and products of photosynthesis in the form of proteins and carbohydrates, illustrating biodiversity in action. Similarly, a mixture of earthworms and arbuscular mycorrhizal fungi improve biomass above ground and nitrogen uptake of clover plants (Zarea et al., 2009; Ammann, 2012; Hunter, 2016). Biopesticides reduce chemical usage, but so far they are not competitive economically. Biocontrol agents, the natural resistance of crops to infection, the biodiversity of the soil microbiome particularly in sub-Saharan Africa, and how certain plants exhibit a systemic acquired disease resistance are topics of incomplete knowledge (Loomans, 2007; Broekgaarden et al., 2011; Fu and Dong, 2013) and future results are awaited with great interest (Chen et al., 2012; van den Oever-van den Elsen, 2016).

Smart villages use agroecology to produce biologically diverse landscapes, minimise pollution of natural habitats by reducing toxic runoff into aquatic systems, modify farming systems to mimic natural ecosystems using mosaics of new and improved perennial crops and agroforests, and use remote sensing for landscape planning and monitoring (Scherr and McNeely, 2008; Dushku et al., 2007). Markets and reward mechanisms for producers of certified sustainable products will need to be developed to provide a supportive framework for smart villages to follow this approach. The landscapes will appeal to Pope Francis, who in the landmark Encyclical *Laudato Si* expressed his preference for the practice of 'agroecology' rather than 'sustainable intensification', though he recognised that neither could claim legitimately to ignore the utility of genetic engineering (Pope Francis, 2015), a topic that has been explored in depth elsewhere (Ammann and Ammann, 2004; PAS, 2009; Potrykus and Ammann, 2010).

Orphan Crops

Smart villages need smart foods (ICRISAT, 2017), yet most of the world's food needs are provided by some 30 species of plants whereas at least 12,000 species have been named as edible. Only three crops – maize, wheat and rice – account for about 50 per cent of the world's consumption of calories and protein, and they attract the biggest amount of research, development, policy support and investment. Understandable concerns have emerged about the possible risks posed by selection that leads to a narrowing of the genetic base from which crops are selected, to a genetic erosion of the crop gene pools, and to a loss of BEF.

Sustainable nutrition has become a United Nations (UN) priority to counter malnutrition which is influenced by environmental degradation, water scarcity and migration of the labour force, among other issues. The African Orphan Crops Consortium (AOCC) (2018) is a partnership that works to make high-nutritional value crops grown by African farmers available to rural and urban consumers. The plan is to undertake genome and transcriptome sequencing, develop tools to assess genetic diversity in crops, and support new breeding programmes. Pigeon pea, an important crop in Asia, Africa and Central and South America which is grown on nearly five million hectares worldwide, is the first orphan crop to have a completed genome analysis (ICRISAT, 2012). Alongside their commercial potential, many of the underused crops provide important BEF as they are adapted to marginal soil and climate conditions.

Smart villages take advantage of the nutritional advantages of crops such as millets because they are high in micronutrients and antioxidants; they are gluten free and can provide the full daily allowance of iron and zinc (ICRISAT, 2017). Millets require 30 per cent less water than maize, grow faster (maturing in half the time of wheat), put less stress on the environment and grow on minimal pesticides/fertiliser. In times of drought they are often the last crop standing, making them potentially critical for addressing the challenges of climate change. While the breeding of millets has received a lot less investment than many other crops, they have the potential to increase yields by up to threefold and produce biomass for alternative use (for example, fodder, biofuels and brewing).

Biofortification of plants helps to overcome human deficiencies in dietary micronutrients through the production of nutrient-dense food fortified with iron, zinc and vitamin A. The process has already been developed in rice, cassava, banana, maize, sweet potato (provitamin A), beans, pearl millet, rice and wheat (iron and zinc). The best-known example of the transgenic approach is 'Golden Rice' fortified with provitamin A, which smart villages may adopt once tendentious regulatory processes have been resolved (Potrykus, 2010). Nonetheless, a diversity in food supplies achieved with orphan crops would complement the need of fortification since a varied diet can be more nutritious.

Organic Procedures

Organic farming continues to be hotly debated because of its claims about the exclusion of the use of most synthetic pesticides and fertilisers, and the benefits for biodiversity compared with the high-yielding methods that rely on genetic engineering and pesticides. Organic yields are typically 19–25 per cent less than conventional ones (Seufert et al., 2012; Ponisio et al., 2015). A meta-analysis shows that on average organic farming increased species richness by about 30 per cent (optimal soils, 5 per cent; bad soils, up to 60 per cent) (Tuck et al., 2014). Plants benefit the most, as do arthropods, birds and microbes, though the effect on soil organisms was less marked. Three-quarters of the studies were carried out in Europe, while three-quarters of the land under organic production is outside Europe. This means that the biodiversity benefits of growing bananas, cassava or cacao beans organically remain to be assessed. Organic methods, therefore, could help smart villages to stem the loss of biodiversity albeit with lower yields but commanding higher prices.

Genetic Engineering

Where they choose to do so, smart villages can gain access to genetically modified (GM) planting materials that take advantage of the knowledge by which we understand in a more systematic way the controls of a world whose mechanisms are complex and delicately balanced. The first-generation techniques successfully modified a few simple input traits in a small number of commercial commodity crops leading to a reduction of chemical usage to control destructive pests and diseases and combat weeds. Second-generation technologies improved consumer benefits through increased food production, better nutritional quality in terms of dietary micronutrients, and greater economic benefits. Third-generation technologies promise new opportunities as genes can be transferred from the same or related species (cisgenesis) instead of different sources (transgenesis), the specific coding region of a gene from the same species inserted, and gene-editing systems used to edit and silence genes by simple 'cut-and-paste' techniques at low cost with great precision – all part of an ever-expanding GM toolbox (Vitale et al., 2008; Beyer, 2010; Morris, 2011; Brookes and Barfoot, 2017; Quéteir, 2016).

Insect-resistant and herbicide-tolerant GM crops stem the loss of biodiversity by decreasing the environmental impact of chemical herbicides and insecticides in the environment. In a meta-analysis of 147 studies, the use of GM soybean, maize and cotton decreased chemical pesticide use by 37 per cent and increased crop yields and farmer profits by 22 per cent and 68 per cent, respectively. The release of greenhouse gas emissions declined through less fuel use, and if 'no tillage' production systems were used more carbon was stored in the soil. Thus there were very significant net global economic benefits at the farm level amounting to $98.2 billion in the period 1996–2012 (Figure 13.5) (Klümper and Qaim, 2014).

Moreover, herbicide-tolerant GM crops that deal with weeds had beneficial effects on soil fertility because conservation tillage meant that there were fewer tractor passes in the field (Fawcett and Towery, 2002). Insect-resistant GM maize did not affect insect biodiversity, and non-target insects including a whole range of butterflies had a better chance of survival than in conventional crop fields. Similar messages came from studies in wheat transformed with different gene inserts (Wolfenbarger et al., 2008; von Burg et al., 2011; Carpenter, 2011; Resende et al., 2016).

The uptake of GM crops as an agricultural innovation has been one of the fastest in history, with LDCs now growing more of them by area than industrial countries (PAS, 2009; Potrykus and Ammann, 2010; Heap, 2016b). As a food market it is expected to grow from the present

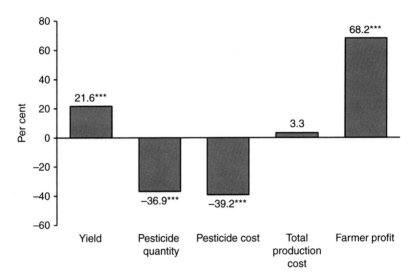

Figure 13.5 Insect-resistant and herbicide-resistant genetically modified (GM) crops stem the loss of biodiversity by decreasing the impact of chemicals on the environment; columns show the percentage difference between GM and non-GM crops. Figure from Klümper and Qaim (2014), used under a Creative Commons BY 4.0 licence.

value of about 112 m to 130 m tonnes by 2021. About 80 per cent of farmers who have adopted GM crops are smallholder farmers because of the attraction of higher yields. The use of more environmentally benign herbicides reduces the pressure to convert additional land into agricultural use, which is good for BES. Smart villages that find that biotic constraints such as pests, diseases or drought are not easily addressed through conventional means may be faced with the prospect of turning to other alternatives such as GM crops to add to practices that aim to close the yield gap and improve their farm income (Figure 13.6) (Zhang et al., 2016; Brookes and Barfoot, 2017).

No evidence of hazards from GM crops has been recorded in terms of human health, environment or food in over 2000 reports (Chassy, 2010; Parrott, 2010; Alessandro et al., 2014). However, a rigorous monitoring regime will be important to ensure that no deleterious effects arise in the longer term through new traits being passed to wild relatives (out-crossing), or a reduced number of preferred varieties that results in greater risks of disease incidence and spread. Some GM

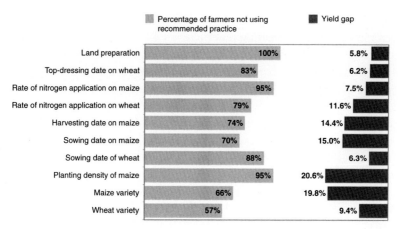

Figure 13.6 Closing the yield gap of crops by using recommended practices (Zhang et al., 2016). Reprinted by permission from Springer Nature from Zhang et al. (2016), 'Closing yield gaps in China by empowering smallholder farmers', *Nature*, 537: 671–674.

technologies that work well today will become less effective as certain insects evolve resistance. Insects that feed on GM crops can, in some cases, start to develop a resistance to the protein that usually kills them, so this is something to keep an eye on in the future. An intriguing option is to merge GM plants with organic agriculture, a synergy that would take advantage of an environment with diminished chemical applications and soil enriched with organic material, respectively (Ammann, 2008, 2009).

The Continuing Tension between Europe and Africa

In the African continent agriculture contributes more than 25 per cent of GDP and employs about 60 per cent of the labour force. The attitude to GM crops is greatly influenced by the European perspective so that only three out of 52 African countries (South Africa, Sudan and Burkina Faso) have enacted the obligatory National Biosafety legislative and regulatory procedures and developed GM crops commercially. Forty-five African countries have ratified the *Cartagena Protocol on Biosafety to the Convention on Biological Diversity* in 2009, a risk-based procedure that ignores benefits, and a prerequisite before GM crops can be considered for commercial production (Heap, 2016b).

The negativity in many European countries toward GM crops has been interpreted as indicating that there is something to fear about the technology and this will restrict the uptake of new technologies in smart villages. Recent reports from Spain, however, suggest that perceptions in Europe may be changing as the benefits from the adoption of GM maize become increasingly apparent. Insect-resistant maize increased yields by 7–10 per cent compared with conventional maize, depending on the geographical area and the pest incidence. Environmental benefits included water savings equivalent to the provision of water for 0.75 m people per year, a reduced hydrological footprint, fewer sprayings with pesticides, less pressure on land use and a net fixation of additional carbon (Areal, 2016; Kathage et al., 2016).

Other Tools for Engineering Biodiversity

Looking to the future, synthetic biology, nanotechnology and genetic engineering offer new solutions to the challenges of biodiversity loss and in due course they could enrich smart villages. While the Earth is in the midst of its sixth mass extinction with 100 species estimated to be disappearing every day, questions are raised about restoring extinct species, usually animals, using new advances in genetic engineering such as the CRISPR-Cas9 revolution (Shultz, 2016). So far, applications of genetic engineering typically concern the transfer of individual genes between cells. Synthetic biology involves the assembly of new sequences of DNA and even new genomes, while nanotechnology can reduce the application of crop protection products and nutrient losses in fertiliser applications, alongside integrated soil fertility management. Some of these technologies build on classical genetic engineering, but many elements are entirely novel. Cells can be equipped with new functions and entire biological systems can be designed so that synthetic organisms have much larger-scale interventions than classical genetic engineering. Current trends show that these technologies can be used to create organisms that could help ecological restoration, combat reservoirs of human viruses, and prevent infectious diseases like white nose syndrome (a fungal disease that affects hibernating bats).

Tools can be provided to better understand biological systems and produce valuable products such as drugs, fuels or raw materials for industrial processes as well as food. For these reasons synthetic biology has been linked to future economic growth and job creation worth billions of dollars (EC, 2016). Gene drive systems that change the genomes of populations of mosquitoes and make them less able to cause malaria (Hammond et al., 2015) could facilitate the rapid spread of genes through wild species, or lessen the threat from invasive species or from other insect vectors of diseases that pose significant threats to BEF (Royal Society, 2015). This world of research has been described as rewriting 'the code of life in the wild', but great care is needed as little is known about how synthetic organisms introduced into the environment will evolve or be degraded, or interact with natural organisms and transfer genetic material to wild populations through horizontal or vertical transfer with adverse effects on native species, habitats or food webs (Redford et al., 2013).

The research pipeline contains a raft of other initiatives relevant to the challenge of stemming biodiversity loss – bees genetically modified to resist pesticides or mites, microorganisms engineered to convert sugars in biomass into biofuels or pharmaceuticals, slow-release fertilisers that enhance plant growth rates, benign life-forms that facilitate the provision of clean water and reduce the stress on BES, and genomic coefficients based on single-nucleotide polymorphisms that give the exact proportion of the genome that is homozygous or shared by two individuals – information that helps to maintain genetic diversity and overcome inbreeding depression (Fernández et al., 2016).

New technologies of the present, and promising solutions of the future, can play a pivotal and positive role in stemming biodiversity loss – but they are not enough. Opposition to technological advances has a long history and can impede application. Belgian philosophers and scientists have turned to cognitive science to try to understand why the opposition to GM crops, for instance, has become widespread despite the positive contributions they can make (Blanke et al., 2015). Typical responses are those of essentialism because technology portrays DNA as the essence of an organism, teleological thinking that portrays GM technology as unnatural and playing God, and romanticism that sees technologies as contamination and interventionist of nature. For smart villages, therefore, technological advances need to be set in the context of a wide range of normative considerations and different ethical demands (CISL, 2016; Blanke et al., 2015).

Comment

Biodiversity has been described as a natural insurance policy against sudden environmental change because it underpins a wealth of beneficial ecosystem services, such as water, soil fertility and pollination, on which all depend. A worldview in the Global South is that nature constitutes an integral part of people's livelihoods and material well-being, so that biodiversity with its ecosystem services and functions is central to their culture, religion and identity, and therefore is rightly conserved (Kaphengst et al., 2014). For some, it is a strong utilitarian argument that matters – the good of the many; for others there is an overriding moral obligation of fairness and technology justice, concerns that people have access to the use of technology. From an environmental point of view, it is how technology can be used in a way that avoids negative effects; the voice of the rural poor who live off the grid has the right to be heard in relation to biodiversity and its services on which they depend.

Georgina Mace (2014) speaks of the changing relationship between nature and people as it has emerged over the past 50 years. Originally, the emphasis was on 'nature for itself' and species, wilderness and protection. It was followed by 'nature despite people' when there was exploitation, habitat loss and extinction that demanded natural resource management. Then 'nature for people' emerged when ecosystem services and functions were seen as commodities that provide food or clean water for growing populations. Today, it is a two-way interaction of 'people and nature', recognising socio-ecology, adaptability, resilience and value systems. It is in this latter frame that we place smart villages, since they can act as significant agents instead of patients in helping to stem biodiversity loss.

Early insights have emerged about smart villages and how they could help the process of development through energy access and also stem biodiversity losses, and we summarise a few of these interim findings (Holmes, 2016).

First, smart villages are attracting international interest and proto-smart villages are under construction in several countries. Not all elements of our smart villages concept have been incorporated into a single prototype, but we see the potential of energy access from renewable sources combined with ICT in helping to stem biodiversity losses and the mitigation of fossil fuel usage. The media have a particular role to play in raising awareness of the potential. Journalists at our South East Asia workshop in Sri Lanka expressed their goals in terms of 'learning about sustainability and energy, contributing to a better quality of life in their countries, improving environmental coverage, gaining skills to write in-depth stories and even books, improving business coverage, and learning from peers about story opportunities and challenges' (Smart Villages Initiative, 2015d).

Second, smart villages and access to energy do not automatically or rapidly solve the challenges of biodiversity loss or rural poverty (Attigah and Mayer-Tasch, 2013; IFAD, 2016). Neither happens in isolation but as part of a broader process of incremental structural transformation, with rising agricultural productivity and productive enterprises in the agricultural and rural non-farm economy. Social impacts of greater life expectancy, improved education and better health care arise from the conditions that help to foster entrepreneurship and the empowerment of women and youth, leading to changes in lifestyle and increased income generation.

Third, symbiotic private and public sector investment with enterprise growth capital funds are needed to de-risk and bridge the financial 'valley of death' if smart villages are to become sustainable and replicable. At the company level there is difficulty in accessing affordable working capital because of the lack of a successful track record. This results in high perceived risk in the finance community and consequently high interest rates, exacerbated by the banking sector's lack of familiarity with off-grid energy. At the domestic level, investment is required for appliances such as sewing machines, food mixers and bread bakers. At the village cooperative level, investment is needed for grinding equipment, welding tools, refrigerators and water pumps.

As Simon Trace, former CEO of the NGO, Practical Action, remarks 'it is an immense injustice that humanity has not managed to ensure universal access to technologies critical to achieving a minimum reasonable standard of living, technologies that have generally been in existence and use for decades and, in some cases, centuries. Technology Justice, in this respect, must mean establishing a global governance process that ensures these gaps in technology access are addressed and closed, something it has long been in our power to do.' Our society chooses to subsidise the coal, gas and oil industries that cause harm to local populations by air pollution and the effects of floods, droughts and storms. Such harmful effects are estimated to cost US$5.5tr each year, in comparison with a woefully low investment in renewable energy of $120bn (Trace, 2016).

Fourth, sustainable education and training in smart villages will be needed at all levels to enable rural communities to climb the energy escalator, to close the yield gap of crops using recommended practices, and to understand the benefits of biodiversity and ecosystem services. These levels range from local farmers and technicians to engineers, product designers to university researchers and local entrepreneurs trained to run a productive enterprise. The financial community needs to familiarise itself with the issues associated with off-grid energy schemes, and government institutions need to build capacity in policymaking and regulation. The mobile telephony industry has a key role as opportunities and responsibilities in LDCs grow exponentially and smart villages become scalable.

Fifth, governments will need to provide supportive policy and regulatory environments to attract private sector capital into smart villages, simplify licensing frameworks, cut red tape and allow sufficient breathing space in respect of taxation regimes for businesses to get off the ground. The Government of India has decreed that any high-value companies have to spend at least 2 per cent of the previous three years' average net profits on Corporate Social Responsibility (CSR) initiatives. Currently, a cumulative sum of US$5.2bn is estimated to be available in India for organisations concerned not only with maximising shareholder value but also with taking steps to improve the quality of life of rural communities and people. As part of CSR, a business can set up renewable energy technologies like solar PV and biogas to serve energy needs, which has significance for smart villages by potentially linking with small-scale farming communities in over 600,000 villages.

The concept of smart villages as a path of rural development is multifaceted and we have focused on potential contributions to stemming biodiversity losses. 'Smart' in this context means using modern renewable energy to replace fossil fuels in rural communities to reduce biodiversity loss and mitigate climate change, improving the efficiency of biomass usage, developing sustainable intensification of food production with high-quality seed and best practices of agronomy, and the protection of genetic resources by the preservation of new and existing stocks aided by a raft of new technologies. Smart villages are sensitive to the socio-economic realities of smallholder farmers who will have lived hitherto off the grid, because indigenous knowledge holds deep value (Clancy and Vernooy, 2016). A full awareness of the benefits of biodiversity is an ethical imperative, particularly with the worrying consumption of the world's cultivable areas by urban expansion estimated to be at the rate of 1 Mha annually (Clancy and Vernooy, 2016; Bren d'Amour et al., 2017), and because of the lack of a directed and integrated international programme devoted to the rural environment and its communities on account of a persistent urban predilection.

Acknowledgements

We are deeply indebted to Professor Klaus Ammann, who gave us access to his comprehensive bibliography on biodiversity, Professor Georgina Mace for her expert advice, and Drs Claudia Canales, Terry van Gevelt and colleagues engaged in the Smart Villages Initiative.

References

African Orphan Crops Consortium. 2018. *Healthy Africa through Nutritious, Diverse and Local Food Crops*. http://africanorphancrops.org/.

Alessandro, N., Manzo, A., Veronesi, F. & Rosellini, D. 2014. An overview of the last 10 years of genetically engineered crop safety research. *Critical Reviews in Biotechnology*, 34: 77–88.

Ammann, K. 2008. Feature: Integrated farming: Why organic farmers should use transgenic crops. *New Biotechnology*, 25: 101–107.

2009. Feature: Why farming with high tech methods should integrate elements of organic agriculture. *New Biotechnology*, 25: 378–388.

2012. Advancing the cause in emerging economies. In D. J. Bennett & R. C. Jennings (Eds.), *Successful Agricultural Innovation in Emerging Economies*: 400–417. Cambridge: Cambridge University Press.

2016. *The Debate on Biodiversity and Biotechnology*. ASK-Force Contribution 11. www.ask-force.org/web/AF-11-Biodiversity/AF-11 -Biodiversity-Agriculture-20160526.pdf.

Ammann, K. & Papazova Ammann, B. 2004. Factors influencing public policy development in agricultural biotechnology. In P. Christou & H. Klee (Eds.), *Handbook of Plant Biotechnology; Part 9: Risk Assessment of Transgenic Crops*. Hoboken, NJ: John Wiley.

Areal, F. J. 2016. *Benefits of Bt maize in Spain (1998–2015)*. Benefits from an economic, social and environmental viewpoint. Madrid, Spain:

Fundacion Antama. www.europabio.org/sites/default/files/2016%20S panish%20benefits%20report-%201998–2015%20-%20english.pdf.

Attigah, B. & Mayer-Tasch, L. 2013. The impact of electricity access on economic development – A literature review. In L. Mayer-Tasch, M. Mukherjee & K. Reiche (Eds.), *Productive Use of Energy (PRODUSE): Measuring Impacts of Electrification on Micro-Enterprises in Sub-Saharan Africa*. Eschborn, Germany: Deutsche Gesellschaft für Internationale Zusammenarbeit (GIZ) GmbH.

Barasa, M. 2015. A way of life: Energy provision in Africa. In R. B. Heap (Ed.), *Smart Villages: New Thinking for Off-Grid Communities Worldwide*: 13–20. Cambridge: Banson.

Beyer, P. 2010. Golden rice and 'golden' crops for human nutrition. *New Biotechnology*, 27: 478–481

Blancke, S., Van Breusegem, F., De Jaeger, G., Braeckman, J. & Van Montagu, M. 2015. Fatal attraction: The intuitive appeal of GMO opposition. *Trends in Plant Science*, 20(7): 414–418.

Bogdanski, A. 2012. Integrated food–energy systems for climate-smart agriculture. *Agriculture & Food Security*, 1(1): 9.

Bogdanski, A., Dubois, O. & Chuluunbaatar, D. 2010a. *Integrated Food Energy Systems – Project Assessment in China and Vietnam, 11–29 October*. Climate, Energy and Tenure Division, Food and Agriculture Organization of the United Nations, Rome. www.fao.org /energy/33467-0140d2e14b981e9923be4670c73e05c95.pdf.

Bogdanski, A., Dubois, O., Jamieson, C. & Krell, R. 2010b. *Making Integrated Food/Energy Systems Work for People and Climate – An Overview*. Environment and Natural Sources Management Working Paper 45, Food and Agriculture Organization of the United Nations, Rome. www.fao.org/docrep/013/i2044e/i2044e00.htm.

Bren d'Amour, C., Reitsma, F., Baiocchi, G., Barthel, S., Guneralp, B., Erb, K.-H., Haberl, H., Creutzig, F. & Seto, K. C. 2017. Future urban land expansion and implications for global croplands. *Proceedings of the National Academy of Sciences*, 114(34): 8939–8944.

Broekgaarden, C., Snoeren, T. A., Dicke, M. & Vosman, B. 2011. Exploiting natural variation to identify insect-resistance genes. *Plant Biotechnology Journal*, 9(8): 819–825.

Brookes, G. & Barfoot, P. 2017. *GM Crops: Global Socio-economic and Environmental Impacts 1996–2015*. United Kingdom: PG Economics Ltd.

Canales, C. 2017. Mixed farming systems and global food security. *Biosciences for Farming in Africa* (blog), May 25. http://b4fa.org/mixe d-farming-systems-global-food-security/.

Canales, C. & Jones, B. 2016. *Livestock Breeding and Other Advances in Animal, Insect and Fish Genetic Research for Africa*, The Genetics for

Africa – Strategies and Opportunities project workshop report, ILRI, Nairobi, September 10–11. London: Science Technology and Innovation for Development Ltd.

Cardinale, B. J., Duffy, J. E., Gonzalez, A., Hooper, D. U., Perrings, C., Venail, P., Narwani, A., Mace, G. M., Tilman, D. & Wardle, D. A. 2012. Biodiversity loss and its impact on humanity. *Nature*, 486(7401): 59–67.

Carpenter, J. E. 2011. Impact of GM crops on biodiversity. *GM Crops*, 2(1): 7–23.

CBD. 1992. *Convention on Biological Diversity*. www.cbd.int/convention /text/.

Chassy, B. M. 2010. Food safety risks and consumer health. *New Biotechnology*, 27(5): 534–544.

Chavan, S. B., Handa, A. K. & Toky, P. 2016. *Innovative Agroforestry for Environmental Security in India*. World Agriculture No. 1613, September. www.world-agriculture.net/article/innovative-agroforestry -for-environmental-security-in-india.

Chen, X., Vosman, B., Visser, R. G., van der Vlugt, R. A. & Broekgaarden, C. 2012. High throughput phenotyping for aphid resistance in large plant collections. *Plant Methods*, 8(1): 33.

CISL. 2016. *Biodiversity and Ecosystem Services in Corporate Natural Capital Accounting: Synthesis Report*. Cambridge: Cambridge Institute for Sustainability Leadership.

Clancy, E. & Vernooy, R. 2016. *Realizing Farmers' Rights through Community-Based Agricultural Biodiversity Management*: 1–8. Rome, Italy: Biodiversity International.

Collier, P. 2008. *The Bottom Billion*. Oxford: Oxford University Press.

2015. *Achieving Sustainability: Should People Be Fitted to Policies, or Policies to People?* Centre for Corporate Responsibility and Sustainability, University of Zurich, March 19. www.ccrs.uzh.ch/Vera nstaltungen.html.

Dale, B. E., Anderson, J. E., Brown, R. C., Csonka, S., Dale, V. H., Herwick, G., Jackson, R. D., Jordan, N., Kaffka, S., Kline, K. L., Lynd, L. R., Malmstrom, C., Ong, R. G., Richard, T. L., Taylor, C. & Wang, M. Q. 2014. Take a closer look: Biofuels can support environmental, economic and social goals. *Environmental Science & Technology*, 48(13): 7200–7203.

Dasgupta, P. 2001. *Human Well-Being and the Natural Environment*. Oxford: Oxford University Press.

Department for Business, Innovation and Skills. 2013. *Smart Cities: Background Paper*. London: Department for Business, Innovation and Skills, UK Government. https://assets.publishing.service.gov.uk/govern

ment/uploads/system/uploads/attachment_data/file/246019/bis-13–12 09-smart-cities-background-paper-digital.pdf.

de Ponti, T., Rijk, B. & van Ittersum, M. K. 2012. The crop yield gap between organic and conventional agriculture. *Agricultural Systems*, 108: 1–9.

Dileepkumar, G. 2014. Knowledge to the poor revolution taking high-end scientific knowledge to the farm fields through innovative ICT tools and knowledge sharing approaches for a food secure future. Proceedings of the Winter School on Livestock Based Livelihood Options: Current Status, Emerging Issues and Future Scenario in Combating Agrarian Crisis, New Delhi, India, November 7. http://oar.icrisat.org/8712/1/dileep_article.pdf.

Dobbs, R., Remes, J., Manyika, J., Roxburgh, C., Smit, S. & Schaer, F. 2012. *Urban World: Cities and the Rise of the Consuming Class*. McKinsey Global Institute Report. www.mckinsey.com/featured-insights/urbanization/urban-world-cities-and-the-rise-of-the-consuming-class.

Dushku, A., Brown, S., Pearson, T., Shoch, D. & Khare, A. 2007. Remote sensing. In *Farming with Nature: The Science and Practice of Ecoagriculture*: 250–264. Washington, DC: Island Press.

EASAC. 2017. *Multi-functionality and Sustainability in the European Union's Forests*. EASAC Policy Report 32, April.

EC. 2016. Science for Environment Policy, 2016. In *Synthetic Biology and Biodiversity*. Future Brief 15. Produced for the European Commission DG Environment by the Science Communication Unit, UWE, Bristol. http://ec.europa.eu/science-environment-policy.

Ehrlich, P. R. & Harte, J. 2015. Opinion: To feed the world in 2050 will require a global revolution. *Proceedings of the National Academy of Sciences*, 112(48): 14743–14744.

El Bassam, N. 2010. Integrated energy farming for rural development and poverty alleviation. In *Resource Management towards Sustainable Agriculture and Development*: 252–262. Jodhpur, India: Agribios International. www.ifeed.org/pdf/Publication_IEF-for-Rural-Development-and-Poverty-Alleviation.pdf.

Energy4Impact. 2016. www.energy4impact.org/10-years-impact.

Fahrig, L., Girard, J., Duro, D., Pasher, J., Smith, A., Javorek, S., King, D., Lindsay, K. F., Mitchell, S. & Tischendorf, L. 2015. Farmlands with smaller crop fields have higher within-field biodiversity. *Agriculture, Ecosystems & Environment*, 200: 219–234.

FAO. 2010. Agricultural biotechnologies in developing countries: Options and opportunities in crops, forestry, livestock, fisheries and agro-industry to face the challenges of food insecurity and climate change (ABDC-10). Current status and options for crop biotechnologies in developing countries. FAO International Technical Conference, Guadalajar, Mexico, March 1–4.

2012. *State of the World's Forests (2012)*. www.fao.org/docrep/016/i30 10e/i3010e.pdf.

2015. *World Deforestation Slows Down as More Forests Are Better Managed (2015)*. www.fao.org/news/story/en/item/326911/icode/.

Fawcett, R. & Towery, D. 2002. *Conservation Tillage and Plant Biotechnology: How New Technologies Can Improve the Environment by Reducing the Need to Plow*. Conservation Technology Information Center. www.ctic.org/media/pdf/Biotech2003.pdf.

Fernández, J., Toro, M. A., Gómez-Romano, F. & Villanueva, B. 2016. The use of genomic information can enhance the efficiency of conservation programs. *Animal Frontiers*, 6(1): 59–64.

Freese, B. 2016. How gene editing will change agriculture. *Successful Farming*. www.agriculture.com/technology/how-gene-editing-will -change-agriculture.

Fu, Z. Q. & Dong, X. 2013. Systemic acquired resistance: Turning local infection into global defense. *Annual Review of Plant Biology*, 64(1): 839–863.

Gabriel, D., Sait, S. M., Hodgson, J. A., Schmutz, U., Kunin, W. E. & Benton, T. G. 2010. Scale matters: The impact of organic farming on biodiversity at different spatial scales. *Ecology Letters*, 13(7): 858–869.

Gebreyes, W. A., Dupouy-Camet, J., Newport, M. J., Oliveira, C. J. B., Schlesinger, L. S., Saif, Y. M., et al. 2014. The Global One Health Paradigm: Challenges and opportunities for tackling infectious diseases at the human, animal, and environment interface in low-resource settings. *PLoS Neglected Tropical Diseases* 8(11): e3257.

Ghosh, A. & Agrawal, S. 2015. *Sustainable Solar Irrigation*. www.business -standard.com/article/opinion/arunabha-ghosh-shalu-agrawal-sustainable -solar-irrigation-115081701282_1.html.

Global Alliance for Clean Cookstoves. 2016. *2016 Progress Report*. http:// cleancookstoves.org/resources/reports/2016progress.html.

Godfray, H. C. J., Beddington, J. R., Crute, I. R., Haddad, L., Lawrence, D., Muir, J. F., Pretty, J., Robinson, S., Thomas, S. M. & Toulmin, C. 2010. Food security: The challenge of feeding 9 billion people. *Science*, 327 (5967): 812–818.

González, C., Schiek, B., Mwendia, S. & Prager, S. D. 2016. *Improved Forages and Milk Production in East Africa*. A case study in the series: Economic foresight for understanding the role of investments in agriculture for the global food system. Cali, Colombia: Centro Internacional de Agricultura Tropical (CIAT).

Gram Oorja. 2015. www.gramoorja.in/.

Gressel, J. 2007. *Genetic Glass Ceilings: Transgenics for Crop Biodiversity.* Baltimore: Johns Hopkins University Press.

Guruswamy, L. 2011. Energy poverty. *Annual Review of Environment and Resources*, 36(1): 139–161.

Hammond, A., Galizi, R., Kyrou, K., Simoni, A., Siniscalchi, C., Katsanos, D., Gribble, M., Baker, D., Marois, E., Russell, S., Burt, A., Windbichler, N., Crisanti, A. & Nolan, T. 2015. A CRISPR-Cas9 gene drive system targeting female reproduction in the malaria mosquito vector *Anopheles gambiae*. *Nature Biotechnology*, 34: 78–83.

Hassanali, A., Herren, H., Khan, Z. R., Pickett, J. A. & Woodcock, C. M. 2008. Integrated pest management: The push–pull approach for controlling insect pests and weeds of cereals, and its potential for other agricultural systems including animal husbandry. *Philosophical Transactions of the Royal Society B*, 363: 611–621.

HCSA. 2016. *HCS Convergence Agreement.* http://highcarbonstock.org/wp-content/uploads/2016/11/Final-HCS-Convergence-Agreement-.pdf.

Heald, P. J. & Chapman, S. 2011. *Veggie Tales: Pernicious Myths about Patents, Innovation, and Crop Diversity in the Twentieth Century.* Illinois Program in Law, Behavior and Social Science Paper No. LBSS11-34. Illinois Public Law Research Paper No. 11-03. http://ssrn.com/paper=1928920.

Heap, R. B. 2016a. *Is Biomass a Sustainable Energy Solution for Off-Grid Villages in Developing Countries?* http://e4sv.org/biomass-sustainable-energy-solution-off-grid-villages-developing-countries/.

2016b. How can genetically-modified (GM crops) help to feed the world? In J. Bicak (Ed.), *On Stars, Oceans and Mankind*, vol. 99: 179–243. Prague: Learned Society of Czech Republic. www.learned.cz/userfiles/pdf/publikace/bicak-text.pdf.

Holmes, J. 2016. *Interim Review of Findings: The Smart Villages Initiative.* http://e4sv.org/wp-content/uploads/2016/04/TR05-The-Smart-Villages-Initiative-Interim-Review-of-Findings.pdf.

Holmes, J. & van Gevelt, T. 2015. Energy for development. In R. B. Heap (Ed.), *Smart Villages: New Thinking for Off-Grid Communities Worldwide*: 13–20. Cambridge: Banson.

Hooper, D. U., Adair, E. C., Cardinale, B. J., Byrnes, J. E. K., Hungate, B. A., Matulich, K. L., Gonzalez, A., Duffy, J. E., Gamfeldt, L. & O'Connor, M. I. 2012. A global synthesis reveals biodiversity loss as a major driver of ecosystem change. *Nature*, 486: 105–108.

Hunter, P. 2016. Plant microbiomes and sustainable agriculture. *EMBO Reports*, 17(12): 1696–1699.

Hurley-Depret, M. 2016. *Terrat, Tanzania: A 'Smart Village'.* http://e4sv.org/terrat-tanzania-smart-village/.

ICRISAT. 2012. http://oar.icrisat.org/9549/1/Pigeonpea%20Genome%20pos ter.pdf.

2017. www.icrisat.org/smartfood/.

IFAD. 2016. *Rural Development Report 2016; Fostering Inclusive Rural Transformation.* www.ifad.org/web/rdr/reports.

Kaphengst, T., Davis, M., Gerstetter, C., Klaas, K., McGlade, K. & Naumann, S. 2014. *Quality of Life, Wellbeing and Biodiversity: The Role of Biodiversity in Future Development.* Final Report submitted to Deutsche Gesellschaft für Internationale Zusammenarbeit (GIZ) GmbH. Berlin: Ecologic Institute.

Kathage, J., Gómez-Barbero, M. & Rodríguez-Cerezo, E. 2016. *Framework for Assessing the Socio-economic Impacts of Bt Maize Cultivation.* European GMO Socio-Economics Bureau 2nd Reference Document. JRC Technical Report, EUR 28129 EN.

Khan, Z. R., Midega, C. A. O., Amudavi, D. M., Hassanali, A. & Pickett, J. A. 2008. On-farm evaluation of the 'push–pull' technology for the control of stemborers and *Striga* weed on maize in western Kenya. *Field Crops Research*, 106(3): 224–233.

Kline, K. L., Msangi, S., Dale, V. H., Woods, J., Souza, Glaucia M., Osseweijer, P., Clancy, J. S., Hilbert, J. A., Johnson, F. X., McDonnell, P. C. & Mugera, H. K. 2017. Reconciling food security and bioenergy: Priorities for action. *GCB Bioenergy*, 9(3): 557–576.

Klümper, W. & Qaim, M. 2014. A meta-analysis of the impacts of genetically modified crops. *PLoS One*, 9(11): e111629.

Kromdijk, J., Głowacka, K., Leonelli, L., Gabilly, S. T., Iwai, M., Niyogi, K. K. & Long, S. P. 2016. Improving photosynthesis and crop productivity by accelerating recovery from photoprotection. *Science*, 354(6314): 857–861.

Lawton, J. H. & May, R. M. (Eds.). 1994. *Extinction Rates.* Oxford: Oxford University Press.

Leonard, D. & Haddad, L. 2008. *Assessing the Policy Prescriptions in The Bottom Billion.* IDS in Focus: research and analysis from the Institute of Development Studies, Sussex. www.ids.ac.uk/files/NewNo1-Overview -web.pdf.

Liang, J., Crowther, T. W., Picard, N., Wiser, S., Zhou, M., Alberti, G., Schulze, E.-D., McGuire, A. D., Bozzato, F., Pretzsch, H., de-Miguel, S., Paquette, A., Hérault, B., Scherer-Lorenzen, M., Barrett, C. B., Glick, H. B., Hengeveld, G. M., Nabuurs, G.-J., Pfautsch, S., Viana, H., Vibrans, A. C., Ammer, C., Schall, P., Verbyla, D., Tchebakova, N., Fischer, M., Watson, J. V., Chen, H. Y. H., Lei, X., Schelhaas, M.-J., Lu, H., Gianelle, D., Parfenova, E. I., Salas, C., Lee, E., Lee, B., Kim, H. S., Bruelheide, H., Coomes, D. A., Piotto, D., Sunderland, T., Schmid, B.,

Gourlet-Fleury, S., Sonké, B., Tavani, R., Zhu, J., Brandl, S., Vayreda, J., Kitahara, F., Searle, E. B., Neldner, V. J., Ngugi, M. R., Baraloto, C., Frizzera, L., Bałazy, R., Oleksyn, J., Zawiła-Niedźwiecki, T., Bouriaud, O., Bussotti, F., Finér, L., Jaroszewicz, B., Jucker, T., Valladares, F., Jagodzinski, A. M., Peri, P. L., Gonmadje, C., Marthy, W., O'Brien, T., Martin, E. H., Marshall, A. R., Rovero, F., Bitariho, R., Niklaus, P. A., Alvarez-Loayza, P., Chamuya, N., Valencia, R., Mortier, F., Wortel, V., Engone-Obiang, N. L., Ferreira, L. V., Odeke, D. E., Vasquez, R. M., Lewis, S. L. & Reich, P. B. 2016. Positive biodiversity-productivity relationship predominant in global forests. *Science*, 354(6309).

Loomans, A. 2007. *Regulation of Invertebrate Biological Control Agents in Europe: Review and Recommendations in Its Pursuit of a Harmonised Regulatory System.* Report EU project REBECA [Regulation of Biological Control Agents].

Lorentz Biopanel Statement. 2016. *Statement of the Lorentz BioPanel.* www .lorentzcenter.nl/lc/web/2016/780/report.pdf.

Mace, G. M. 2014. Whose conservation? *Science*, 345(6204): 1558–1560.

Marsh, T. L., Yoder, J., Deboch, T., McElwain, T. F. & Palmer, G. H. 2016. Livestock vaccinations translate into increased human capital and school attendance by girls. *Science Advances*, 2(12): e1601410.

McFarland, W., Whitley, S. & Kissinger, G. 2015. *Subsidies to Key Commodities Driving Forest Loss: Implications for Private Climate Finance.* London: Overseas Development Institute. www.odi.org/sites/odi.org.uk/files/odi -assets/publications-opinion-files/9577.pdf.

Morris, A. L., Guégan, J.-F., Andreou, D., Marsollier, L., Carolan, K., Le Croller, M., Sanhueza, D. & Gozlan, R. E. 2016. Deforestation-driven food-web collapse linked to emerging tropical infectious disease, *Mycobacterium ulcerans*. *Science Advances*, 2(12): e1600387.

Morris, E. J. 2011. Modern biotechnology: Potential contribution and challenges for sustainable food production in sub-Saharan Africa. *Sustainability*, 3(6): 809–822.

Ozturk, I. 2016. Biofuel, sustainability, and forest indicators' nexus in the panel generalized method of moments estimation: Evidence from 12 developed and developing countries. *Biofuels, Bioproducts and Biorefining*, 10(2): 150–163.

Ozturk, I. & Bilgili, F. 2015. Economic growth and biomass consumption nexus: Dynamic panel analysis for sub-Sahara African countries. *Applied Energy*, 137: 110–116.

Parrott, W. 2010. Genetically modified myths and realities. *New Biotechnology*, 27(5): 545–551.

PAS. 2009. *Transgenic Plants for Food Security in the Context of Development*. PAS Study Week, Vatican City, May 15–19. www .casinapioiv.va/content/dam/accademia/pdf/multilanguagestatement.pdf.

Pereira, M. G., Freitas, M. A. V. & da Silva, N. F. 2011. The challenge of energy poverty: Brazilian case study. *Energy Policy*, 39(1): 167–175.

Pickett, J. A., Woodcock, C. M., Midega, C. A. O. & Khan, Z. R. 2014. Push–pull farming systems. *Current Opinion in Biotechnology*, 26: 125–132.

Ponisio, L. C., M'Gonigle, L. K., Mace, K. C., Palomino, J., de Valpine, P. & Kremen, C. 2015. Diversification practices reduce organic to conventional yield gap. *Proceedings of the Royal Society B*, 282: 20141396.

Pope Francis. 2015. *Laudato Si': On Care for Our Common Home* [Encyclical]. Vatican City, Italy: Vatican Press. http://w2.vatican.va/con tent/francesco/en/encyclicals/documents/papa-francesco_20150524_en ciclica-laudato-si.html.

Potapov, P., Hansen, M. C., Laestadius, L., Turubanova, S., Yaroshenko, A., Thies, C., Smith, W., Zhuravleva, I., Komarova, A., Minnemeyer, S. & Esipova, E. 2017. The last frontiers of wilderness: Tracking loss of intact forest landscapes from 2000 to 2013. *Science Advances*, 3(1): e1600821.

Potrykus, I. 2010. Constraints to biotechnology introduction for poverty alleviation. *New Biotechnology*, 27(5): 447–448.

Potrykus, I. & Ammann, K. (Eds.). 2010. Transgenic plants for food security in the context of development. *New Biotechnology*, 27(5).

Pradhan, P., Fischer, G., van Velthuizen, H., Reusser, D. E. & Kropp, J. P. 2015. Closing yield gaps: How sustainable can we be? *PLoS One*, 10(6): e0129487.

Quétier, F. 2016. The CRISPR-Cas9 technology: Closer to the ultimate toolkit for targeted genome editing. *Plant Science*, 242: 65–76.

Ray, D. K., Ramankutty, N., Mueller, N. D., West, P. C. & Foley, J. A. 2012. Recent patterns of crop yield growth and stagnation. *Nature Communications*, 3: 1293.

Redford, K. H., Adams, W. & Mace, G. M. 2013. Synthetic biology and conservation of nature: Wicked problems and wicked solutions. *PLoS Biology*, 11(4): e1001530.

Resende, D. C., Mendes, S. M., Marucci, R. C., Silva, A. d. C., Campanha, M. M. & Waquil, J. M. 2016. Does Bt maize cultivation affect the non-target insect community in the agro ecosystem? *Revista Brasileira de Entomologia*, 60: 82–93.

Robinson, T. P. & Pozzi, F. 2011. *Mapping Supply and Demand for Animal-Source Foods to 2030*. FAO Animal Production and Health Working Paper 2. Rome: Food and Agriculture Organization. www.fao.org/doc rep/014/i2425e/i2425e00.pdf.

Rodriguez, D. 2011. *New Holland Agriculture's Clean Energy Leader Strategy*. www.climateactionprogramme.org/press-releases/new_hol lands_clean_energy_leader_strategy.

Royal Society. 2009. *Reaping the Benefits: Science and the Sustainable Intensification of Global Agriculture*. RS Policy Document 11/09. London: The Royal Society.

2015. *Trends in Synthetic Biology and Gain of Function and Regulatory Implications*. Sackler Forum, Royal Society, DES 4538. London: The Royal Society.

Satterthwaite, D. 2008. Cities' contribution to global warming: Notes on the allocation of greenhouse gas emissions. *Environment and Urbanization*, 20(2): 539–549.

Scherr, S. J. & McNeely, J. A. 2008. Biodiversity conservation and agricultural sustainability: Towards a new paradigm of 'ecoagriculture' landscapes. *Philosophical Transactions of the Royal Society B: Biological Sciences*, 363(1491): 477–494.

SCOPE. 2015. Bioenergy and sustainability: Bridging the gaps. In G. M. Souza, R. Victoria, C. Joly & L. Verdade (Eds.), *SCOPE Report 72*. Paris. http://bioenfapesp.org/scopebioenergy.

Seufert, V., Ramankutty, N. & Foley, J. A. 2012. Comparing the yields of organic and conventional agriculture. *Nature*, 485: 229–232.

Seward, P. 2015. *Farm Input Promotions Africa Ltd*. http://fipsafrica.org/.

Shultz, D. 2016. Should we bring extinct species back from the dead? *Science: Biology, Plants and Animals*. www.sciencemag.org/news/201 6/09/should-we-bring-extinct-species-back-dead.

Smart Villages Initiative. 2015a. *Smart Villages: The Gender and Energy Context*. http://e4sv.org/wp-content/uploads/2015/08/03-Technical -Report.pdf.

2015b. *Sustainable Dissemination of Improved Cookstoves: Lessons from Southeast Asia*. http://e4sv.org/wp-content/uploads/2016/03/WR13 -Sustainable-Dissemination-of-Improved-Cookstoves-Lessons.pdf.

2015c. *Smart Villages in Southeast Asia: Kuching Workshop Report (2015)*. http://e4sv.org/wp-content/uploads/2015/06/04-Workshop -Report-low-res.pdf.

2015d. *South Asia Media Dialogue: Colombo Workshop Report*. http://e4 sv.org/wp-content/uploads/2016/04/WR12-South-Asia-Media-Dialogue -Colombo-Workshop-Report-DRAFT.pdf.

Sole, R. V. & Montoya, J. M. 2006. Ecological network meltdown from habitat loss and fragmentation. In M. Pascual & J. A. Dunne (Eds.), *Ecological Networks: Linking Structure to Dynamics in Food Webs*: 305–323. Amsterdam: Elsevier.

Sun Moksha. 2015. *Smart Village Nanogrid*™. www.nanosoftremote.com /ChhotkeiSmartNanogrid/.

Swanson, T. 1999. Conserving global biological diversity by encouraging alternative development paths: Can development coexist with diversity? *Biodiversity & Conservation*, 8(1): 29–44.

Trace, S. 2016. *Rethink, Retool, Reboot: Technology as If People and Planet Mattered.* Rugby, UK: Practical Action. www.developmentbookshelf.com /doi/pdf/10.3362/9781780449043.

Tuck, S. L., Winqvist, C., Mota, F., Ahnström, J., Turnbull, L. A. & Bengtsson, J. 2014. Land-use intensity and the effects of organic farming on biodiversity: A hierarchical meta-analysis. *Journal of Applied Ecology*, 51(3): 746–755.

UN. 1987. *Report of the World Commission on Environment and Development: Our Common Future.* Annex to document A/42/427, Development and International Co-operation: Environment. www.ask-force.org/web/Sustai nability/Brundtland-Our-Common-Future-1987-2008.pdf.

UNA-UK. 2015. *Global Development Goals: Leaving No One Behind.* www.una.org.uk/global-development-goals-leaving-no-one-behind.

UNEP. 1997. *Global Environment Outlook-1* (GEO1). United Nations Environment Programme. Global State of the Environment Report 1997. www.grid.unep.ch/geo1/.

van den Oever-van den Elsen, F., Lucatti, A. F., van Heusden, S., Broekgaarden, C., Mumm, R., Dicke, M. & Vosman, B. 2016. Quantitative resistance against *Bemisia tabaci* in *Solanum pennellii*: Genetics and metabolomics. *Journal of Integrative Plant Biology*, 58 (4): 397–412.

van de Wouw, M., van Hintum, T., Kik, C., van Treuren, R. & Visser, B. 2010. Genetic diversity trends in twentieth century crop cultivars: a meta analysis. *Theoretical and Applied Genetics*, 120(6): 1241–1252.

van Gevelt, T., Holmes, J., Marcheselli, M., Safdar, T., Price, M. & Heap, B. 2016. Energy for off-grid villages: The Smart Villages Initiative. In J. Bicak (Ed.), *On Stars, Oceans and Mankind*, vol. 99: 179–243. Prague: Learned Society of Czech Republic. www.learned.cz/userfiles /pdf/publikace/bicak-text.pdf.

van Ittersum, M. K., van Bussel, L. G. J., Wolf, J., Grassini, P., van Wart, J., Guilpart, N., Claessens, L., de Groot, H., Wiebe, K., Mason-D'Croz, D., Yang, H., Boogaard, H., van Oort, P. A. J., van Loon, M. P., Saito, K., Adimo, O., Adjei-Nsiah, S., Agali, A., Bala, A., Chikowo, R., Kaizzi, K., Kouressy, M., Makoi, J. H. J. R., Ouattara, K., Tesfaye, K. & Cassman, K. G. 2016. Can sub-Saharan Africa feed itself? *Proceedings of the National Academy of Sciences*, 113(52): 14964–14969.

Vianello, M. 2016. *A Review of Cooking Systems for Humanitarian Settings*. Toolkit for the Moving Energy Initiative. London: Royal Institute of International Affairs. www.chathamhouse.org/sites /default/files/publications/research/2016-05-19-mei-review-of-cooking-systems-vianello.pdf.

Vitale, J., Glick, H., Greenplate, J. & Traore, O. 2008. The economic impacts of second generation Bt cotton in West Africa: Empirical evidence from Burkina Faso. *International Journal of Biotechnology*, 10(2–3): 167–183.

von Burg, S., van Veen, F. J. F., Álvarez-Alfageme, F. & Romeis, J. 2011. Aphid–parasitoid community structure on genetically modified wheat. *Biology Letters*, 7(3): 387–391.

Weindl, I., Lotze-Campen, H., Popp, A., Müller, C., Havlik, P., Herrero, M., Schmitz, S. & Rolinski, S. 2015. Livestock in a changing climate: Production system transitions as an adaptation strategy for agriculture. *Environmental Research Letters*, 10(9): 094021.

Wolfenbarger, L. L., Naranjo, S. E., Lundgren, J. G., Bitzer, R. J. & Watrud, L. S. 2008. Bt crop effects on functional guilds of non-target arthropods: A meta-analysis. *PLoS One*, 3(5): e2118.

Wunder, S., Engel, S. & Pagiola, S. 2008. Taking stock: A comparative analysis of payments for environmental services programs in developed and developing countries. *Ecological Economics*, 65(4): 834–852.

WWF. 2012. *Living Planet Report 2012: Biodiversity, Biocapacity and Better Choices*. www.worldwildlife.org/publications/living-planet-report-2012-biodiversity-biocapacity-and-better-choices.

2016a. *Living Planet Report 2016: Risk and Resilience in a New Era*. Gland, Switzerland: WWF International.

2016b. *Conserving Forests to Combat Climate Change: What Is REDD+, How Was It Created and Where Is It Going?* Washington, DC: World Wildlife Fund. www.worldwildlife.org/publications/conserving-forests -to-combat-climate-change.

Zaman, T. 2016. *It Is Not a Village but People: Long Lamai, a Case Study of a Smart Village*. https://e4sv.org/not-village-people-long-lamai-case -study-smart-village/.

Zarea, M. J., Ghalavand, A., Goltapeh, E. M., Rejali, F. & Zamaniyan, M. 2009. Effects of mixed cropping, earthworms (*Pheretima* sp.), and arbuscular mycorrhizal fungi (*Glomus mosseae*) on plant yield, mycorrhizal colonization rate, soil microbial biomass, and nitrogenase activity of free-living rhizosphere bacteria. *Pedobiologia*, 52(4): 223–235.

Zhang, W., Cao, G., Li, X., Zhang, H., Wang, C., Liu, Q., Chen, X., Cui, Z., Shen, J., Jiang, R., Mi, G., Miao, Y., Zhang, F. & Dou, Z. 2016. Closing yield gaps in China by empowering smallholder farmers. *Nature*, 537: 671–674.

14 The New Design Condition

Planetary Urbanism + Resource Scarcity + Climate Change

JOHN T. HOAL

The New Design Condition

It is the confluence of three human agency trends – planetary urbanism, resource scarcity and climate change – that will have a profound impact on the manner in which we occupy and relate to the planet and each other. This confluence is unparalleled in world history. We are entering unknown territory with little knowledge as to how these three trends will interact in complex, unpredictable and unprecedented ways. However, we do know that this confluence is upon us and it will continue to create a NEW DESIGN CONDITION to which we as a planetary community need to respond.

We also know that this new design condition has and will continue to accentuate the already intractable social, environmental and economic issues. Challenges such as inequality, poverty, public health, malnutrition, migration, inadequate housing, and natural resource and biodiversity loss and fragmentation will only be exacerbated as the full impact of the confluence of these three trends emerges. It is further understood that the current socio-economic paradigm for planetary living is not only unsustainable in its own right but cannot and does not adequately respond to this confluence of planetary urbanism, resource scarcity and climate change.

This discussion paper explores this confluence and suggests that cities as the primary habitat for humans today are the greatest driver of prosperity, creativity and innovation; consumption of materials and energy; producer of waste; polluter and destroyer of our natural capital; emitter of greenhouse gases (GHG), and they fundamentally change the climate, while remaining the place in which we define who we are as a community and a civilisation. Since cities are the largest sites of human settlement today and are increasingly acting as critical nexus points of social, economic, ecological and technological change, it is critical that cities be the focus of the challenge.

This is especially evident in the Global South, where growth is most rapid, and where future sustainability challenges will be most severe – all this in the light of growing inequalities and poverty; the pervasiveness of slums and informality; governmental and societal inefficiency; and a lack of responsive planning and design. In the face of these challenges, it is critical we reconsider the planning and design of cities as the focus for sustainability and resource generation. Cities are truly the greatest locus of the challenge and opportunity!

The Confluence of Planetary Urbanism + Resource Scarcity + Climate Change: Key Characteristics and Challenges

Planetary Urbanism

The first trend is planetary urbanism, resulting from the projected global population increase from 7.3 billion in 2015 to 9.7 billion in 2050, and to between 9.5 and 13.3 billion in 2100, layered with the fact that the majority of people will continue to select cities as their preferred habitat for reasons of opportunity, work, survival and/or personal choice (UN, 2015). In fact, since 2007 the majority of the world's population has been living in cities, and over the past 20 years, world urban population has grown by more than 60 per cent. Today 54 per cent of the world's population live in cities and by 2050 it is projected that 70 per cent of the 9.7 billion people in the world will be living in cities, i.e., 6.8 billion people. By 2100 it is projected that 84 per cent of people, an approximate total of 9 billion or more people, will live in cities, and this represents more than a doubling of the number of people living in cities between now and the end of the century. However, it is not only the scale but the speed with which this is happening that will be challenging. It is understood that the world is growing at 83 million people per year and although not everyone will live in a city, together with the increasing rural to urban migration, the urban population growth implies 4 metropolitan New Yorks per year, or 9 Greater Londons per year, or 19 metropolitan Romes per year would need to be designed, constructed and serviced additionally every year for the next 35 years.

Globally urban growth is projected to comprise primarily of extensions to and rebuilding of existing cities rather than completely new cities. In terms of existing cities, growth will occur roughly equally in both large (one million plus) cities and in medium (below 0.5–1.0 million) sized cities (UN, 2015). The most impactful growth will occur in association with those existing cities that will emerge as dominant economic global megacities with 10 million or more inhabitants (research has shown that the larger urbanised regions have a bigger per capita ecological footprint). Today, there are 25 megacities, and it is projected that in 2050, there will be 55 megacities and 85 megacities in 2100 – a 340 per cent growth of megacities in the world over the next 80 years.

In addition, there will be the emergence of multiple hyper-city regions with populations exceeding 20 million plus inhabitants. The largest city today is Greater Tokyo with approximately 36 million people, but within 80 years – one person's lifetime – the largest city-region is projected to be Lagos, Nigeria with nearly 90 million people – over twice the size of Tokyo today. In perspective, only 15 countries today have populations larger than 90 million people. So in the future the world will need to design, build, operate and service cities of unprecedented sizes, for which there is little knowledge and expertise, and in many case these cities will be self-built.

This challenge is accentuated by the location and age differential of the population growth, with Asia and Africa as the centres of population growth and urbanisation. Africa in particular has a very youthful and growing population. The most populated continent will remain as it is today, with Asia's population growing from 4.3 billion in 2015 to 5.3 billion in 2050 and then declining slightly to 4.9 billion in 2100. India is expected to become the largest country in population size, surpassing China around 2022. Europe is projected to lose population, and the Americas will have modest growth. In relation to cities, by 2100, of the top largest cities, 15 will be in Africa, 9 in Asia and 1 (New York) in the US. It is the Global South that will be home to nearly three-quarters of the world's urban population and most of the world's largest and fastest-growing cities (UN, 2015).

The Global South cities will see the majority of this unprecedented population growth dispersed over tens of thousands of urban areas. Africa, Asia and Latin America will be the home of approximately 90 per cent of the added urban population and therefore the location of city building. However, the key challenge for cities will be Africa, which is currently the fastest urbanising continent in the world with a 2.55 per cent growth rate for the foreseeable future. Africa is expected to more than double its population by 2100, increasing from 1.2 billion in 2015 to 2.5 billion in 2050 and 4.4 billion in 2100 (UN, 2015). Africa currently accounts for 16 per cent of the global population. The UN expects that proportion to rise to 25 per cent in 2050 and 49 per cent by 2100. Nigeria's population could surpass the US by 2050, and by 2100 contain the world's largest city Lagos of 90 million people. Thus Africa, with some of the world's most important hotspots of biodiversity but with one of the most undeveloped economies and infrastructures, as well as significant political fragmentation and exploitation, natural resource depletion and/or degradation, and high rates of poverty, illiteracy and disease, will certainly be the most challenged continent to design, develop, manage and service ecologically responsible and humane cities.

However, planetary urbanism is not just the number, size, location and speed of city growth driven by the number of people to be housed in cities; it also incorporates the understanding that not only will the majority of the world's population live in cities, but more importantly that those that do not live in places defined as cities will be increasingly directly or indirectly involved in assuring the existence of the city, or will be dependent upon the city. This implies that there is a physical network of various sizes of cities, towns and villages supported by separate functional zones of specific land uses such as agriculture, fishing, mining, industrial, conservation areas and wilderness. From the natural capital perspective, planetary urbanism also implies that the ecological and biological resources and services needed for the existence of the city (e.g., clean air, carbon dioxide sequestration) are being drawn from increasingly further afield and cities are having an increasingly larger spatial footprint and ecological footprint. This expanded footprint also occurs with and supported by a social and economic network of inter-relationships through people's work, seasonal migratory patterns, disjointed locations of work and home, and family and community.

So as a totality, these complex and multi-layered functional and personal relationships have become increasingly disparate, loose, global and transitory within the city, between city and peripheries and with other cities and their peripheries, as well as with the specialised land use functional zones. This implies that planetary urbanism must be understood as an urban to wilderness transect. Increasingly cities are dependent upon these highly specific functional zones for the supply of food, water, energy and air quality, all of which are increasingly far away. An example is the emergence of the global agricultural trade. China, with a quarter of the world's population and only 9 per cent of the arable land, requires agricultural land and products from places within Africa like Mozambique which is using only 15 per cent of its agricultural land. Another indicator of the impact of cities is their increasingly larger water footprint. Although urban areas cover 3 per cent of the Earth's land surface, their water footprint covers 41 per cent, and the watersheds of the 100 largest cities cover over 12 per cent. Thus, the impact of cities on global resources is increasing and will continue to increase, most often with detrimental impacts on planetary natural resources and biodiversity conservation.

Finally, city building correlates with improved living standards for many but not all of its residents. Over recent history, city building has been used as a national, regional and local economic development strategy and one that was intended to alleviate poverty and provide humane living conditions for all. This has not necessarily been achieved. It has been the middle class and wealthy people that have benefited most from city building through rising incomes and greater levels of consumption. In parallel with the growth of cities the global middle class will increase from 1.8 billion to 4.9 billion people by 2050, an increase of 3 billion middle income people over the next 35 years (OECD, 2010). The net impact for urbanisation is that the city's ecological, social and economic footprint exponentially increases as a result of the combination of urbanisation and the rising middle income class due to the substantially increased consumption patterns per person. As an example, with the increased urban middle class there is typically a change of food diet. Projections suggest that food production will need to increase by 50 per cent by 2030 and 100 per cent more by 2050 to meet forecast demand. This will bring enormous demand stresses to the water and energy sectors, and will result in major competition between different land uses – between cities, agriculture (food), cropland (fuel and feed), natural resource conservation and carbon sinks. Cities are already consuming some of the more productive agriculture lands and natural areas.

From an overall global perspective, the size, number, speed and location of cities that need to be designed, developed, managed and serviced over the next 80 years to accommodate the projected increases in population and the growing middle class presents a huge challenge. In my opinion, this, together with the economic, ecological and social resources and governmental structures in said locations, results in a condition that the 'formal economy' will not be able to deliver the necessary urbanisation at the needed pace to match the population growth. The implication is that people at the lower ends of the economic spectrum will self-build their communities and informal urbanism will be an essential element of many, if not all cities. Informal urbanism (known as slums) already exists and has existed in parallel to major cities for decades; however it is projected to become an even more significant component of urbanisation in the future. Estimates suggest that 40 per cent of the world's urban expansion is taking place in slums. Informal urbanism is expected to increase from one billion people to two billion people by 2030 and will be increasingly associated with formal urbanism (UN-Habitat, 2003).

This intractable flow into cities, and the pattern of formal and informal urbanism spatially, socially and economically coexisting, is already well established in the Global South. For example, Lagos, Nigeria; Accra, Ghana; Mexico City, Mexico; San Paulo, Brazil and Buenos Aries, Argentina are examples of mature urbanisation patterns that incorporate both formal and informal urbanism with varying degrees of success. The challenge in this case is to decouple informal urbanism from poverty, inequality and a lack of opportunity, education and basic services such as sewerage, water, waste, food and health and social services. We need to understand informal urbanism as a legitimate form of urbanism – as an emergent city in which communities and people themselves will have to be the agents of urbanisation.

Thus, embedded in planetary urbanism as currently practised are a set of uneven and unequal patterns of development and processes of inequality and social/environmental justice. Broadly, the current difference between the Global North and Global South will be accentuated with most of the cities being built in the Global South in places that are challenged by degrading environmental resources, ineffective governmental structures and a lack of necessary skills. There are high levels of poverty and insecurity, including insecurity of food, tenure, water, shelter and health; and this comes with all the implications of the most vulnerable people living in the highest risk areas of cities with the lowest levels of services. Overall, this implies that this challenging trend of urbanisation needs to be understood as an opportunity to completely rethink the very nature of how we plan cities today.

Resource Scarcity

The second of the two human agency trends is resource scarcity, which results from the extraction, pollution and fragmentation of the world's natural resources and ecological systems, as well as the current consumption patterns of the middle income and wealthy classes, and the reliance on the free market to determine the planning and use of the world's finite resources. In this regard, the world has already moved from an era of city building in a resource abundant age to an era of city building where resource scarcity is and will be increasingly a major constraint. Scarcity will not only mean some products are in short supply but many will become cost prohibitive and/or the availability will be significantly less predictable, all of which will exacerbate the current social and economic challenges, and further environmental degradation. As such, the building, rebuilding, operation, maintenance and servicing of the projected cities over the next 80 years housing 9 billion people will be constrained by the available ecosystem services and natural resources, especially in terms of biomass (this includes materials, energy, oil, water, feed and food).

The predominant global city morphology of urban sprawl is accentuated by the growing middle class lifestyle, with its increasing average floor area per person and material consumption footprint. This results in urban land worldwide growing at a faster rate than population within cities (Seto et al., 2012). Currently, cities occupy 3 per cent of the world's land surface and produce 50 per cent of global waste and 60–80 per cent of global carbon emissions while consuming 75–80 per cent of natural resources. It is anticipated that with the projected urbanisation, the overall land area for cities will triple by 2050, with the resultant negative impact on natural capital. This implies that urban land consumption rates worldwide are increasing at least twice as fast as urban populations, and in some places, three and four times faster (Angel et al., 2011; Seto et al., 2011). As a result of this growing urbanisation and rising middle income class, and unless there is a substantive change in approach to resource utilisation and the design of cities, by 2050 there would need to be a 70 per cent increase in food production, 80 per cent more energy and a 55 per cent increase in clean water demand, which would result in an unprecedented and unsustainable demand on biological resources and ecosystems (Cohen, 2004).

These projections are reflective of the current model of city planning and design – autocentric sprawl and planning in a resource abundant era. To bring about global change in levels of urban consumption, waste output, and natural resource conservation, preservation and restoration, there will need to be a focus on the design and development of cities, particularly as they relate to the density of inhabitants. The general assumption is that high-density cities have the opportunity to become less car dependent, to generate lower emissions and to reduce energy consumption by shifting mobility to walking, cycling and public transport, reducing trip distances through mix of uses, and reducing the total number of trips through proximity, while improving urban vitality and providing a high quality of life. Currently, research has mixed results and has not necessarily fully supported all the anticipated environmental benefits. However I believe that much of the research indicates that compactness alone will not necessarily achieve the full benefit unless it is matched with public policy, funding and investment. The UN has established a target of 15,000 inhabitants per sq. km for a resource efficient and sustainable city. Currently only 10–15 cities (urban areas) in the world reach the UN target overall, so there is a tremendous opportunity to densify our cities without consuming additional land. For instance, Dhaka, the capital of Bangladesh, is the most densely populated urban area in the world with a density estimated at 44,000 people per square kilometre. All of Dhaka's urban population of 15.4 million fits into a land area equal to that of the municipality of Portland with a population less than 600,000. Overall, the US has the highest number of larger cities (with populations greater than 2.5 million) with the least dense areas.

In addition, today cities are typically planned, developed and maintained with a complete lack of sensitivity to the integration and consideration of biological variables, and as such biodiversity within the city is threatened by a vast array of anthropogenic factors. The form and character of urbanisation as currently implemented homogenises the biota as native ecosystems are replaced by pavements and buildings; the natural soil is covered with areas dominated by non-native ornamental species; and wetlands, forests and other peripheral ecosystems are removed, fragmented or invaded by non-native species. As a result, urbanisation produces some of the greatest local extinction rates and frequently eliminates the majority of native species, with the result that non-native species invasions often occur (Kowarik, 1995; Luniak, 1994; Marzluff, 2001; Vale and Vale, 1976). Finally, urbanisation is often more lasting than other types of habitat loss (Stein et al., 2000). However, clearly the opportunity exists and there is an essential need for city planning to be inclusive of habitat preservation, biodiversity and ecosystem services. The services provided by natural ecosystems to cities can be categorised as follows: (1) provisioning services, i.e., the provision of oxygen, food, water and raw materials; (2) regulating services for carbon capture and sequestration, water management and waste water treatment, air purification, pollination, biological control; (3) supporting services, by providing habitat for flora and fauna, maintaining genetic diversity and nutrient cycling; and (4) cultural services contributing to mental and physical health in human beings, as well as recreation/tourism, and spiritual benefits (TEEB, 2011a, 2011b).

While there are uncertainties around the forecasts of urban population growth, there is even greater uncertainty about where and how much urban expansion will take place in different parts of the world over the next few decades. The manner in which the magnitudes of future urban expansion will vary across the world have important implications for biological productivity and biodiversity particularly in the Global South. What is clear is that the current modes of city planning and design, which facilitate the sprawling urban morphology and the increasing consumption footprint of the growing middle class, are a primary factor in the utilisation of land and have a negative impact on biodiversity. Thus one of the most significant challenges to biodiversity and natural resource preservation and conservation is the form of the city itself, as well as the urban residents' consumption patterns, and not necessarily the number of people living in the city. It is increasingly essential to build ecologically performative compact cities.

This becomes more important since of the 34 biodiversity hotspots in the world, all contain some form of urban area (CI, 2011). Examples of such cities include Berlin, Brussels, Cape Town, Chicago, Curitiba, Frankfurt, Kolkata, Mexico City, Montreal, Nagoya, New York City, Sao Paulo and Singapore. Over 50 per cent of the world's plant species and 42 per cent of all terrestrial vertebrate species are endemic to these 34 biodiversity hotspots, and most face extreme threats and/or have already lost 70 per cent of their original natural vegetation (CI, 2011). Given the anticipated growth of existing cities to accommodate increased populations, these hotspots are particularly threatened in two ways by urbanisation. First, the expansion of the city physically destroys and/or alters the habitat, biodiversity and biological resources of the area (McKinney, 2002). Second, with the expansion of cities, the distance between protected areas and cities shrinks, further negatively impacting the biological resources and ecological functionality of resources adjacent to the city. This secondary negative impact is derived from biophysical changes associated with urban components and materiality, such as impervious surfaces which modify energy and water partitioning and thus influence local and regional surface climates (Hansen et al., 2001; Kalnay and Cai, 2003). Built environments not only trap heat and influence local precipitation patterns, but they also degrade air quality by changing atmospheric chemistry (Stone, 2008).

This urban-biodiversity challenge can clearly be seen in numerous cities within these rich biodiversity hotspots, and especially with sprawling cities. A great example of this is Cape Town, South Africa which is located in the Cape Floristic Region biodiversity hotspot. Cape Town has 50 per cent of South Africa's critically endangered vegetation types and approximately 3000 indigenous vascular plant species. It has increased its population by 3 million people over the last 75 years, a 490 per cent growth rate. The population is expected to double before 2050 placing an increased pressure on these natural resources. Importantly, the spatial morphology of Cape Town has been a sprawling low-rise formal and informal urban form, which has resulted in its having one of the lowest population densities of the largest 15 cities in Africa. It has also meant that the urban areas and the impact of urban life have expanded into some of the most sensitive habitats and biodiverse areas in Cape Town, resulting in their current level of critical endangerment.

Thus, with the projected growth of the middle class and their increased consumption patterns, acting alongside the growth of cities many of which are located in rich biodiverse regions, there is a serious question as to whether the natural resources and the ecosystem services that they provide can survive. Similarly, in terms of the ability of the world's natural resources to provide the necessary ecosystem services, it must be noted that the 2005 United Nations Millennium Ecosystem Assessment found that 15 out of the 24 key ecosystems that human survival is dependent on were degraded and/or subject to unsustainable use. The consequence is that 1.3 billion people currently live in ecologically fragile environments, mostly in the Global South. There is no doubt that resource scarcity and degraded ecosystem services will combine to bring about complex challenges in unique ways in different urban contexts. Cities need to be design, developed, managed/operated and maintained in 'ways that they can lessen their pressure on the environment by being more self-sufficient'. Not only must cities include ecosystems and biodiversity within the cities themselves, but they also need to be designed to lessen their metabolic impact on the remainder of the resources of the Earth, i.e., to retain, conserve and produce 'biodiversity elsewhere'.

Climate Change

The third of the three human agency trends is climate change. Climate change acts as the background context for both planetary urbanism and resource scarcity. While we can dispute the degree to which the climate is changing due to natural variability versus human agency, there is no denying that the climate is changing to a significant degree through human agency, and that this will continue to have tremendous impacts both locally and globally on cities, on the biological resources and on the carrying capacity of the Earth. Cities as the planet's human habitat are and will continue to be the very focus and nexus of the human tragedy of climate change, be it through natural disasters, migration and/or social and economic instability and turmoil.

Currently, climate disasters are both the biggest financial liability and the most urgent public health risk facing the world. In the coming decades of rapid urbanisation in an age of resource scarcity, all cities will continue to experience intensified and unpredictable shocks and volatility of many kinds as a result of climate change, including extreme weather, heat waves, heavy precipitation, intensified droughts, tropical storms and the migration of people, flora and fauna, etc. A particular challenge is the fact that climate change impacts are likely to be highly unpredictable, non-linear and characterised by sudden shifts as key GHG thresholds are passed. These changes will impact the provision of food; water and energy availability; air quality; public health;

poverty and inequality; disease potentiality; natural resource performance; and they will amplify risks posed by normal hazards. All of
these will increase the difficulty of managing and servicing cities, and
point toward the critical importance of resilience as a fundamental
design and planning parameter for cities. All of these risks and vulnerabilities present the greatest risk to poor people and countries which
have the least capacity to cope with shocks or to adapt to new realities.

This condition will be further accentuated due to the location of the
major megacities. Typically, megacities with the highest concentrations
of people are located in places of high vulnerability to climate change,
in particular along the coast. There is a coevolution of urbanisation and
vulnerability and risk. These megacities are engines of economic
growth and centres of innovation for both the global economy and
the hinterlands of their respective nations. The foundations of prosperity and prominence for most megacities lie in their long-standing commercial relationships with the rest of the world. To facilitate trade,
most primary cities are located on or near the coast. They are also often
located in low-lying areas near the mouths of major rivers, which
served as conduits for commerce between interior agricultural and
industrial regions and the rest of the world. These locations place
megacities at greater risk from current and projected climate hazards
such as cyclones, high winds, flooding, coastal erosion and deposition,
and sea level rise (Nicholls, 1995; Rosenzweig and Solecki, 2001). This
implies we will need to plan and design for environmental risks, including chronic and catastrophic forms of 'natural disaster' as part of the
urbanisation process (Hewitt, 1983; Castree and Braun, 2001).

To further compound the challenge, the poorest and least empowered populations tend to be located in the areas of highest vulnerability
within these cities. Natural and climate change disasters bring attention
to the inequalities of the current socio-economic systems and requisite
planning models, and by 2050 it is anticipated that 54 per cent of the
urban poor will live in cities. Currently approximately one billion
people are living in informal settlements (this will grow to 2 billion or
more), and many of these settlements are located in highly exposed
areas including coastal zones, floodplains and steep hillsides, all with
low-quality infrastructure and high degrees of poverty, with no areas
for retreat nor the ability to retreat to safety.

Urban disasters cannot be resolved with technical short-term
repairs and solutions alone. Rather the nature of disaster risk is

constantly being redefined as changes to urban landscapes and socio-economic characteristics emerge. Urbanisation affects disasters just as profoundly as disasters can affect urbanisation. There is a co-evolutionary pattern of changing human and environmental processes acting in and through the city. The cascading effects of these disasters on humans vary from the short-term interruption of the movement of goods to the long-term impact on public health. There is no simple one-way line of causality in the production of human or environmental conditions: 'nature' does not cause 'natural disasters'; rather risk in the city is an outcome of a myriad of feedback loops, thresholds and competing ideas, mechanisms and forms. In this way, the breaching of a critical threshold – perhaps by a relatively minor initial event – can initiate a cascading series of knock-on effects with wide repercussions throughout the planetary urbanism system (Castree and Braun, 2001; Hewitt, 1983; Nicholls, 1995; Rosenzweig and Solecki, 2001).

As of today, 70 per cent of cities are already dealing with the impacts of climate change, and nearly all cities are to some degree at risk. Importantly, the manner in which cities are currently designed, built, managed, operated and serviced, together with their use, consumption and production patterns and impacts, is one of the major contributing factors to climate change. A leading indicator of the extent to which cities impact climate change is their greenhouse gas emissions. Overall, it is generally understood that cities already account for well over half of global greenhouse gas emissions, with some research indicating that this could be as high as 70 per cent of all global greenhouse gas emissions. This implies that cities generate a disproportionate amount of the world's greenhouse gas emissions. However, detailed analyses of urban greenhouse gas emissions for individual cities suggest that, on a per capita basis, urban residents tend to generate a substantially smaller volume of greenhouse gas emissions than residents elsewhere in the same country. For instance, in 2007 New York's per capita emissions were estimated to be 7.1 metric tonnes of CO_2, whereas per capita for the US it was 19.24 metric tonnes of CO_2. In addition, the per capita GHG emissions of cities have typically been reduced at a more efficient rate. For example, New York City's per capita emissions have gone down from 7.1 metric tonnes of CO_2 in 2007 to 5.8 metric tonnes of CO_2 in 2014 (a reduction of 18.3 per cent), whereas per capita emissions for the US went down from 19.24 metric tonnes of

CO_2 in 2007 to 16.4 metric tonnes of CO_2 in 2014 (a reduction of 14.8 per cent).

With the emergence of the consumption-based accounting system for GHG emissions, early research is indicating that all these figures should be substantially higher. Consumption based GHG emissions include all the goods and services a city consumes that are produced both inside and outside city limits, including such things as food, clothing, electronic equipment, air travel, delivery trucks and construction materials and industries. It also excludes the exports from a city. These components outside the city limits and exports were not included in the previously stated figures. This demonstrates the importance of understanding the city as both a productive and consumptive economy, and allows a better comparison of how cities differ in their generation of GHG, based upon their economies. This form of GHG accounting supports an understanding of how an increase in residents' living standards increases the GHG emissions of a city. It corroborates the well-established correlation between high per capita GHG emissions for cities and high-income consumption based service economies. It also highlights the importance of the ongoing management of operations and services in cities to reduce the GHG impacts. Thus, although there are large differences between actual cities in terms of their carbon dioxide emissions, cities generally have an opportunity to reduce their GHG emissions and climate change. As such, if we consider the overall planetary condition of increasing urbanisation, then the design, development and management of the city has the potential to deliver the biggest cuts in GHG emissions, potentially providing the greatest opportunity to impact the climate change trajectory.

Urbanism Is the Opportunity: Connected, Compact + Humane

It is clear that planetary urbanism, resource scarcity and climate change form a confluence of overlapping trends in time and space, and are integrally linked in a complex set of relationships that is yet to be fully understood. This confluence implies a NEW DESIGN CONDITION that is the unique condition of our era to which we need to respond. No longer is it possible to continue to plan, develop and operate the most important human habitat – cities – in the manner that we are doing today. No longer is it possible to build cities to cater for the aspirational middle income urban lifestyle, with its high levels of consumption, while accommodating an additional 4 billion people in cities in the next 80 years. Instead, I suggest that there is an opportunity in the very manner in which we respond to this need to build cities in an age of resource scarcity and climate change, which could result in the conservation and regeneration of the planet's biosphere and an improved quality of life for all people. I suggest that the greatest opportunity to deal with all the issues before us is through the design, development and management of the city.

The design of cities defined in its broadest sense (inclusive of the physical design and management of built and natural systems, and the governance, societal and economic systems) is a key driver for global sustainability, including the conservation of biodiversity and the maintenance of biological resources and biocapacity. Equally, the survival of the Earth's biological resources, biodiversity and ecological carrying capacity are essential to the provision of the human habitat of planetary urbanism. Importantly, the Earth's biological resources, biodiversity and ecological carrying capacity will only survive if the design of cities fundamentally changes. No longer can nature and city be seen as separate and distinct – they are completely interconnected and interdependent upon each other for survival. This requires a holistic integrated planetary strategy delivered at scale and high performance!

For the most part, current city-building practices are destructive to the planet's ecological and biological resources, and do not respond to the predicted climate change implications, as well as being instruments of social, economic and environmental injustice. With the current paradigm there are and will continue to be winners and losers. In fact, this urban planning failure has been identified in the 2015 Global Risk Landscape Report by the World Economic Forum as a risk factor in creating social, environmental and health challenges. So, if we ask the question 'Can the world double the urban population over the next 80 years using our current paradigm of city-making, and at the same time can all people achieve the idealised urban lifestyle?', the answer in my opinion is negative. Moreover, there are now serious questions being posed as to whether there are sufficient biological and natural resources to complete the required urbanisation, given the population projections and today's urban consumption patterns. I believe we are at a breaking point. In response, I suggest that there is a need for a new set of performance criteria for cities at both the local and global scale. These performance criteria need to be inclusive of the essential functionality, performance and conservation of the planet's ecological systems, biodiversity and biocapacity. The relationship between urbanisation, climate change and biodiversity is multifaceted and complex, and is most likely a 'wicked problem', so the definition of these performance criteria will be a continuous research and monitoring project. At the moment there is clearly insufficient knowledge of the interrelationships between cities and ecosystems and how these function together as adaptive systems.

Thus, with the confluence of these three trends, there is an immediate need for a fundamental reconceptualisation and new methodologies and approaches to the design of cities, with an innovative approach to generating knowledge before, during and after the process of urbanisation in an adaptive, holistic and integrative mode.

Here I would like to suggest this is a design problem where design must be understood in its broadest sense. Instrumental is a complete rethinking of our understanding of city and nature. It is no longer possible to separate city and nature; rather we need to understand city and nature as a co-evolving socio-ecological metabolising complex adaptive system, with a multi-scalar layered network of nodes (cities) of varied morphologies based on their location, size, geography, climate, history and culture. We need to eschew all categories of traditional urban theory and research, in particular the ideas of the definitions of urban to suburban to rural, city to nature and city to metropolis/megacity. We need to hybridise the clarity of these understood discrete and distinctive forms with an understanding of the continuous dynamic and adaptive flows and processes of interdependent systems. This implies that we need new methods of analysis to fully understand the interrelationship between the morphology and metabolism of all the urban socio-ecological systems and how they adapt to the ever-changing climate conditions that make up the context of planetary urbanisation. It further implies that the methodology must be driven by a series of collectively agreed upon values and principles of urbanism at local, regional and global scales.

We need to change the design of cities from the destructive forms and flows of today and develop new understandings of urban forms and processes such that cities are a generative condition for the good of the environment and society – i.e., for people and planet. To this end, a focus on the generative design principles of a connected metabolism supporting a compact urban morphology that affords a humane urbanism as a way of life is primary. In this way cities can be designed such that ecosystem services are maintained and resources are conserved through the use of a resource efficient approach using a circular metabolism model. In this context, spatial planning plays a key role in the preservation of natural resources through promoting compact urban forms that are less resource intensive, protect agricultural land and preserve areas of ecological importance. Incorporating natural systems into the early stages of planning can restore and/or preserve the ecosystems in and around cities. These ecosystems provide many natural services that cities depend upon, while safeguarding biodiversity hotspots and improving landscape connectivity.

The historic concept of city and nature needs to be replaced with this new understanding of planetary urbanism as a dynamic closed loop system, which interfaces at the global, continental and the eco-regional scales and integrates the morphology and metabolism of the socio-ecological adaptive systems of different 'place types' (cities). The design and development of the different 'place types' (cities) at the various scales must integrate the formal morphological characteristics with the performative requirements of the circular metabolism, taking account of the projected changes resulting from climate change. This will require a city to be understood as a multi-scalar human and biological habitat that is responsible and accountable for the generative conditions of its immediate biosphere as well as its ecological, economic and social footprint within a planetary system. It will also require the acceptance of spatial and urban planning and design as one of the tools for shaping a sustainable and equitable future simultaneously with reinventing the discipline to adequately address twenty-first-century challenges.

References

Angel, S., Parent, J., Civco, D. L., Blei, A. & Potere, D. 2011. The dimensions of global urban expansion: Estimates and projections for all countries, 2000–2050. *Progress in Planning*, 75: 53–107.

Castree, N. & Braun, B. (Eds.). 2001. *Social Nature Theory, Practice, and Politics*. Oxford: Blackwell.

CI. 2011. Data Basin: Biodiversity Hotspots Revisited, Conservation International, 2011. Conservation Synthesis, Center for Applied Biodiversity Science at Conservation International, Washington, DC.

Cohen, B. 2004. Urban growth in developing countries: A review of current trends and a caution regarding existing forecasts. *World Development*, 32(1): 23–51.

Hansen, J., Ruedy, R., Sato, M., Imhoff, M., Lawrence, W., Easterling, D., Peterson, T. & Karl, T. 2001. A closer look at United States and global surface temperature change. *Journal of Geophysical Research – Atmospheres*, 106(D20): 23947–23963.

Hewitt, K. (Ed.). 1983. *Interpretations of Calamity: From the Viewpoint of Human Ecology*. Risks and Hazards Series 1. Boston: Allen and Unwin.

Kalnay, E. & Cai, M. 2003. Impact of urbanization and land-use change on climate. *Nature*, 423(6939): 528–531.

Kowarik, I. 1995. On the role of alien species in urban flora and vegetation. In P. Pysek, K. Prach, M. Rejmánek & P. M. Wade (Eds.), *Plant Invasions – General Aspects and Special Problems*: 85–103. Amsterdam: SPB Academic.

Luniak, M. 1994. The development of bird communities in new housing estates in Warsaw. *Memorabilia Zoologica* 49: 257–267.

Marzluff, J. M. 2001. Worldwide urbanization and its effects on birds. In J. M. Marzluff, R. Bowman & R. Donnelly (Eds.), *Avian Ecology in an Urbanizing World*: 19–47. Norwell, MA: Kluwer.

McKinney, M. L. 2002. Urbanization, biodiversity, and conservation. *BioScience*, 52.

Nicholls, R. J. 1995. Coastal megacities and climate change. *GeoJournal*, 37 (3): 369–379.

OECD. 2010. *The Emerging Middle Class in Developing Countries*. Paris: OECD.

Rosenzweig, C. & Solecki, W. D. (Eds.). 2001. *Climate Change and a Global City: The Potential Consequences of Climate Variability and Change – Metro East Coast*. Report for the U.S. Global Change Research Program, National Assessment of the Potential Consequences of Climate Variability and Change for the United States. New York: Columbia Earth Institute, Columbia University.

Seto, K. C., Fragkias, M., Guneralp, B. & Reilly, M. K. 2011. A meta-analysis of global urban land expansion. *PLoS One*, 6(8).

Seto, K. C., Guneralp, B. & Hutyra, L. R. 2012. Global forecasts of urban expansion to 2030 and direct impacts on biodiversity and carbon pools. *Proceedings of the National Academy of Sciences*, 109(40): 16083–16088.

Stein, B. A., Kutner, L. & Adams, J. 2000. *Precious Heritage*. Oxford: Oxford University Press.

Stone, B., Jr. 2008. Urban sprawl and air quality in large US cities. *Journal of Environmental Management*, 86(4): 688–698.

TEEB. 2011a. *TEEB Manual for Cities: Ecosystem Services in Urban Management*. London: Earthscan.

2011b. *The Economics of Ecosystems and Biodiversity in Local and Regional Policy and Management*. London: Earthscan.

UN. 2015. *World Population Prospects: The 2015 Revision, Key Findings and Advance Tables*. Working Paper No. ESA/P/WP.241. New York: United Nations, Department of Economic and Social Affairs, Population Division.

UN-Habitat. 2003. *The Challenge of Slums: Global Report on Human Settlements*. Nairobi: Earthscan.

Vale, T. R. & Vale, G. R. 1976. Suburban bird populations in west-central California. *Journal of Biogeography* 3: 157–165.

Index